Paradoxes of
POLICE WORK

SECOND EDITION

Paradoxes of
POLICE WORK

SECOND EDITION

By Douglas W. Perez, Ph.D.

DELMAR
CENGAGE Learning

Australia • Brazil • Japan • Korea • Mexico • Singapore • Spain • United Kingdom • United States

DELMAR
CENGAGE Learning™

Paradoxes of Police Work, 2nd edition
Douglas W. Perez, Ph.D.

Vice President, Career and Professional Editorial: Dave Garza

Director of Learning Solutions: Sandy Clark

Senior Acquisitions Editor: Shelley Esposito

Managing Editor: Larry Main

Product Manager: Anne Orgren

Editorial Assistant: Danielle Klahr

Vice President, Career and Professional Marketing: Jennifer Baker

Marketing Director: Deborah S. Yarnell

Marketing Manager: Erin Brennan

Marketing Coordinator: Jonathan Sheehan

Production Director: Wendy Troeger

Production Manager: Mark Bernard

Senior Content Project Manager: Betty Dickson

Senior Art Director: Joy Kocsis

Library of Congress Control Number: 2009939340

ISBN-13: 978-1-4354-9682-8

ISBN-10: 1-4354-9682-5

Delmar
5 Maxwell Drive
Clifton Park, NY 12065-2919
USA

Cengage Learning is a leading provider of customized learning solutions with office locations around the globe, including Singapore, the United Kingdom, Australia, Mexico, Brazil, and Japan. Locate your local office at:
international.cengage.com/region

Cengage Learning products are represented in Canada by Nelson Education, Ltd.

To learn more about Delmar, visit **www.cengage.com/delmar**

Purchase any of our products at your local college store

Notice to the Reader
Publisher does not warrant or guarantee any of the products described herein or perform any independent analysis in connection with any of the product information contained herein. Publisher does not assume, and expressly disclaims, any obligation to obtain and include information other than that provided to it by the manufacturer. The reader is expressly warned to consider and adopt all safety precautions that might be indicated by the activities described herein and to avoid all potential hazards. By following the instructions contained herein, the reader willingly assumes all risks in connection with such instructions. The publisher makes no representations or warranties of any kind, including but not limited to, the warranties of fitness for particular purpose or merchantability, nor are any such representations implied with respect to the material set forth herein, and the publisher takes no responsibility with respect to such material. The publisher shall not be liable for any special, consequential, or exemplary damages resulting, in whole or part, from the readers' use of, or reliance upon, this material.

Printed in United States of America
1 2 3 4 5 6 7 12 11 10 09

**For
Bananaphone and Woofie**

TABLE OF CONTENTS

ABSTRACT

The second edition of the *Paradoxes of Police Work* is focused around a central theme: that police work is an endeavor replete with paradoxes. Taken together, these paradoxes make the police experience one that can be frustrating for police officers, police managers, and citizens alike. Part One discusses the individual police officer's paradoxical experience and the consequent formation of a tightly-knit subculture—known both for its solidarity and for its feelings of isolation from the public. Part Two considers police organizational styles. There is no one, particular way to organize police systems. There are multiple means of prioritizing police militarism, law enforcement, order maintenance, and service functions, each rife with paradoxes. Part Three engages the many paradoxes inherent in the administration of police organizations. Part Four discusses contemporary and future developments in police work—again driven by a concern for paradoxical dynamics in the field. The work is designed to function in two ways: (1) as a reader for cadets going through the police academy experience and (2) as an accompanying reader for several types of criminal justice courses. It has more of a liberal arts and sociological focus than books written for "nuts and bolts" courses of the "how to be a police officer" variety, and it was conceived as a more practical and real-world-driven text than others composed for theoretical and social science–oriented courses.

ACKNOWLEDGEMENTS

My thanks go out to J. Alan Moore and Sandy Muir for sharing with me their insights—not only on this work but on my numerous academic endeavors—their profound understanding of the human experience, and their loyal comradeship over many years. Jerome Skolnick has also affected my studies of the police in important ways by challenging my assumptions at critical moments.

For allowing me into their organizations, and for graciously finding time to discuss many of the ideas herein, thanks go to Chief John Hart, Chief Dashel Butler, Chief John Terry, Chief Kevin Scully, Chief Norm Stamper, Chief Joseph McNamara, and Sheriff Richard Rainey. For their insights into the individual police officer experience, I have far too many practitioners to thank—but John Gackowski, Mike Barkhurst, Al Salerno, Nolan Darnell, Bill Moulder, Jim Simonson, Skip Stevens, and Joe Colletti must be singled out here.

To my ever-faithful, personal editor Darlene Wood and to Abe Brennan of Pre-Press PMG, who did the final, meticulous editing, go my profound thanks. Also from Pre-Press PMG, Dewanshu Ranjan (Project Manager) and from Cengage, Anne Orgren (Production Manager) and Shelley Esposito (Senior Acquisitions Editor) were instrumental in assuring that the work was finalized. Without their commitment to seemingly endless hours of editing and analysis this second edition would never have reached fruition. I must also thank the hundreds of students in my police classes who, over the course of more than 30 years, have helped me hone my understanding of how best to describe and illuminate the paradoxes of police work.

—*Douglas W. Perez*
April, 2009

The author and Delmar Cengage Learning would like to thank the following reviewers:

Clea Andreadis,
Middlesex Community College,
Bedford, MA

Brian R. Johnson, Ph.D.,
Grand Valley State University,
Allendale, MI

Dr. Robert N. Diotalevi, Esq.,
LL.M., Florida Gulf Coast
University, Fort Myers, FL

Pamela Spence, ABD,
Holmes Community College,
Ridgeland, MS

Dr. Richard M. Hough, Sr.,
University of West Florida,
Pensacola, FL, and Criminal Justice
Academy, George Stone Vocational-
Technical Center, Pensacola, FL

INTRODUCTION

Police work is not what it appears from the outside. Every day on the streets of America, police officers are faced with numerous functional dynamics and practical realities that operate contrary to conventional wisdom, police intuition, or, even, common sense. The police are committed to maintaining the freedom of individuals in our democratic society, and yet they are licensed to take away that freedom in the pursuit of that goal. The police stand opposed to the forces of violence on the streets of America, and yet they often must resort to violence themselves in order to control incorrigible citizens. The police appear to be very powerful public officials, and yet they often have difficulty controlling the behavior of apparently powerless individuals. The police ought to be the foremost champions of the American due process–oriented legal system, and yet they are sometimes so frustrated by its operations that they take the law into their own hands and work against the system (Klockars, Dirty Harry Problem). In these, and several dozen other ways, American police officers are confronted with paradoxes at every turn.

This is a book about police work that differs from similar texts in two distinct ways. First, our analysis is driven by an understanding that the paradoxes of police work are everyday in evidence—not only on the streets, but also within police organizations themselves—and that no complete understanding of this work can be developed without consistently addressing these paradoxes. Throughout our discussions about the individual police officer experience, the formation of the police subculture and its solidarity, styles of police organization, police systemic dynamics, and administrative problems faced by police officers and police managers, we will always acknowledge the paradoxes of police work. These paradoxes not only color the job experience of officers and administrators, but they impact the administration of justice on the streets every day. And, thus, the paradoxes of police work directly affect the lives of millions of American citizens.

Second, this book is about more than *just* the police. That is, our discussions provide a broader context for the dynamics these powerful individuals experience. For example, when considering stereotyping, we examine how all people stereotype and the pluses and minuses of doing so. When discussing discretionary

BOX I.1

DEFINITION OF A PARADOX

A paradox is an assertion or a dynamic in life that seems to operate contrary to common sense but is nevertheless true in fact.

decision-making, we look at how all people who apply rules to others exercise this sort of power. When analyzing the difficulties powerful individuals can have coercing the ostensibly less powerful, we use examples that aren't just police-related. When evaluating the importance of media imagery in contemporary America, we emphasize how slants taken by various media entities affect more than just the police.

Along the way, then, in order to develop a broader and deeper understanding of police work, we compare and contrast the police experience with that of other public and private power wielders. It is no exaggeration to suggest that the numerous paradoxes, operational dynamics, and pragmatic realities faced by police officers are unique. We will engage this idea shortly below. But it is also true that students of the police and of police organizations can learn a great deal about the law, American public institutions, power, and life outside of police work by making connections between the police and other public and private actors.

So we focus on the police as our primary topic of concern but often provide the reader with many non-police examples. Let us begin here by delineating, in more specific terms, this idea that police work is replete with paradoxes—paradoxes that color the individual police officer experience and mold and drive police organizational and subcultural dynamics on a daily basis.

AN EXAMPLE: ONE PARADOX OF POLICE WORK

One of the most important paradoxes in all of police work is the fact that the police are hired, trained, and disciplined to behave in a way not necessarily conducive to accomplishing their multiple jobs. People expect the police to always observe the letter of the law. One of our Founding Fathers, John Adams, is credited with coining a critical phrase that states America is supposed to be a land "ruled by laws and not men" (Adams 106). This statement embodies one of the important ideals of both our country and Western Liberalism—that unless the agents of the state, in this case the police, cleave to the letter of the law, the machinations of our government are not morally defensible (Wolfe).

The paradoxical problem is that the law does not always provide the police with sufficient tools to accomplish their numerous tasks. Put another way, what "works" is not necessarily legal, and, conversely, that which is legal does not necessarily "work." Police officers must consistently utilize non-legal, quasi-legal, and semi-legal means to deter crime, keep the peace, and maintain order in society. Crime can be—*and is*—effectively deterred in any number of ways irreconcilable with the clean, sanitized, pure sense of legality and civility often possessed by members of the public.

Lawrence N. Blum has pointed out that while espousing support for local police in a theoretical way, the public often "turn on" them, evincing contempt when confronted with the practical reality of how the police behave. This suggests a dynamic that has haunted the police for decades now—that the American police officer is society's fall guy. Our culture expects officers to deal with violent people and almost impossible situations in a legally defensible way. When they do not adhere to our idealized notions of how the law should work—even if they accomplish their tasks effectively—we rail against police "excesses" and demand they behave themselves.

To some extent, the police take up the slack and fill in a large gray area on the streets of America. Society depends on them to behave in many high-handed, intimidating, and sometimes ugly ways and to accomplish the rather "dirty" job of making the streets safe for the rest of us (Muir 45). But when the police are guilty of excesses, society effectively blames them for being out of control. People want it both ways; they want effective policing, but they also want clean and pure legality. The police must deal with gun-toting gangsters, deranged psychopaths, serial rapists, child molesters, and violent individuals of all types. The public wants the police to take effective action in creating a social order wherein there are fewer guns, drugs, gangs, and crime. People expect the police to do "whatever it takes" to achieve these goals.

But here is the paradox: for as much as people might assert their faith in the pristine dictates of the law, for as much as they might pontificate about how only the objective machinations of the law should determine the fate of citizens facing their government, and for as much as they might rail against police excesses, people want results from the police. Often, they do not much care how the police achieve them. They will not tolerate growing crime and disorder. They will not tolerate gangs and guns and drugs. They will not tolerate unsafe streets. In general, they will not tolerate deviant behavior. But when the police utilize ugly (yet pragmatic) tactics, they are often accused of incompetence, ignorance, and unprofessionalism.

Often the machinations of the entire legal system do not work effectively to deter would-be criminals. Laws printed in books that rest on legal library shelves are not effective deterrents. The threat of a waiting jail cell is not an effective deterrent. The degradation involved in being dragged into a courtroom filled with judges, attorneys, juries, and witnesses is not an effective deterrent. Even the threat of a life sentence is not an effective deterrent. And all of these potentialities taken together—partly because they are so remote from life on the street—may not deter a citizen from perpetrating a crime.

But the police *can* deter crime. There is no doubt about this: the police, acting as state-sponsored "bullies," can deter crime quite effectively. Answering to police officers—who threaten to harm incorrigibles—can keep people from perpetrating crimes against others. Every police officer knows this. As Crank puts it: "A cop uses force on the streets because it does the job, solves a problem" (Crank 65).

And there is more than the power of *threats* to harm. Police officers know that using violent "curbside justice"—roughing up a suspect, for example—can effectively deter crime. In other words, the use of force, the threat of force, and the application of ongoing harassment—"tools" that people want the police to avoid—can and do work to deter crime. No amount of denying these dynamics will change reality.

Here is a true life example. A professional burglar was apprehended several times in the act of committing thefts only to be set free due to legal technicalities. The local beat officers were appalled. But they did not give up. They began to harass the burglar mercilessly. They stopped him, on foot or in his car, whenever they saw him. When they stopped him, the police ran extended records and warrants checks, thus taking up a lot of his time. When he had his driver's license suspended, they cited him every time they saw his car in motion for "Driving without a License." They cited him 14 times in two weeks, twice in one day. The burglar eventually moved away from their beat, and local burglary statistics were cut in half.

The police were obviously harassing this man. If he had made a citizen's complaint, any fair investigation would have found the police guilty of misconduct (Perez). They had singled out one citizen and been profoundly unfair in their treatment of him. But—and herein lies the paradoxical problem—it worked. Harassing this man got the job done; it lowered the neighborhood's crime rate and made its streets marginally safer. Put succinctly, the law failed, but police intimidation worked.

So, paradoxically, while society expects the police to behave in legal and proper ways, it is quite often the case that they can be effective by ignoring the law. This is just one example, albeit a critically important one, of the paradoxes of police work—dynamics that work in a different way than logic or legal requirements might dictate. Our discussions will illustrate that such paradoxes are often in operation, on every beat, in every police department, all over America—and much of the time.

Unrealistic Expectations

When a young woman or man first puts on a police uniform and steps onto the street as a police officer, he or she has certain expectations about how things will operate on the job. These expectations are gleaned from viewing television programs and movies about the police, from experiencing personal interactions with the police, from observing the police in action at a distance, and possibly from classroom discussions about law and justice and so on. But there is a major problem with these preconceived notions about police work: police officers who are new to the street invariably find that their expectations are unrealistic. Things are more complicated than they had imagined. Police work is far more ambiguous and frustrating than they had intuitively believed it to be. There are numerous, overlapping frustrations experienced by rookies that can cloud their judgment and make them lose sight of their overall goal: to administer justice on the streets of America.

Now we must be clear about one thing here: the individual police officer's job is not comprised of an endless string of frustrating, paradoxical encounters and experiences. Day-to-day police work can be psychologically rewarding, intellectually stimulating, and even emotionally engaging. There is much in police work that is positive and enjoyable. Our discussion will take note of this along the way. But *some* of the time (to the individual officer it can often appear to be *most* of the time), the paradoxical nature of the experience can be almost overwhelming. The paradoxes of police work can lead officers to question their commitment to the profession. They can lead to personal problems, both on the job and at home, that have a tremendous, negative impact upon the police officer's psyche. They can foster an "us against them" mentality toward the very citizens they are supposed to protect and defend (Crank 198). These paradoxes can lead to any number of counterproductive behavior patterns on the part of police officers—patterns that are deleterious to the interests of the administration of justice in America.

In Chapter Six, we engage, in a prolonged discussion, the unrealistic imagery placed in the minds of Americans by the media. Our treatment here is meant only to indicate that police officers themselves can suffer frustration due to unrealistic expectations about the nature of police work. Often, American police officers enter the profession unprepared for the paradoxical nature of the job.

Threads Drawn Through the Work

There are several overarching topics of concern that we visit so often throughout our discussions that it behooves us to outline them briefly here. These are the substantive topics, or "threads," that will be drawn through the book. They are the central issues being debated in contemporary policing. Two of them—the drive toward genuine professionalism and the movement to move the philosophy of modern policing toward what is called "Community Oriented Policing"—have to do with ongoing change. And two of them—paramilitarism and "The Dirty Harry Problem"—create resistance to that change.

Professionalism: A critical topic for our consideration has to do with the ongoing efforts, now almost 100 years old, to move the American police in the direction of becoming genuine professionals. In Chapter Fifteen, the final chapter, we combine various strands from other chapters that inform this effort. For now, we merely note that police work in America is moving toward becoming a profession, even though the police have yet to achieve the expertise, history, and status of other professionals. Furthermore, it is important to note that forces within the police subculture, and even within American society as a whole, tend to inhibit the realization of this dream of professionalism for our police. This is the central paradox associated with professionalism.

Community Oriented Policing (COP): Parallel to the drive toward a genuine professionalism is the change—in motion almost everywhere in America today—toward a new philosophy of policing, that of "Community Oriented Policing" or "Community Based Policing." In Chapter Ten we specifically define this new philosophy, outline some specific operational dynamics, and then critique it. We find that COP makes logical sense and is being instituted in many places for that reason. But we will see that it has yet to be inculcated sufficiently within the psyche of the American police for it universally to be considered the optimum form of contemporary policing. The same factors that tend to inhibit genuine professionalism can also work against COP. In Chapter Ten, we examine several related paradoxes while developing an understanding of this new philosophy in action.

Paramilitarism: One paradox central to police work involves paramilitarism. As we discuss in Chapter Eight, almost everything about paramilitaristic policing is bad. The negatives associated with police behaving like an occupying army are numerous. And because of this, paramilitarism needs to be limited as much as is possible. However, the paradox is that under certain, unusual circumstances—such as riots, hostage situations, or mass shootings—the police *have* to operate like a military organization. Even though the situations that call for paramilitarism are extraordinary, the police must change—sometimes in an instant—from a group that eschews a militaristic mindset (in favor of a more community-friendly focus) into an efficient, effective, accountable military organization. A central paradox for police work is that a great deal of time is spent preparing for such unusual, violent occurrences—and this time is often wasted.

The Dirty Harry Problem: Dirty Harry is the title of a movie and the name of a fictional character from (and several other movies from the 1970s). While the movie is quite dated, Harry is important, because about 20 years ago the criminologist Carl Klockars wrote an article entitled "The Dirty Harry Problem." In it, Klockars illuminated what had become a major difficulty within the police subculture: the propensity for some officers (too many, really) to become involved in "framing" citizens to get them off the streets. If the job of the police includes, among other things, "cleaning up the streets," then this can be accomplished in illegal ways and, equally, it can be rationalized as a necessary part of the job. Dirty Harry Callahan "got the job done" by obtaining evidence in illegal ways and treating people he determined to be bad actors (in whatever way he saw fit to determine this) in a dishonest and unjust manner. This type of police behavior on the street is called "noble cause corruption" (Perez and Moore 133), because even though it is illegal, such conduct is done in the pursuit of the noble cause of making the streets safer. In Chapter Thirteen we discuss different types of police misconduct, and we find that this particular type—specifically because it is considered to involve a noble cause—is the most difficult sort of misconduct to deter.

The Historical Eras of Policing: In most policing textbooks, an entire chapter is spent covering the history of policing (Peak 1; Roberg, *et al.* 35; Walker 19). While some of this history is interesting, most is irrelevant to the development of an understanding of today's police. So in this work we simply list the historical eras of policing and note how our above threads are related to them (see accompanying box).

When the American police first formed, they were controlled directly by political organizations, then called political "machines." We call this the "Political Era" of policing (Lyman 42). Corruption was rampant, morale was low, effectiveness was limited, and the police enjoyed little status in America. Calls for reform, begun during the Progressive Era of American politics, resulted in change (Diner). In an effort to make the police more effective and efficient, as well as to do away with the corruption of the times, the second era of policing, the "Reform Era," was instituted (Lyman 46).

Reform did not come all at once. Indeed, city by city, corruption scandal by corruption scandal, American policing slowly changed into a different institution. Civil Service examinations were instituted to make selection more fair and objective. Police academies were invented and serious efforts begun to train officers both before and after they assumed a beat. Police accountability was taken seriously for the first time. In general, police organizations were made more "tight" and responsive to the law and the interests of justice. The methods utilized to introduce these changes involved altering police work and moving it in the direction of paramilitarism. In Chapter Eight, we engage the pros and cons of paramilitarism. Suffice it to say here that in a paradoxical way there was good and bad news associated with these changes.

The good news was that the paramilitarism of the Reform Era did away with corruption almost everywhere. The tactic worked. The police became more effective, more efficient, and more accountable. Almost immediately, they began to enjoy more status in the minds of American politicians and citizens. Unfortunately, after several decades of such paramilitaristic policing (longer in some places) the bad news was that people began to rail against its excesses. The citizenry began to dislike the aloofness of the police. They began to oppose the rigid, occupying army–type carriage of officers. Business owners did not like the fact that they had

BOX I.2

THE ERAS OF AMERICAN POLICING

- **The Political Era (1840s–1920s)**
  From the invention of the uniformed police until reform. During this time frame, the police were controlled by political machines; corruption and ineptitude were rampant.

- **The Reform Era (1920–40)**
  As a response to corruption and ineptitude, city-by-city the police were reformed. What eventuated was paramilitarism. Some mislabeled this as "professionalism."

- **The Professional Era (1970–)**
  A new philosophy, "Community Based Policing," drives efforts to instill genuine professionalism in policing.

(Lyman 28–60)

no ongoing relationship with their local beat officer(s). Minorities distrusted the paramilitaristic police almost more than they had distrusted the police of the Political Era. Hence, further changes were in order.

Thus, our modern era, the Professional or Community Oriented Era, evolved out of the excesses of the paramilitarism of the Reform Era (Lyman 56). Driven by concerns about skyrocketing crime in the 1960s and '70s, the inner city riots of that era, and the drawbacks of paramilitarism, people began to call for something new and different. Out of this set of concerns came the impetus to create a new philosophy. The pressure exerted by those who called for change eventually drove police scholars and practitioners to develop community policing. And it is within the Professional or Community Oriented Era of policing that we now reside.

These are the important topics we engage through our discussions of the many paradoxes of police work. Understanding these several issues and movements, their strengths and weaknesses, their pros and cons, will illuminate our understanding of contemporary American policing in a crucial way.

Before beginning Part One, we take a moment here to outline the sequence of the work and how each chapter is meant to fit into the whole.

The Sequence of the Book

A word is in order about this book's structure. It is a "reader," not a textbook, per se. It is designed for easy reading and thus does not burden the reader with copious footnotes. At the end of each chapter, there is a set of discussion questions, a list of key terms (in boldface type throughout the work), and an essay suggesting additional reading. The bibliographical essay aims to direct the reader toward some classic, additional readings without being synoptic or all-inclusive. The texts suggested are meant to enhance understanding of the important topics in each chapter without listing so much in the way of references as to overwhelm a reader. The discussion questions can be utilized in either a classroom setting, amongst a group of readers, or as tools—exercises to some extent—for an individual reader's edification.

Part One focuses on the experience of being a police officer on the street. In this section of the book, we begin by discussing several paradoxical dynamics associated with the day-to-day realities of working a beat. At the end of Part One, we synthesize our understanding of these paradoxes to formulate an appreciation of the individual police officer's experience that then, in turn, will serve as the basis for a discussion of the police subculture.

Chapter One confronts the fact that the goals (and therefore functions) of the police are multiple, conflicting, and vague. While it appears that the police should know precisely "what they are doing out there," in fact, what to prioritize (and how to accomplish it) is often in doubt. Chapter Two discusses stereotyping. All people stereotype as a way of making life easier. But the police officer stereotypes much more often than does the average person, because he or she must make quick decisions about potentially violent people and dangerous situations.

Unfortunately, as illustrated in Chapter Two, the police are quite often wrong about the potential of violence. And, thus, they generate a great amount of antipathy on the part of citizens who see them as paranoid and overly aggressive.

Chapter Three engages a common topic in all books about the police: police discretion. We examine what police discretion is, why it is necessary, and the paradoxical drawbacks of its exercise. Even when taking the utmost care to exercise their discretionary power in the interests of justice, the police are often seen to be prejudiced and unfair when making decisions in front of citizens. Chapter Four confronts important paradoxes that relate to the operations of the due process system. While it may appear that the police should feel themselves the primary champions of the America legal system, they are often frustrated by its focus upon procedural guilt as opposed to factual guilt. When factually guilty criminals go free due to procedural error(s), the police can become not only disenchanted with the due process system but they can actually begin to work against it. Chapter Five analyzes the paradoxes of coercive power. These involve circumstances under which seemingly powerful police officers have difficulty coercing (controlling) ostensibly far less powerful citizens. The four paradoxes of coercive power present profound difficulties for police officers when dealing with a wide variety of citizens and situations.

Chapter Six targets images of police officers and police work that are media-created and construct impossible expectations for the police. The dynamics associated with these unrealistic images tend to make both police officers and citizens alike dissatisfied with the realities of the criminal justice system. Chapter Seven incorporates all Part One discussions and analyzes the development of the police subculture. Known for its solidarity and isolation from the public, the police subculture is at once an understandable consequence of dealing with the paradoxes of police work and a counterproductive construction that can make things worse for the delivery of justice in the long run.

Part Two focuses on varieties of police organization. Its discussions point out numerous paradoxes associated with how police systems are structured around the priorities of several different system types. Chapter Eight begins Part Two with a consideration of police paramilitarism. The central paradox engaged is the fact that while paramilitarism has numerous negative consequences for police and citizens alike, and therefore should be avoided in its most excessive forms, the police in fact do need to behave like an army on certain, infrequent occasions. Chapter Nine focuses directly on the three different types of police organization that have historically been employed in America. Differentiating between these three classic styles of policing, this chapter notes that each has its drawbacks and, in fact, the search for the "perfect" style of police organization is thwarted by the negative dynamics associated with each type.

Chapter Ten is about the new philosophy of policing, Community Oriented Policing (COP). This new doctrine has spawned a great deal of positive change in American policing in the recent past. But, paradoxically, it has its drawbacks, and it is possible that COP might degenerate into the 19th century–style of policing known for its corruption. Furthermore, numerous influences exerted by the police subculture, by police middle managers, and even by the media and the citizenry work to mitigate progress toward this new philosophy.

Part Three is about police administration. It works its way logically through various topics associated with how police departments are administered, from selection through training through accountability. Chapter Eleven covers police selection. While there is no one way selection is accomplished, our discussion engages the "standard" types of barriers over which potential police officer candidates must pass in order to be sworn into office. In evaluating how things tend to be done, we confront several paradoxical dynamics at work that inhibit police selection systems from choosing (perhaps) the best candidates for the job. Chapter Twelve looks at police education and training. While virtually everyone calls for expanded efforts in this field, in some places paradoxical forces work against enhanced sophistication in police education and training. Chapter Thirteen closes Part Three with a discussion of police accountability and the paradoxes associated with attempting to hold the police accountable for their conduct.

Part Four embraces several discussions about the future of police work in America. Chapter Fourteen engages the rather vague and amorphous concept of "leadership" in general and the paradoxes associated with attempting to lead a group of powerful individuals, each of whom exercises not only discretionary arrest/ no arrest powers, but even—on occasion—life and death powers over individual citizens. Chapter Fifteen covers the development of police professionalism. As we speak, police work is changing from an "occupation" to a genuine "profession." And there are paradoxical dynamics involved in the attempts of thousands of people, both inside and outside of police work, to professionalize the police.

NEW TO THIS EDITION

The Second Edition of the *Paradoxes of Police Work* has been thoroughly reorganized and expanded. The format has been completely changed. Each chapter includes Boxes that provide practical examples from police work on the street, questions for discussion purposes, and summations of topics in progress. In addition, there are several charts inserted for clarification and illustration. At the end of each chapter are three new elements. First, there is a set of "Discussion Questions," for utilization in a classroom format or for the consideration of individual readers. Second, there is an inventory of "Key Terms," listing definitions for important words and phrases in boldface type throughout the chapter. Finally, there is an essay suggesting "Additional Reading." This essay is written in lieu of traditional endnotes. The substance of the work is also greatly expanded. While the first edition engaged the paradoxes associated with the individual police officer experience only, this now makes up only Part One (7 Chapters) of a four-part, fifteen-chapter work. The remainder of the book now discusses the paradoxes associated with police systems organization and administration, police leadership, Community Oriented Policing, and the drive toward genuine professionalism in police work. The chapter-by-chapter treatment of the paradoxes of police work has been reorganized and expanded in the following ways;

- **Introduction:**—A substantial Introduction outlines the concept of the paradox and discusses, as an example, one of the central paradoxes in police work. The Introduction also includes brief discussions of four major topics addressed throughout the book. It concludes with a short explication of the history of policing in America and of the flow of the entire work.

- **Chapter 1: What Are We Doing Out There?**—This chapter includes an expanded analysis of the importance of mission statements, the police as bureaucrats, and the conflict between police goals and functions. New additions include a debate about why the uniformed police were created in the first place, how the police actually spend their time on the job, and the suggestion that "law enforcement" is an inaccurate term for describing police work.

- **Chapter 2: Stereotyping**—This chapter has expanded discussions of the dynamics of stereotyping, why bureaucrats stereotype more than most people, and why police officers stereotype more than most bureaucrats. Expanding on the concept of potential violence, the new edition adds considerations of "normal crime," how police officers work their beats, and how rookie officers utilize stereotypical jargon in an attempt to appear "salty."

- **Chapter 3: Discretion**—The discussion of the rule of law now includes an analysis of the idea that "the police are the law." An imaginary "Discretionary Decision Making Continuum" is included (in chart form) and "Khadi" justice is defined at length. Of critical importance are the debates over the meaning of "justice" and why full enforcement is neither practical nor desirable.

- **Chapter 4: The Due Process System**—The chapter's initial discussion about the concept of due process has expanded to include an explanation of how the overarching principle is distilled for application on the street. Also expanded are the analyses of noble cause corruption and substantive due process. Regarding the latter, examples are given of catch-all statutes and anti-gang ordinances.

- **Chapter 5: Coercive Power**—Chapters 4 and 5 from the original work have been compressed into a new Chapter 5 that illustrates Muir's paradoxes of coercive power with non-police examples. Important are discussions about the paradox of detachment, given its salience for the contemporary "War on Terrorism," and the paradox of irrationality's explanation for the "crazy cop" idea.

- **Chapter 6: Media Imagery**—The chapter begins with a brief consideration of the myth of the "liberal media" in America and of its importance for police work. Discussion then covers unrealistic, media-generated images troublesome for the police, including the "RCMP Syndrome," Dirty Harry as hero, "Cosmetized violence," and *mis*information about Miranda warnings.

- **Chapter 7: Subculture**—This chapter discusses subcultures in depth and engages stress-related problems for police officers, such as alcohol usage, divorce, and suicide. It also analyses several norms of the subculture that often work to create an acceptance among the police of "overkill," noble cause corruption, the "never explain, never apologize" dynamic, and others.

- **Chapter 8: Paramilitarism**—This expanded discussion of paramilitaristic policing includes reference to the fact that this type of organization was a response to the corruption of the Political Era. The chapter includes considerations of the logical, practical reasons for paramilitarism, the numerous criticisms of it, and the paradoxical situation in which police at all levels find themselves in contemporary times—needing to be efficient as a military unit but only on limited, extraordinary occasions.

- **Chapter 9: Three Traditional Styles of Police Organization**—This chapter begins with Wilson's classic differentiation of organizational styles. The chapter proceeds to discuss the pros and cons of each style, making the point that many police organizations today still cleave to one of these types, despite the movement toward community oriented policing. The difficulties of deciding which system is "best" and attempting change from one system to another are considered.

- **Chapter 10: Community Oriented Policing**—The historical roots of COP are investigated, and the major elements of the philosophy are discussed. A critique is offered of COP in theory and in practice, and paradoxes associated with COP are explored. Practical, specific COP-oriented programs are briefly discussed.

- **Chapter 11: Selection**—Beginning with a discussion of what an ideal candidate might look like, this chapter then focuses on the near-impossible attempts by selection systems to pre-determine a candidate's character on the street. Affirmative action is explained and debated. The Civil Service process is described, including tests, certified lists, and the rule of 3. Then specific elements of the selection process are outlined and critiqued.

- **Chapter 12: Education and Training**—This chapter begins by discussing the sort of "patchwork" quilt that police educational requirements include. It further engages the debate over what type of higher education is required in the modern police world. The police academy and FTO programs are then discussed and criticized. The chapter ends with a brief consideration of in-service training.

- **Chapter 13: Accountability**—This chapter discusses the multiple standards of conduct to which the police must answer. It then analyzes the causes of police misconduct—including a typological table explaining different forms of police deviance. Limits of reform are discussed, presenting the substantial roadblocks that hamper police review systems, and explanation and comparative analysis of police review systems follows.

- **Chapter 14: Leadership**—Discussion begins by explaining the traditional command and control model and establishing why it does not fit well in today's police work. Subsequent sections treat police leadership as coaching, the Sergeant as teacher, middle management paradoxes, and, finally, Muir's conceptualization of the "vulnerable and corruptible" Chief.

- **Chapter 15: Professionalism**—This chapter discusses different definitions of "profession," from a simplistic, lay definition, to the paramilitaristic definition, to the sociological definition. It considers whether or not the police are true professionals, concludes that this is not yet the case, and ends with a discussion of the future of the professionalization movement. Specific reference is made to what steps need to be taken for policing to achieve the status of a genuine profession.

Having established the importance of the paradoxes of police work, and having provided a brief roadmap for the work here, let us engage in Chapter One our first discussion about the mission of the police. Consider the fact that, at the outset, it is not completely clear what it is the police should be doing on the streets of America.

PART ONE

In the Bag: The Police Officer's Experience

Part One is about the individual police officer's experience on the street. Each of the first six chapters engages an important element of that experience and, in turn, highlights important paradoxes that inform and complicate the policing endeavor. At the end of this set of discussions, Part One will conclude with an analysis that integrates the previous topics. Chapter Seven will endeavor to both illustrate and explicate how and why the police subculture is created, how it functions, and what its norms and values entail.

CHAPTER 1

What Are We Doing Out There?

Chapter One Outline

In this book we discuss a group of individuals known as "the police." We will attempt to analyze their individual and collective experiences, their subcultural norms and values, and the operations of their systems and organizational dynamics. First we must define who and what it is we are talking about. Who are the police? What differentiates police officers from other workers in other occupations? More specifically, what makes the police stand out from other public service agents—from firefighters and welfare workers and nurses and teachers? What are the police licensed to do? Why is it so important to so many people that they understand, analyze, evaluate, and control the police?

In this chapter, we set out to discuss two topics. First, we define who the police are. Second, and more importantly, we analyze what the goals of the police are. In discussing these goals, we will define the functions of the police—functions that are aimed at the pursuit of those goals. The first endeavor, defining the police, is a rather straightforward enterprise. It is relatively easy to do. But in engaging the second question, we will find that a paradox appears: while most people live their lives with the understanding—in the back of their minds—that they know what it is the police are supposed to accomplish, it turns out that defining the goals (and, thus, the functions) of the police is *not* such an easy task. The goals of the police are numerous and, at times, confusing. And the confusion over what it is the police are supposed to accomplish out on the street can frustrate not only the public and individual police officers but police administrators as well. How difficult is it to operate within a complex organization that does not always know what it is supposed to be doing? The answer is that it is extremely difficult—at times, frustrating and debilitating. And thus, the paradox is that what appears to be the case—that it is easy to understand the goals of police work—is not at all true.

DEFINING "THE POLICE"

Who are the police? The Criminologist Carl Klockars wrote a short but very important and thoughtful book about the police entitled *The Idea of Police*. In this now classic introductory discussion, he began with a cogent definition of who the police are. We will use his definition here. Klockars's definition included three main points (Klockars, "Idea of Police" 12). He noted first that the police use **coercive force** and do so legally. They often attempt to control the behavior of others by using threats. There are two types of threats the police use on a regular basis, that they implicitly bring to any and every interaction with the public: the threats of arrest and violence. The police use these threats to control situations and individuals. Of course, others use coercive force in our society, too, but they do so at their own peril, because coercing others is a crime. Attempting to manipulate people through the use of threats is **"extortion,"** plain and simple. And extortion is a felonious offense listed in every state's penal code.

BOX 1.1

KLOCKARS'S DEFINITION OF "POLICE"

- The Police possess the right to use coercive force.
- They are licensed by the State to do so.
- They may do so anywhere, at any time, within their domestic jurisdiction.

(Klockars, *"Idea of Police"* 12)

But there is more. Since others use coercive force, Klockars added a second part to his definition: the police are *licensed by the State* to use coercive force. While the use by a citizen of coercive force against another is a crime (again, extortion) and the use of force itself—going beyond the *threat* to do violence—is also a crime (**assault**, or **battery**), when the police use such force it is almost universally acceptable. As long as the police are using force to overcome the *illegal* use of violence by citizens, the use of force by the police is not a crime. It is accepted as an ongoing, day-to-day part of the job of policing.

However, other people in our society are, on a limited basis, also licensed by the State to use force. Teachers, when they are working, may use minimal amounts of force upon students in order to maintain classroom discipline. Orderlies at hospitals are also so licensed. As Klockars points out, so are football players, prison guards, and parents ("Idea of Police" 11). So Klockars added his final part to the definition: the police may use force at any time and anywhere in their domestic jurisdiction. While these other public workers are licensed to use force on a very limited basis—only when they are on the job and in the classroom/emergency room/mental hospital—the police are not so limited. Their coercive powers extend everywhere, at all times (Klockars, "Idea of Police" 16).

This definition is pretty straightforward. It makes logical sense, and there is little room for debate about it. This is who the police are, and no one has any reason to dispute such a definition. However, as we now move to discuss the goals of police and the consequent functions of police organizations, confusion and frustration can occur. For the goals and functions of the police are not so easily reduced to a succinct, clear, and understandable definition.

 ## BUREAUCRACIES—DEFINING THE MISSION

In any complex organization, it is absolutely critical to have a specific and detailed understanding of the overall focus of one's enterprise—the mission of the organization. It might sound obvious, but people cannot accomplish much of anything unless they initially know what it is they are trying to *get* accomplished (Maier). So attempting to formulate **Mission Statements** is an important endeavor

(Abrahams). Such statements outline the major goals of complex organizations in specific terms. The idea is to allow everyone everywhere in an organization to focus upon the overall mission whenever deciding something becomes troublesome.

As odd as it might sound, the process of developing a specific understanding of what an organization is supposed to be doing can be difficult at times. For clubs, fraternities, private companies, and corporations, a mission statement is often easy to produce. An organization's mission might be summed up quickly in a declaration: "Our mission, here at International Flange Corporation, is to make flanges and to maximize profits while doing so." Simple.

But for **public institutions**—those bureaucracies that provide services to citizens (Goodsell)—it is not always easy to agree upon what the mission of the organization is. And when any organization has trouble defining its mission, difficulty in administering its operations is guaranteed. Mission confusion within a public organization can generate chaos for top policymakers, middle management, those who deal directly with the public, and, by extension, for the public itself.

Here is an example. During the Great Depression, a number of public bureaucracies were created to help millions of Americans deal with job loss, an inability to take care of their families, a loss of faith in the system, and, generally, with their inability to participate in the pursuit of the "American Dream." One such **bureaucracy** involved putting together, on a state-by-state basis, departments that provided unemployment insurance. The idea was simple to begin with: employers that laid off people would be taxed. The taxes would be paid into a fund used to help support laid off workers—for brief periods of time—while they were out of a job. On the employer's side of things, the more people any given employer laid off, the more taxes they would pay. The payments would support jobless workers and their families on a limited basis until these workers obtained another job. The mission of unemployment insurance departments was fairly clear, and an unemployment insurance department's Mission Statement at the time might have read: "To provide limited support, on a temporary basis, for people who are out of work through no fault of their own (workers that have been laid off, as opposed to having been fired from or quit a job) while they obtain a new job."

But, over time, things changed in America. In the recent past, not only have people been laid off temporarily because of a lack of work at one place or another, but entire industries—in manufacturing in particular—have been closed down. People are being laid off from jobs at factories that will never operate again. These workers lose the ability to utilize workplace skills that have taken a lifetime to develop. They are—by the millions, over time—being left without either a job or a marketable skill. As these changes have come into play in the past several decades of American history, the job of unemployment insurance departments has been expanded. Their work now often involves assisting people with financial support for longer periods of time. It also (now) involves helping people obtain new training in new fields. Unemployment for millions of Americans is no longer a "sometime problem" of limited duration.

These developments have created an odd situation; the mission of unemployment bureaucracies is no longer straightforward, no longer something that can be easily defined in one sentence. Unemployment insurance departments still give people support for limited timeframes when a jobsite temporarily closes down. But now they *also* provide support for extended periods of time so workers can relocate and find new positions. They are *also* involved in helping people plan long-term strategies for obtaining new careers. They are *also* involved in re-training and re-education and a host of other endeavors aimed at reorganizing the American work force.

So there are now several vaguely defined missions—multiple missions—for unemployment bureaucracies to perform. Such multiple missions can be confusing for complex organizations. To make matters worse, sometimes these missions conflict with each other. When this happens, it becomes difficult to know where to focus energies, fiscal support, and program priorities. And it becomes difficult to agree upon which goals to prioritize when faced with finite resources.

Now these problems are not limited to the field of unemployment insurance. Disability insurance departments, workmen's compensation bureaucracies, social welfare programs of various kinds, and a host of other public organizations all suffer from the problem of defining, specifically, what it is they are supposed to do. As the famous political scientist Aaron Wildavsky of the University of California at Berkeley wrote a generation ago, such public bureaucracies all suffer from a number of counterproductive organizational dynamics associated with the fact that their goals (and functions) are **"multiple, conflicting, and vague"** (Wildavsky 48). When an organization has this problem, it is difficult to know who to hire, how to train them, how to discipline them, how to prioritize the organization's use of resources, and so forth.

Police Goals and Functions

Upon first glance, it may not appear that police organizations suffer from the problem of having multiple, conflicting, and vague goals. A simplistic overview of the function of the police might conclude that they "protect and serve." But what does that mean? The police protect what? They serve who? How? When? Where? It turns out that the police do have multiple, conflicting, and vague goals (and functions) and that they always have. And the difficulties associated with this dynamic are numerous.

Those who study police work have long observed that there are three, overarching sets of goals (and functions) for the police: **law enforcement**, **order maintenance**, and **service** (J. Wilson 4). As it is for police administrators and managers, it is important for us to define these three different focuses of the job. Then too, we must spend some time discussing how they often conflict with each other and how numerous difficulties are created by the confusion thus created.

Law Enforcement: Clearly, police work involves some measure of law enforcement. The police receive reports of crime and construct written reports that are,

CHART 1.1

THE GOALS AND FUNCTIONS OF THE POLICE

- Law Enforcement
- Order Maintenance
- Service

in fact, legal documents. They investigate reported crimes and do their best to find out who is responsible for criminal acts—transgressions against the law. When appropriate, they make arrests, taking away people's freedom and putting them in jail. Later on in the criminal justice process, the police testify in court. They serve warrants, transport prisoners, and—if they work for sheriff's departments—operate local jails. They are **legal actors** in every sense of the word.

This is so much the case that many people—perhaps most people—consider "law enforcement" the appropriate label for the field of police work. This was not always the case. Before the dawn of what is now called the "Reform Era" of policing, and before the "War on Crime" and "War on Drugs" metaphors were created, police work involved much more of what we would today consider social welfare–type work. Back in the 19th century, police precincts in big American cities ran soup kitchens for the poor and provided temporary shelter for people during times of economic downturn. The police ran **Police Athletic Leagues (PAL)** and were involved in a host of community-related functions that have only recently been revisited in our current era of **Community Oriented Policing (COP)**. It has only been in the past several generations that the goals and functions of the police have largely been defined as involving "law enforcement" as a top priority. (We will discuss the problem of emphasizing law enforcement as the top priority of the police below.)

Order Maintenance: While the police are certainly involved in enforcing the law on the streets, it is apparent that this focus is only part of what they do on a day-to-day, minute-to-minute basis. While there is some debate about how much time the police spend on enforcing the law, it is generally agreed that this part of their job involves only a fraction of their time and efforts. The police spend much, much more time generally maintaining order in society than they do in enforcing the letter of the law. On a regular basis the police are detailed to handle domestic disturbances, deal with homeless people, break up bar fights, defuse tense crowd situations, monitor high school and community dances and athletic events, contend with public drunkenness, limit loitering, quiet loud parties, and perform many, many functions whose goals are to keep the peace on the streets. Many, if not most, of these daily, routine details involve nothing in the way of law enforcement. They are critical functions, to be sure, but they do not bring into play the dictates of the law in any direct way. Using common sense, intuition, training, and (even) "sixth sense," the police regularly maintain order in society without referring to the law (Crank 97, Understanding ...). Order maintenance is ever-present as an essential goal for the police and, thus, maintaining order is also a top priority function.

Service: But there is more. Aside from enforcing the law when it has been broken and dealing with potentially volatile situations when the peace and order of society are threatened, the police often engage in providing services to their communities. The police direct traffic around accidents and emergencies of various kinds; they aid EMTs and firefighters on a regular basis; they mentor teenagers in an attempt to keep them away from lives in crime and gangs; they provide first aid; they check on the welfare of elderly shut-ins; they are involved in **D.A.R.E.** –type programs; they give directions to lost citizens and tourists; they find lost children; they aid stranded motorists; and they deal with death and bereavement. The police often—very often—help to calm the hysterical, orient the confused, comfort the victimized, educate the ignorant, and so on. In these and a thousand other ways, the police provide indispensable services to their communities—services that have absolutely nothing to do with enforcing the law or maintaining order.

While police goals and functions are multiple for the above reasons, it is also true that there is no one specific, universal kind of police work. Varying amounts of crime, calls for service, and disorderly conduct are presented to the police in different locations. And, thus, the mix between these multiple functions varies. Policing is done in cities with huge populations, diverse and competing ethnic groups, and high crime rates. In these environments the police spend a significant amount of time enforcing the law and maintaining order. As a result, urban policing involves less in the way of service to the community than policing elsewhere. Even if a strong desire to serve their community exists, in some urban areas the police quite simply lack the free time to do so.

Policing is also done, however, in rural areas, with small, largely **homogeneous populations**. In the country there is often almost no crime. Policing there involves very, very little law enforcement, some order maintenance, and a great deal of service. Rural police officers engage their communities in a number of ways that are informal and non-threatening and, in essence, are service-oriented in their minute-by-minute approach to the job. Of course crime—when it occurs—is taken quite seriously by rural police officers. But the call for crime fighting and law enforcement almost never comes. In fact, the job of policing in rural areas can be quite boring for young police officers in particular, specifically because there is so little for them to do.

Policing is also done in suburban areas that are, in every sense, something in-between these two polar opposites. The suburbs are homogenous, like the country. There is far less crime in the suburbs than in the city—again, making suburban policing much like it is in the country. There is less call for law enforcement in the suburbs than there is in the cities. But, on the other hand, there are far more calls for service coming from the suburban public than there are in the country. Suburban Americans demand more "work" from their police than do country citizens.

So the mix of functions for police in the suburbs is something unknown to either urban or rural police officers.

As we shall see in Chapters Nine and Ten, there are differing styles of police organization in America, and these styles emphasize these three functions differently. But in all police organizations, in all jurisdictions, and for all police officers in America, the conflict between these three sets of functions presents a set of paradoxes that are ever-present in the workplace.

THE CONFLICT

It is obvious that the goals and functions of the police are multiple because there are three sets of them. It is also obvious that these sets of functions are rather vaguely defined. One could spend a great deal of time arguing whether any given type of police action involves law enforcement, order maintenance, or service. Take the fairly common example of the police being called to handle a loud party. When detailed to do so, are they involved in law enforcement—because they are concerned with potential violations of noise ordinances? Are they maintaining order—because their main focus is to keep a major disruption from breaking out? Or are they providing service—because they are keeping noise levels down so that the work-a-day people in a neighborhood can go to sleep at a reasonable hour? It is hard to tell. (More on this later.)

But the "multiple" and the "vague" parts of Wildavsky's formulation are not remotely as troublesome as the "conflicting" part. Because the goals and functions of the police regularly conflict with each other, presenting difficult situations. On the one hand, enforcing the law can sometimes create disorder. On the other hand, in attempting to maintain order, the law often does not provide the police with the necessary tools to accomplish this function. Several illustrations are in order.

Box 1.2 provides a true-to-life (this really happened!) example of how law enforcement can conflict with order maintenance. While policing huge concerts

BOX 1.2

A MARIJUANA BUST AT A LARGE CONCERT

A few years ago, at a Grateful Dead concert, a rookie police officer waded into a crowd of over 70,000 people in an attempt to arrest someone for smoking marijuana in public. Now the officer's actions were certainly legal, in the sense that smoking marijuana is a crime, and he was taking action to stop that crime. But in attempting to enforce the law "to the letter," he exhibited extraordinarily bad judgment. Even though the crowd was made up largely of mature, middle-aged "former hippies from the '60s," the officer's efforts led to an altercation that quickly got out of hand; it almost degenerated into a riot. This is a classic example of how enforcing the law can create disorder.

is not a task often experienced by most police, the point is illustrative; very often, in working a beat, police officers are confronted with situations wherein enforcing the law exactly the way it is written is not the best course of action. In attempting to enforce noise ordinances at loud parties, make drug busts at rock concerts, arrest drunks in bars, apply curfew regulations when confronted with large groups of juveniles, or apply any number of disturbing-the-peace–type ordinances at postgame athletic celebrations or parades, they may very well create disorder. And if they do so, they then work directly against one of their primary goals: maintaining order on the streets.

It is important to realize that this conflict between law enforcement and order maintenance is not obscure. It is not something confronted on a limited basis. The police are forever dealing with situations where enforcing the law as it is written might very well encourage counterproductive, *dis*orderly dynamics out on the beat. Arresting *all* college students making noise and being disruptive on a Saturday night, arresting *all* the drunks in a rowdy bar, taking *all* of the juveniles out after curfew to **Juvenile Hall**—each of these is an example of everyday situations that the police must handle. Situations where "law enforcement" (to the letter) might be a very bad idea.

But the direct creation of disorder is only a part of the problem. For in enforcing the law to the letter, the police can also work against the interests of "justice" in society. For example, should the police arrest each and every shoplifter that comes to their attention? What about arresting a 13-year-old shoplifter with a clean record who is clearly embarrassed and, even, afraid when confronted by a shop owner? Is it "best" to take such a child to Juvenile Hall where she will interact with kids who have been involved in far worse offenses? Best for whom? Is it in the interests of justice to make an official arrest and enter the child in the justice system's databank as a "criminal?" Justice for whom? Can we not make the argument that handling such a detail in an informal manner—by taking the child home to Mom and Dad, for example—is in the long term best interests of the child, of the shop owner, and of society in general? If Mom and Dad "handle" the situation effectively within the family unit, and the kid is deterred from future shoplifting, is that not best? Would not enforcing the law in this case work against the interests of every party concerned, including the public?

We will revisit this idea when we explore the use of police discretion in Chapter Three. For now, suffice it to say that since law enforcement and order maintenance can directly conflict with each other in these and a thousand other ways, the police are presented with a paradox: doing their job in one way can inhibit doing their job in another way.

But if it is true that enforcing the law can create disorder or inhibit the delivery of justice on the street, it is equally true that in maintaining order and attempting to administer justice the law is often inadequate. The official, legal tools provided are often just too limited to provide the police with the authority to take action where action is needed. Box 1.3 illustrates this point.

BOX 1.3

DETAIL AT A CONVENIENCE STORE

A 70 year old, semi-retired man is working at an all night convenience store in order to make ends meet. In the middle of the night, he is confronted by a group of a dozen teenaged boys who are local high school seniors. They arrive in two carloads. The youths enter the store, mill around, and buy nothing. They go out into the parking lot and mill around some more. They come back into the store. They are not drunk, and they have not stolen anything. And because they are 18 years of age, they are not guilty of violating curfew. The clerk nonetheless feels uneasy about the situation and calls the police for assistance. Most people would agree that the elderly clerk has a right to expect the police to do "something" about the "situation." But what? What can the police do legally? What laws have been broken? Is this not America, a "free country," wherein such young men have the right to spend their evenings "just hangin' out"? In this instance, the police might be moved to take some sort of action in order to get the youths to "move along" and stop worrying the clerk. But such action would have to be "non-legal," "semi-legal," or "quasi-legal," because there is nothing the police can do according to the letter of the law.

These types of paradoxical situations confront police officers often. They are not unusual circumstances by any means. Police work is fraught with paradoxical instances that involve wrestling with what to do. The police must often decide which set of goals to prioritize and how to handle anything and everything with an eye toward delivering justice on the streets. This is a central reality for the everyday police officer.

UNUSUAL CIRCUMSTANCES

When confronting this problem of the multiple, conflicting, and vague goals and functions of the police, Klockars suggests an interesting way to think about it. He puts our two problems together to create a sort of "axiom" about police work. Facing both sides of our dilemma here, **Klockars' Axiom** suggests that the police must attend to:

1. Situations which ought not to be happening . . .
2. About which something ought to be done . . .
3. NOW!

In assertion Number One, Klockars points out that all sorts of strange, odd, uncomfortable, bizarre, and (at times even) dangerous situations that do not necessarily relate to the breaking of any codified laws present themselves to the police on a regular basis. The police are the recipients of all manner of requests for action that have to do with citizens' fears and frustrations as they attempt to make sense of life's confusion.

Life on the streets of a diverse society is complicated. The behavior of people is at times inexplicable. And citizens call upon the police to deal with anything and everything out of the ordinary. Aside from the obvious requests relating to violence and theft and gangs that come in on a daily basis, the police get calls about UFOs, chickens on the highway, inexplicable noises ("things that go bump in the night"), unfamiliar street vendors, loitering strangers, barking dogs, unattended children, teenagers with "bad attitudes," and a host of other out-of-the-ordinary events and situations. There is just no end to the unusual circumstances that present themselves to citizens as they go about their daily lives and with which the police must be engaged. And, again, many of these unusual circumstances have nothing to do with laws being broken (remember our example from above about the convenience store clerk).

Klockars's second point is that while the police should do something about such unusual circumstances, the action that they take may have absolutely nothing to do with enforcing the law, making arrests, or acting as legal officials. The police must do *something*, but the action they take is often driven by nothing more sophisticated than common sense and intuition. Police work, some have suggested, is all about common sense, and Klockars here points out how often non-legal, semi-legal, and quasi-legal action must be taken by police in the pursuit of their charge. The police must somehow get the teenagers to move along and leave the convenience store clerk alone, but they don't have the law on their side when they do so. They must solve such a situation utilizing informal means of persuasion.

But there is more—something that makes police work unique. Other actors in public organizations face similar realities. Social welfare workers, for example, are often confronted with situations that ought not to be happening, about which something should be done, when they encounter (as a classic example) destitute families that do not "fit" into the rules and regulations of their bureaucracies. A social worker will often want to do something to help a family that is new in town, but the family does not "qualify" for local aid under existing bureaucratic rules. Under such circumstances, the social worker may take semi-legal, non-legal, or quasi-legal action to help. This problem can confront welfare workers, unemployment insurance administrators, tax accountants, disability workers, and a host of other public agency employees.

But the police are constrained by time. As Klockars notes in assertion Number Three, they must decide what to do and take action "now." They don't have the luxury of waiting until tomorrow, or the day after, or next week. When citizens call the police for help, it usually involves an immediate problem that requires immediate action. And so police work's paradoxical mission difficulty (the multiple, conflicting, and vague problem) is ever present and suggests that police work is not as straightforward an endeavor as the lay person might believe it to be. Police work, like life itself, is messy and uneven. And it demands an extraordinary amount of common sense, empathy, and creativity if it is to be done well.

THE HISTORY OF POLICING

It might seem that efforts to succinctly identify the mission of the police would be aided by considering why they were invented in the first place. In other words, if we discovered why organizations of uniformed police were created initially—through studying the history of the police—we might find that our search for one set of goals, for one mission, would be easier. Unfortunately, this is not the case. While some dynamics associated with the invention of the police are agreed upon, others are not. And when considering two separate sets of explanations for why the police were initially created, we find that the mission-oriented confusion gets murkier. Even agreeing upon the *initial* mission of the police—when they were first invented—is problematic.

There has been "policing" of one kind or another since the invention of uniformed codes of law. Once **Hammurabi's Code** (the first written code of laws in human history) was written in the 18th Century BCE, people have had to work at enforcing laws (King). But for many, many centuries there was little need for uniformed, professional groups of individuals to be set aside in society as law enforcers. Largely due to a lack of criminal behavior, there was no need to "invent" the police until the early 19th century. Before that time, people generally policed themselves. Some systems were established utilizing citizen-based policing on occasion, such as both **The Constable System** and **The Night Watch System** in England (Miller, W.). But generally there was no need for a specific group of people to do this work as a regular job.

The first police in the Anglo-American world were the London Police, created by **The Metropolitan Police Act** of 1829 (Peak 11). Police invention in America followed shortly thereafter with the creation of the Boston Police in 1837 and the New York Police in 1841. Why were these police forces invented? Can we help ourselves understand the goals and functions of the police today by visiting what scholars of police history have said about those original forces? The answer as to why police were invented comes in two sets of rationalizations, and the argument between which of them is more accurate illustrates an interesting fact about the American police: people have been debating why the police exist and what they are for (what their goals and functions should be) for more than 150 years now.

The more conservative explanation for why the police were first invented—underwritten in 1829 by the debate in the English Parliament over the passage of the Metropolitan Police Act and in America very shortly thereafter—has to do with maintaining order within huge metropolitan populations (Lane). The newly invented police (in London, Boston, and New York) had to deal with the steadily increasing levels of crime associated with mass industrialization. Also, sufficient

BOX 1.4

WHY THE AMERICAN POLICE WERE INVENTED

"CONSERVATIVE" RATIONALIZATIONS

To deal with increased street crime associated with the industrial revolution, overcrowding, and the newly created "slums" of major cities.

To deal with already existing (and powerful) street gangs.

To deal with tensions between groups of ethnic immigrants.

To provide social services in an age when other public organizations were yet to be created.

"CONFLICT THEORY" RATIONALIZATIONS

To protect elites from increased street crime.

To maintain a stable work force.

To provide a domestic military for the purpose of destroying the burgeoning union movement.

To provide an "occupying army" in the streets for the purpose of both everyday and extraordinary control over the "dangerous classes."

manpower (only men policed in those days) was needed to meet the problem of ethnic tensions between various minority communities with sufficient force to deter what we now refer to as race riots. In America, there were still two more reasons for the invention of the police. They had to confront the power of street gangs that, by the mid 19th Century, had already existed (and were a problem) for fifty years. Then, too, the police of that century performed any number of social welfare–oriented tasks in a world bereft of any public welfare organizations. The police of the 19th century ran soup kitchens, housed the homeless, and provided several other sorts of services for which there were just no other municipal, public employees to perform.

These rationalizations for the invention of the police make perfect sense, and they were the arguments made at the time. But they are not the only arguments that make sense. Since the 19th century, **Marxists**, analyzing society through the lens of what we today call "Conflict Theory," have suggested a very different set of reasons for the initial creation of police forces (Cooper; Johnson). Conflict theory, generally driven by the idea that society—its norms and values, institutions, and operational principles—is controlled by elites at the expense of the underclasses, suggests that the police were (and are today) a behavior control mechanism aimed at keeping those who lack wealth and power "in their place." The police were (and are) needed to keep the underclass from victimizing the elites of society. Furthermore, the police are needed to generally keep tabs on the underclass, providing day-to-day, minute-to-minute control over the masses on the street.

In doing so, the police protect wealthy interests by striving to maintain a stable working class. By keeping crime at minimum levels in places where the underclass resides, the police maintain enough stability so that workers who do the jobs elites would never deign to—cleaning toilets, cutting grass, working in factories, and so forth—continue to go to work and live their lives, as conflict theorists would put it, "repressed by the system." And finally, throughout more than a century's worth of American history, the police worked to prohibit the organization of labor into a cohesive body. Labor unions were broken up and individuals who attempted to provide a framework for the development of unions were oppressed and even—on occasion—murdered by the police. (None of this is "opinion," by the way. It is historical fact (Brody; Hirsch).)

This is not to suggest that the reader accept all of these rationalizations and become a Marxist. It merely behooves the thoughtful person to reflect upon the logic of these arguments. The conflict theorists, in other words, make several good, solid, logical points about what the police have been doing for the 180 years since they were invented in the Anglo-American world.

And so delving, albeit very briefly here, into the history of why the police were invented does us no good in terms of coming up with an understanding, acceptable to everyone, of what initial police functions were. Thus we are presented with the problem of multiple, conflicting, and vague goals and functions— because ideas over who the police are, why the police were invented, and what the police are supposed to do have always been up for debate.

HOW THE POLICE SPEND THEIR TIME

In discussing the problem of multiple goals for police, it is important to stop for a moment and reflect upon how they actually spend their time on the street. How much time is spent on law enforcement? What percentage of hours in a day? How much time is spent on order maintenance? On service? Most important in this regard is the amount of time spent on law enforcement. Since students of the police universally agree that law enforcement does not take up very much police time (Roberg *et al.* 224), it is important to contemplate what does. But here again there is some debate among those who have attempted to put the numbers together.

One item not particularly controversial in these calculations is the estimated time the police spend on law enforcement. Some scholars suggest that merely 8 or 10 percent of police time is spent on law enforcement (Wilson, J.). Others have suggested that close to 40 percent of specific calls for police service from citizens involve law enforcement (Wrobleski and Hess). But that statistic is misleading; calls for service may make up 40 percent of the police "workload," but how does that

CHART 1.2: How the Police Spend Their Time

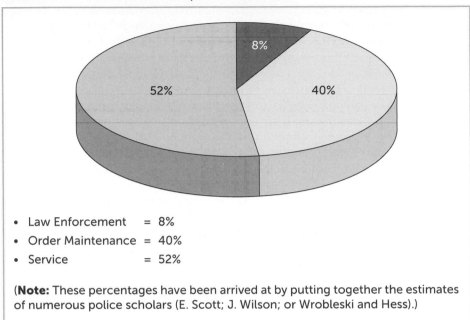

- Law Enforcement   = 8%
- Order Maintenance = 40%
- Service   = 52%

(**Note:** These percentages have been arrived at by putting together the estimates of numerous police scholars (E. Scott; J. Wilson; or Wrobleski and Hess).)

translate into time spent on the job? How often do police officers spend time on specific calls from citizens? As expressed in minutes, hours, and seconds? The answer is that such calls make up a small amount of police workload. We must remember that America is a huge country, with more than 300,000,000 people in it, in which policing goes on 24 hours a day, 7 days a week, all the time, everywhere. Viewed from that perspective, the amount of time spent on law enforcement must be very, very minimal—perhaps even less than 8 percent (E. Scott).

How can this be? In most places, the graveyard shift (for example) involves little or no law enforcement, 7 days per week, year round. This is true not only because police do not encounter much activity patrolling on night shifts but also because few calls come in from the public during the hours between midnight and morning. Furthermore, we cannot ignore the fact that a great deal of policing occurs in rural and suburban areas, where even during the day watch and swing shifts there are often very few calls for service and little in the way of crime fighting to be done. Adding up all of the hours on the clock, day in and day out, during which the police are on routine patrol and answering no calls whatsoever, we come to this conclusion: the police spend a very small percentage of the hours in their day on law enforcement.

As Wildavsky mentioned with regard to the goals of public bureaucracies, these three sets of goals are vaguely defined (45). It is difficult to know, for example, whether the police are maintaining order or providing community service when they are, say, directing traffic. Or when they are solving domestic disputes. Or when they are calming down loud parties. Which of these specific functions fits into which category? There is no one, single, definitive answer to that question. And so analysts who have tried to calculate the numbers—the percentages of time spent on one goal or another—have had some trouble in agreeing upon their results.

Somewhat confusing in this debate about how the police spend their time is the consideration of what "routine patrol" means. On routine patrol, between specific calls for service and assigned details, are the police maintaining order or providing community service? Since routine patrol involves a huge percentage of what the police do, it is an important question if we are to attempt an analysis of how the police actually spend their time. Again, no matter how we attempt to add it up, and irrespective of this debate between order maintenance hours and service hours, the fact is that the police in America spend very, very, *very* little of their time on law enforcement.

ONE LAST WORD ABOUT LAW ENFORCEMENT

Even if it is true that the police do not spend much of their time on law enforcement, why is this point so important? Why dwell upon this for so long in our discussion? The answer is that a focus upon law enforcement is not just inaccurate—in a substantive sense—it is troublesome in several ways that impact police officers, police systems, and the administration of justice. If mission statements are important—because they focus and direct organizations and the individuals inside of them—they can be so in both positive and negative ways. An inappropriate mission statement can lead to inappropriate organizational behavior and individual behavior and, thus, to confusion. And it is most definitely true that focusing upon law enforcement as the primary focal point of police work in America—whether in official mission statements or just generally within the subculture and within police organizations—can have any number of deleterious effects upon police work.

Emphasizing law enforcement can drive police recruitment and selection procedures in an inappropriate direction. It can draw to the profession people who are "gung-ho" to go out and to fight in a "War on Crime" or a "War on Drugs." Such people may be selected in lieu of people who are more prone to see the service side of the job as being important. Fighting wars involves struggling with an "enemy." And in an era of Community Oriented Policing (see Chapter Ten), viewing substantial numbers of the general public as "the enemy" is counterproductive to the new, modern philosophy of American policing.

Emphasizing law enforcement can drive police training in an inappropriate direction. Training can focus upon teaching the criminal law and crime fighting strategies to the exclusion of teaching about any number of dynamics that prepare young police officers for a life of service. Young officers can fall into a mindset that suggests "real police work" only involves putting handcuffs on people and taking them off to jail. Policing in a community-oriented way involves mentoring youths, interacting with business owners and neighborhood leaders, counseling couples, calming fears of elderly shut-ins, maintaining order at public events, developing anti-gang strategies, comforting aggrieved families, understanding the psychology of drug and alcohol addiction, and a host of other endeavors that have next-to-nothing to do with law enforcement. If training emphasizes law enforcement, young officers might eschew accomplishing these other tasks. And the central problem with this is that these other tasks make up the bulk of the police workload.

Emphasizing law enforcement can drive police administration and accountability mechanisms in an inappropriate direction. It can reward the war-oriented, overly aggressive officer instead of acknowledging the efforts of the more agent-of-change–based, problem solving, community-oriented type of police officer. Nothing could be more inimical to the development of good police-community relations, of long-term, problem-solving relationships between police and local leaders, and of a general pro-police, "we-are-all-in-this-together" type of focus in the minds of citizens than having police officers on the street who focus solely on making arrests and fighting wars on crime and drugs. Fighting these wars in an aggressive way, being law enforcement–oriented all of the time, implies that the police are an occupying army out on the beat. And all of this is bad.

For these, and a dozen other reasons (some of which will be explored in Chapter Eight when we engage paramilitaristic policing), it is important for students of the police, police administrators, and the police themselves to understand how negative a "law enforcement first" type of mentality can be. For the remainder of our discussions in this book we label our topic as "police work"—that is what we will call it—rather than calling it "law enforcement." We do this to remind ourselves on a consistent basis why law enforcement is an inappropriate focal point for the police as a central mission.

SUMMATION

In this chapter, we have found that while it might be easy for us to define who the police are, it is an entirely different story when we attempt to focus upon the goals and consequent functions of the police. Prioritizing goals and functions is next-to-impossible. The police officer on the street is forever presented with situations requiring that action be taken. Yet those situations often involve nothing in the way of criminal conduct. And they often require little in the way of law enforcement. While millions of people—perhaps most people—call what the police do "law enforcement," that label is not accurate. Little of what the police do has anything to do with law enforcement, and focusing upon law enforcement as the primary mission of the police can be deleterious for the interests of American citizens and justice in general.

Having discussed our first paradox, and a central, all-encompassing one at that, it is time to move on to engage several dynamics of police work that include

CHAPTER ONE PARADOX BOX

At the very beginning of our study of the police we have our first, important paradox; while it appears that the goals and functions of the police are clear, specific, and generally agreed upon, this is not the case. They are "multiple, conflicting, and vague." And this complicates everything about police work; the individual police officer's experience, the job of police management, what citizens experience when they encounter the police, and the administration of justice on the streets of America.

other paradoxes. The first of these discussions is about stereotyping. While all people stereotype, police officers do so much more often than average citizens. And though it is understandable to see why they do so, their propensity to stereotype creates problems for the police, for the citizen on the street, and for the administration of justice in America.

 DISCUSSION QUESTIONS

1. Think about the term "law and order." People often refer to themselves or to politicians as being in favor of law and order. Given our discussion in this chapter about the conflict between law enforcement and order maintenance, discuss how this phrase—"law and order"—is actually a non sequitur and logically inconsistent with itself.

2. The police are called to a loud fraternity party in a small college town. They arrive to find several hundred college students drinking inside of the fraternity, out on the front lawn, and even on the sidewalk. It is obvious that more than 100 of the drinkers present are under 21. What should the police do? What would "the law" suggest that they do? If they invoke the law will they create disorder? What would common sense dictate? Discuss the fact that there is no one, "perfect" response to any of these questions.

3. Box 1.2 tells the true story of a rookie officer attempting to make an arrest for smoking marijuana at a rock concert. Are the rookie's actions reasonable? Are they legal? If someone made a citizen's complaint about the rookie's poor judgment, should such a complaint be upheld? Was the rookie guilty of "misconduct" in utilizing so little in the way of common sense? Discuss.

4. Box 1.4 suggests several rationalizations for the invention of the police that are products of conflict theory. Discuss these rationalizations. Which are true? Can you come up with other examples of why you think the police were invented? Which are not true? How might you argue against the ones with which you do not agree?

KEY TERMS

Assault: The attempt to use force on another (a misdemeanor).

Battery: The use of force on another (a misdemeanor).

Bureaucracy: A state-run organization that provides services to the public.

Coercive Force: The use of threats to harm to control behavior.

Community Oriented Policing (COP): A new philosophy of policing—discussed at length in Chapter Ten.

The Constable System: A system in Old England involving citizens policing small villages.

D.A.R.E.: Drug Abuse Resistance Education—an anti-drug program for grammar school children.

Extortion: The unlawful exaction of money or property through intimidation or undue exercise of **authority (a felony)**.

Hammurabi's Code: The oldest code of laws in the world—dates to the 18th Century BCE.

Homogeneous Populations: Populations with common demographics, norms, and values.

Juvenile Hall: Criminal Justice facility for the detention of juveniles who are either without parental supervision, incorrigible, or who have perpetrated what would be "crimes" if committed by adults.

Klockars' Axiom: Statement of what sorts of issues the police must attend to.

Law Enforcement: One of the three major functions of the police—involves the enforcement of the law as written in penal codes, vehicle codes, and so forth.

Legal Actors: Public employees who represent the law in dealings with citizens.

Marxists: Those who follow conflict theory—the idea that the struggle between economic classes explains societal norms, values, institutions, and individual behavior.

The Metropolitan Police Act: The 1829 act that created the Metropolitan Police in London, England.

Mission Statement: A statement of the overall goals of a complex organization.

Multiple, Conflicting, and Vague: Wildavsky's idea about the interplay between goals and functions in complex, public organizations.

The Night Watch System: The last citizen-operated policing system that pre-dated the invention of the uniformed police in England.

Order Maintenance: One of the three major functions of the police—involves maintaining order on the streets through multiple means not necessarily relating to the law.

Police Athletic League (PAL): Sports league run by the police both during the Political Era of policing and now, again, during today's COP Era.

Public Institutions: State-run bureaucracies providing service to citizens.

Service: One of the three major functions of the police—involves being of service to the community in various ways.

ADDITIONAL READINGS

An excellent discussion about the need for specific, focused goals in complex organizations can be found in Norman Raymond Frederick Maier's work entitled *Frustration: The Study of Behavior Without a Goal* (Greenwood Press, 1982). It is one of the works often cited in discussions about not only the general requirement of having specific goals but the need for mission statements in particular. Aaron Wildavsky's classic point about public bureaucracies having goals that are multiple, conflicting, and vague was published in many forms over the course of Wildavsky's life. Perhaps the most sophisticated and well-developed explication by Wildavsky can be found in *Speaking Truth to Power* (Transaction Publications, 1987).

Carl Klockars's police-specific ideas about the three major functions of the police, and also his notions about those situations to which the police must attend, are found in *Thinking About Police* (McGraw-Hill, 1983) and another excellent, short work by Klockars, *The Idea of Police* (Sage, 1985). A more contemporary and elaborate discussion about the problematic nature of police goals and functions is found in Cyril D. Robinson, Richard Scaglion, and J. Michael Olero's *Police in Contradiction: The Evolution of the Police Function in Society* (Greenwood Press, 1993). Former Police Chief Anthony V. Bouza's book *The Police Mystique: An Insider's Look at Cops, Crime, and the Criminal Justice System* (Perseus, 2001) includes an argument relating to the slippery slope that the police can encounter when focusing upon arrests and statistics to explain and evaluate what it is that they should accomplish. Given how little law enforcement is involved in police work, the argument contends that focusing upon such numbers misses the point of what the police should prioritize.

Counterposed to these treatments of the complex nature of defining the goals, functions, and mission of the police is perhaps the foremost textbook in the world of "nuts and bolts" police studies, Thomas F. Adams's *Police Field Operations 7th Ed.* (Prentice Hall, 2006). In this work, Adams assumes that the goals and functions of the police are specifically defined and well understood by all. This is usually the case in all similar "police operations-oriented" works.

A synoptic compilation of many arguments and studies of how the police actually utilize their time can be found in Charles J. Edwards's *Changing Policing Theories for 21st Century Societies* (Federation Press, 2005). Edwards engages this topical area in contemporary terms using recent analyses and research.

Finally, throughout our work, we will refer to police jargon on numerous occasions. A fun book about police slang—and one that can bring a more focused understanding to the student who either lacks police officer experience or has few contacts in the police world—is *Cop Talk: A Dictionary of Police Slang* (IUniverse Publishing, 2000) by Lewis Poteet and Aaron C. Poteet. We mention it here, but it has relevance to our discussions throughout this book.

CHAPTER 2

Stereotyping

Chapter Two Outline

In this chapter we will discuss a dynamic present in everyday life on a regular basis: the propensity to stereotype. We will analyze how and why all people stereotype and embrace the reality that bureaucrats stereotype more often than the average person. Finally, we will consider why police officers stereotype even more than other bureaucrats. It is part of the on-the-job, working personalities of police officers to stereotype and to attempt to do it quickly and efficiently. This discussion will present us with still another, central paradox of police work: in order to accomplish tasks on the street, police officers must stereotype for rational, understandable reasons—often involving efforts to protect themselves from harm—but this propensity creates numerous dubious dynamics that impact upon police community relations in a negative way. Put differently, police **stereotyping** is understandable, rational, and important for the accomplishment of the police officer's task, but, at the same time, it is often counterproductive to the interests of the police themselves.

Before discussing the psychological dynamics of stereotyping, it is important to remind ourselves that the word "stereotyping" conjures negative connotations. In our contemporary American world, we tend to think of stereotyping as a deplorable dynamic that should be avoided as often as possible by enlightened and intelligent individuals. Racial and religious prejudice, in particular, come to mind when we hear the word "stereotyping," and we therefore tend to react to the word in a negative way, driven by our modern understanding of what it means to be a good, moral person.

But stereotyping is not necessarily a negative or bad thing. In fact, stereotyping is a necessary part of life. The stereotyping of persons, places, events, and things is an absolutely essential element of how people understand their world and operate within it. Let us begin this discussion with a brief consideration of how stereotyping is accomplished by the human brain.

HOW PEOPLE STEREOTYPE

Our propensity to stereotype begins very early in life. When we come out of the womb we are immediately shocked—frightened would be a better word—by the light and the noise and the cold with which we are confronted. This, along with the physical trauma of coming through the birth canal, is why babies almost universally cry at birth. Very, very shortly thereafter—so early on in life that none of us ever remembers it happening—a baby's little brain begins to attempt to make sense of its new environment. In making sense of the world, the baby's brain stereotypes; it groups together experiences and stores them for future reference. Here's how it works.

Our brains receive all sorts of external stimuli. All five senses—touch, taste, smell, hearing, and sight—receive these stimuli on a regular basis. Using a computer metaphor, this is the raw "data" out of which our brains create information. The stimuli are screened through mental constructs in our brains and "dropped" into categories—stored in mental "boxes" of sorts. These boxes in our brains are called

BOX 2.1

AN EXAMPLE OF POLICE STEREOTYPING

In the Sacramento Valley, a Sheriff's Deputy stops a vehicle in the middle of the night on a lonely road. Over the radio she calls in the location and description of the vehicle. A few moments later, she calls in the name and date-of-birth of the driver, asking for a records and warrant check. Immediately after she ends her transmission, another officer comes on the air and says: "That guy's a 245B." In California, the Penal Code section 245B refers to the crime of "Assault with a Deadly Weapon Upon a Police Officer." Using this code, a stereotypified communication occurs—the officer making the stop immediately knows she is not making a "normal" stop and takes appropriate action to protect herself. Here is a classic example of police stereotyping involving distilling a dangerous reality into just a couple of numbers. It illustrates why police stereotyping is a logical, practical, handy tool of the police trade.

"**diagnostic packages**" by psychologists who study how we learn and think. Once a diagnostic package has been created, our brain uses it forever as a "**perceptual shorthand**" (another label from the world of psychology); we see something, reference it to pre-existing categorizations, recognize what it is, and act accordingly. This is how we store absolutely everything we know in life (Schneider).

For example, when people are young, they learn that when a certain stimulus enters their brain through their sense of sight they need to relate it to a stereotypified idea previously stored as a diagnostic package. They perceive "the color red." They know it to be the color red because they have learned from their parents that this is the word associated with this type of data. (Of course, if people speak Spanish, they learn to categorize the same data as the color "rojo," and if they speak French they learn to categorize the same data as "rouge" . . . and so forth.) If the stimulus comes in from, say, a red jacket, people will recognize it to be red and they will also recognize it to be a jacket. They can then act toward this object in a logical way.

The important point here is that this is how we store *all* information—all of the knowledge that we have in the world. Because this is the case, stereotyping goes on all of the time, and, indeed, it is at the heart of how we learn and utilize anything and everything we know. To have knowledge—to be able to recognize anything, event, person, or concept—and to act effectively upon this knowledge recognition is to stereotype.

So stereotyping makes life easier, simpler, more understandable. Stereotyping is something with which we are all familiar and without which none of us could go through life. But as we shall see in a moment, stereotyping is done for reasons other than this basic one of making life simple and understandable.

WHY PEOPLE STEREOTYPE

Stereotyping is more than a way to make life easier. It is much more than that. For as much as stereotyping involves categorizing people, things, events—all knowledge—to operate effectively in life, we take it further. People use their stereotyping skills for more than these basic human operational requirements. And it is here that stereotypification becomes troublesome and negative. People stereotype others in many ways not merely aimed at keeping them separate and straight in their minds. People stereotype to make themselves feel comfortable and superior to others. We stereotype human characteristics and create what we believe to be meaningful beliefs about social groups (McGarty, et al).

In other words, we tend to develop a perceptual shorthand that conveys much more than "this person is Fred" and "that person is Kate." We also tend to develop a shorthand that suggests "Fred is black" and "Kate is white" or "Fred is Jewish" and "Kate is Muslim." And along with these two types of stereotypification (regarding race and religion) can come many dynamics that have brought unbridled harm and evil into the world throughout human history. In addition to these simple differentiations concerning race and religion (and sexual orientation and so forth), socially constructed negatives that have been and can be deleterious to the maintenance of positive human relationships have developed.

Stereotyping other groups of people can make a person feel comfortable as a member of the "us" as opposed to being a member of the "them." In other words, stereotyping groups of people—our group and the other group—can create social solidarity. It makes us feel good to be a part of the "in" group (of "us"), and it can create in the individual a level of comfort that allows us to be a part of something greater than just ourselves. So much is this a part of everyday human dynamics that many people have studied the propensity to create in foreign groups of people the fearful concept of "**the evil other**" (Aho). Later in this discussion we will reflect upon the tendency of the police subculture to think in these "us against them" terms. And we will consider at great length the destructive consequences of police officers thinking in such ways. For now, though, it is merely important

BOX 2.2

WHY DO PEOPLE STEREOTYPE?

- To simplify life—to make things easier.
- To categorize knowledge into understandable elements.
- To feel comfortable about their lives and themselves.
- To feel superior to others.

to remember that while stereotyping is not *necessarily* a negative thing, it most certainly can be. It can fashion a troublesome reality by turning this logical and practical dynamic of life into inappropriate prejudice.

It is but a short step from this propensity to label an "us" and a "them" in life—for comfort and a feeling of belonging—to creating a feeling of superiority to others. The construction of an "us" group can begin to take on profoundly disturbing implications. The group of "us" can be perceived as composing the good, the honest, the loyal, the righteous, the intelligent, the worthy, and the just. The group of "them," concomitantly, can be thought to include people who are wicked, dishonest, disloyal, stupid, worthless, and evil. And because we are good and they are bad, it is acceptable (or it can be *seen* to be acceptable) to confront the evil others in the world not only with contempt and disdain but with hatred and violence.

So stereotyping can at once be a necessary, important, logical part of everyday life and also develop into counterproductive, vicious, and (even) evil ways of thinking and behaving. This is a paradox of life, not just of police work. Stereotyping can be good and utilitarian, but it also may be bad and counterproductive. It might often make us feel good about ourselves, but it can also create animosity, tragedy, and genuine evil in the world.

While each and every person stereotypes, there are occupations and endeavors that amplify this human propensity. One such occupation is working in a bureaucracy.

BUREAUCRATIC STEREOTYPING

So all people stereotype—putting people, things, places, and events into categories in their minds. They then can utilize this perceptual shorthand to make life simpler. So far, so good. But a bureaucrat, it turns out, stereotypes far more often than the average person. The very nature of bureaucracy demands it (Perrow). And since police officers operate within a bureaucracy, they inherit this bureaucratic propensity (White 129–132).

Why do bureaucrats stereotype much more often than other people? For one thing, bureaucrats deal with large groups of people. They deliver services to the public, and in doing so they must apply rules on a regular basis. They meet citizens, analyze their situations, apply bureaucratic rules to the situations they confront, and make decisions about how to treat citizens. Does this person qualify for unemployment insurance? Does that person qualify for disability payments? Does this person qualify as a dependant? Does that person qualify to enter into this program? How should I deal with this unusual, out-of-the-box–type situation? It doesn't fit well into the rules and regulations, so what should I do? These are the types of questions with which bureaucrats are confronted. And the answers come with numbers attached to them: this person or that person is eligible or ineligible under this or that numbered rule (or law).

Thus bureaucracy is all about taking everyday situations and everyday people and applying rules to them. While attempting to provide social welfare services to needy citizens, the bureaucrats of a state's Department of Social Services, as an example, will deal with applicants and decide if their situations qualify them for services. Then they determine which services might be relevant and effective. Then they deliver the appropriate services. Sometimes they will question eligibility as time goes on. Sometimes the services provided are modified due to policy changes at the state, local, or federal level. Sometimes they might reevaluate provided services based on changes in a client's life situation. This is the essence of bureaucratic work. Because of this central reality, bureaucrats tend to think along very rigid and structured lines when dealing with the public; people fall into categories. So much so that people can become "cases" in the minds of bureaucrats. And the cases have numbers. These numbers don't just represent a given case or citizen/client, they also represent the type of rule or situation under which a client is served.

In police work, details (assignments) are numbered in the same several ways as in a welfare agency. To begin with, every call for service is given a number by those in charge of taking calls from the public. So each and every call has its very own number. In order to keep calls for service separate, in order to develop accountability (making sure that all citizen calls are, in fact, handled), and in order to track police time spent statistically, each and every call is assigned this number initially upon its reception.

But there is also a number assigned that indicates the *type* of call received. Either from the Penal Code or from some other code (Vehicle Code, Welfare and Institutions Code, Business and Professions Code, etc.), a number is automatically associated with any call into the police. This is not done just for the sake of efficiency and simplicity. In the criminal justice system, every actor, or set of actors—the

BOX 2.3

"NORMALIZING" CRIME

The sociologist David Sudnow once wrote that criminal justice practitioners had to "normalize crime." Crime, by its very nature, involves deviant behavior. That behavior can be strange, odd, inexplicable, and frightening. But no matter how bizarre or extraordinary a given type of deviance is, professionals working in the system must come up with a number for it, a section in the penal code (or some other code) that quantifies or stereotypes the deviant behavior. A murder becomes a "187." A robbery becomes a "211." A suspicious circumstance becomes a "415." And so forth. Thus, paradoxically, while deviance is *ab*normal, it must be "normalized" if the criminal justice system's bureaucrats are to deal with it efficiently.

(Sudnow)

police, prosecutorial staffs, judges, correctional officers, and so forth—must always focus on the principle of *habeas corpus* embedded in American jurisprudence. This principle has several different applications in our legal system, but one idea that it represents is this: anyone arrested must be brought before a magistrate and charged with a specific crime. Police officers may at times jokingly suggest that a person was arrested for "failing the attitude test." But in fact, anyone brought to any jail—for even a moment—must be charged with some specific act. Thus police officers are consistently translating the facts that present themselves in any given detail into (potential) code sections that number specific violations of the law.

In this way, all of the strange, crazy, mixed up, irrational, disgusting, bizarre, violent, and generally deviant types of behavior into which some citizens might fall become "cleaned up," to some extent, and normalized—stereotyped with a coded number. And, of course, this code-oriented number is given (when a detail is assigned) to a police officer whose beat is also numbered. And further, the police have a numbered, three-pronged approach to how details should be handled relative to the nature of what sort of priority they deserve: Code 1 details are handled "at the convenience of the officer"; Code 2 details are handled "as quickly as possible"; and Code 3 details are "emergencies" handled with blue lights and sirens and so forth.

But there is more. Not only are penal and vehicle code numbers applied to police details, but the calls for service come over the air—on the radio or on a prowl car's computer—in codified fashion using a police radio code. In most departments, the **10 Code** is used. Every minute of every day a police officer is on the street, police details, citizen behavior, and operations are being consistently codified and stereotyped and translated into 10 Code numbers. An officer is "10-8" when he or she is "in service." An officer arrives at the scene of a detail, gets out of the car to handle it, and "goes 10-97." And officer having his or her lunch break is "Code 7." And so it goes, day and night, minute by minute. Police service is forever broken up into these stereotypically codified radio code sections.

In modern day police work, there are even more numbers than these three types. Statistics of various kinds are produced by police departments and computerized so patterns can be determined—patterns of criminal behavior, patterns of police calls for service, and patterns that reflect the amount of police time spent in one way or another. This set of computer-oriented numbers is, in most locations today, something into which all modern police operations must be translated. And finally, as is true with other bureaucrats, the police must keep financial numbers in order to develop, administer, expand, or contract budgets.

Put bluntly, the police—like all bureaucrats—are always counting things, numbering them, keeping track of calls, arrests, time utilized, and dollars spent. They are forever stereotyping anything and everything in different ways; they construct codified images that simplify what are often the extraordinarily complicated activities of citizens in their jurisdiction and the police themselves, of crime and

BOX 2.4

NUMBERS IN POLICE WORK

Any call for service from a citizen may end up being given at least four numbers. For example, a domestic disturbance call might be given:

- A case number for the call itself (that reflects the date, time, and type of call).
- A penal code number: 415 (a California code, as an example).
- A radio code number: "1Y22, you have a 415-Family—handle this Code 2."
- A computer code number, entered later into the department's computer system.

criminals and budgets as well. They keep statistics on just about everything, and they do so as an integral part of what their jobs are all about.

So the propensity for all people to stereotype is exacerbated in the bureaucrat. But police officers are a special kind of bureaucrat. They work within a bureaucracy driven by dynamics that are foreign to all other public service organizations.

POLICE STEREOTYPING

Police officers, as noted above, stereotype people and events as part of their bureaucratic charge. But there is more. Police officer stereotyping is more rampant, more ever-present, and more necessary than stereotyping by other bureaucrats. In a sort of overlapping way, the tendency of all humans to stereotype is amplified among bureaucrats and exponentially amplified among police officers—who literally work at honing their ability to stereotype (Lieberman; Navarro, Karlins).

Police officers spend a great deal of time "working their beats." That is, in between handling specific calls for service, serving warrants, investigating cases, responding to accidents, and so on, they are relatively free for "routine patrol." Routine patrol involves monitoring the streets of their communities, looking for anything and everything suspicious, unusual, out of the ordinary, disturbing, disruptive, and—potentially—related to crime or disorder. It is the job of the police, at all times, to enforce the law, maintain order, and provide service to their communities, even when citizens have not called for a specific response. And in accomplishing this general task of working the beat, police officers are moved to stereotype all of the time.

The Sociologist Jerome Skolnick once wrote that police officers develop what he called a "**working personality**" (Skolnick 41–58, Justice Without...). This personality involves developing techniques for handling certain types of details, creating particular methods for investigating crimes, constructing ways of inter-rogating people, and developing strategies for monitoring and maintaining peace, quiet, and order on their beats between specific details. As a part of the officer's working personality, she or he develops unique approaches to routine patrol and personal philosophies of policing. No two officers are the same, and no two work-ing personalities approach the job in an identical way. (Indeed, part of what makes the job of policing interesting and alluring is this latitude—the ability to construct one's own working personality.) But one thing is common to all police officer working personalities: in an effort to know who or what is "**wrong**" on their beat, police officers must know who is "right" or who "belongs."

In the locker room, much is made of the police officer's "sixth sense" (Crank 102, Understanding . . . ,). Knowing that something is "up" or amiss is an impor-tant element of a good police officer's repertoire. A good tool of the trade is this ability to sense that things are not the way they should be. Translated into police jargon, this is all about knowing who is "wrong." When telling a story in the locker room, a police officer may sometimes joke that someone was stopped because they were "wrong." Other officers know what this means. On the witness stand, in open court, the reason for a vehicle stop (as an example) might be related to the legal principle of **probable cause**, and an officer will testify to that effect: "I had probable cause to stop the vehicle because . . . " But to other police officers, all that need be said is that the vehicle was wrong.

In order to know who and what is wrong, an officer must know who and what is right. And, thus, the job of working a beat involves paying attention, on a daily basis, to who moves about at what time of day or night. When does this business open and when does that business close? Who operates legitimately at night, behaving themselves and acting legally? At what times do kids get out of this or that school? At what time does the local plant change its shifts? In addi-tion, police officers must learn who the local trouble makers are. What cars do they drive? Where do they live? Where do they "belong?" What are their records? Who are the local burglars, bullies, and thieves of various kinds? What ongoing problems plague one neighborhood or another? With regard to domestic distur-bances, who are the "regulars"—the families that generate calls on Friday nights, when paychecks or welfare checks have been cashed, leaving people with money to get "loaded?" At which bars do people drink to excess and look for trouble, and at which bars is there normally not very much in the way of drunkenness and fighting?

These and a hundred other questions need to be asked and answered before an effective officer knows what the beat looks like under normal circumstances. Once this normal picture is painted, then those people or occurrences or alterca-tions or suspicious circumstances that do not fit into the normal picture stick out and are easily confronted. It is as if in the process of working the beat, a police officer must make up a template of sorts in her or his mind—that involves what normal life appears to be like—and then place that template over the activity and interactions that are observed . . . and, now and then, someone or some activity

BOX 2.5

BEING "WRONG"

A Field Training Officer (FTO) is parked in a strip mall, explaining the last detail to a rookie, who is writing up the report about it. As they talk, the officer notices a local troublemaker who he knows to be a burglar walking across an open field, on the other side of the roadway, about 100 yards or so from the patrol unit. The FTO explains to the rookie who this burglar is, that he (the burglar) lives miles away, that he owns no vehicle, and, thus, that he does not "belong" here. Right in the middle of this explanation the young burglar drops something he is toting in his left hand. He drops it in the field and continues walking. The FTO and his rookie drive across the street to investigate and discover that the youth was carrying a stereo amplifier labeled as belonging to the local middle school. Sure enough, a quick look at the middle school uncovers the fact that a burglary has just occurred. An arrest is made—strictly on the strength of knowing who the young man was and that, in this circumstance, he was "wrong."

doesn't fit the template (again, in the police officer's mind) and is labeled "wrong." Anyone and anything wrong deserves police attention. It is that simple.

So in working a beat, police officers attempt—in a conscious way, as a part of their craft—to stereotype everyone and everything. This is the essence of working the beat, and how it is done forms the central element of the working personality. This is what police officers are paid to do, and, thus, there is a pronounced propensity for police officers to stereotype and work at doing it effectively.

There is another, somewhat unique dynamic operational in the police subculture that moves young officers in particular to *work* at stereotyping. On a regular basis, rookies consciously attempt to hone their police-geared stereotyping abilities with the goal of becoming expert at them. This is driven by the realities surrounding the rookie experience. In any occupation, profession, or (even) athletic endeavor, people do not like to be rookies. Being a beginner can give a person excuses, to some extent, for ignorance and incompetence. And such excuses can allow latitude as rookies learn their trade or sport—latitude that allows them to commit errors and be ineffective. But the self-respecting rookie wants to shed the title as soon as possible. Being a rookie in any enterprise carries with it a certain amount of negative stigma; rookies are the brunt of jokes by veterans on the playing field as athletes, in the office as bureaucrats, and on the beat as police officers. And most people do not appreciate being made the fool. So they work hard to gain acceptance into the veteran group as soon as possible.

In police work, this propensity is even more pronounced than in other arenas of life. The police subculture is known for its solidarity and, even, for its isolation from the rest of the world. (In Chapter Six, we will discuss the subculture at length.) Because of a dozen dynamics that make the police feel as if "it's us against them out there," police officers cleave to one another and form a bond that is solid and almost impenetrable (much more on this in Chapter Seven). Given this isolation, and given the dangers associated with the job, police officers who are new to the field want to avail themselves of the psychic sustenance—not to mention physical safety—that comes with the feeling of "belonging" within the subculture. So rookies strive to appear more experienced than they really are. One way they do this is to pick up subcultural jargon quickly and behave as if they (rookies) have been around.

Thus rookies work at appearing "**salty**" (experienced) veterans. In order to shed the rookie label or image, young officers memorize the 10 Code and penal code numbers quickly. They talk—sometimes more so than veterans—using such stereotypical communication modes. They learn who the local "bad actors" are and make a point of sharing this knowledge with everyone who will listen. Often, in the locker room or on the beat, young officers act boisterous beyond their years—indicating a sort of jadedness that is inappropriate given their lack of experience. Since they *want* to appear jaded by their street experience, they pick up on locker room humor and, at times, laugh a bit too long and too loudly at cynical stories. Finally, rookie police officers tend to await—in an almost anxious way—the day when a new crop of rookies arrives. New rookies, of course, come into the locker room at the bottom of the totem pole. And the appearance of the latest group of newcomers can elevate the now not-so-inexperienced last group of arrivals to a new status: that of veterans (if only in their own minds). Spouting jargon—code numbers and so forth—accelerates the rate at which young officers become accepted.

We have discussed here several dynamics operational in police work that motivate officers to stereotype more than average citizens and, even, other bureaucrats. But there is one more, critically important dynamic to discuss, and it is so important that it deserves its own, separate subsection in our discussion.

POTENTIAL VIOLENCE

Largely because of Hollywood-driven imagery (that we will discuss at length in Chapter Six), people often think of police work as an extraordinarily dangerous occupation. Perhaps this is because the danger to police officers comes from other human beings—rather than equipment or Mother Nature—and, thus, it has an odd, eerie feel to it. But police work is not the most dangerous occupation in America. It is not even close. Those who fish, log, fly airplanes, and work with iron and steel are far, far more prone to die on the job. In fact, police work resides at the very bottom of the top ten most dangerous occupations. Chart 2.1 indicates which occupations are *truly* the most dangerous in America.

CHART 2.1

THE MOST DANGEROUS OCCUPATIONS, 2007

(Deaths per 100,000 workers each year)

1. Fishing   = 111.8
2. Logging   = 86.4
3. Flying   = 70.7
4. Iron/Steel Working   = 45.5
5. Farming/Ranching   = 39.5
6. Roofing   = 29.4
7. Electrical Line Working   = 29.1
8. Driving (Trucks/Sales)   = 28.2
9. Refuse/Recycling   = 22.8
10. Policing   = 21.8

Source: U.S. Bureau of Labor Statistics, U.S. Department of Labor, 2009

But even though these statistics indicate that the job is not necessarily very dangerous, police work *seems* fraught with peril. It seems as if danger lurks at every turn. In one of the first and most important books ever written by a social scientist about the police, *Justice Without Trial*, Jerome Skolnick notes that every day of police work, on a minute-by-minute basis, is filled with **"potential violence"** (Skolnick 67). This potential for violence motivates police officers to be careful, sometimes to the brink of paranoia. It influences police training. It drives the entire subculture to withdraw within its metaphorical shell in order to protect brother and sister officers from potential evils that await them.

Police officers learn on the street to watch people carefully. They learn any number of little tricks of the trade aimed at maintaining officer safety levels as high as possible. "Never trust another officer's search" (meaning, re-search any suspect handed over to you). "Never stand in front of a door when knocking." "Never sit with your back to the door." "Always keep yourself at least an arm's length from any citizen." These and a dozen other axioms are part of what police officers learn early in their on-the-street education.

Skolnick suggests that while police work is not particularly dangerous, police officers are nevertheless prone to look at citizens as potentially violent—at all times—and to search for actions or postures that might indicate volatility and aggressiveness in a citizen. Certain behaviors or attitudes indicate the potential for assault in a person, and Skolnick suggests that officers therefore are forever looking for **"symbolic assailants"**—people who *might* turn violent at any moment (Skolnick 67).

So the police watch people's eyes. They search for glazed-over, drugged-up looks and drunken stupors. They watch for crazed, maniacal visages. They observe hands, ordering people to keep them where they can see them, not to put their hands in their pockets, or to put something down and leave it alone. They are careful to keep citizens in view—always in front of them. When police officers go out of service for a while, to have a cup of coffee or a meal at a coffee shop, they survey areas they enter. They never sit with their backs to a door. They position themselves so that they can watch all who enter and leave a room. These and a thousand other "rules" are taught to police officers—both at the academy and by **Field Training Officers (FTOs)** (see Chapter 12)—in order to make them careful and prepare them for dealing with symbolic assailants.

Now some of what the police do to protect themselves from potential violence is logical and obvious. It makes such sense that even citizens observing from a distance understand when the police exhibit careful and cautious behavior—when they order citizens to remain in their vehicles at traffic stops, for example. Or when they order a suspect to stand still when talking to him. Or when their positioning allows them to see everyone in a room. Common sense explains these actions.

But some police behavior, from the perspective of the citizenry, appears driven by artificial paranoia. Certain actions—aimed at self-protection—appear unnecessary. For example, police officers never stand in front of a door when knocking on it. They stand to the side. They do this to avoid being shot. But while it is *possible* someone might blast them with a shotgun through a door, it is not probable. Has it ever happened? Even once? Is this type of concern logically based on facts or reasonable probabilities? Or are the police driven by some odd persecution complex?

Herein lies the problem. For the police can be seen by the public to be in a "war-like" frame of mind, even when accomplishing the most common of their everyday tasks. This can develop a great amount of antipathy in the hearts and minds of the citizenry, because the police appear to be playing some sort of artificially constructed, romantically unrealistic, Hollywood imagery–driven "game." Worse, the police can be seen as the enemy by citizens in exactly the same way police officers sometimes see citizens. (More on this in a moment.)

The classic example of these dynamics occurs when officers make traffic stops. Police training teaches rookies that, when stopping vehicles on the street, they are extremely vulnerable to assault (see Chapter Twelve). If someone wishes to harm a police officer, and they are armed with a weapon, the officer is essentially defenseless when standing outside a vehicle on the roadside. When officers die at the hands of motorists, as several did in Oakland during the writing of this book, all police officers everywhere become even more prone to be on their guard.

So the police are taught to turn on their high beams and flood a stopped vehicle with the additional lighting of the spotlight. They are taught that two spotlights flooding a car are better than one. This is because even if an officer is alone, turning on the right side (of the patrol car) spotlight *implies* there are two officers present. They are taught to approach all vehicles cautiously, with one hand on a flashlight—to point into the eyes of the driver—and one hand on their sidearm.

All of this is done to protect police officers from assault. It is logical and understandable. Since several dozen police officers die each year at the hands of motorists who have been stopped merely for vehicular violations, the police are on edge at all car stops. And they should be. It is rational for officers to believe "this might be one of those dangerous, lethal stops" when they approach a curbed vehicle. To behave in any other way would be unintelligent.

But there is a problem here. In a country of over 300 million citizens, with over 800,000 police officers working the streets (Department of Justice [DOJ], Bureau of Justice Statistics [BOJS]), there are literally millions of car stops each year that proceed without incident. In fact, the chance of a police officer being killed at a vehicle stop is so remote that it is statistically insignificant; several dozen deaths, out of millions and millions of stops, is so few that one can say accurately that death at such a stop "almost never happens." Almost. But "almost" is not the same as "never." And unless it were true that police officers *never* died at traffic stops, then the police will (and should) continue to treat vehicle stops as potentially dangerous situations.

In a substantive, realistic sense, the police are wrong about potential violence—and they are wrong most of the time. No amount of rationalizing police concern and caution by pointing out the yearly death toll of police officers killed by citizens mitigates the fact that millions upon millions of traffic stops, specific details, and police interactions with citizens occur without anything dangerous or even potentially dangerous happening.

Therefore, we have this paradox operating: while it is perfectly logical for the police to treat car stops as potentially violent situations, they are almost (literally) always wrong when they believe this to be the case. Again, and not to belabor the point, but to emphasize how critically important this reality is with regard to its impact upon police–community relations, the police are almost universally mistaken when they believe a car stop to involve a symbolic assailant–type of situation. And the paranoid image that people develop of police officers under these circumstances produces much of the anti-police feelings among the American public.

One can argue that being concerned about potential violence leads police officers to stereotype even more than all of the above dynamics put together. Since an officer's life hangs in the balance, searching for symbolic assailants—however statistically improbable an encounter might be—is an ongoing, logical part of police work that creates a gulf between officers and citizens. We are herein confronted with the fact that good, understandable police practice operates to create bad, and equally understandable, antipathy toward police in the minds of many citizens.

BEING STEREOTYPED

In this chapter's discussion, we have been focusing upon the predilection for police officers to stereotype people and situations in order to accomplish their tasks. Particularly disconcerting in this discussion has been the realization that the police

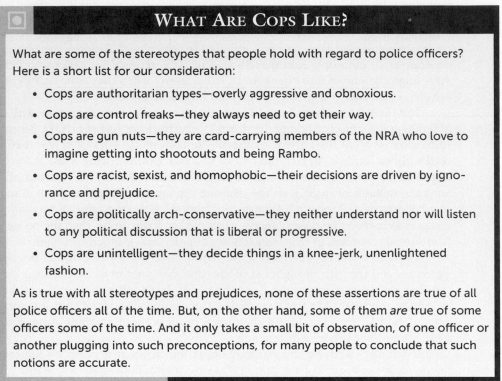

BOX 2.6

WHAT ARE COPS LIKE?

What are some of the stereotypes that people hold with regard to police officers? Here is a short list for our consideration:

- Cops are authoritarian types—overly aggressive and obnoxious.
- Cops are control freaks—they always need to get their way.
- Cops are gun nuts—they are card-carrying members of the NRA who love to imagine getting into shootouts and being Rambo.
- Cops are racist, sexist, and homophobic—their decisions are driven by ignorance and prejudice.
- Cops are politically arch-conservative—they neither understand nor will listen to any political discussion that is liberal or progressive.
- Cops are unintelligent—they decide things in a knee-jerk, unenlightened fashion.

As is true with all stereotypes and prejudices, none of these assertions are true of all police officers all of the time. But, on the other hand, some of them *are* true of some officers some of the time. And it only takes a small bit of observation, of one officer or another plugging into such preconceptions, for many people to conclude that such notions are accurate.

are wrong—not just some of the time, but most of the time—when they consider citizens to be threats. So stereotyping works to alienate police officers and citizens.

But the problems associated with stereotyping are even more complex. In this case, the act cuts both ways: not only do police stereotype citizens and situations, but the general public also stereotypes the police. In a way that officers sometimes consider unfair, citizens hold stereotypes about police officers that drive anti-police feelings even further in a negative direction. Box 2.6 exhibits merely a few prejudices (stereotyped ideas) about police that are considered true by large numbers of the population.

Police officers see and hear these stereotypes on a regular basis. They may joke about it from time to time, but such prejudicial ideas can cut to the heart of a police officer. Understanding that theirs is a tough job, often underappreciated by the general public, police officers can rail against being treated in this unfair, prejudicial way. Police officers can say to themselves, "How dare people think that I'm prejudiced in my decision-making! I'm out here doing the best that I can, in a difficult situation. I make decisions based upon logic and my training and education. And furthermore, I put my life on the line every day at work—for THEM!"

While no definitive research has been conducted on it, there is intuitive reason to believe that experiencing this stereotyping might be most difficult for white, male police officers. One can argue that female and minority group officers may very well have experienced prejudice directed at them in their pre-police work lives. Without making light of experiencing prejudice, it might be that minority and female officers are more used to being treated unfairly just because of their personal characteristics—and, in some sense, they might be more adept at dealing with prejudice. It is possible that white, male officers—having little experience on the receiving end of prejudice—might rail against this type of citizen stereotyping with even more vehemence than their fellow minority and female officers.

So at the end of our discussions about stereotyping, we are left with one additional problem that exacerbates poor police-community relations: police officers themselves can react to being stereotyped in a way that further alienates them from the public. This can, in turn, push them further in the direction of feeling isolated from and unappreciated by the people for whom they work.

SUMMATION

In this chapter, we have confronted a significant reality of life for human beings: all people stereotype as a part of their everyday lives, and stereotyping is not necessarily a negative dynamic. It is a means by which we learn about and cope with life. We have engaged the reality that working in a bureaucracy requires people to stereotype events and situations more so than when they are not working as public servants. We have considered that in addition to stereotyping because they are human beings *and* bureaucrats—prone to dealing with the public and codes, statistics, and budgets—police officers are even more likely to stereotype because of the specific nature of their job. In a layered sort of way—one need to stereotype being amplified by another and then another—the police stereotype much more often than others…and with good reason.

Stereotyping people and situations as they do—in an effort to be efficient in performing their duties and also in an attempt to protect themselves from harm—the police are often wrong. In fact, with respect to perceived threats, they are wrong most of the time. Not only that, but their efforts to protect themselves

CHAPTER TWO PARADOX BOX

Police stereotyping is absolutely necessary, not only for police officers to perform their duties efficiently, but for officer safety. But it makes the police prone to pre-judge people and situations, often incorrectly, and it creates great community–police antipathy.

inadvertently create a negative image in the minds of the citizens they serve. Finally, we have acknowledged the fact that negative police–community relations can also develop because the police themselves tend to be stereotyped, and they tend to react with righteous indignation.

In keeping with Part I's established theme of analyzing the individual police officer experience and the numerous paradoxes involved in that experience, we now address discretionary decision-making in Chapter Three. Again we will be confronted with practical realities that present paradoxes: exercising discretion is an important and necessary part of police work that nonetheless produces negative dynamics. These dynamics include, among other things, creating even more antipathy toward police in the minds of citizens.

 ## DISCUSSION QUESTIONS

1. The propensity for people to search for and even to require an "evil other" in their lives is universal. It happens in all societies throughout all of history. Discuss this universal tendency. Why is this so? What is it about such an "other" that makes people feel better about themselves and their world? How does the "other" help us define ourselves?

2. Police officers must "normalize" their beats. They must construct an image of who is "right" in order to understand who is "wrong." Picture the main street in your town in the middle of the night—at, say, 3 A.M. Discuss what it would look like under "normal" circumstances. Who is out and about? What activity is there? What would a police officer be looking for—that is "wrong"—at that time of night?

3. Police work is not really dangerous. Many other occupations are more dangerous. Discuss why it is that people think of police work as being dangerous. What makes it seem so? Where do people get such ideas? Why is there so much talk about police work stress when there should be more stress in fishing or logging?

4. American citizens tend to hold all sorts of stereotypical notions about police officers. Discuss these notions. What are they? What are cops like? What do cops think? What kind of worldviews do cops have? What sorts of personality types? Discuss all of these questions from the perspective of people on the street. Finally, which notions do you consider to be the most unfair to the police? The most dangerous?

 ## KEY TERMS

10 Code: A standard police radio code—used by a majority of police departments.

Diagnostic Packages: Term that refers to how humans store learned information in their brains in "boxes" of sorts.

The Evil Other: The enemy; the devil; the nemesis; the foe; the rival.

Field Training Officers (FTOs): Officers with whom rookies must spend time on the street when they first come from the Police Academy.

Habeas Corpus: Latin for "you have the body." A legal principle requiring that the evidence against a suspect be produced and brought before a magistrate.

"Normalizing" Crime: David Sudnow's idea that criminal justice practitioners are required to take all forms of deviant behavior and "fit" them into legal code sections.

Perceptual Shorthand: Psychology term for the process by which people apply pre-constructed stereotypes to human experience.

"Potential Violence": A term, developed by Jerome Skolnick, that refers to dangers police officers are vulnerable to and for which they are always on guard.

Probable Cause: Legal standard required for police officers to obtain warrants and to confront citizens.

"Salty": The idea of experience. A "salt" is a veteran, in police work and other occupations or sports experiences.

Stereotyping: The human propensity to codify things, places, people, and events.

"Symbolic Assailants": Skolnick's term for people who might pose a threat to the safety of police officers.

Working Personality: Skolnick's term for each police officer's individual way of working a beat and approaching the job.

"Wrong": Police term for anyone who does not "fit" into the normal activity on their beat.

ADDITIONAL READINGS

The basic, modern "tour de force" with regard to how and why all people stereotype is *The Psychology of Stereotyping* by David J. Schneider (Guilford Press, 2005). The study of how social group prejudice is accomplished, and its utility for people, is explained in *Stereotypes as Explanations: The Formation of Meaningful Beliefs About Social Groups* by Craig McGarty, Vincent Y. Yzerbyt, and Russell Spears (Cambridge University Press, 2002). Regarding the construction of "The Evil Other," James Aho's *This Thing of Darkness* (University of Washington Press; 1995) is the study in the field.

There are several basic "how to" books about honing individual stereotyping skills. David J. Lieberman's *You Can Read Anyone* (Viter Press, 2007) is a generic work on the subject while Joe Navarro and Marvin Karlins have studied it from a police-specific perspective in *What Every Body is Saying: An Ex-F.B.I. Agent's Guide to Speed-Reading People* (Collins Living, 2008).

Regarding whether or not police officers are in fact more prone to stereotype than most people, *Blue vs. Black: Let's End the Conflict Between Cops and Minorities* by John L. Burris and Catharine Whitney (St. Martin's Griffin, 2000) makes the point that while high-handed police deeds often seem racially slanted, American society in general still suffers from a racial divide that cannot be blamed upon the police. In *Are Cops Racist?* (Ivan R. Dee Publications, 2003), Heather MacDonald goes further. Her thesis is that statistics do not bear out the idea that police decision-making is racially biased. MacDonald suggests that great progress has been made in this regard, not just generally in American society but among police officers. She posits that contemporary media ignore some studies indicating a lack of police officer prejudice because these studies do not conform to conventional media wisdom.

In our discussion, we pointed out David Sudnow's idea that criminal justice bureaucrats must normalize crime as a part of performing their duties. His theory came to light first in 1965, and to study it one can read *Normal Crimes* (Irvington Publications), later published in 1993. Regarding police stereotyping in particular, *Basic Patrol Procedures* by Tim Perry (Sheffield Publications, 1998) discusses the need to normalize the officer's beat.

Jerome Skolnick's classic work is *Justice Without Trial* (John Wiley and Sons, 1966), wherein he creates the ideas of the police officer's working personality, potential violence, and symbolic assailants. Confirmation of the dynamic reality that the police focus upon such concepts as a self-defense mechanism appears both in *Vehicle Stops, 3rd Ed.* (Stipes Publications LLC, 2000) by Greg Connor and Gregory Connor and *Surviving Street Patrol: The Officers' Guide to Safe and Effective Policing* (Paladin Press, 2001) by Steve Albrecht.

CHAPTER 3

Discretion

Chapter Three Outline

This chapter's discussion is about a subject critical to any person who applies rules of one kind or another to the behavior of others: discretionary decision-making. To exercise **discretion** in applying the law involves using common sense or discernment. Discretion is defined as "individual judgment; undirected choice." Employing judgment and making choices is the essence of the rule administrator's job. In this chapter we will analyze discretion and discuss how, like stereotyping, it is both essential to a police officer's job and, at the same time, potentially counterproductive to police-community relations.

On the one hand, rules are rigid. They are predetermined, codified, and specifically defined. Rules are meant to be applied to everyone in an equitable manner, without prejudice or favoritism. That is the central, basic, driving purpose of having rules in the first place. But, on the other hand, because rules are applied to the complex patterns of life, there is always some latitude in their use. Between the specificity of what a law (or rule) says and the variety of what people do in real life there is the need for judgment, lest the spirit behind any given law be lost in its application.

Every book written about the police includes a discussion about discretionary decision-making (Davis). This makes perfect sense. While discretion is exercised by everyone who administers rules, the people who police the streets of America—who walk amongst the citizens and apply society's laws on a daily basis—exercise so much in the way of discretionary power that their decisions about how to do this have a profound impact upon the lives of millions of citizens. How the police decide to apply the law can affect the life of a particular individual, a family, or a neighborhood. It can define how society works, which norms are respected, which get ignored. Discretionary decision-making can, in effect, legalize one type of behavior and make another illegal. And in impacting life on the street in these important ways, police discretionary decisions can change the world for better or for worse. This is why the topic gets so much attention when anyone studies the police, analyzes the law, or discusses justice.

In our discussion, we will note an ongoing tension between two ends of an imaginary continuum: on one end, there is **complete discretion** or the absence of absolute rules, and on the other end, there is **zero discretion** or the application of rules without interpretation. Somewhere between these extremes lies the appropriate mix or balancing point between rigidity and latitude. In our analysis of discretion, we will discover how dangerous it is for law appliers to exercise either too much or too little discretion—because the point where the appropriate mix of rigidity and discretion occurs is the point where justice resides.

THE IMPORTANCE OF POLICE DISCRETION

Discretion exists at every step in the criminal justice system. Public prosecutors exercise a great deal of discretion. As a part of the **plea bargaining** system (Skolnick, Justice), they construct "deals" that influence the lives of hundreds of thousands of people every year. They have the power to change official criminal charges and to make felonies into misdemeanors or vice versa. They have the power to consolidate charges by making five into one or vice versa. The discretion that they exercise sometimes sets people free and sometimes incarcerates them for extended periods of time. They even have the power to drop charges completely, releasing people from the criminal justice system's operations.

Judges, too, exercise discretion. They can do all of the things prosecutors can because they must accept and pass judgment upon all plea bargains. In administering trials, they make decisions about evidence: what to include and what to exclude. They exercise sentencing discretion. With regard to juveniles, they have almost complete power over how the system treats the underaged.

Likewise with probation officers, parole officers, and correctional employees. Each of these criminal justice system actors has discretionary power of different sorts. Their decisions affect the lives of citizens on a regular basis and, again, can exercise an influence upon individuals for better or worse. But police discretion is more important than that exercised by these other actors. This point has been agreed upon by virtually every analyzer of the U.S. criminal justice system.

Why is it so often asserted that the police's discretionary decision-making power is the most important and critical element of the system of discretion that permeates the criminal justice system? The answer is that the police exercise an extraordinary power possessed by no one else in the system, not even judges: the power to do nothing. When police decide not to act—or, more specifically, not to invoke the dictates of the law—then the impact upon the citizenry is profound. The police are the only people within the criminal justice system who can decide to keep a citizen completely out of that system.

Any given case against a citizen can be dropped by a prosecutor or a judge. They can exercise their discretion and end the state's efforts in a criminal case. But for a case to arrive before these legal actors, it must first become an official part of the system. That is, only after the police make an arrest and write a report does a given citizen become a suspect and experience being labeled as such. That suspect then has an arrest record. Even if things are dropped at that point, a person is still in the system and "labeled" forever. This labeling as a criminal suspect with an arrest record can have deleterious consequences for a citizen's future. In fact, in the world of criminology, there is an entire branch of inquiry called "**labeling theory**" that seeks to explain the ramifications of such labeling (Becker).

First, there are operational norms in some occupations that negate a person's ability to get a job if they have an arrest record. Opportunities in the educational world can forever be limited by arrest. People can be excluded from graduate schools, especially law schools, if they have conviction records. They can even lose forever the chance to obtain student loans for college and so forth. Even if a case is later dropped—and a person is never convicted of a crime—having "only" an arrest record can be troublesome. Only the police, through deciding to take no action (if that is what they choose to do), can exercise discretion in a way that avoids such future ramifications in the life of a citizen.

BOX 3.1

LABELING THEORY

Among other ideas, this theory states that when youths are officially "entered into the system" at an early age they become labeled as "trouble makers" or "delinquents." This has several negative effects:

- Such "labeled" youths tend to live up to their labels, for a number of reasons, and thus the fact that they have been labeled as deviants becomes a "self-fulfilling prophesy."
- Decisions made by criminal justice practitioners, especially police arrest / no arrest decisions, take these labels—in the form of arrest records and conviction records—into consideration. Thus, the "trouble maker" is more and more often arrested and his or her record grows.
- If they are arrested often, young people tend to "graduate" from petty offenses to more serious crimes due to what they learn and with whom they interact behind bars. Time spent with other deviants makes deviance grow.

Second, future arrest, no-arrest decisions are sometimes made by police officers utilizing previous records. The police do this all of the time. In the middle of the night, confronted by a minor offense, officers will run records checks on suspects and utilize the information they obtain to decide between taking action and not taking action. When a detained suspect has an arrest record, they are much more likely to be arrested than if they have no such record. This is because police officers, looking for patterns of behavior, will tend to determine that a person with an arrest record is a "bad actor" and deserves, in some sense, to be treated as such.

So when the police decide against taking action, they exercise a profoundly important power over individual citizens. The impact and importance of this power can outweigh all other machinations of the criminal justice system combined.

THE RULE OF LAW

In the Introduction, we referenced John Adams' axiom that America is a country "ruled by laws and not by men." (Adams) This axiom reminds us that the historical roots of America's fight for freedom against English oppression run deep. Driven by the principle of limited government, our institutions have always attempted to cleave to a concept that was part of the **Age of Enlightenment** (Berlin) and the development of **Western Liberalism** (Bramsted): instead of having tyrannical powers—the latitude to treat citizens however they want to—representatives of any morally defensible government should be directly controlled by written laws. The power of the state over the individual is to be limited by codified laws administered on the street exactly as they were written. This principle seeks to take power away from those who administer the law—the police, for the purposes of our discussions—and give it to those who construct the law: the representatives of the legislative branch. This is because unlike the police, the representatives in our legislative branches are directly controlled by the people in a democratic way. So "The People," and not the police, make the rules that govern the lives of individual citizens.

Thus, as Americans, and believers in the principles of Western Liberalism, we believe in the ideal of limiting the power of legal administrators (the police). But there is a problem with this ideal. For we also must be realistic and acknowledge that for the law to be just and to effect logical decisions in the lives of individual citizens, there must be at least a modicum of latitude within which legal administrators (again, the police) can operate. So while we want to emphasize here that as good Americans we believe in the **rule of law**, we must also concede that discretion has its place in our system of laws and of government.

Practical reality suggests that we must also allow that the "rule of men" (the police) has its place on the streets. That is, often the law as written dictates a certain

BOX 3.2

DISCRETION IN ACTION

During Christmas week, a large music store calls the police three times in just two days to report that they have detained shoplifters. In each case, the thieves are caught "red-handed" stealing CDs. One suspect, who exhibits no remorse for being caught, has a long record of thievery. He regularly shows up at the local flea market on weekends to sell CDs, DVDs, and other property that is obviously stolen. A second suspect is a local sorority girl who is clearly excited by the "thrill" of attempting to shoplift "for fun." She sees the entire experience as a lark or a fling of sorts. A third suspect is a single mother, without a job, who is embarrassed and almost hysterical about being apprehended as a thief. She is stealing the CDs in order to provide Christmas presents for her children.

These situations are exactly the same in an objective, legal sense. But are they really the same? Should the police treat them in the same way? Or would it be more "just" to consider these to be three separate and distinctly different sets of circumstances?

course of action that, upon reflection, may not be best for an accused citizen, the victims of a criminal act, *or* a community in general. A first-time teenaged shoplifter with a clean record, who indicates a genuine remorse for having stolen something from a store, may very well be treated more "justly" by being given a stern lecture and a warning than by being arrested. Under such circumstances, it might very well be best in the long run for the teenager, for the shop owner, and for society that these informal sanctions be utilized.

Our American heritage makes us leery of the "rule of cop" on the street. Beginning with our fear of the power of "**King George's Men**," Americans have railed against placing too much power in the hands of those who police the citizenry. And so, as a free people, we Americans tend to be affronted, more so than citizens of many other countries, by the assertion that "the police are the law." This dictum rules the streets in many dictatorial countries around the world, but as Americans we do not like the sound of it.

But there is a problem here. We Americans may be affronted by the assertion that the police are the law, but a realistic appraisal of the discretionary decision-making power of the police on the street suggests that it might often be true. The decisions made by police officers—to apply the law as it is written or not, to arrest or not, to use force or not—do, in fact, make up the reality of what law means on the streets. And, thus, we must confront an awkward reality: the police breathe life into the law with their discretionary decision-making, and that this is not necessarily a bad thing.

THE POLICE *ARE* THE LAW

Our section title here may suggest an open invitation to police officers to be egocentric, to do whatever they feel is appropriate on duty, and to avoid taking the rule of law seriously. We appear to be saying that the rule of cop is what is important because, on the street, what they say goes. We seem, in other words, to be confirming the police locker room idea that operating on this basis is at once realistic and morally defensible. Is this true? Because they make thousands of important, life-changing decisions every day, often alone and unsupervised, is it true that the police are the law?

The answer is both yes and no. On the one hand, the police must apply the law fairly, evenhandedly, and with a view to promoting justice. Laws are created by legislatures that pass them in the name, and presumably the best interests, of all of the people. The police cannot think or act as if they are completely free, by themselves, to define legal and illegal, to decide who the inherently good people and the inherently bad people are, or to rule the streets as an occupying army. This is exactly what law enforcement personnel do in "police states," against which America has fought any number of wars. In such countries, the police have so much power that the law, as written, is largely irrelevant to the lives of millions of people. Citizens in these countries are subject to the whims of absolute police power.

BOX 3.3

AN EXAMPLE FROM THE WORLD OF SPORT

In the sport of basketball, there is a rule against "traveling." That rule applies (among other instances) when a player attempts to score a "lay-up." Put simply, when moving toward such a shot, a player may not take more than "one step and a half," or else she or he is guilty of "traveling." This rule is the same—in the rule book—for high school, college, and professional basketball. But any basketball fan will tell you that the professional players of the NBA (National Basketball Association) are allowed to take two steps instead of one. This is completely different from requirements placed upon players at the amateur level. The difference is due to how the referees call the game . . . how they interpret the traveling rule. Thus, the game is played differently at different levels due to referee discretion. This is an example of how people who administer rules (laws) define what those rules (laws), in fact, are—through discretionary decision-making.

When the police act, they must understand the underlying concept of the rule of law, and they must behave in a way that does honor to it. Thus, the streets of America must be ruled by laws that are applied fairly. The law treats people differently because of their behavior, sanctioning them when they perpetrate crimes. That is, the law treats people differently if they are labeled as "burglars" than if they are not. This is one of the jobs of the law—to treat people differently because of their personal behavior. But the law cannot, in an ethically or legally defensible way, treat people in different ways because of their personal characteristics—their race, religion, sexual orientation, manner of dress, political views. Thus, from this perspective, the law is absolute.

On the other hand, the actions of the police, to a great extent, do, in fact, determine what the law really means. The police put the American legal system into practical application. If the laws the police uphold are the skeleton, then the on-the-street discretionary decisions of the police put flesh and blood on that skeleton. The police make the written laws of the penal code come to life for the public.

The above assertion confirms what a number of analysts and well-informed, intuitive police officers have pointed out for a very long time—no matter what the law states, no matter how penal code sections read, no matter what training teaches, and no matter what police leadership may want to tell us, the true meaning of the law on the street is determined by police officers.

When officers decide on a day-to-day basis where to focus their attention, whom to arrest, and when to use force, they determine the effect the legal system will have on the lives of individual citizens. This means that police officers bear a tremendous and unique responsibility. If they either overlook or overemphasize certain types of crime, they can, in effect, change criminal law. If, for example, in a college town, the police look the other way when college kids are involved in underage drinking, then underage drinking has, in effect, been decriminalized in that town. If police in any given jurisdiction decide not to worry much about local gambling rooms, then gambling has been decriminalized de facto.

These two examples—ignoring underage drinking and gambling—involve police deciding not to invoke the law. But the police can, equally, appear guilty of unfairness and arbitrariness through rigorous application of the law. If, for example, the police decide that, in an effort to thwart the growth of local gangs, they will stop every teenage driver they see—to make records and warrants checks, to ask for information, and generally to make things uncomfortable for gang members—then the police have effectively created a new, separate set of unique laws that apply to one segment of the population.

In these two ways, exercising discretion in both aggressive and passive manners, the police define what the law means on the streets of America.

AN IMAGINARY CONTINUUM

This brings us to the consideration of an imaginary continuum that stretches from something called "**full enforcement**" on one end to something called "**Khadi justice**" on the other. Conceptually understanding this "**discretionary continuum**" (see Chart below) helps illustrate the nature and importance of police discretion.

One of the pioneers of modern sociology was Max Weber. Among the concepts for which he became famous was his analysis of absolute discretion. Weber engages what he labels "Khadi justice" when discussing the expansion of discretion in the extreme (Schlossberg). Too much discretion, he warns, means an end to rules and laws altogether. It places so much power in the hands of legal administrators that the operations of democratic systems became irrelevant.

Until the Age of the Enlightenment several hundred years ago, authority figures in the English class structure—kings, earls, dukes, and other members of the aristocracy—had absolute, life and death power over those beneath them. Because they exercised total power, they did not have to refer to any particular law, rule, or even custom when they dealt with their "inferiors" and meted out justice on their estates. Before the age of equality and the written law (the age of Liberalism), this was the type of absolute power possessed by the aristocracy.

About 100 years ago, Weber's analysis found that in Muslim law this type of absolute discretionary power still operated. In some places in the Muslin world there existed something he called "Khadi justice." The male Khadi (law-giver) was not bound to make his judicial pronouncements in concert with any preexisting, written rules. Such codified rules did not exist nor were there expectations that judicial rulings had to follow any particular form of law. The Khadi made rulings in concert with whatever religious, political, or ethical values he himself chose to observe.

So Khadi justice refers to the absence of rules or, put another way, absolute discretion. Since Weber's time, anyone in the world of law who exercises unlimited power over others and is not bound by codified rules is considered to be exercising Khadi justice. Parents, for example, are almost never bound by law (unless they are genuinely abusive) when deciding how to discipline their own children. People, again bound only by the requirement of avoiding genuinely abusive behavior, exercise unlimited discretion when they deal with their pets or livestock. In historical terms, slave holders were also so empowered. Each of these examples suggests the exercise of Khadi justice.

As our chart indicates, Khadi justice resides on one end of an imaginary continuum—the continuum of discretionary decision-making. At the other end, opposed to the absolute discretion of the Khadi, sits zero discretion. In police circles, zero discretion is called "full enforcement," and it refers to making arrests every time a suspect surfaces, without attempting to analyze or judge suspects on the street. "Everyone goes to jail" or "everyone gets cited" is the rule here. The law is enforced to its fullest extent and no latitude exists. People who call for full enforcement are, normally, those who distrust the power given to administrators. This mistrust fuels an urge to remove as much discretion as possible. Suggesting full enforcement where the police are concerned is, in essence, suggesting that the police cannot be entrusted with the power to make decisions in the best interests of justice.

In recent American history, there is an example of politicians attempting to turn the concept of full enforcement into law. It is the **"zero tolerance"** idea—relating to the Drug War—that came about during the Reagan administration (Punch). Reagan and his political allies pushed the idea to the public that the only way to make headway in the War on Drugs was to institute a policy wherein any amount of drugs—even a trace—was sufficient to warrant arrest. Before that time (in the mid 1980s), drug arrests for possession of a controlled substance required there to be a "useable amount" of whatever drug was involved. After the institution of zero tolerance, that standard changed. Today, the smallest trace of illegal drugs in connection with a suspect is enough to warrant arrest. The zero tolerance policy is similar to the idea of full enforcement in the sense that it forbids the police from exercising any discretion whatsoever.

So again, our theoretical continuum stretches from "Khadi Justice" to "Full Enforcement." This illustration will hopefully aid the reader in comprehending the difference (and distance) between the two extremes. In actuality, neither end of the

Discretionary Continuum

"Full Enforcement"
(Zero Discretion)

Actual Discretion Exercised
(Somewhere in the Middle)

"Khadi Justice"
(Complete Discretion)

spectrum exists. No police officers, anywhere in the world, have so much power that they are free to do precisely as they please. Pretty much everywhere, even in totalitarian states, some limitations are placed upon the powerful, would-be Khadis of today. Similarly, full enforcement does not exist in the real world, either. As we shall soon see, for several practical, logistical reasons, full enforcement is an impossibility. But even if it *could* be administered, it isn't necessarily something one would want to create. Attitudes toward the concept of full enforcement are largely driven by how one defines justice.

WHAT IS "JUSTICE?"

So far we have been taking the concept of "justice" for granted. It behooves us here to discuss definitively what it is. If the efforts of the police and the entire operations of the criminal justice system are to be effectively focused and morally defensible, then they must be driven by a concern for this sometimes amorphous concept. Police discretionary decision-making *must* be directed and controlled by the ideal of justice in both the short and long terms.

What is justice? What is meant by that word? If the system within which the police operate is indeed the criminal *justice* system, what is it that this system is supposed to accomplish? What are its major tasks? Is there merely one definition of justice? If not, how many are there? What are these definitions? The answer to this set of questions is that there are, indeed, various definitions of justice. Philosophers have, for several thousand years now, debated what the essence of justice should be. For the purposes of our discussion, we will engage two classic definitions. We do this with an eye toward developing an understanding of how the police wrestle with still another paradox in their work-a-day lives: the fact that while people assume the police have one, definitive understanding of what justice means, there are two very different and competing ways of looking at it—and of prioritizing what it is the criminal justice system is supposed to accomplish (Perez and Moore).

One of the central principles of Western Liberalism, and one of the most important principles of American institutions, is that of equal treatment. Our Constitution preserves for all citizens the right to "**equal protection of the law**." This is a principle that guides much of American political and legal life. In fact, so central is equality to our thinking as Americans that it is credited around the world as being one of the basic American principles. And so it is no surprise that one definition of "justice" often popular with Americans resides in the straightforward notion of "**justice as equality**" (or equal treatment) (Pollock 80). This would entail treating all people and situations alike and being evenhanded when doing so.

Several hundred years ago, one of the answers to the ancient problem of the unchecked, unlimited power of kings and lawgivers was the invention of the idea of the written rule. In lieu of a world wherein Khadi justice reigned supreme, the new paradigm ushered in during the Enlightenment—the world of modern

Liberalism—was driven by the concept of power being exercised equitably. No matter what a person's race, color, creed, ethnic identity, sexual orientation, or gender, our post-Enlightenment world is spurred by the idea that everyone has a natural, "God-given" right to equal treatment. At the very heart of the reason for having rules in the first place is this modern desire for equity. And therefore, a perfectly understandable, acceptable, and morally defensible definition of justice is "equity."

But there are other definitions, and this next one is just as powerful, understandable, and morally defensible. In terse terms, this second concept says "Justice is fairness." (Pollock 80) This is a common thread drawn through many philosophical discourses and political treatises. What does "justice is fairness" mean? To be fair is to be objective, honest, unbiased. But it means something more. Fairness involves taking into account, without personal prejudice, all sides of a given situation before attempting any action or developing any potential solution. Fairness is the key concept in what is called distributive justice. **Distributive justice** seeks to answer a question: "What is due to each person?" (Fleishacker) The difference between the two concepts may seem slight, but each can lead to very different outcomes when applied by those who administer justice. Box 3.2 above provides an example.

Box 3.2 describes the arrests of three different shoplifters. If we consider our definition of justice to be equity, then the appropriate way for a police officer to handle these cases would be to treat each shoplifter equally—that is, in the very same way. Either they should all be taken to jail; they should all be cited; or they should all be let go with a warning. If justice is equity (and, again, that is a perfectly defensible definition), then it would be unjust to treat the professional shoplifter, the thrill-seeking sorority girl, and the single, unemployed mother in different ways.

On the other hand, if we define **justice as fairness**, then an analysis of the situation might very well suggest the attending police officer do different things with these three different people. The professional thief might very well be taken to jail, with "no questions asked." The sorority girl might be given the chance to reflect for and, perhaps, to acquire some sort of deferential and apologetic attitude. Then she might be cited and released. And the poor, single mother might find the attending police officer intervening on her behalf and convincing the store owner to drop the charges. If justice is fairness, then all of these actions are just; they are logically defensible. The fact that three thieves are treated in an *in*equitable manner does not matter. They are all treated fairly.

This section's brief discussion may appear to be strictly an academic exercise. But the difference in these two conceptualizations of justice is critical. Every day, police officers are confronted with situations that require them to wrestle with these two definitions and use their hearts and minds in an effort to employ the most just of the two. As we shall see, this ongoing debate (in the hearts and minds of police officers) is an integral part of grappling with the difficulties and paradoxes presented by police discretion.

BOX 3.4

TWO DEFINITIONS OF "JUSTICE"

- Equality: "Justice" requires equal treatment; people are considered to be precisely equal and, therefore, they should receive exactly the same treatment.
- Fairness: "Justice" requires fairness; people are understood to be differently situated in life and, therefore, may receive different treatment according to what they are "due" or what they "deserve."

THE IMPOSSIBILITY OF FULL ENFORCEMENT

In Anglo-American politics—in all modern Western nations, in fact—Montesquieu's conceptualization of three separate branches of government has been the standard way of thinking for 250 years now. This French philosopher is largely given credit for creating the idea that laws should be made by a legislative branch, interpreted by a judicial branch, and administered by an executive branch of government (Montesquieu). In America, the state legislatures make penal laws, the state courts interpret them, and the police—members of the executive branch—enforce or administer these laws.

Our **Founding Fathers** agreed with this line of reasoning. They believed that the legislative branch should have most of the power and make the laws because they (the Founding Fathers) possessed immense faith in the power of representative democracy. Furthermore, as members of the affluent upper classes, they believed in the logic and intelligence possessed by people with elite educations. And the judicial branch would be entrusted to these elites. After all, those who became judges and justices would hail from the same social and political class as the Founding Fathers. And so they had great faith, too, in the judicial branch.

But they possessed a great deal of doubt about placing too much power in the hands of the executive branch. Driven by remembrances of **King George of England**, our Founding Fathers sought to create an executive that had little in the way of real power. The executive was "merely" to enforce laws while having nothing whatsoever to do with policy development or legal interpretation.

This lack of faith in the executive branch has made its way down through American history, in a circuitous way, and today manifests in a lack of faith in the police possessed by those who call for full enforcement of the laws. As noted above, the concept of full enforcement refers to requiring the executive branch to arrest or cite anyone suspected of any crime and then allowing the judicial branch to make decisions about guilt or innocence. People who call for full enforcement possess little faith in police and, therefore, are moved to expect full enforcement despite the fact that it is a logistical and practical impossibility.

There are any number of reasons why full enforcement is impossible. To begin with, the concept carries with it an assumption: laws can be written in such a way as to allow for no interpretation by police officers. For full enforcement to work, laws would have to include within them contingencies that cover absolutely each and every possible kind of human behavior. That is, laws would have to be so complicated and so specific that they provided those who applied them with solutions to every single circumstance life could possibly present. And since this is impossible, full enforcement will never be a reality.

To illustrate how impractical the writing of such specific laws would be, let us take what might be considered the most straightforward (and unimportant) of laws: those that cover parking meter violations. What could be simpler than to write a law that explains what do to about a lapsed parking meter time limit? Surely this would be easy to do. Surely we could agree upon how such a law would look. Under the full enforcement philosophy, the function of such a law would be to leave no discretion to an officer making a to-cite-or-not-to-cite decision.

For a parking meter violation, such a specific, non-interpretable law might read: "If the parking meter red flag has come up, write a ticket. If the red flag has not come up, do not write a ticket." This would be our "full enforcement / zero discretion parking meter law." Simple. However, this law might not necessarily live up to the "spirit" of parking meter laws with which most people would agree. And that is our point here.

While this law sounds specific enough, it is relatively easy to come up with circumstances under which we might very well *not* want a citation written, even if the red flag *had* come up. What if the parking meter is located in front of a hospital, and the driver who parked there was taking a bleeding child into the emergency room when he parked? What if a police officer comes upon a mother in the process of strapping two children into different car seats when the red flag springs up? What if a police officer comes upon a fire truck parked in a red-flag-up parking metered slot? What if a police officer sees a driver park a car and forget to put money in the meter, but then sees him turn around after a few paces, come back, and put money in the slot? What if a police officer comes across someone who has just parked and who asks the officer for change . . . and then, not receiving it, goes immediately into an adjacent convenience store to get some? Under each of these examples, our law would tell the officer to write a citation. Should a citation be written? For the parent of a bleeding child? For a fire fighter? For a person honestly attempting to obtain change for the meter?

In this simple example, it is impossible to write an all-encompassing parking meter law specific enough to cover all contingencies while simultaneously allowing police officers zero discretion. If parking meter laws present such problems, how impossible would it be to write a penal code section stipulating when and when not to make arrests in dealing with domestic quarrels? How many variables

BOX 3.5

"FULL ENFORCEMENT IS IMPOSSIBLE BECAUSE"

- Of the "Specificity of Rules" Problem—rules cannot be written that are so clear and understandable that they do not afford any room for interpretation.
- The System Would Be Impacted—if absolutely every person suspected of criminal behavior were arrested or cited, jails and courts and prisons would overflow and the system would grind to a halt.
- Pragmatic Legal System Realities—some witnesses are unreliable, some physical evidence is excluded, some confessions are thrown out . . . these and other pragmatic realities make arresting everyone a waste of time and money.
- The Delivery of "Justice"—sometimes the law's specific dictates are *not* sufficient to deliver "justice" on the street, and police discretion—particularly the discretion not to take action—is required.

could we come up with in attempting to write a specific law for any and all domestic disturbances any police officer could ever observe? How about disturbing the peace? How about curfews? How about disorderly conduct? Returning to the example of the CD store, how about a petty theft law? The difficulty in making laws specific enough that they limit discretion completely—the **"specificity of rules problem"**—is insurmountable (Groeneveld).

The second difficulty with instituting full enforcement is the logistical problem it would bring to the criminal justice system. Arresting and citing each and every individual ever suspected of anything would present more than a "problem"—it would be an absolute nightmare. Where would the system get enough holding cells in police departments? Enough county jail cells and jail guards? Enough Public Defenders? Enough Public Prosecutors? Enough Judges? Enough courtrooms? Enough prisons? Enough Correctional Officers? Enough Probation Officers? Enough Parole Officers? Even musing on the problems full enforcement would visit upon the system is a breathtaking endeavor. The American criminal justice system already suffers from such overcrowding that we have a **"revolving door"** problem (Pittman and Gordon). People come in the front door of the penal system at such a rapid rate and in such numbers that others have to be let out of the back door, no matter their crime or how much of their sentence they have served.

A third problem relates to certain pragmatic realities of the criminal justice system. Being students of the system themselves, police officers often know a great deal about how trials work and about evidentiary law. They know a poor witness—someone who will be unhelpful on the stand—when they see one. They know poor evidence when they see it. They understand what conflicting statements can mean in court. They know what a "bad" search is. Because of such realities, wouldn't we want the police to save time and taxpayer money by acknowledging such troublesome pragmatics and eschewing the pursuit of cases bound to waste either one or both (time and money)? Certainly we would.

Finally, in discussing the impossibility of full enforcement we come to the topic considered in the previous section. Police officers work within something called the criminal *justice* system. The key word, of course, is justice. The system is supposed to dispense justice on the streets of America. How could it possibly do so if we took away all discretion from today's modern, intelligent, educated, and well-trained police officers? While the police may fall short of these expectations at times in real life, in theory we want police officers to use both head and heart when dealing with the public. We want them to be as logical and analytical as is humanly possible, and, equally, we want them to be as empathetic and understanding as they can be. Full enforcement—even an attempt to implement it—takes away the police officer's ability to infuse the dictates of the law with common sense, humanity, empathy, pragmatism, and insight. Justice demands that they do so. Full enforcement demands that they do not.

Taken together, this set of arguments against full enforcement suggests that while some who lack faith in the police might want to call for the implementation of full enforcement, it is, in reality, an illogical and counterproductive idea.

DONALD BLACK: HOW THE POLICE DECIDE

While it is quite dated, a very important study of police discretionary decision-making was conducted years ago in New York City by Donald Black (the findings of which continue to be analyzed, cited, and replicated) (Black "The Social…"). After many scholars had addressed police discretion and agreed upon its importance for the rule of justice on the streets of America, Black decided to ascertain exactly how police discretion was used on the streets. Utilizing research assistants trained in evaluating police decision-making, Black's study charted the arrest / no arrest decisions made by dozens of New York City officers over an extended period of time. Gathering all of the data, he analyzed what criteria officers used when making such decisions. His findings are illustrative for our discussion in several ways.

It turns out that the police use four major sets of criteria for making such decisions. First and foremost in importance, they consider the strength of the evidence. All other things being equal, the stronger the evidence of guilt presented to officers on the street, the greater the likelihood police will make arrests. This initial finding was good news for students of the legal system who believe in the rule of law. It indicated that officers were prioritizing exactly that criterion which the dictates of the legal system would logically suggest. Out on the street, the police were imagining courtrooms and trials. They were evaluating evidence and making decisions based upon how strong, in a legal sense, a case was. This was good news

BOX 3.6

BLACK'S STUDY OF POLICE DISCRETION

Black's study of police arrest / no arrest decisions found that officers took the following into account when making their decisions; the considerations are listed in order of importance, with the top consideration being the primary or most important:

- The strength of evidence.
- The seriousness of the crime.
- The distance between the Victim and the Suspect.
- The attitude of the suspect(s).

because the police were behaving in a logical and appropriate manner. Prioritizing this criterion was legally defensible from any reasonable perspective.

Second in importance was the seriousness of the crime. Given equally authoritative evidence, the police were more prone to make arrests for serious crimes than they were for lesser ones. Again, this was good news. It indicated that police officers understood how the criminal justice system prioritized crime. The police understood that the more serious the victimization of either an individual or society itself, the more prone to arresting someone they ought to be. Again, this process was legally defensible from a reasonable perspective.

Third, there was the "distance" between the victim and the suspect. This consideration was based upon a very pragmatic view of reality on the streets of America. These New York officers knew, from experience, that citizens often attempt to utilize the criminal justice system to "get back at" their enemies, to right some civil wrong not handled by the system, or to maintain power over other individuals in their neighborhoods. Put succinctly, they knew that some citizens tried to manipulate the system for their own purposes. So these New York City officers thus prioritized making arrests when alleged perpetrators and victims were unknown to each other, as opposed to when they were acquaintances or "friends." This was a third piece of good news, as it indicated a high level of sophistication on the part of the police; they understood not only the legal dictates of the system but, also, practical reality.

Finally, fourth in its significance was the attitude of the suspect or suspects. If a suspect (or suspects) showed deference to police authority, they often weren't arrested. If they did not show respect for the police, they were more prone to be arrested. This finding proved interesting in that it was a scientific, research-oriented confirmation of what is called "the attitude test" in police-officer parlance. While the first three findings provided positive feedback about police competence and knowledge, this fourth finding was somewhat disconcerting. Even though people knew intuitively that attitude had a great deal to do with how police officers behaved toward suspects, it was uncomfortable for some scholars to read this aspect of Black's findings. However, the good news (again) was that while police officers used the attitude test to determine arrest/no arrest decision-making on occasion, it was the fourth and least important criterion used. While dated, Black's research has never been contested by any research since.

After defining and analyzing the concept of discretion, we have seen how the police in fact exercise their discretionary powers. Black's research is good news for our discussion, as it indicates that police on the street behave in a way that is legally rational, ethically defensible, and logistically practical. Their operational norms are clearly in concert with how we would wish them to behave, in the interests of justice.

SUMMATION

We have seen that discretion is an important tool that police officers use in accomplishing their numerous tasks. In fact, it is impossible to imagine the police effectively administering anything we could fairly label as "justice" without utilizing a significant amount of discretion.

However, we have also seen that discretion can be troublesome. Mistrust of the police abounds in America. We see this manifested in those who place such little faith in the police that they call for the impossible policy of full enforcement. People who mistrust police to begin with, for whatever reason, are prone to have that mistrust amplified when they see officers making discretionary decisions. Even if they are not knowledgeable about police work (or the law), people sense when the police make these decisions. And when such people witness discretion in action, they can construe what they see as, in fact, the "rule of cop" on the streets of America.

So we are left with this chapter's major paradox: while discretion is absolutely necessary, it can create citizen-police antipathy (in much the same manner as with police stereotyping). Furthermore, while we want the police to be cognizant of the importance of the rule of law, we also must acknowledge that they—the police—*are* the law in a very real sense.

CHAPTER THREE PARADOX BOX

Police discretion is absolutely critical to the delivery of justice on the street. But it can be resented by citizens and make the police appear lawless. As a society, we want the "rule of law" . . . but in essence, "the police *are* the law."

Let us now turn to what some consider a fascinating paradox relating to how the due process system works in America. In Chapter Four, we will discuss how the operations of the due process system can actually create not just frustration and cynicism in police officers, but police misconduct.

DISCUSSION QUESTIONS

1. Consider Box 3.2. How would you handle these several suspects? How should the police handle them? Why? Is it morally defensible to treat them differently? Or not? Discuss.

2. Police decisions define the law. If the police deemphasize something, they can effectively decriminalize it. What are the limits to this reality? Should the police decriminalize underage drinking in a college town? Should they decriminalize gambling in an inner city area where it has been part of the local culture for a long time? Should they decriminalize marijuana smoking where it is commonplace? What is the difference between these types of crimes? Is there any? Discuss.

3. Our book juxtaposes two different definitions of "justice." Consider the differences between justice as fairness and justice as equality. Which is best? Which is your personal philosophical view on the subject? Can people agree with both philosophies—using one at one time and one at another time? Discuss.

4. Consider the specificity of rules problem. Try to construct a rule dictating what a police officer should do when he or she sees a person staggering down the street at night. Make the rule "tight," such that there is no discretion involved—the arrest / no arrest options are absolutely clear cut. Then see if you can construct circumstances under which you would *not* want the rule to be so "tight"—where even though the rule demands an arrest you would not be in favor of that outcome.

KEY TERMS

Age of Enlightenment: The historical era when English aristocratic tradition was challenged and then replaced with Western Liberalism.

Complete Discretion: A lack of rules; Khadi justice.

Discretion: Using judgment; for our discussions, it pertains to those who apply rules to the behavior of others.

Discretionary Continuum: An imaginary spectrum that moves from absolute discretion (Khadi justice) to zero discretion (full enforcement).

Distributive Justice: The philosophical principle suggesting that justice involves giving what is "due" each person.

Equal Protection of the Law: American Constitutional Principle included in both the 5th and 14th Amendments.

Full Enforcement: The application of rules without discretion; for the police, this involves arresting or citing "everyone."

Founding Fathers: Those who led the American Revolution, signed the Declaration of Independence, or helped frame the Constitution.

Justice as Equality: The idea that justice involves treating everyone in exactly the same way, irrespective of exigent variables.

Justice as Fairness: The idea that justice involves treating people fairly—and not necessarily equitably.

Khadi Justice: The absence of rules; the Khadi is an absolute lawgiver who has no accountability to anyone.

King George of England: King of England at the time the American Revolution broke out; responsible for many of the excesses that led to the Revolution.

King George's Men: The "Redcoats" who applied English law in the American Colonies.

Labeling Theory: A school of criminological theory suggesting that those who get arrested and put into the system when young tend to end up hardened criminals, while those who avoid arrest (and labeling) tend to end productive, law-abiding citizens.

Plea Bargaining: Part of the practical operations of the criminal justice system under which trials are rarely held and bargains are made instead that determine criminal guilt and appropriate punishment.

Revolving Door: The contemporary idea that our correctional system must deal with so many new convicts that those inside state and federal prisons must be released—regardless of the time left on their sentences.

The Rule of Law: The idea that rules control the law in a rigid way, and that human discretion has no place in the legal system.

Specificity of Rules Problem: The idea that it is effectively impossible to construct rules so specific that they obviate the need for discretion completely.

Western Liberalism: The set of principles that ushered in the modern era of our "meritocracy"—it replaced the ancient European system of aristocracy.

Zero Discretion: Application of rules rigidly without reference to exigent circumstances.

Zero Tolerance: The idea that zero discretion be used in the pursuit of drugs—that everyone gets arrested no matter how minor their drug offense.

 ## ADDITIONAL READINGS

The topic of discretion is covered in every thoughtful book ever written about police by social scientists. The first seminal treatment of discretion was done by Kenneth Culp Davis in 1977 in his book *Police Discretion* (West Publishing, 1977). A discussion of how important discretion is in the modern police officer personality is engaged in ***Thinking Cop, Feeling Cop: A Study in Police Person-alities, 3rd Ed.*** by Stephen M. Hennessy (The Center for Applications of Psychological Type, 1998). Another modern treatment detailing how police leaders need to be cognizant of discretion, its positives and its negatives, is included in Thomas E. Baker's ***Effective Police Leadership*** (Looseleaf Law Publications, 2005), which focuses upon the importance of discretion right from its introduction.

Our work has touched briefly upon the subject of labeling theory, and the interested student may wish to investigate this criminal justice theory in more depth. To do so is to engage the ideas of Howard S. Becker, who first posited the concept. Initially discussed in 1963, a much more recent and synoptic treatment of Becker's ideas can be obtained in ***Outsiders: Studies in the Sociology of Deviance*** (Free Press, 1997).

The idea of the continuum of police discretionary decision-making is analyzed in William Terrill's ***Police Coercion: Application of the Force Continuum*** (LFB Scholarly Publishing, 2001), which focuses upon the use of force but suggests the utility of the continuum conceptualization. Regarding the two ends of the continuum, ***Zero Tolerance Policing*** by Maurice Punch (Policy Press, 2007) discusses the evolution of the idea of full enforcement first discussed in connection with the Drug War during the Reagan years. This policy is now the subject of much controversy in many areas of public policy, including that of school conduct rules. At the other end of the continuum, Herbert Schlossberg explains Weber's ideas about "Khadi Justice" in ***Idols for Destruction*** (Thomas Nelson, 1983).

There are as many discussions about the two classical ideas of justice (justice as equity and justice as fairness) we engage in our book as there are philosophers in the world. For a police-specific discussion that is terse and yet utilitarian, see Douglas W. Perez and J. Alan Moore's ***Police Ethics: A Matter of Character*** (Cengage Publishing, 2002). For a more in-depth treatment of the specificity of rules problem, see ***Arrest Discretion of Police Officers: The Impact of Varying Organizational Structures*** by Richard F. Groeneveld (LFB Scholarly Publishing LLC, 2005).

Finally, Donald Black's original study of the arrest / no arrest decisions of New York City police officers was first published in "The Social Organization of Arrest" (Stanford Law Review, 1971, Vol. 23, pp. 1087–1111). Black later developed an all-inclusive theory of the application of rules by legal practitioners that was published in what is now considered the classic work in the field: ***The Behavior of Law*** (Academic Press, 1980).

CHAPTER 4

The Due Process System

Chapter Four Outline

Our American criminal law system operates on what is called the **due process** principle. This principle goes back even before our Declaration of Independence and our Constitution. It suggests that the state may take away a person's life, liberty, or property only under certain specific, unusual circumstances. Only when there is a formal process in place, and each and every step of that process is scrupulously observed, can the state take away any of these rights or possessions. The due process principle itself, and the procedural rules put in place to make its generalizations more specific, is aimed at promoting one of the most important underlying principles of American government and politics: that of limited government (Locke). When put into action, these principles make up the "rules of the game" to which agents of the state must adhere when dealing with citizens. These rules provide personal protection to every American citizen from the abuse of governmental power.

This makes sense in a logical way. It is a hedge against the government exercising the sort of absolute power the English exercised in America prior to our Revolution. The due process principle was so important to our Founding Fathers that obtaining the right for every citizen to have access to such procedures was one of the reasons for that revolution. It is a bedrock American principle—a part of who we are and what we stand for.

However, the due process system is cumbersome and can be frustrating. It is artificially complicated, making the task of holding criminals to answer for their deviant behavior much more difficult than it has to be. No other country in the world goes about processing criminals in as byzantine a fashion as we do in the United States. Every other country on earth has a criminal justice system that is more straightforward and easy to follow. Sometimes it seems as if the American criminal justice process is some sort of "full employment program" for lawyers because of its multifaceted, intricate, and perplexing practices.

In this chapter, we will consider both views of the due process system. We will discuss the positive and logical rationalizations for it and remind ourselves that only in America does every citizen have the kinds of rights and protections that it provides. We will also analyze its negative and almost irrational realities and how unwieldy and ponderous it can be.

Let us begin with some definitions and reminders about how the system operates in general.

THE PROCEDURAL LAW SYSTEM

Included in several places in the United States Constitution—the Fifth and Fourteenth Amendments, to be precise—the due process principle is meant to guarantee that procedures are always in place to protect individuals from the abuse of governmental power (Orth). At the same time, the principles in place work to protect the logic, consistency, and integrity of the very system itself.

The due process system operates through a sort of layering effect that begins with the over-arching principle of due process and then gets progressively more

BOX 4.1

MAKING THINGS DIFFICULT—ON PURPOSE

The due process system puts artificially created, procedural "roadblocks" in the way of police officers. At times, it seems to work directly against the police. It is the job of the police to deal with crime, crime scenes, victims, and survivors and to find out who was, in fact, "guilty" when a crime occurred. After they solve a crime and make an arrest, the machinations of the due process system go into effect. Rights and procedures rule that system. And it sometimes appears to the police as if no one else in the system really cares about factual guilt; attorneys and judges and juries seem to focus exclusively upon procedural guilt and upon legal technicalities instead of criminal culpability and the rights of those who are the victims of crime.

specific as the layers of the process unfold (Bodenhamer). Let us discuss this layering idea for a moment before we analyze and critique the system.

"No person shall be . . . deprived of life, liberty, or property without due process of law." This phrase comes from the Fifth Amendment, and it is echoed, word-for-word, in the Fourteenth Amendment. The pronouncements and guarantees of the Fifth Amendment were meant to limit the power of the federal government, and those of the Fourteenth Amendment were meant to limit the power of state and local governments. Taken together, these principles echo similar language in the writings of not only Thomas Jefferson (author of the **Declaration of Independence**) but also John Locke, the political philosopher and ideological forerunner of the Founding Fathers and all of our institutions.

But what does it mean? What does the phrase "due process" signify in action? The words themselves do not give us much to go on. They merely require that *some* kind of process needs to be in place that will limit the power of the government and protect what both Locke and Jefferson called the "natural rights" ("unalienable rights" in the Declaration of Independence) with which all persons are born.

To enumerate the ideal of due process with more clarity, the Constitution presents many specific principles important in-and-of themselves (Roach). They outline the general processes that the system must have in place in order to define its operations more precisely. Thus, accused persons have the right to a trial by jury, to have the advice of counsel, to remain silent when on trial, and to protection against double jeopardy. And there are even more specifics—a list of particular rights that is more substantive than procedural. Aside from more politically oriented rights, such as the right to assemble freely, or the right to freedom of speech, or the right to exercise the religion of one's choice, all citizens have the right of protection against unreasonable searches and seizures. The Constitution was specific about warrantless searches because its framers remembered King George's men making searches without any specific cause whatsoever. They did so under what were then called "**writs of assistance**," which were open-ended instruments provided to the Redcoats by the King (Otis).

The Fourth Amendment's pronouncements about **unreasonable searches and seizures** are absolutely critical to the part of the criminal justice process that relates to police officers (Long). Searches and seizures happen constantly in police work and the law surrounding them is studied consistently by the police. It is appropriate to focus upon the Fourth Amendment's pronouncements about searches and seizures in our discussion here, precisely because it is so much a part of the policing endeavor.

But there is a specificity problem with the Fourth Amendment. It guarantees one's right against "unreasonable" searches and seizures, but this is somewhat amorphous. What does it mean? What does "unreasonable" signify? What kind of searching is unreasonable and what kind is reasonable? In order to make sense on the street of this generalized principle, police officers need still another level of clarification. Specific rules defining what police officers may do on a minute-by-minute basis must be determined. These further delineated rules have to be still more specific than the Fourth Amendment with regard to vehicle stops, personal searches, wire tapping, and a host of other forms of governmental intrusion.

And so we have case law. In the case of ***Terry v. Ohio (1968)***, for example, the U.S. Supreme Court laid down specific rules to be followed by police officers if they wished to search a suspect but possessed no grounds for arrest. *Terry* allows officers to make limited, external pat-searches of suspects on the street. The Supreme Court's decision in *Terry* was the final, end-result ruling that put it all together—all three layers of the process. A generalized right to something called due process, the first layer, had been further codified by something labeled a right against unreasonable searches and seizures, the second layer. This, in turn, had been further defined by a case before the Supreme Court that embodied the nuts and bolts of police work on the street (searching a suspect without a warrant and without a charge), which was the third and final layer. This three step system of defining criminal justice procedures is the essence of the due process system.

This system makes logical sense. Beginning with the more general, over-arching right to due process, then focusing more specifically upon a Constitutional Amendment's pronouncements, the everyday police officer ends up with something tangible in the Court's definition of what he or she can do with regard to pat searching a suspect. One step follows the other in the process of making clear what rights a citizen has and what a police officer can and cannot do.

Now that the due process ideal is a bit clearer, it is time to critique this system as it is made operational in the American courtroom. Police officers are often extremely critical of the system, and it is toward a consideration of why this is true that we now turn.

THE DUE PROCESS SYSTEM AS "THE ENEMY"

On the surface, it might appear that police officers would be the members of the criminal justice system most prone to be supportive of its due process focus. To some extent, the police are the symbols of the system. Their authoritative carriage on the streets is emblematic of the power of the law. They are its messengers, walking amongst us, in uniform, representing the government, the legal process, the Constitution, and the justice system in general. In theory, they would be the champions of due process.

But this is seldom the case. Often, the police feel stymied by the system in operation. Modern, intelligent, educated, well-trained officers understand the rational reasons for due process. But in reality, most officers are frustrated by how it works *some* of the time. And some officers, as we shall see later, are frustrated by how it works *most* of the time. Being unsupportive of the system that they represent—at least some of the time—is commonplace among contemporary police officers.

Why is this so? Why does the due process system become, to some extent, the "enemy" of the average police officer? The answer comes in the form of the most important procedural rule in all of American criminal law: the **exclusionary rule** (Krantz). Because of the pragmatic realities of how the exclusionary rule is applied in our system, police officers can become frustrated, cynical, and even diffident out on the street. Following is a brief primer about what exclusion is and how it works:

Going back in American history about 100 years, the courts of this country—the Supreme Court of the United States in particular, being the primary protector of the Constitution—were asked to do something about police lawlessness. In particular, they were asked to take some kind of action that would force police officers to take notice of the Fourth Amendment's pronouncements

BOX 4.2

THE EXCLUSIONARY RULE

The United States of America is the only country in the world with an exclusionary rule. We are the only people who have decided that as a part of the operational principles of our criminal justice system we will "pretend" that evidence does not exist if it is obtained illegally. If any evidence—physical or confessional—is obtained in a way inconsistent with the procedural laws of the system, it is ignored in a criminal courtroom. This means that some factually guilty criminals will be set free by the system. And this is very disconcerting for many. As Justice Cardoza once commented, dissenting against the rule, "The criminal is to go free because the constable has blundered."

about unreasonable searches and seizures. The police in those days were, to some extent, out of control; they regularly ignored the Fourth Amendment, making thousands of warrantless searches each year and generally behaving as if the Constitution had no relevance to their work-a-day jobs. Since there was no recourse for citizens abused by the brazen exercise of police power, the Court was asked to step in.

In 1914, in the case of **Weeks v. United States**, the Court put into place a rule aimed at stopping police abuses of the Constitution at the federal level. Knowing that they were not police chiefs, that they could not hire police officers, train them, and discipline them, the members of the Court decided to take the only action they could: they decided to put into place a procedural rule that would "punish" the police when they abused their power and when they made mistakes. This was to be done by excluding evidence in the courtroom if it had been obtained in violation of the Fourth Amendment's dictates. Metaphorically speaking, illegally obtained evidence was considered to be the "**fruits of the poisoned tree**." Such fruits would poison the purity of the criminal justice system if they were admitted into court. In this metaphor, of course, the "poisoned tree" is the illegal search and the "fruits" are the evidence obtained (Lyman and Geberth).

In *Weeks* the Court took a limited step—it required exclusion in federal cases only. But by 1961, frustrated by several more generations of police misconduct, the Court put exclusion into place at the state and local levels. That year, in **Mapp v. Ohio (1961)**, the Supreme Court made the practice of excluding illegally obtained evidence the law of the land in every criminal case in America. Since that time, the exclusionary rule has been the singularly most important procedural rule in American criminal law. And since no other country has followed suit, America is the only country on the face of the planet with this rule as its primary procedural safeguard against police misconduct.

Here is how exclusion is supposed to work. The police make an arrest and begin the process of moving a case through the system. But evidence has been obtained in an illegal way. Perhaps an "unreasonable" search has been conducted—violating the Fourth Amendment's admonitions. Or perhaps a suspect was interrogated and a confession was obtained in an illegal fashion—violating the suspect's Fifth Amendment right against self-incrimination. When the evidence is reviewed by a court, the court will exclude it from the trial process. The evidence is kept from the jury's view and the trial proceeds as if it (the evidence) never existed. Or, if the evidence is absolutely critical to the case, the case is dropped completely—before the trail process even begins—because of the evidentiary problem. The police officers involved in the case will then hear about this. They will be "punished" in a sense, because they will have lost the case and be subject to the embarrassment and reputation tarnishing that can result from botched police work. They then reorganize their thinking. They learn never to make the sort of illegal search (or to conduct the sort of illegal interrogation) that caused the exclusion. That's how exclusion is supposed to work to require that police take note of the Constitution and "behave themselves."

The law is what the judge says it is.

This all makes sense, especially from the perspective of the justices of the Supreme Court. They were frustrated by police lawlessness and, as they saw it, they had no other options. But the operational realities of the system are such that exclusion creates a great deal of consternation, and even antipathy, in the hearts and minds of many police officers—an antipathy directed squarely at the criminal justice system's due process realities. For what happens is this: factually guilty criminals walk free on the streets of America because of legal technicalities. That is the effect of exclusion.

So while the police might be expected to act as the champions of the due process system, they are often moved to consider it the enemy. Due process works against the police in that it makes their job much more complicated than it has to be. On occasion, it negates their hard work by turning loose those who they have found to be factually guilty of victimizing the good citizens the police are sworn to protect. Put simply, the police do not like this reality.

It should be noted here, albeit briefly, that in other countries, police can be chastened for misconduct in numerous ways that do not involve exclusion. But in no country other than America are guilty citizens freed when a constable blunders.

THE DIRTY HARRY PROBLEM

In reacting to the frustrations created by the operations of the due process system, some police officers are moved to "take the law into their own hands." That is, they are prone to ignore the dictates of due process and to "do whatever it takes" to put those who they determine to be bad actors behind bars. If **procedural law** is so complicated that the police feel they cannot do their jobs in a way that avoids exclusion, one thing they can do is become involved in what has been labeled as **"noble cause corruption"** or "Dirty Harry-like" behavior (Perez and Moore). They can manipulate the system in such a way as to insure that people who are factually guilty will be put away instead of being turned loose by exclusion.

How can Dirty Harry (see Box 4.3) clean up the streets by using illegal tactics? This can be accomplished in several different ways. First, the police can "plant" evidence on citizens. This often involves placing drugs on people believed to be bad actors in an effort to "put them away." The evidence is planted and the case proceeds as if the suspect was guilty. From the perspective of the Dirty Harry–like police officer, the end result is that one more bad actor is removed from the streets. Since it involves cleaning up their beats, making the streets safe from criminals, police officers involved in this type of behavior consider it to be "just doing the job out there."

Second, after an incident on the street, police officers can become involved in what is sometimes laughingly referred to in police circles as "creative report writing." Basically, creative report writing involves lying on paper. In an effort to insure

BOX 4.3

WHO WAS DIRTY HARRY?

We refer in the text here numerous times to "Dirty Harry." Who was he? "Dirty Harry" was the title of a movie filmed in the 1970s starring Clint Eastwood as the title character, Dirty Harry Callahan. Eastwood went on to play the same character in several more movies. The reason this fictional character is important with regards to the criminal justice system is that Harry was made out to be a "hero" because he cut corners—he broke procedural law, making warrantless searches and torturing a prisoner to get information—to get the bad guy. The Harry character became so famous that his name became synonymous with the problem of police officers misbehaving in this way. This is why the famous criminologist Carl Klockars chose Harry for his now classic article **"The Dirty Harry Problem"** about "noble cause corruption."

(Klockars, 1980)

that prosecutors will pursue cases they might otherwise ignore or throw out, police officers change case facts by adding or subtracting something. They can change the sequence of events in order to make an otherwise illegal search into a legal one. Or they can just make something up entirely—a statement by a witness or a confession by a suspect, for example.

Third, in addition to (or instead of) the above, police officers can lie on the witness stand. This happens often enough that it has been christened "testilying" by criminologists (Mollen). If police officers are willing to lie on the witness stand, then all other efforts of the due process system to make things not only fair but logical can go by the wayside. Testilying is, perhaps, the most repulsive of the various types of misconduct associated with Dirty Harry.

Finally, some police officers use excessive force to obtain information from suspects. Thinking that "the end justifies the means," some officers are willing to use force to find out what they need to know—or think they need to know. Dirty Harry did this in the movie, and it is unfortunately still a part of police work today.

Going over this litany of the types of misconduct associated with noble cause corruption is not meant to imply that law enforcement is full of Dirty Harrys. As we shall see in Chapter Thirteen, police misconduct is on the wane in contemporary America. Far less misconduct—of all sorts—exists today than in the past. But that does not mitigate the fact that in attempting to understand American police, we have to embrace the Dirty Harry reality. It is real, and it is a problem with major implications for the delivery of justice on the streets.

Before moving on to consider concerns about still another form of due process—substantive due process—it makes sense to review the arguments made against exclusion. Any synoptic understanding of the dynamics of exclusion in

America today must include this important discussion. Furthermore, since the exclusionary rule is the most important operational principle in the American criminal justice system, and since a large majority of police officers are against exclusion, it behooves us to understand their arguments.

ARGUMENTS AGAINST EXCLUSION

In one sense, one might be moved to tell police officers who make so much of the impact of exclusion to "get over it." After all, the exclusionary rule went into effect in 1961, so virtually every police officer on the street today has worked their entire career under its auspices. It is nothing new, and it came long before today's police officers were hired and trained. Also, as noted in Box 4.4, exclusion does not result in criminals going free very often. The American criminal justice system has operated in an effective manner since the onset of exclusion—so much so that our prison population is now more than five times what it was in 1961. Logic suggests that if exclusion made it impossible to obtain convictions—not just more difficult but impossible—then this increase in the size of the prison population would not have occurred.

But the police do have a point. There are a number of reasons for believing that exclusion works against what it was designed to do—that is, guarantee police officers respect the rights of individual citizens and not violate the dictates of our Constitution. Furthermore, there is reason to believe that exclusion sometimes works in odd and even counterproductive ways. In the ongoing debate about exclusion, the Supreme Court has come close—in recent years—to overturning its dictates. Our Supreme Court has become arch-conservative in the past few decades. It can be argued with conviction that we now have the most conservative court in American history (Toobin). In the 40 years since the election of President Nixon, only two Justices, Ruth Bader Ginsburg and Stephen Breyer, have been appointed by Democratic presidents. The rest have been appointed by Republicans. Since exclusion is viewed as a procedural rule that works against the police, and can thus be characterized by some as a liberal policy, today's court may overturn the rule.

BOX 4.4

HOW OFTEN DO THE GUILTY GO FREE?

So much has been made of the exclusionary rule, and of the noble cause corruption it tends to rationalize, that numerous studies have been conducted to determine how many criminals actually *do* go free under its application. The answer? Not many. A federal study found that federal courts exclude evidence only 1.3% of the time. A California study found that evidence is excluded in that state only 4.8% of the time.

(U.S. Controller General, 404)

There are several logical and prudent reasons for reassessing exclusion (Hatch). The first, as noted earlier, is that it allows factually guilty people to go free. In some sense, exclusion does not work in the way it is supposed to because it punishes the public instead of errant police officers. Thus, the police don't "learn from" making the mistakes that lead to exclusion. This is the number one reason police rail against it.

A second argument against exclusion also relates to the lack of a learning connection between its operations and the errant police officer. Exclusion occurs in one of two ways. Evidence can be excluded behind closed doors in negotiations that are a part of the plea bargaining system. The strength of the prosecution's case can be negatively impacted by exclusion, and, because of this, sometimes prosecutors end up having a less-potent hand when playing the poker game involved in plea bargaining. Exclusion can also occurs as part of a case that makes it into open court. A judge can throw out evidence during a trial.

The logical problem here is that in either event the process of exclusion happens in a way never communicated to the police. Prosecutors and judges do not contact them and explain what they did wrong. They neither contact individual officers nor the police department in general. So how could "police learning" possibly occur? When or where would it be that the police would find out about exclusion? We have to conclude that exclusion does not "teach" police officer(s) anything. There is, quite simply, no logical way such learning could occur.

Third, exclusion does not deter the police from harassing American citizens. We must recall that the Founding Fathers were a rather affluent and conservative group. They put the Fourth Amendment into place in order to deter future government agents from harassing honest, hard-working, legitimate business people—such as themselves. This was something that King George's men had done before the Revolution, and it was at such harassment that they aimed the amendment. There is every reason to believe that if members of the Founding Fathers were to rise from their graves and see how exclusion operates today—in shielding factually guilty criminals from prosecution—they would protest that this wasn't what they had in mind at all!

While exclusion operates to throw evidence out of court, and thus to negate prosecutions, it does nothing to stop the police from harassing citizens if they wish to do so without any aim to prosecute. In other words, if the police want to harass someone, or a group of people, in order to deter them from one thing or another, as sometimes occurs, there is nothing in the operations of exclusion that prohibits this. If, for any reason whatsoever, they are moved to do so, the police are not deterred by exclusion from harassing suspects, from using excessive force, or from applying curbside justice in any number of ways. They may do so with impunity, reverting in a sense to the type of police conduct commonplace during the Political Era's time of incompetence and corruption. And it was exactly this type of misconduct at which the Supreme Court aimed its exclusionary rule in the first place.

Fourth, on the heels of the above point, exclusion can motivate police officers to behave in Dirty Harry–like ways. Such noble cause corruption can be rationalized in an oft-repeated mantra: "I did it because the system was going to let the bum go free." If police officers are willing to lie on the witness stand in order to "get the job done," and unfortunately some of them are, then exclusion guarantees more "testilying" on the witness stand in American courtrooms. Or more creative report writing. Or there more evidence planting. Frustrated officers willing to perjure themselves are in no way deterred by exclusion. So exclusion can create a general disrespect for the law among police officers. But there is more.

The operations of exclusion can work to create a general disrespect for the law among not only police officers but also members of the general public. Often driven by politicians attempting to sell themselves as being "tough on crime," citizens can learn about exclusion and become disgusted with the system's operations. As we shall see in Chapter Six, Hollywood does America no favors in this regard; Dirty Harry–like characters did not cease to exist once Clint Eastwood stopped playing that particular role in the 1970s. On a regular basis, movies and television programs about the police—always popular and viewed by large audiences—sell the noble cause corruption–related message criminal justice system operations are illogical and perhaps even dangerous. Often the police officer hero in the entertainment world is sold to the public as someone they should look up to because he or she "bends the rules to get the job done." And so Dirty Harry still lives on the screen and probably will for a long, long time.

We have so far been exclusively focused on what is called "procedural" due process. Procedural due process involves rules for members of the criminal justice system. But there is also something called **"substantive due process"** that is also part of the guarantees afforded to all Americans by our Constitution and institutional principles.

Before discussing this, let us remind ourselves of the central paradox here that relates to the procedural side of the due process system: while in some sense the police ought to be champions of the due process system, the dynamics associated

BOX 4.5

SUMMATION OF THE ANTI-EXCLUSION DEBATE

The numerous reasons in favor of doing away with the exclusionary rule include:

- Exclusion allows guilty criminals to walk free.
- The reasons for evidentiary exclusion are not communicated to police officers.
- Exclusion doe not stop overt harassment.
- Exclusion encourages Dirty Harry–like behavior.
- Exclusion encourages a general disrespect for the legal system.

with exclusion create a situation wherein the police can come to see due process as their enemy and, even, work against the integrity of the system by engaging in Dirty Harry–like behavior.

SUBSTANTIVE DUE PROCESS PROBLEMS

The Constitution provides that all citizens have the right to due process. This idea has two sets of separate implications for the criminal justice system and the police. In our discussion so far, we have analyzed the procedural side of due process. We have engaged the fact that when they deal with citizens, members of the criminal justice system must follow certain procedural rules in order to avail citizens of their due process rights. We have, in essence, been exclusively focused upon the rules of the game for criminal justice practitioners.

But there is a different, substantive side to due process, too. Substantive due process includes many different concepts, including those related to the principle of eminent domain (Keynes). With regard to the operations of the criminal justice system, substantive due process is about the substance of what is included in penal code sections (and, indeed, in any codified set of rules or laws). To simplify for our immediate discussion, it is about the substance of what can be made illegal. That is, there are certain things that cannot be included in criminal law pronouncements. There are limitations to what rules legislatures can make for citizens to follow.

For example, can the federal government, a state, or a local city make it a crime to play rock and roll music? This would be illogical and unreasonable. But if a legislature *were* to pass such a law, then, undoubtedly, someone would challenge it. And such a law would be overturned by some appeals court somewhere. The basis upon which such a decision would rest is that the passage of an act that makes the playing of rock and roll music a crime violates people's due process rights in a *substantive* sense. Given that the First Amendment protects a person's right to freedom of speech, some appeals court (at either the state or federal level) would

BOX 4.6

THE CHICAGO ANTI-GANG STATUTE

As has been the case in many cities in America in the past 20 years, the City of Chicago passed an anti-gang ordinance in the 1990s. The law made it a crime for three or more people to stand in the street "with no apparent purpose." On the grounds that it was overly broad and gave unlimited discretion to police officers, the United States Supreme Court declared this ordinance unconstitutional in 1999 in the case of *City of Chicago v. Morales*. This was a classic example of a substantive due process decision.

unquestionably decide that playing rock and roll music was just the sort of freedom the Founding Fathers meant to protect with this amendment. Therefore, the law itself would be unconstitutional.

Now this example might seem silly. Who would outlaw rock and roll music? Furthermore, why would they do such a thing? But case decisions in the area of substantive due process are a serious matter. When a substantive due process decision is handed down, it pits justices sitting on appeals courts directly against the legislative representatives of the people. It pits the decisions of judicial officials who are appointed rather than elected—and appointed for life, in the case of federal justices—against the decisions of people accountable to the population. Put another way, substantive due process pits an elitist group, to some extent, against the will of the people. This is an ancient stand-off: society's elites against "the people." Thus, substantive due process decisions can be extraordinarily controversial.

Flag burning cases provide an example. In 1989, in the case of ***Texas v. Johnson (1989)***, the United States Supreme Court ruled that a state cannot make it a crime to burn an American flag in protest (Goldstein). In 1990, in the case of ***United States v. Eichman (1990)***, it then ruled that the federal government also cannot make flag burning a crime. The Court's decision was based on a rational argument: burning a flag in protest is "symbolic speech," and free speech is protected by the First Amendment to the Constitution. But millions of Americans were outraged. So politically volatile and emotionally charged is the issue of flag burning that this set of substantive due process decisions has been controversial ever since they were handed down.

For our purposes, focusing upon the police as we are, the substantive due process cases that relate to police practices are about penal code sections found to be either too "vague" or too "overly broad" to pass constitutional scrutiny. What does this mean? One of the central principles of substantive due process involves the idea that the substance of the law must be fair to citizens in the sense that laws must be easily understandable. The general principle is this: citizens who are of average intelligence and attempt to live by the dictates of the law—so as not to create "trouble" for their government or for their community—should be able to read any criminal law and 1) understand it and 2) behave in such a way as to avoid being arrested. As is true with all of the extrapolations that come from the general principle of due process, this requirement is about limiting the power of the government over the individual.

Substantive due process suggests that for criminal laws to be understandable and fair, they have to do two things at once. First, they have to be specific enough that a person of average intelligence can understand them and avoid committing whatever crime(s) they delineate. Second, they have to be narrowly focused enough that they don't give too much power to the police. If codified laws do not follow these two general guidelines, then they are in danger of being declared unconstitutional on substantive due process grounds—because they are too **"vague and overly broad"** (Boychuk). The vagueness problem relates to the fact that the law should be understandable to the average citizen. The overly broad problem relates to the fact that the American principle of limited government requires that the police not be given the power to "arrest whomever they please." If a law is adjudged to give the police this power, it may be struck down, as was the case with the Chicago Anti-Gang ordinance (Box 4.6).

In practice, what kinds of criminal laws come under this sort of substantive due process scrutiny? What sorts of laws can be accused of being too vague and of giving too much power to the police? An example is the New York State Penal Code's section for "**Disturbing the Peace**." Within a law that goes on for more than 100 words, this code section defines disturbing the peace as (among other things) making "loud or unusual noise" and using "vulgar, profane, or indecent language within the presence or hearing of women or children, in a loud and boisterous manner."

This one little section of one penal code presents the intelligent person with about a dozen questions, due to its vagueness and breadth. What does "loud" mean? What does "unusual" mean? What does "vulgar" mean? How are these words defined, both for the citizen who wishes to avoid being arrested and for the police who should not be given carte blanche to arrest whomever they wish? We can continue. In today's contemporary society, what constitutes "indecent" language? Isn't this code section unacceptably sexist for suggesting that vulgar, profane, and indecent language can be used in front of men but not in front of women? Is that fair to men? Doesn't it imply that women are not adults? And furthermore, what is meant by "boisterous"? There are certainly enough questions to wonder how this penal code section passes judicial scrutiny. If the constitutionality of it were questioned on substantive due process grounds, would this section be declared unconstitutional because it is vague and overly broad?

All penal codes include at least one or two of these seemingly open-ended sections (see Box 4.7). They are often referred to as "**catch-all**" sections by police officers. The police know how broad such sections are and how much power they allow them to exercise. When officers talk with a citizen, they tend to like having

BOX 4.7

EXAMPLES OF "CATCH-ALL" LAWS

- Disturbing the Peace
- Disorderly Conduct
- Malicious Mischief
- Loitering
- Outraging Public Decency

Note: This last section (California P.C. Section 650 1/2—"Outraging Public Decency") was declared unconstitutional—thirty years ago—due to being "vague and overly broad."

"**levers**" over the citizen. The word "lever" is another piece of subcultural jargon. Having a lever refers to possessing the ability to arrest the citizen—in effect, it refers to having leverage. If a citizen has done something illegal, but it isn't something serious or felonious, then the police will have an easy time getting the citizen to cooperate with whatever they are attempting to do. The officer knows that if the citizen does not cooperate he or she can be arrested. So catch-all sections provide police officers with levers on a regular basis. And the police appreciate having such leverage, because it makes the job easier.

However, there is a problem here. Since they are of only marginal legality, the police cannot abuse the use of catch-all sections. They cannot make too many arrests for Disturbing the Peace or **Disorderly Conduct** lest they get themselves into trouble with appeals courts. The police must be judicious in their application of catch-all sections, or they may lose the right to use them completely, due to such sections being declared unconstitutional. So while catch-all sections are of great utility to police officers, they can be troublesome in their application. This presents another paradox for the police. Such laws are utilitarian, but they cannot be utilized very often. In Chicago, the police made the mistake of making thousands of arrests using this anti-gang ordinance. There is reason to believe that if they had refrained from making so many arrests, they might have been allowed to use the ordinance indefinitely.

We have now seen the other side of due process—the substantive side. And as was the case with procedural due process, substantive due process considerations present the police with difficulties that complicate their job.

SUMMATION

In this chapter we have engaged two different sides of the due process principle of American government and politics. On one side, the procedural side, the police are confronted by the paradox that the system they serve presents so many artificially

CHAPTER FOUR PARADOX BOX

Procedural Due Process:

While the due process system is based upon important American principles and is both rational and ethically defensible, it can actually operate to *create* illegal police tactics and police misconduct . . . and a set of rationalizations for both.

Substantive Due Process:

While the police utilize catch-all laws in penal codes all of the time—and appreciate the utility such laws give them—these marginally legal laws are often challenged with regard to their constitutionality for being too vague and overly broad.

created obstacles to their endeavors (particularly because of exclusion) that they are sometimes moved to consider due process an unprincipled enemy. And what is more, some officers end up being moved to participate in noble cause corruption—to become Dirty Harry–like—in an effort to get around the dictates of the system and get the job done. On the other side, the substantive side, the police are afforded a great deal of latitude and power over the citizenry by catch-all sections of the penal code. But in the performance of their duties they must exercise a great deal of caution in using these tools lest they lose them (the catch-all sections) altogether.

Now we shall turn to the exercise of police power. In Chapter Five, we will find that while the police appear as incredibly powerful individuals they are, in fact, often faced with paradoxes that relate to the use of coercive power . . . paradoxes that can make them feel ineffective, power*less*, and impotent.

DISCUSSION QUESTIONS

1. Discuss the exclusionary rule. How does it work? It makes things hard on the police and upon others in the criminal justice system—what is the logic behind this? What is at stake when we talk about such due process concerns? Why is there such concern about the process? Why were the founders of our country so concerned with such processes?

2. Among the criticisms of exclusion is the argument that the process does not prevent the police from harassing citizens. What does this mean? Why might the police harass citizens—not because they personally dislike them but as a strategy of some kind? What do police officers (sometimes) think gets accomplished through overt harassment?

3. Thirty years ago, section 650 ½ of the California State Penal Code was declared unconstitutional. This section had made "outraging public decency" a crime. What did that mean? What is "outrageous" conduct? Might the definition of outrageous conduct differ from place to place? Is it different in the suburbs than in the city? Is it different in the country than in a college town? How could a citizen read that phrase and know what it is they were not supposed to do? Discuss these questions and why such a law is unfair to citizens.

4. Several loitering statues have been declared unconstitutional over time for being too broad—for giving too much power to the police. Discuss allowing the police to arrest someone who is on a public sidewalk "without apparent purpose." Is this reasonable? Is it just? Is it the type of power that we wish to give to our police? Or is it something that might be, in the long run, dangerous?

 KEY TERMS

Catch-all: Refers to the type of penal code section which is vaguely defined and, thus, which allows great latttude to the police with repect to allowing them arrest powers. An example of a "catch-all" section is Disturbing the Peace.

City of Chicago v. Morales (1999): The case that resulted in the striking down of the Chicago anti-gang ordinance making it a city violation for "three or more people" to stand on a streetcorner "without apparent purpose."

Declaration of Independence: Written by Thomas Jefferson, this was the pronouncement of independence from Great Britain by the American colonies.

Dirty Harry Problem: Coined by Carl Klockars, this is the idea that substantial numbers of American police officers break procedural laws in order to convict people who they consider to be worthy of incarceration.

Disorderly Conduct: A crime included in most penal codes sometimes considered to be vague and overly broad (a misdemeanor).

Disturbing the Peace: A crime in most penal codes sometimes considered to be vague and overly broad (a misdemeanor).

Due Process: The general legal principle requiring that procedures be followed before the government can take away a citizen's life, liberty, or property.

Exclusionary rule: The rule that any evidence obtained illegally is unacceptable in an American criminal court.

Fruits of the Poisoned Tree: Metaphor for exclusion; the fruits (evidence) of a poisoned tree (unconstitutional search or interrogation) are unacceptable in a court of law.

Levers: Penal code sections and city ordinances that allow the police leverage over citizens because they allow citizens to be arrested for vague crimes.

Loitering: A crime in most penal codes sometimes considered to be vague and overly broad (a misdemeanor).

Malicious Mischief: A crime in most penal codes sometimes considered to be vague and overly broad (it involves vandalism).

Mapp v. Ohio (1961): The United States Supreme Court case that applied the exclusionary rule to all criminal prosecutions in America at all levels.

Noble Cause Corruption: The idea that breaking procedural rules in order to find citizens guilty of criminal conduct is a morally acceptable endeavor.

Procedural Law: The "rules of the game" that must be followed by criminal justice system practitioners in order to find a citizen guilty.

Substantive Due Process: The area of constitutional law that has to do with the acceptability of the substance of crimes.

Terry v. Ohio (1968): United States Supreme Court case allowing police officers to make limited, external "pat searches" of citizens if officers believe the citizens to be potentially dangerous.

Texas v. Johnson (1989): United States Supreme Court case making it unconstitutional for a state to make flag burning a crime.

United States v. Eichman (1990): United States Supreme Court case making it unconstitutional for the federal government to make flag burning a crime.

Unreasonable Searches and Seizures: Phrase from the Fourth Amendment having to do with requiring the police to obtain warrants to conduct searches.

Vague and Overly Broad: Legal phrase under which civic ordinances or state penal laws are sometimes declared unconstitutional on substantive due process grounds.

Weeks v. United States (1914): United States Supreme Court case applying the exclusionary rule to the federal government.

Writs of Assistance: Warrants provided to the British Redcoats before the American Revolution allowing them unlimited search powers.

ADDITIONAL READING

John Locke is the father of the political philosophy followed by Jefferson that is the bedrock of all American institutions and political ideals. His classic work is *Two Treatises of Government* (Kessinger Publishing, 2004). The concept of due process, a basic principle that springs from Locke, Jefferson, and the Constitution and around which this chapter rotates, is outlined cogently but briefly in *Due Process of Law: A Brief History* by John V. Orth (University of Kansas Press, 2003). It is more synoptically treated in *Fair Trial: Rights of the Accused in American History* by David J. Bodenhamer (Oxford University Press, 1991). Contemporary developments in this field are covered in Kent Roach's *Due Process and Victim's Rights: The New Law and Policies of Criminal Justice* (University of Toronto Press, 1999), wherein Roach makes the argument that the negative, and at times vehement, reaction to the excesses of due process since *Mapp* is gaining ground, especially in the area of victim's rights.

Exclusion is very well covered in *Mapp v. Ohio: Guarding Against Unreasonable Searches and Seizures* by Carolyn N. Long (University of Kansas Press, 2006), although the student should understand that this is a constitutional law treatise and not as easy a read as many works cited herein. In our discussion of the criticism of exclusion we noted that today's American Supreme Court is perhaps the most conservative in all of our country's history—in *The Nine: Inside the Secret World of the Supreme Court* (Doubleday, 2007) by Jeffrey Toobin, this arch-conservatism is discussed at length in a balanced and forthright way.

With regard to Dirty Harry, it must first be suggested that students interested in the idea of Harry and noble cause corruption are well advised to rent the movie if they have never seen it (or if they have not seen it in a long while).

Watching the movie with an eye toward discussions in this book can be most illuminating. Klockars's initial article "The Dirty Harry Problem" was published in 1980 (*The Annals of the American Academy of Political and Social Sciences*, Volume 452, Number 2, 33–47). An excellent, contemporary discussion of this problem is included in *Criminal Justice Ethics: Theory and Practice 2nd Ed.* by Cyndi Banks (Sage, 2008).

Some suggestions about the types of excesses and abuses that the police fall into when behaving like Dirty Harry, such as sweeps and raids, are presented by Anthony V. Bouza in *Police Unbound: Corruption, Abuse, and Heroism By the Boys in Blue* (Prometheus, 2001). The research into how often exclusion occurs and, thus, how often Dirty Harry is given the excuse to misbehave, has been brought together cogently in Sheldon Krantz et al's book *Police Policymaking* (Lexington Books, 1979).

Substantive due process is explained and put into historical perspective in *Liberty, Property, and Privacy: Toward a Jurisprudence of Substantive Due Process* by Edward Keynes (Pennsylvania State University Press, 1996).

CHAPTER 5

Coercive Power

Chapter Five Outline

Perhaps the singularly most important and insightful book ever written about the police is *Police: Streetcorner Politicians* by William K. Muir Jr. In later chapters, we will visit Muir's conceptualizations as part of our discussions about the idea of professionalism and with regard to the leadership of both sergeants and chiefs of police. But in our discussion about the exercise of **coercive power**, Muir's ideas will take center stage. He theorizes about a reality that has haunted police officers for generations: the feeling that even though they are supposed to be powerful individuals, they have trouble coercing apparently powerless people. This feeling of powerlessness on the part of police officers is a mystery to both those within the police subculture and those without. In fact, it is extremely difficult for those who have never been police officers to understand how this group of power wielders could possibly feel impotent.

Muir changed that, at least for those who read his book. In the midst of a book about the many paradoxes of police work, perhaps our discussion in this chapter will be the most intriguing and educational—because of how hard it is to understand the precarious position occupied by police officers with regard to the exercise of power in general.

We begin our consideration of police power paradoxes with a brief discussion that defines power itself and reflects upon the three kinds of power in the world. Then we will focus more directly upon coercion and paradoxes associated with it. Throughout the chapter, we will make connections between different power-wielding people, one of the things Muir's work does so well. Muir reminded us that in terms of the dynamics involved in the administration of power and the operational realities of the paradoxes of coercive power, there is little difference between being a parent, being the President of the United States, or being a police officer. All of these people enjoy the same advantages when dealing with those who appear to have less power than they (children, weaker countries, and citizens), and yet they all suffer equally from the limitations of coercive power.

POWER DEFINED

This is not a political science book, so we will not attempt a protracted discussion about different definitions of **power** (Hawkins). For the purposes of this chapter and this book, we define power as "behavior control": when one exercises power over another, one changes the other's behavior in a desired direction. To be powerful is to make people behave in ways they otherwise would not.

Three Types of Power

Now there are three basic kinds of power in life—three ways to influence the behavior of others: exhortation, reciprocity, and coercion. To begin our discussion, we define each, emphasize the fact that all power-wielding people may utilize all three types, give examples, and then focus on coercive power. We do this because the police are licensed to exercise this type of power, and they do so on a regular basis. But we also focus on the coercion of others because it is an enterprise so replete with difficulty that it creates animosity toward anyone and everyone who coerces.

The police coerce others legally in ways that are criminal for civilians. In fact, so omnipresent is this license that most people associate the police with their coercive powers as if those powers were *the* critical element of police work. And because people very much dislike being coerced, it is the sort of power that creates anti-police feelings in the hearts and minds of millions of Americans. But let us not get ahead of ourselves. Let us first consider the three types of power.

Exhortation: Exhortative power involves convincing people to do what you want by using words (Wrage; Yellin; Cialdini). One person can control another by motivating them to do something because it is the right and ethical thing to do. Or because it is the good and proper thing to do. Or because it is the rational and intelligent thing to do. If one knows another's religion, one might influence their behavior by appealing to their religious beliefs—convince them it is the Christian thing to do or that Allah would want them to it. And so on.

When using exhortative power, one plays into previously internalized values. If the person one wants to influence has been socialized with a value or belief system important to them, then exercising power over them only takes some creativity on the part of anyone who wishes to influence their behavior. The would-be power wielder simply appeals to the value or belief system, and the goal of behavioral influence can be achieved.

Parents—good parents—use exhortative power all the time. Parenting is all about molding youngsters into good people by influencing their behavior in positive directions. Even when dealing with a very small child, parents want to motivate him or her to do the right thing, the intelligent thing, and, often, to behave like a good Christian or a good Muslim or a good Jew. While some people rail against the idea of utilizing power against children, that is precisely what is involved in parenting—on a daily basis.

Presidents, too, use exhortation as often as possible. A good president will try to get Congress to cooperate by suggesting that what is being asked is the right thing to do for the good of the country. Or a good president will attempt to motivate a foreign leader to do this or that because it is in the best interests of good relations between nations. For as much as we consider the American president to be "the most powerful person in the world," wielding power in an aggressive manner is always in the background of good presidential politics; exhortation is the means by which an intelligent president wants to accomplish goals. All thoughtful power wielders will attempt to utilize this type of power—the power of positive motivation—as often as they can.

The police utilize exhortation on a regular basis. In order to control them, an intelligent police officer can appeal to a father's love for a child, a mother's commitment to her family, a person's vanity, a man's machismo, a woman's empathy,

BOX 5.1

EXPECTING PEOPLE TO BE GOOD

Sometimes police officers can become jaded about life. Since they regularly see the worst in people, they can come to *expect* only the worst. But oddly enough, the police are often quite effective in controlling people and situations by utilizing exhortation—by reminding people of their own values and notions of right and wrong. Exhortation only works when people are intelligent, thoughtful, moral, pious, or kind. For exhortation to work for them, the police have to depend upon people having these values already internalized into their personalities. And it turns out that exhortation often does work for the police, no matter how much they may be driven to think it will not.

and or to many other internalized elements of a citizen's personality. A drunk can be convinced to "go home and sober up." An angry significant other can be convinced to "go out and have a drink." A shoplifter can be convinced to apologize to a shop owner. A father can be convinced to calm down because his child is becoming upset. Noisy teenagers can be motivated to quiet down and move along. In these and a hundred other ways, an intelligent and creative police officer can solve any number of problems on the beat. To be an effective exhorter merely takes imagination, the ability to innovate, and the time necessary to make one's case.

Reciprocity: The power of reciprocity is the **power of trade** or **barter**. One can control the behavior of another by giving them something in exchange for the behavior desired (Kolm). Of course, one can give money in exchange for desired behavior. In fact, this is why much of the world goes to work every day. Most people—the overwhelming majority of them—are not lucky enough to work at doing something they love to do. They only go to work in exchange for money. They do not like or enjoy their jobs. If they did not get paid for it, they would not be moved to be involved in what they do on the job week in and week out, year in and year out. So in this way, people's behavior is controlled by their employers. And this means that their employers have power over them. To control someone reciprocally, it is not necessary that one use money to make the exchange possible. It is equally effective to exchange goods and services, information, or, even, "favors" to create a reciprocal power relationship. Reciprocity is the "I'll scratch your back, you scratch my back" type of human interaction.

Parents are using reciprocal power when they motivate their children to behave by offering a reward for good behavior. "If you do this, we'll go out and get ice cream." "If you do that, you'll get a special treat." As is true with exhortation, utilizing reciprocity is a positive way to control the behavior of children. And good parents seek to reciprocate with their children as often as they can because, again, it is a positive, supportive, civilized way to achieve desired ends.

Similarly, presidents, when dealing with members of Congress, will engage in what is called **"log rolling"** in politics (Merriam-Webster 495). A president will make a deal that involves supporting one piece of legislation in exchange for obtaining support for another, unrelated act. Or a president will make trade-offs with foreign leaders in any number of ways. They will encourage desired behavior by forgiving debts, opening trade routes, creating foreign aid packages, and so forth. This is the essence of politics; compromises are made in one area and then reciprocated in another arena.

Police officers can control the behavior of citizens utilizing reciprocity by doing favors for them—locating information about outstanding warrants, finding out about relatives who are in jail, or determining probation or parole status. Most often, when using reciprocity, the police allow people latitude with regard to minor criminal offenses. In an effort to create on-going relationships wherein citizens "owe them something," police officers often allow little transgressions to go without sanction. This is done in anticipation of handling future situations using the stored up stock of what is owed to the police. An officer might say, "I'll let you slide on this one. Remember it." Then too, narcotics officers influence people directly by "paying them" with money or drugs. In these and other ways, the police exercise power over people through reciprocity.

Coercion: Coercive power involves controlling people by using threats to do harm. We will spend more time in a moment carefully illustrating the dynamics that need to be in place for this to happen—for the coercive power transaction to occur between a coercer and the victim of coercion—but for now we will merely suggest that coercing another involves picking out something of value to them and then threatening to do harm to it. It is a much more negative form of power wielding, and, therefore, it is not as constructive or optimistic as exhortation and reciprocity.

Good parents avoid coercion whenever possible. Threatening one's children on a regular basis is not conducive to maintaining a positive relationship with them. Whether they be misbehaving toddlers, disrespectful "tweenagers," or incorrigible teenagers, coercion does not go over well with children. Nevertheless, at times parenting boils down to, "Johnny, if you don't stop that you'll get a time out." Or "Mary, if you don't behave yourself you'll get a spanking." It is quite impossible to raise children without ever stooping to coercion, no matter what a parent's intentions might be over time.

Presidents are equally able to coerce, of course. At times they may threaten to bring the full force of the American military to bear upon an overly aggressive nation that threatens the peace. Or they might sanction uncooperative nations with economic embargos or high tariffs on imports. In their interpersonal relationships with foreign leaders, American presidents may threaten to bring their power to bear in order to motivate other nations to "straighten up and fly right."

Coercive power is often what we think of when we think of the police—and rightfully so. Because the police are uniquely licensed to coerce, people outside of police work often believe that coercing people is what they do *most* of the time, not just some of the time. People observe the confident carriage of the police, see their militaristic uniforms, focus upon their weapons, and reflect upon the symbolic meaning of their badges—and in noticing all of this, they perceive the trappings of coercive power. People therefore believe that the police are almost exclusively involved in controlling people through the use of threats. When the police show up, their very presence brings with it two implicit threats: the threat of arrest and use of force. These two threats are ever-present when the police are around.

There are some important lessons power wielders need to understand to avoid depending upon coercion all of the time. First, an intelligent power broker learns to avoid coercion if at all possible. Intelligent parents seek to avoid coercing their kids if they can utilize exhortation or reward to control them. It is not good parenting to spend your time threatening your kids on a regular basis. Presidents, if they are intelligent about it, will seek to use exhortation or log rolling to influence congress members or foreign powers before they resort to threats.

The intelligent police officer—or the intelligent mother or President—will not want to depend exclusively upon coercion. This is because people do not like to be coerced and rail against it. But it is also because the more one coerces, the more one tends to run into situations where one's bluff is called and coercion fails. This is dangerous ground upon which to tread as a power wielder, as we will find out shortly.

Secondly, the intelligent exerciser of power wants to prioritize the use of the three different types of power. Mothers, Presidents, and police officers should exercise exhortation, reciprocity, and coercion *in that order of priority*—if they at all can. Of course, it is not always possible for police officers to utilize the three types of power in that specific order. Often when the police are called to solve a problem, the situations to which they respond have gone well past any ability to use, for example, exhortation. The police are often called because people's internal value systems have already failed. Attempting exhortation—which depends upon those very same value systems to work—is a lost cause under such circumstances. But when it *is* possible, any power wielder should attempt to use the three types of power in this specific order.

Exhortation should always be attempted first when time and circumstances permit. This is for two reasons. First, people do not resent being exhorted. In fact, quite the opposite is the case. When someone decides to do something because it is the right or logical or Christian thing to do, they feel good about themselves. They feel good about their decision. It has been their choice to behave in an appropriate manner, not someone else's, and they enjoy having acted like a good or logical or Christian person. Second, exhortation doesn't cost the power wielder anything. To exhort someone to do the right thing merely costs the time it takes to make one's pitch—to explain the situation and to ask for appropriate behavior. In essence, exhortation is "free" to the power wielder.

If exhortation does not work, reciprocity should always be attempted second, because it costs the power wielder something. But reciprocity is still positive. That is, when someone decides to do something because of a trade, they have made the decision themselves and feel good about it. They have made a calculation and come to the conclusion that "it's worth it" to do what they are being motivated to do. So reciprocity comes second.

And of course, coercion comes last. Coercion should be avoided if at all possible because people don't like to be coerced. Furthermore, it can cost the power wielder dearly. In a moment, when we discuss the four paradoxes of coercive power, we will find out just how much coercion can cost. But let us now discuss coercive power in depth and analyze the dynamics involved in its successful application.

COERCIVE POWER

We now come to the major focal point of this chapter's discussion; coercive power. To coerce someone is to influence their behavior by utilizing what Muir calls "threats to harm." The formula involved is not difficult to understand, but it is important that we work our way through it slowly, taking care to be clear about each dynamic involved. Once we have done this, our discussion of the four paradoxes of coercive power will easily follow.

Exercising coercive power is the equivalent of committing **extortion**, a crime in the penal code (Wrage). The crime of extortion involves "the gaining of property or money by almost any kind of force, or threat of (1) violence; (2) property damage; (3) harm to reputation; or (4) unfavorable government action." For what Muir calls "the extortionate transaction" to occur, several dynamics and participants must be in place. There must be a **Coercer** (the person attempting to exercise coercive power), a **Victim** (the person being coerced), a **Hostage** (something or someone of value to the Victim), and a threat. Furthermore, for the transaction to proceed, several steps must be taken in a particular order.

First, the Coercer must take a Hostage. We are familiar with the concept of the Hostage because we are familiar with how kidnapping works. In kidnapping, the Hostage is a person. But for our purposes here, the Hostage can be anything of value to the Victim of the coercion. A Hostage is merely something that can be threatened. A student can be coerced by threatening them with an "F" for a grade. A child can be coerced by threatening them with being grounded. A country can be coerced by threatening it with invasion. A citizen can be coerced by threatening arrest. And so on.

Second, the Hostage must be of significant value to the Victim. The Victim must care about the harm threatened to the Hostage. The student (Victim) must care about his or her grades. The child must care about being grounded. The country must not want to be invaded. And the citizen must care about being arrested.

BOX 5.2

STEPS IN THE EXTORTIONATE TRANSACTION

- The Coercer takes a Hostage.
- The Hostage is of significant value to the Victim.
- The Coercer makes a believable threat to harm the Hostage.
- The above is communicated effectively to the Victim.
- The Coercer demands a ransom.

And, if all of the above is in place . . .

- The ransom is paid.

Third, the Coercer must make a believable threat to harm the Hostage. The threat must involve something that the Coercer *can* do. The threat must also involve something that the Coercer *will* do. This is an absolutely critical element to the extortionate transaction. In a moment we will analyze in depth what can happen if a threat is not believable (or reasonable).

Fourth, all of the above must be communicated to the Victim. In other words, the Victim must "get it." There is no way for the extortionate transaction to operate smoothly if the Victim does not understand what is happening: what the Hostage is, what is being threatened, and so forth.

If all of these participants and elements are in place, and if each of these steps has been taken, then the Coercer makes a demand for a "**Ransom.**" The Ransom is whatever the coercer wants the Victim to do. And—again, only if everything is in place—the Ransom is paid. It is paid by the Victim behaving in the way that the Coercer wishes. When this occurs, the Victim has been effectively coerced.

Here is an example: A police officer says to a drunken student outside of a fraternity party, "Go back inside . . . get off of the street . . . or you're going downtown." The police officer is the Coercer. The student is the Victim. The Hostage is the Victim's freedom. The threat is that of arrest. The ransom demanded is that the student go inside and get off of the public street. This is how the extortionate transaction works when successfully accomplished. Simple.

Having put together this picture of how coercive power is exercised, it is now time to confront one of the most important sets of paradoxes in the world of the police: the paradoxes of coercive power. This discussion involves coming to the realization that there are circumstances under which the apparently powerful can have difficulty coercing the apparently powerless. That is, an apparent disparity of power between two people does not necessarily mean that the *apparently* more powerful person can coerce the *apparently* less powerful person with ease. Since police officers are apparently powerful people, interacting on a regular basis with people who apparently possess a great deal less power, it would seem that they can coerce citizens at will. But this is not the case. And Muir's breakdown of why it is not the case is one of the most insightful pieces of analysis ever written about the police.

The Paradoxes of Coercive Power

Unfortunately for the police, their power to influence others through threats to harm suffers from four major paradoxes. These paradoxes relate to each of the first four steps of the extortionate transaction process discussed above. We will engage the paradoxes, one by one, as we "walk" through the above list of steps. The paradoxes are those of Dispossession, Detachment, Face, and Irrationality.

The Paradox of Dispossession: The first step in the extortionate transaction involves the Coercer taking a Hostage. But what if there is no Hostage? What if a person is so disenfranchised as to have nothing to threaten? Is it possible to coerce such a person? The answer is no. This is because, "the less one has, the less one has to lose," which is the **Paradox of Dispossession** (Muir 4). Muir's police-related example here has to do with dealing with the homeless. The homeless are so disenfranchised that they have neither jobs nor careers nor homes nor community status. For a police officer, what is there to threaten if a detail requires that a homeless person be made to "move along?" Not even a night in jail is necessarily much of a threat to the homeless in some locales. In some places, the weather is so harsh that a night in jail means a warm night and having something to eat (for which the arrested homeless person does not pay). This does not constitute much of a threat. Add to this paradox the subcultural reality that police officers can actually lose status in the locker room if they use force on the homeless or if they cannot deal with the homeless without arresting them. These are signs of extreme incompetence. Taken together, these two realities mean that the police will have trouble controlling the homeless. This is, in essence, because the homeless lack Hostages.

The Paradox of Detachment: What if someone has Hostages, but does not care about them? What if a person is successful at consciously detaching themselves from worrying about any harm coming to their hostages? They would then be difficult if not impossible to coerce. The **Paradox of Detachment** states: "The less the Victim values a Hostage, the less coercible the Victim is" (Muir 4). Muir's police-related example has to do with people involved in domestic disturbances. Often, a person is so upset about something done by their significant other that they will detach themselves from caring about arrest—either their own or the arrest of their significant other. When this occurs, the police lose their ability to handle a domestic disturbance through utilizing the threat of arrest. In the case of the Paradox of Detachment, a person makes himself or herself un-coercible through conscious effort. (As noted in Box 5.3, Muir's paradox of detachment has some profound implications for America's contemporary **War on Terrorism**.)

BOX 5.3

CONTROLLING TERRORISTS

In today's America, it is important for all thoughtful citizens to understand the Paradox of Detachment even if they are not students of the police. This is because this paradox informs us of the difficulties involved in attempting to fight a "War on Terror." Suicidal terrorists are, by definition, prepared to die for their beliefs. They are thus detached from valuing what is usually a person's most cherished possession: their own life. Because of their detachment, attempting to coerce such people effectively is impossible. For as much as we might like to think that exhortation or reciprocity or coercion might help in deterring terrorists, there is only one way to stop them effectively: kill them. As distasteful as this might sound to some, it is the reality of dealing with terrorists. And the paradox of detachment explains to the intelligent person why this is the case.

The Paradox of Face: When we talk about coercing someone, we often talk about how threats are sometimes "bluffs." While coercers must be careful not to stick their metaphorical necks out too far—they should always endeavor to make threats that they can carry out—it is true that sometimes a threat does not work and a bluff is "called." In that event, the coercer has to go through with the action(s) threatened. One can get away with bluffing only so many times before it becomes a problem—a bluff is called and then the arrest or the violence threatened *has* to be forthcoming. If a coercer is found to be bluffing on a regular basis, their threats lose integrity in the hearts and minds of those whom they attempt to coerce. And their ability to coerce in the future becomes lost.

In no type of police detail is this reality more apparent then when they have to deal with crowds. Always outnumbered by crowds, and not wishing to be "called" on their threats, the police must hone their ability to show a tough "face" to a crowd. They must look tough enough and appear serious enough about what they are asking people to do in order to make people do what they are told. ("Alright, everybody outa here . . . clear it up . . . you all go home now . . . nothing to see here . . .")

Lucky for the police, the **Paradox of Face** can be an ally under such circumstances (Muir 4). This paradox says, "The nastier your reputation, the less nasty you really have to be." This means that a great deal of behavior control can be instituted through the application of a nasty reputation. In reality, people do not often challenge the police—not physically at any rate. If when a bluff is called police officers go through with whatever they have threatened, their police department can build the sort of reputation that regularly controls situations. As Muir found by following Oakland police officers on the street for several years, a police organization with a reputation for standing behind its threats will not often have to prove what their reputation promises. A "bad ass rep" usually does the work for them.

The Paradox of Irrationality: Of course, all of this has to get through to the Victim. If the victim does not understand the circumstances involved—the value of the Hostage, the seriousness of the threat, the future implications of calling the bluff of the police—then the whole formula can fall apart. Muir uses the example of dealing with juveniles. Kids (teens) are often too young and too naive to understand what is happening when the police threaten them and, in particular, what the long term ramifications are of being arrested.

Here is an example: Suppose a police officer finds drugs on an 18-year-old girl but is willing to let her off with a lecture. By "playing around" with the situation, the teenaged kid can make a life-changing decision by getting herself arrested. The teenager doesn't "get it" and, because of this irrationality, becomes un-coercible. Such an 18-year-old—being given a "break" by the police officer—can make a life-altering decision if she acts like a brat and disrespects the threat. Being convicted of drug possession can keep the teen from getting in to schools in the future (law school in particular), from obtaining certain kinds of jobs, and from getting student loans for college. But the irrational girl may very well call the police officer's bluff and ruin her own life forever.

The **Paradox of Irrationality** has two sides to it (Muir 4). The first half states: "The crazier the Victim, the less effective the threat." Of course, Muir's use of the term "crazy" might not necessarily be accurate in describing the average teenager. But his point is that anyone who doesn't understand a situation is, largely, un-coercible. Think, for a moment, of the people with whom the police interact on a regular basis who, for one reason or another, might not understand what is happening when they are threatened. We are talking not only of juveniles

BOX 5.4

WHY K-9 UNITS ARE SO EFFECTIVE

The Paradox of Irrationality helps explain why police K-9 units are so effective at controlling large numbers of people. A dog is irrational. It therefore presents an impressive threat to do violence. No matter how much a person might know about dog training—and believe that police dogs are in fact under control—a snarling dog that pulls violently against its owner's leash is scary. Any sane person knows that a dog is not worried about making sergeant some day, about receiving a citizen's complaint, or about keeping its uniform clean. A dog is an irrational animal and, therefore, frightening.

but also of drunks, people on drugs, people who don't speak English as their first language, people frightened out of their wits, the elderly, people distraught and out of control of their emotions, and so on. These people, and a host of others, do not get what is happening when the police threaten to arrest them or deal with them physically. Thus, these people are uncontrollable. They are not coercible under any circumstances.

But there is more to this paradox. For the other side of the formula—the coercer's side—can also involve irrationality. The second half of this paradox states: "The crazier the Coercer, the more effective the threat." Think about it. How intimidated are we when, just walking down the street, we are confronted with someone who we believe might be mentally unstable? We want to steer clear of such a person, do we not? Now imagine how much more intimidating a "**crazy cop**" might be. If people really thought that a police officer, armed the way he or she is, was genuinely crazy, then how effective might that officer be in coercing members of the public? How scary are threats made by mad people? As noted in Box 5.4, the element in police work that best illustrates this side of the Paradox of Irrationality is the K-9 unit. Because dogs are irrational entities, K-9 units are extraordinarily effective at coercion. In fact, in the world of policing, it is estimated that the **coercive power of the K-9 Unit** is so great that a dog can intimidate about 100 people.

So there are four main paradoxes operative when police officers attempt to initiate an extortionate transaction in an effort to control citizens. These paradoxes place extraordinary limits upon the police. And in an odd way, because members of the general public have absolutely no way to understand these dynamics, police-community relations are impacted in a negative fashion by the paradoxes of coercive power. People believe that the police are powerful and that their job is easy. And when the police fail to coerce effectively, citizens can believe that the police are incompetent.

BOX 5.5

REVIEW OF THE PARADOXES

- Dispossession: The less one has, the less one has to lose.
- Detachment: The less the Victim values a hostage, the less coercible is the Victim.
- Face: The nastier your reputation, the less nasty you really have to be.
- Irrationality:
    - The crazier the Victim, the *less* effective the threat.
    - The crazier the Coercer, the *more* effective the threat.

(Muir 44)

ANALYSIS

The paradoxes of coercive power present tremendous challenges to the police. Muir's analysis presented the world of police studies with important information upon which to reflect. Furthermore, he aided the police to some extent by explaining something that police officers had experienced, and yet had not been able to comprehend completely, for a long time—their propensity to feel powerless out on the street.

In analyzing these paradoxes, there are several key points. To begin with, we must remind ourselves that the ability of the police to accomplish their tasks is inhibited by the paradoxes. In general, the police suffer from the paradoxes of coercive power. But there are two exceptions to this. First, the police can use the Paradox of Face to their advantage if (and only if) they have generated a reputation for being tough over the course of time. Under such circumstances, the police need only make a threat and they will develop cooperation among the citizenry. Second, we must note that the second half of the Paradox of Irrationality can also work for the police. If they can successfully generate the idea in the minds of citizens that they are crazy, then they are quite intimidating.

Of course, all sorts of negative drawbacks can develop if all police worked at appearing crazy. Such a dynamic would generate a loss of respect among the citizenry. But if *just* one police officer appeared to be crazy, then that could present a most intimidating formula for coercion. A true-to-life example of this dynamic may be illuminating.

Many years ago now, in a Sheriff's Department in California, one particular officer developed a reputation for being "just plain nuts." This occurred in a tough area that had a lot of crime. More than just a high crime rate, the area had several sets of competing minority groups that did not get along well. On Friday and Saturday nights in particular, groups of youths would gather together to fight each other on a regular basis. The police had trouble with this problem because—as is almost always the case—when attempting to handle these volatile situations they were highly outnumbered. But one thing they had going for them was the reputation of this particular "crazy cop." When he showed up to would-be riots, it was clear that just his attendance had a substantial impact upon the proceedings.

This particular officer would arrive in a cloud of dust on purpose—complete with squealing tires. He would jump out of his patrol car, grab his night stick, and scream at the assembled gangs of teenagers. He banged his night stick on the hoods of cars, gyrated in a very animated way, and directly challenged the teens to fight. "Come on! Let's get it on, you mother f___ers! It's the same thing every Friday night . . . all talk and no action! Come on, let's fight, you chicken s___ a__holes!" He ranted and raved. If the group did not disperse right away, he might challenge a particular individual to "get it on." Of course, over time, the other officers learned he was anything *but* crazy; he had come up with an "act" of sorts, which he knew was profoundly intimidating. Even though this story occurred years before Muir wrote his book, when this particular officer (now the Warden of a Prison) read Muir's work he laughed about how he had understood the Paradox of Irrationality long before Muir.

An additional—critical—piece of analysis for our discussion has to do with how often the police suffer from these paradoxes. We must remember that the examples Muir uses are not obscure details in police work. Handling homeless people, solving family beefs, confronting crowds, and dealing with the drunk, the stoned, the frightened, the hysterical, the old, the young, and so forth . . . all of this is the essence of what the police do. What Muir found out, in other words, was that the police have difficulty coercing people *much* of the time, not just under extraordinary circumstances. The list of those who the police have trouble coercing is a veritable "who's who" of citizens police meet on the street.

It does no good to note that the police can coerce the overwhelming majority of citizens in America because most citizens have jobs and homes and reputations (Hostages). It does no good to remark that most citizens neither wish to be arrested nor are prepared to deal with the police physically. It does no good, in other words, to note that "Mr. and Mrs. Middle America" are eminently coercible. Because even though this happens to be true, the police spend only a fraction of their time dealing with Mr. and Mrs. Middle America. The people with whom the police spend their time are the people most difficult to coerce. Thus, this discussion about the paradoxes of coercive power is one of the most important discussions of our entire work. It is about everyday police work. It is about the most common details to which the police are sent on a regular basis.

BOX 5.6

HOW OFTEN ARE THE POLICE INVOLVED IN THESE PARADOXES?

The paradoxes of coercive power involve the following kinds of police details:

- Dealing with the homeless.
- Dealing with domestic disturbances.
- Dealing with crowds.
- Dealing with the young, the old, the mentally impaired, or people who don't speak English.
- Dealing with people who are drunk, stoned, frightened, or hysterical.

These are not obscure details in the police world. They involve the very core of police work and bring the police into contact with those whom they encounter every day.

Before ending this chapter, we need to engage an interesting twist Muir brought to his work. This twist does not relate to the difficulty that police officers have coercing others. Rather, it has to do with the police themselves being coerced.

THE POLICE AS "VICTIMS"

An additional frustration having to do with the dynamics of coercive power is visited upon the police in America; it involves the police being coerced. Muir pointed out that while the police might seem to be the supreme practitioners of coercion, in fact they are frequently its victims (Muir 45). Citizens tend to enjoy certain advantages when dealing with the police amidst the extortionate transaction. And because this is true, the police can *be* coerced themselves. For the police, this adds still another layer of frustration that comes from the paradoxes of coercive power.

Citizens are more dispossessed than the police. The police have hostages. Each and every police officer, by definition, has a job. The police have careers. They want to keep their records clean and, for most, advancement is something that they covet. They tend to have homes and families and car payments. The police are most assuredly not disenfranchised.

Citizens are more detached from their hostages. The middle class police officer, with familial and professional responsibilities, simply cannot detach himself or herself from valuing their hostages. Detachment—the conscious process of devaluing hostages in an effort to insulate one's self from coercion—is just not an option for the police officer. Police work is how they feed their families and, thus, they cannot under any circumstances treat their careers with anything short of focused concern.

BOX 5.7

COERCING THE POLICE

Some citizens are capable of coercing the police. This reality can be driven by just knowing that police officers want to avoid citizen's complaints because they want to move up in the police world. Most police officers either want to become sergeants at some point in their careers or they just generally want to keep a clean departmental record. Then, too, the ability of citizens to coerce the police can be driven simply by an understanding that the police are outnumbered on a regular basis and have trouble dealing with crowds. Finally, and this may sound repellent to some extent, there are people—normally alcoholic "street people"—who know that the police don't want to put them in their cars at all because of the odors that tend to surround the street person's lifestyle. For these reasons, some people can coerce the police out of taking action that they would otherwise take; they exercise power over the police.

Citizens are nastier than the police. While the set of powers possessed by police officers is imposing and their ability to intimidate can be impressive, citizens have the ability to show face in ways that police officers cannot. A police officer or a police department might develop a reputation for being tough, physical, and aggressive. But think of how limited that reputation is when compared to the reputation for toughness possessed by the meanest, nastiest members of society. Think of how intimidating, say, gang members can be? In large numbers. Think of how intimidating a group of professional athletes can be, say, football players from the NFL. Think of how intimidating military people can be; they too have uniforms, but they carry automatic weapons and grenades and so forth. Any number civilians can show a more impressive and intimidating face than the police.

And finally, citizens are crazier than the police. We have shared the story of the "crazy cop" of course. But this was an isolated incident. In general, because of the job they do, police officers on the street must restrain themselves, act with dignity, and exhibit a level of sobriety and sanity that is palpable. They cannot be drunk or stoned on duty. They cannot be so naive or so old or so young as to misunderstand what is happening around them. And, again, this can make them vulnerable to being coerced by citizens who can act crazy and can *be* crazy.

For each of these reasons, the police can be coerced out of making arrests. They can be coerced out of taking action. They can be coerced into allowing even some criminal behavior to go without response. In general, the police can become (once again) frustrated because they are vulnerable to being coerced by citizens. And this reality adds still another layer of frustration to the imposing list of dynamics that can create disgust, frustration, impotence, and even hopelessness in the hearts and minds of police officers.

 ## SUMMATION

This is not to say that police work is always disgusting, frustrating, and hopeless. If that were the case, then there would not be any police officers left. No, our efforts here involve making the dynamics of the individual police officer's experience clear to both students of the police and to future police officers themselves. If we are aware of a troublesome dynamic in life, then there is every reason to believe that as intelligent and thoughtful people we can deal with it effectively.

CHAPTER FIVE PARADOX BOX

The apparently power*ful* police officer is often confronted with circumstances wherein he or she is, in effect, power*less*. These circumstances occur every day, on every beat—they are at the heart of the policing experience. Furthermore, while apparently being the supreme practitioner of coercive power, the individual police officer is often its victim.

In this chapter we have engaged in an absolutely critical discussion for anyone who seeks to understand the police in America. We have seen that these apparently powerful people often suffer from the paradoxes of coercive power in a way that can make them feel impotent and ineffective. And, concomitantly, we have seen that the police can feel frustrated not only by their inability to coerce others but by being coerced themselves. We will revisit the issues engaged in this chapter throughout the remainder of our discussions, so central are they to our endeavor.

Let us continue with our treatment of the individual police officer's experience by embracing the effect of media imagery upon police officers and upon the job they do. In Chapter Six, we will see that numerous unrealistic expectations created for police by news and entertainment media not only tends to impede the job police officers attempt to accomplish but, equally, can frustrate citizens too.

 ## DISCUSSION QUESTIONS

1. We have suggested that whenever possible the power broker should endeavor to use exhortative, reciprocal, and coercive power *in that order*. Discuss how a police officer might utilize exhortation or reciprocity to control the homeless, keeping in mind the limitations of the paradox of dispossession. How might police officers be "creative" power brokers by honing their skills at reciprocity in particular?

2. It is important for all educated, thoughtful American citizens to understand the Paradox of Detachment because of its relationship to the War on Terrorism. Discuss why it is that this war is so difficult to win, due to this paradox. How *can* suicide bombers or hijackers be stopped?

3. In general, police officers suffer from the paradoxes of coercive power. But there are two dynamics discussed in this chapter that the police can "use." The Paradox of Face and the second half of the Paradox of Irrationality can be used by the police to gain an advantage over citizens. Discuss how and why this works.

4. The list of those who it is difficult for the police to coerce is a veritable "who's who" of those with whom the police must deal. On a regular basis, the police will have trouble coercing all sorts of people. But they have no trouble at all coercing "most" American citizens. The average citizen is eminently coercible. Discuss how this reality can lead to unreasonable expectations on the part of most people about the exercise of power by the police.

 ## KEY TERMS

Coercer: One who attempts to control another's behavior through coercion.

Coercion: The act of utilizing coercive power to control the behavior of others.

Coercive Power: Controlling behavior through the use of threats to harm.

Crazy Cop: A particularly intimidating and effective power broker because of the Paradox of Irrationality.

Detachment (Paradox of): The less value the Victim places upon the hostage, the less coercible is the Victim.

Dispossession (Paradox of): The less one has, the less one has to lose.

Exhortation: The power of persuasion through the use of words.

Extortion: The gaining of property or money by almost any kind of force or threat of violence.

Face (Paradox of): The nastier one's reputation, the less nasty one has to be.

Hostage: That which is threatened by the Coercer in any coercive power interaction.

Irrationality (Paradox of): The crazier the Victim, the less effective the threat; the crazier the Coercer, the more effective the threat.

K-9 Unit (Coercive Power of): A particularly intimidating and effective power broker for the police due to the Paradox of Irrationality.

Log Rolling: The legislative equivalent of reciprocal power: doing favors in exchange for other favors.

Power: Behavior control; influencing the behavior of another in a desired direction.

Power of Trade/Barter: Reciprocal power; obtaining desired behavior in exhange for goods, services, money, or favors.

Ransom: That which is demanded of the Victim of coercion; this can be any type of behavior desired by the Coercer.

Reciprocity: A method of behavior control that is created through exchange; see The Power of Trade/Barter above.

War on Terrorism: War against those who are not afraid to die (*e.g.*, suicide bombers); such people are impossible to coerce due to the Paradox of Detachment.

ADDITIONAL READING

To begin with, there are any number of excellent works that engage the topic of power generally. David R. Hawkins analyzes power in *Power vs. Force: The Hidden Determinants of Human Behavior* (Hay House, 2002). Two works that are sort of "how to do it" books about the exercise of power are *Get Anyone to Do Anything: Never Feel Powerless Again* by David J. Lieberman (St. Martin's Griffin, 2001) and *Concise 48 Laws of Power, 2nd Rev.* by Robert Greene (Profile Books, 2002). These books are not police officer oriented at all but, rather, are aimed at a general treatment of the subject in an abstract way.

In *Bribery and Extortion: Undermining Business, Government, and Security* (Praeger, 2007), Alexandra Addison Wrage discusses the concept in a more criminal justice–oriented way by suggesting that extortion is the focal point of coercive power. Of course, William K. Muir's *Police: Streetcorner Politicians* (University of Chicago Press, 1977) is the seminal work on power and on the paradoxes of coercive power in particular. Cited by literally every treatment written since it was published, this work should be the very first additional reading engaged by any student who wishes to expand their understanding in the field.

Engaging exhortative power in particular, Keith Yellin discusses how soldiers have been motivated to make what sometimes turns out to be the ultimate sacrifice (of their own lives) on the battlefields of the world throughout history in *Battle Exhortation: The Rhetoric of Combat Leadership* (University of South Carolina Press, 2008). Along these same lines, but a more general work, Robert B. Cialdini also engages the power of exhortation in *Influence: The Power of Persuasion* (Collins Business Publications, 2006).

Understanding Police Use of Force: Officers, Suspects, and Reciprocity (Cambridge University Press, 2004) by Geoffrey P. Alpert and Roger G. Dunham focuses upon the use of reciprocal power by police officers (among many other topics). In *Reciprocity: An Economics of Social Relations* (Cambridge University Press, 2008), Serge Christophe Kolm engages the same topic in a generalized work that does not relate specifically to the police.

Finally, the use of force by police officers in contemporary times is analyzed by Howard Rahtz in *Understanding Police Use of Force* (Criminal Justice Press, 2003). In this work, Rahtz argues that the use of force by police officers in America has declined substantially in the past 25 years.

CHAPTER 6

Media Imagery

Chapter Six Outline

In this chapter, we will focus upon a critically important, ever-present reality in modern day America: the impact that the media have upon everyday life. We live in a society permeated with **media imagery**—imagery that constructs a view of reality that is embraced and accepted by millions of American citizens (Parenti, Inventing Reality). Much of this imagery is merely meant to entertain, and often this is clearly the case. But the line between what is entertainment and what is fact is blurring in contemporary America. Some of what used to be considered "**hard news**" is packaged as entertainment. Some of what is constructed purely for entertainment purposes is misconstrued to be real. Much of what the average person believes to be true about contemporary life and the world is made up of media-constructed imagery that is only marginally related to reality.

The fact that reality and myth are coming together in the hearts and minds of Americans is both fascinating and disturbing. Living a life controlled by myth can be entertaining, because myth can lend an extra importance, drama, and even romance to life. But it can also lead to trouble, to confusion, and even to the creation of beliefs that are silly and counterproductive in life.

Here is an example: Millions of people believe the media-perpetuated myth that Americans are taxed at an extremely high level. This is patently false, as viewed from any knowledgeable perspective. Americans are taxed at a rate that is *by far* the lowest in the industrialized world. But this misconception does not tend to do much harm. In fact, if it is focused in the direction of keeping taxes down in America, it might very well be considered by many to do some good. In other words, it is not a bad thing when Americans believe in such a myth.

But it is quite another thing when people believe the media-perpetuated myth that Americans are the most educated people in the world. This is not even close to being true. The literacy rate in many countries, including Cuba, to use one example, is much higher than it is in America. This myth can have deleterious consequences for our country when it creates complacency about American education. We do not have an educational system that competes equally in the international marketplace, and this reality can be perpetuated—our system can fall further behind—because of such mythological beliefs.

As we shall see later in this chapter, the blurring of the line between fact and fiction has unfortunate implications for the police in America. It drives all sorts of misconceptions that impact upon police-community relations in a negative way. Being as fascinated as they tend to be about police work, each year most Americans watch hundreds of hours of television programs and Hollywood movies about it. Therein, they "learn" things that are either exaggerated or that are just not true. And the false "knowledge" obtained in this way has important, and even disturbing, consequences for the police. Since so much of "what we think we know" today is constructed for us, by television in particular, devoting one chapter to its analysis is the very least we can do in our effort to understand policing in America.

Of course, there is nothing wrong with being entertained. But when even the news becomes laced with half-truths—and morphs, at times, into misleading nonsense, nonsense that drives the opinions of millions—then analyzing American media is a reasonable enterprise for anyone discussing any issue in the world of public policy.

Our treatment of the media in this chapter will begin with some generalized reflections upon its power, upon who owns and operates it, and upon how certain agendas are packaged and sold to us all. Then, with this framework in place, we will delve into a discussion about the unrealistic, media-constructed images of police officers and police work that make the job of policing far more difficult than it has to be.

"WHAT WE THINK WE KNOW"

Americans no longer read. They do not read books as much as they used to. More important for our discussion, they do not tend to read newspapers anymore. To be more accurate about it, when Americans read newspapers, it is not to obtain news—hard news about what is really going on in the world—but to obtain entertainment. For hard news, the average person depends upon the **"talking heads"** of the television world. In addition, but to a lesser extent, younger people have begun to depend upon the internet's blogosphere. This did not use to be the case. As recently as two generations ago, television had yet to achieve the stranglehold that it now has over our view of the world. And the internet had not yet been invented. But that has changed. And this is an absolutely critical turn of events.

Until recently, newspapers existed in far greater numbers than they do today. Because there used to be so many, they tended to present a diversity of opinion

BOX 6.1

URBAN MYTH: THE MEDIA ARE "LIBERAL"

We often hear—in the media, ironically—that the media in contemporary America put a "liberal" slant on things. From "hard" news to talk shows to television dramas, we are told that there is an unrealistic bent to things that favors the liberal side of the political agenda. We hear that something exists called **"the liberal media."** Nothing could be further from the truth. The media in America are owned and operated by corporations. Newspapers, magazines, radio stations, television stations, and Hollywood movie companies are all operated by large, powerful corporations. And the advertising that supports several forms of our contemporary media is paid for by other corporations. Unlike what is being sold to us by these corporate entities, the media are in fact slanted in a conservative direction, as any reasonable analysis of the politics of American corporations would suggest. Parenti, in *Dirty Truths*, also discusses these ideas about how and by whom the media are controlled.

that the thoughtful person could utilize in order to become enlightened about what goes on in life. There were liberal and conservative newspapers and, again, anyone wishing to be genuinely educated about events in the world could read different points of view and balance one perspective against another. Experts on different sides—genuine experts—debated policy and provided context for the intelligent observer.

Today, depending upon television and the internet as we do, we have two problems. The first has to do with the blogosphere. People who blog online are by no means experts. To qualify to put "information" on the internet, one has only to own a computer. On the internet, there are no entry-level requirements with respect to education, experience, or intelligence that are utilized to cull out silliness, prejudice, and falsehood. Much of what is produced, read, and believed online is based upon myth, supposition, and ideology. But millions of people believe what they read there to be true.

The problem here—in the blogosphere—has to do with how unrealistic much of the information presented is. It is not "slanted" in any particular direction, but rather inaccurate in many directions ... all at once. On television, the problem multiplies because not only is much of what we see there inaccurate, but it is purposefully slanted in an effort to present particular ideas and political agendas.

The "Liberal Media" Myth: Much more important than the blososphere, as it effects many, many more people, are the images presented by the corporate interests that manage and operate television. On television we see and hear only a limited, narrowly slanted view of what goes on in the world. And this view, unbeknownst to many, slants in a conservative direction. The myth that the media are liberal—something we hear every day—is a preposterous bit of nonsense, constructed and disseminated by the media themselves in an effort to make sure we accept their perspective and "buy" certain agendas. The media, being universally owned and operated by huge corporations, tend to favor policies and embrace perspectives that favor the interests of major corporations. Their editorial policies are constructed and applied by extremely affluent people. In general, and understandably so, they possess and support corporate-friendly political views. And both corporations in general and extremely affluent people as individuals tend to hold conservative, rather than liberal, viewpoints (Parenti, Inventing Reality).

Thus, the television media in contemporary America are not liberal. No one who has an ounce of sense and who spends even a moment in serious reflection upon it believes this. But this is a central piece of mythology—that of the liberal media—that constructs and drives the worldviews of millions of people today.

Why does this matter? Why is it important for us to understand that the media are most definitely not liberal but, instead, conservative in their approach to the world? That they are controlled by corporate interests? It is important in general because the intelligent person wants their worldview to have some definitive relationship with reality. The thoughtful individual will, on occasion, attempt to question their own assumptions, their own perspective, and their own prejudices

BOX 6.2

THE C.I.A. AND DRUGS

An example—perhaps a "classic" example—of the media being conservative and ignoring issues and stories that might make conservative political agendas look foolish has to do with the relationship that the Central Intelligence Agency (C.I.A.) has had with drug dealers for more than two generations now. In exchange for having drug dealers run (and support) covert operations that underwrite anti-communist and pro-corporate agendas around the world, the C.I.A. has worked to facilitate drug dealing. In essence, the C.I.A. has worked against the efforts of the Drug Enforcement Administration (D.E.A.) and police agencies all over the world—even in the United States. This is not someone's "opinion." It is a fact, supported by dozens of books, hundreds of eye witness accounts, and several major governmental investigations. This reality is reported occasionally by the mainstream press but, in general, it is kept out of the limelight. This is because it would make the agency itself, the government, and numerous corporations look bad. It is, in other words, a major story with immense implications that is suppressed because the media are conservative—in this case, arch-conservative.

(Levine and Kavenau-Levine; Scott and Marshall; Stich)

in life. This is extremely difficult to accomplish, especially when "what we think we know" is a combination of images with which we have been bombarded by people who want us to think a certain way. And believing a myth that permeates society is something that the intelligent person does not want to suffer. Furthermore, and as we shall visit in the next several sections, this conservative slant to things can work against the police. Particularly where Dirty Harry is concerned: unrealistic images of Harry's one man crusade against the evil system tend to inhibit the development of police professionalism by encouraging noble cause corruption.

We must be careful with this discussion and note to the reader that we do not mean to imply there is something wrong with being conservative. What we mean to point out is that corporate control over what Americans think is growing steadily. This type of corporate control over media imagery presents a world to viewers wherein one and only one point of view is appropriate.

The pro-corporate bias of the media has several particularly unfortunate implications for our study of the police. First, one agenda that the media push in today's America has to do with their traditional anti-governmental views. They sell the idea that people who are involved in business—any business of any size, from the corporate world to the small business world—are capable, intelligent, and able to accomplish great things. By selling this idea for the past several decades, corporate America has been given a free hand in operating without governmental interference. And that freedom has resulted in the near-collapse of the American economy due to corporate greed and incompetence. This fact is an important one for intelligent Americans to know, though it is only tangentially connect to police work. Our next point, however, has a great deal to do with police work.

Second, and in parallel with the above point about the competence of private business, the media sell the idea that the government is operated by self-serving, incompetents who never accomplish anything of value. This idea is used to keep taxes down. While there's nothing wrong with having lower taxes, provided the money to pay for police, fire, schools, and other forms of infrastructure and services comes from somewhere, this "government is always incompetent" idea has impacted negatively upon police work in recent years. Police budgets have been cut across the board, as they have been in other areas of municipal government, resulting in layoffs in some places. In an era of increased tensions on the streets of America, this can only mean bad things for the citizenry and for the administration of justice.

Third, this anti-governmental attitude fosters the revitalizing of an old, almost Wild West type of myth: "**the individual against the system**" (Parenti, Inventing Reality). Since government "accomplishes nothing good," the individual must always struggle against it. This, too, leads to deleterious consequences for the police. It lends added support to the lunatic fringe–type of separatist movements that gives us the likes of Timothy McVey (the man who bombed the Federal Building in Oklahoma City, killing hundreds, including small children) and Branch Dividian–type paramilitary groups that arm themselves and practice for a future war against the federal government and the police.

Corporate-driven policies are also responsible for the fact that "cop killer" bullets are available for purchase in American gun shops. "It's nothing personal, it's just business" is a mantra often heard from those free market capitalists who lobby to keep such ammunition in the hands of whomever wants to purchase it.

There are two types of televised information sources from which we obtain our view of the world in today's post-reading era. The first are the news media. The second are the entertainment media. Intelligent individuals often say to themselves that people ought to be smart enough to know that entertainment should not be taken seriously as a source of news to inform one's worldview. Nevertheless, an increasing numbers of Americans ignore this. Some people use the Daily Show and The Colbert Report, two comedy programs that report "fake" news, to obtain their information. Some use the Oprah Winfrey Show. Some use numerous programs on VH1, a music-related channel. These are the "definitive" sources that millions of people use to learn about world events. Let us discuss these two media entities separately.

The News Media: In today's world there are no longer merely the three major networks of a generation ago: ABC, NBC, and CBS. Today we have the continuous, non-stop reporting of FOX News, MSNBC, and CNN. Then too, an increasingly large number of people depend upon public broadcasting (PBS) for information, as PBS is known for spending more time on stories (not having to worry about commercial interruptions) and has, arguably, a more balanced approach. Furthermore, many people even use the BBC from England (now available on PBS and on some cable networks) as their major source of information.

While it may appear that this menu of alternatives is more diverse than in bygone days, this group of media outlets is still controlled by the small number of major corporations that own them and purchase advertising time. With the exception of PBS (where there are no commercial interruptions), these corporate-driven news media spend their time putting a spin on things that tends to favor the interest of what some are calling today's "**corporatocracy**"—the contemporary "rule of corporations" that threatens to replace our democracy (Grupp). This is no place to settle the debate about whether or not we in fact have a corporatocracy in America today. Suffice it to say that many argue that the influence of the thousands of paid lobbyists that now crowd the halls of Washington, D.C., and state capitals is so great, and the amount of money spent on influencing legislation so impressive, that corporations not only "rule" legislatures but spend their time and money on television convincing millions of Americans that their worldview is correct. One does not have to buy the entire argument to see that there is at least some truth to it.

BOX 6.3

WHO CONTROLS THE NEWS MEDIA?

Aside from the reality that the media are owned and operated by major corporations—which suggests something about how their perspective will slant—there is the question of how the specific content of media coverage is influenced on a daily basis. The content of media in today's America is controlled in the following ways:

- Television content is controlled by advertising dollars—that come from major corporations.

- Radio content is controlled by advertising dollars—that come from businesses and corporations.

- Newspaper content is controlled by advertising dollars—that come from small businesses and large corporations—and public demand.

- Internet content is controlled by any and all of the above, because they sponsor the major internet locations that influence people today.

The thrust here is that the content of news in America, no matter what type, is controlled by the world of local businesses—which tend to be conservative, but are not so universally—and by major corporations, which *are* universally conservative. See Parenti, *Inventing Reality*, for more on these ideas.

The point upon which we should focus is that television, radio, and printed news is controlled by the editorial policies of the corporations that own them. And these corporations are, almost exclusively, conservative in their worldviews (above).

Hollywood Entertainment Media: Oddly enough, much more important than news coverage with regard to police-related imagery are the images portrayed regularly on television and movie screens. Even though intelligent people will often note that viewers *should* know that television shows and Hollywood movies are fantasy creations, we often have to remind ourselves that people watch so many screen images over the course of their lives that they begin to believe imaginary characters are real and fictional stories are factual. So much is this the case that Hollywood celebrities are often elected to political office on the grounds that they actually *are* the characters that they portray.

Millions of people voted to elect Ronald Reagan, a Hollywood actor, to be Governor of California and then President of the United States. Pollsters reported that many people voted for him "because he was a hero in the war" (World War II)—even though he only played roles in movies about World War II and didn't actually see combat. Recently, millions of people in California voted to elect Arnold Schwarzenegger, another Hollywood actor, to be their Governor "because he's a tough guy" and he says things like "hasta la vista, baby." Both Reagan and Schwarzenegger possessed absolutely no experience in government and politics when first elected. Yet their name and face recognition—again, because they had been in movies and played tough guys—was so great that they were catapulted into power on the strength of their ability to "pretend" to be someone or something people liked. (There are many more examples, liberal and conservative alike.)

BOX 6.4

WHO CONTROLS THE CONTENT OF HOLLYWOOD MOVIES?

While we have argued that the content of news media coverage is most definitely controlled by corporate interests, the content of Hollywood movies is different. The success or failure of a motion picture is not determined by advertising dollars but, instead, by public demand. If people go to a certain type of movie then, in the long run, that sort of movie is successful. If they do not attend another type of movie then, in the long run, that sort of movie fails. The entire industry rises and falls in this way. Thus, movie content is driven by the likes and dislikes of the general public. Oddly enough, this makes movie content much more "liberal" than news content. The general public in America is more liberal than are corporate executives, and that is why this occurs.

We do not want to turn away readers who are Reagan and Schwarzenegger followers. But even if a person supported one or both of these politicians or thinks that they were or are effective politicos, the point here is still valid. Their lack of experience, credentials, and qualifications for the positions that they attained is fact. And the point is that image, "**spin**," and fantasy are replacing reality in some senses in American life. And this change has consequences for the police on the street and for the administration of justice. We shall see below that as fantasy replaces reality in today's world, the list of unrealistic expectations that people hold for the police grows and grows.

Police-Related Imagery

There is good news and bad news with regard to the images of police officers and police work portrayed on television and silver screens in America. The good news is that TV and motion picture police officers are almost always portrayed as being intelligent, competent, and honest. They always solve crimes; they do whatever it takes to get the job done; they treat suspects with kid gloves when it comes to interrogation and Miranda warnings; and they are rough-and-ready individuals capable of super-human feats when it comes to dealing with violence. By and large, they are portrayed as heroes.

But the bad news is that there are about a dozen things wrong with this. These images create unrealistic expectations in the hearts and minds of citizens—expectations that are almost never achieved by the real police in real life. Furthermore, they frustrate the police indirectly because of the displeasure or even contempt that citizens develop when the real police seem to let them down. Finally, American police officers are citizens themselves. They do not arrive here from Saturn and then become police officers. They have watched television and movies themselves over the course of their pre–police service lives. They are raised on the same media-generated expectations as average citizens. And when rookie police officers embrace the realities of police work on the street, they often find themselves unhappy about how often they do not—*cannot*—live up to the images that both they and the public hold in their minds.

Here are just a handful of specific examples of the expectations we are talking about. The next several subsections illustrate only the tip of the iceberg with regard to unrealistic, media-generated expectations for the police.

The RCMP Syndrome: The Royal Canadian Mounted Police of Canada live by an adage that is more than 100 years old. It says: "The Mountie always gets his man." This is a clever little phrase, of course, but the idea has importance for our discussion here. Even though Mounties are not American police officers, when we refer to the "**RCMP Syndrome**" we are referring to this motto. We are suggesting that there is a profoundly important and unrealistic propensity for Hollywood—both on television and in the movies—to present millions of Americans every day with the idea that crime is always solved by the police. The idea that the Mounties always solve each and every crime with which they are confronted is mirrored in American media imagery.

Now this is totally understandable from the perspective of the entertainment media. They want people to watch their programs and movies so that they can make money. This is rational enough. With hundreds of options on television today, and with the price of going to the movies skyrocketing in recent years, it makes sense that the competition for the entertainment dollar is fierce. And it also makes sense that any program or movie that shows the police *not* solving crimes will not be received well; people simply do not want to watch police-related dramas that end in frustration, without a solution and without the cathartic experience of seeing bad people receive their just desserts.

As understandable as all of this is, there is a problem with it. It may make sense to the purveyors of fantasy that they have to show the police solving every crime, but this imagery tends to be translated into the real world in the minds of American viewers. People expect the police to solve each and every crime because that is what they see on the screen all of the time. Beginning when they are small children, people regularly watch police dramas that end in the arrest, if not the conviction, of "the bad guys." This may be comforting and it may help people sleep at night. They can become comfortably wrapped in the understanding, albeit artificially and unrealistically constructed for the purposes of entertainment, that the police are so vigilant and competent that they will solve any and all crimes.

But this bears no resemblance whatsoever to reality. In the real world, the police are often unable to solve crimes. In fact, a majority of the time crime goes unsolved. In today's police world, **"clearance rates"** are calculated to indicate what percentage of reported crimes are solved (U.S. F.B.I.). The number of crimes reported in any given jurisdiction is divided into the number of crimes actually solved and the resulting percentage is the clearance rate. These rates are calculated locally, on a state-wide basis, regionally and nationally. Clearance rates are collected and published each year by the Federal Bureau of Investigation (FBI) in their annual Uniform Crime Reports (UCRs) (U.S. F.B.I.). And they are taken seriously as an indication of how effective the police are.

The problem for today's police is that clearance rates are substantially lower than the media lead Americans to believe (see Chart 6.1). While the majority of homicides and aggravated assault cases are solved, these crimes make up an infinitesimal percentage of the crimes with which the police must deal. The overwhelming majority of crime involves nonviolent and even minor offenses, such as petty theft and vandalism. And these crimes are almost *never* solved. The citizens with whom the police interact on a daily basis, driven as they are by such unrealistic expectations, can tend to consider their local police to be incompetent when they report a crime and find that the real police are unable to solve it.

So in the short run, media-generated imagery might very well help people sleep at night, secure in the knowledge that "NYPD Blue" or "C.S.I. Miami" are

CHART 6.1

CLEARANCE RATES

Just as an example for the purposes of discussion, here are the FBI's clearance rates for the year 2007:

Homicide	= 61.2
Aggravated Assault	= 54.1
Forcible Rape	= 40.0
Robbery	= 24.9
Larceny	= 18.6
Motor Vehicle Theft	= 12.6
Burglary	= 12.4

Source: U.S.F.B.I. Uniform Crime Reports: 2007

out there solving each and every crime ever committed in America. In the long run, however, people can lose faith in the *real* police when they discover that, unlike their screen heroes, the local police are unable to be effective all of the time—or even much of the time.

Selling Dirty Harry: The character of Dirty Harry was, of course, a media creation. Inspector Harry Callahan was not a real person. Clint Eastwood, an actor, played the part on the silver screen. But the selling of the idea of Dirty Harry is something that has taken on a life of its own in the 30 years since the movie came to theaters. Dozens and dozens of movies and television programs that have come along since Harry was created have played up the idea that to get the job done in today's America, the good, hard working, heroic police officer has to "bend" or "break" the rules. We are sold the general idea that **Dirty Harry is a "hero."**

What Harry represents is important. He stands for the idea that the due process system is so complicated, so focused upon legal technicalities, so uninterested in the plight of victims, and so devoid of concern for the factual realities of crime on the streets that to get the job done, police officers have to be renegades. Harry also underscores the idea that to be effective, today's police officer must fight the aforementioned "individual against the system"–type of Hollywood-constructed battle. This might be a romantic notion, and it might sell tickets to motion pictures, but it is unrealistic. Not only does it sell a romantically impractical idea, but it also endorses police misconduct—noble cause corruption.

There is an interesting scene in the original Dirty Harry movie wherein Harry is confronted by a District Attorney who tells him that the case Harry is working on is going to have to be dropped. This is because Harry has obtained evidence in violation of the 4th Amendment. And the evidence will have to be excluded. The D.A. says, "That's the law." And our hero Harry responds, "Well then the law's crazy." This may very well make viewers want to stand up and cheer the hero; after all, he's only trying to get the job done. But the whole scene—and the idea that it portrays—is troublesome for the administration of justice in two ways.

First, it suggests—again—that the good police officer must work *against* the American legal system in order to be effective. Second, it implies that police ignorance about how the law works is acceptable. The movie was produced ten years after the *Mapp v. Ohio* decision. By that time, any competent and intelligent police officer should have learned about exclusion, how it operates, and how to work within the system legally. While Hollywood wants us to consider Harry a hero (and people pretty much do), Harry is, in fact, an incompetent, lazy, ignorant officer. Holding him up as a hero is troublesome because it sends the message to the public and to young police officers that old-fashioned, "Western-type" justice is what's important, and that modern, intelligent, educated policing is a waste of time.

Cosmetized Violence: In an interview more than 20 years ago, the great fiction writer Joseph Wambaugh, who was once an L.A.P.D. sergeant, complained that the entertainment media trivialized violence by creating what he labeled "**cosmetized violence**." Wambaugh meant that on television especially, a great deal of violence was acted out in a way that was so unrealistic as to make it appear inconsequential and even romantic. Actors are regularly shot, stabbed, pummeled, and strangled without showing anything remotely approaching what such action does to the human body in real life. He pointed out that this numbs the viewer in a way (Wambaugh, Interview).

Police dramas are particularly vulnerable to falling into this dynamic. Police programs on television are replete with high-speed automobile chases, prolonged gunfights that approach the intensity of pitched battles, and constant physical altercations between police and citizens. Viewers are left with the idea that police work is not only dangerous but consistently exciting and something akin to ongoing warfare.

Such cosmetized violence socializes viewers into thinking that the consequences of violent behavior are far less horrific than they really are. It desensitizes us all in a way—by suggesting that resorting to violence is not something that should be eschewed or avoided if at all possible. Not only are people desensitized by the *type* of violence portrayed in this unrealistic way, but also by the *amount* of violence portrayed on television. One study a number of years ago suggested that the average five-year-old child entering Kindergarten had already seen more than 4,000 people "die" on television.

In the movies, of course, violence is much more realistic. In recent years in particular, the level of graphic violence has escalated. Today's war movies, such as

BOX 6.5

CHILDREN AND TV VIOLENCE

American children watch an average of three to four hours of television daily. Television can be a powerful influence in developing value systems and shaping behavior. Unfortunately, much of today's television programming is violent. Hundreds of studies of the effects of TV violence on children and teenagers have found that children may:

- Become immune or "numb" to the horror of violence.
- Gradually accept violence as a way to solve problems.
- Imitate the violence they observe on television.
- Identify with certain characters, victims, or victimizers.

Source: American Academy of Child & Adolescent Psychiatry,
Bulletin #13, November 2002 (at *www.aacap.org*)

"Saving Private Ryan," show much of the gore and horror of war in a graphic and realistic way. Many argue that such violence is gratuitous and unnecessary. It has become "entertainment" in every sense of the word. It has spread to video games and into the worlds of music lyrics and music videos. And it has impacted the realism of violence on television, increasing it exponentially due to the competition for viewers that drives the entertainment industry.

This type of pretend violence affects the police for several reasons. First, normalizing violence and everyday brutality in this way suggests to young people that violence is romantic and sexy. There is every reason to believe that this increases the amount of violence on the streets of America. This in turn means that there is more violence with which police officers must deal.

Second, television and motion pictures create an image of the average, everyday police officer as a super-human martial arts expert. Some people, perhaps the more gullible among us, come to expect this from the police. While police officers are given training in the area of "defensive tactics," there are no super-human police officers out there. None. And the inability of real life police officers to live up to this imagery can move citizens, once again, to believe that their local police are incompetent.

Finally, police work is not filled with action and violence and confrontation on a minute-by-minute basis. As has been said by many people over the years, a shift out on the street for a police officer often involves "three hours of paper work, four hours of boredom, an hour's worth of action, and three minutes of terror." Even this statement romanticizes police work, since the three minutes of terror is seldom visited upon the average police officer in the average shift. The point here is that police work is so often filled with boredom and a lack of action that the police are quite often surprised by violence. The fact that violence so seldom occurs can build up a certain complacency in police work that exhibits itself when the police are unprepared for physical confrontation. When officers are caught off guard, they appear, in still one more way, to be ineffective and incompetent.

Miranda Warnings: The singularly most difficult case to teach in American Constitutional Law classes is ***Miranda v. Arizona (1966)***. This is because unlike virtually every other case in such a course, students believe they already understand *Miranda* when the topic is first breached. Thus, they have trouble listening when it is discussed. Having seen the case's findings illustrated a hundred times on television or motion picture screens over the course of their lifetimes, students tend to let their minds wander when *Miranda* is analyzed. This is more than a little disconcerting for professors of constitutional law.

The problem with this is that what Hollywood tells us about *Miranda* is wrong (Hrenchir). Students almost universally misunderstand the case because of the unrealistic Hollywood images with which they are familiar. And it is not just students who hold misconceptions about the case. American citizens in general harbor expectations about Miranda warnings that are flawed and that lead them to believe that their local police are incompetent and dishonest.

Hollywood teaches the *substance* of the Miranda warnings correctly. Anyone who has taught constitutional law knows this, because any group of American students can recite its warnings verbatim. Ask the average American to chant along with you, and they will give the speech correctly, word-for-word: "You have the right to remain silent. Anything you say can and will be . . ." And so forth. So far, so good.

But the problem here does not relate to the substance of the admonitions, it lies in widely held misconceptions about the *process*. For Hollywood is mistaken about *when* a suspect hears the warnings, and that creates citizen-police antipathy. Hollywood universally portrays the image that Miranda warnings are given to all suspects who are arrested at the time of arrest. But this is not the holding in the case. What the case *actually* says is that the police have to admonish a person when he or she (1) becomes the focal point of an investigation as a "suspect" and (2) is going to be interrogated. The moment of arrest has nothing to do with the admonitions per se.

Since uniformed officers on the street rarely conduct interrogations—leaving that to the Detectives whose job it is to do so—those who make arrests rarely admonish suspects. When citizens observe this, they tend to think that their local police are either incompetent or treating arrestees unfairly. This dynamic creates an unnecessary bit of antipathy toward the police. And this antipathy has been constructed by Hollywood.

BOX 6.6

MIRANDA WARNINGS

Hollywood "teaches" millions of citizens that the Miranda warnings are given to suspects at the moment of arrest, right out on the street. Unfortunately, this is not correct. In the real world, the uniformed police almost never give Miranda warnings. And this reality leads a great many citizens to think that their local police are lazy, biased, and unintelligent. Or, perhaps worse, many people believe that their police are incompetent. Hrenchir also discusses this idea in "Miranda Warnings Lack Hollywood Spin."

Scandal "Sells"

There is a paradox operational in the coverage that news media give to the police in general. On a regular basis, from day to day, when reporting on police-related stories and issues, the contemporary press in America are extremely supportive of the police. Media coverage of the police is almost effusive with its praise about the police. On the other hand, when anything out of the ordinary or scandalous rears its head, the media can be troublesome. Live stories about hostage situations, investigations that are "fresh," upper level hirings and firings, and especially scandals of any kind get a completely different type of coverage than that utilized for the daily police story. Put bluntly, **scandal sells** (Parenti, Dirty Secrets).

Under normal circumstances, the news media consistently take the side of the police and generally work to put a good face on their local police organizations. This occurs for two reasons. The first has to do with one of the major themes of this chapter: the fact that the media in America are extremely conservative. Being conservative as they are, the media will support the local police whenever and wherever they can because to do so is to underwrite the status quo. This is perfectly understandable from a conservative point of view. The police are, after all, a part of the establishment. As such, they are rarely the targets of any form of critical and insightful reporting.

The second reason for the glad-handing between the police and the news media has to do with how the media construct their crime-related news. Put bluntly, the media ask the police for their perspective on crime-related stories and they report it without question. This happens all of the time. A report on a homicide, a burglary, an armed robbery, a drug bust, a gang-related crime, and so forth is reported to the public just as the police report it to the media.

One of the reasons this happens has to do with laziness on the part of the press. The hard work that sincere investigation and follow-up on police-related stories would encompass is ongoing, time-consuming, and most often boring. It is far easier for media reporters on the police beat just to ask the police to tell them what has happened. Then, reporters take what the police have said and report (or publish) it word for word. This is exactly what happens; the police, effectively, write the news.

In small towns, where the only police-related news is usually the local "police blotter" report, that report is constructed by the police and reported word-for-word by the local media. In larger cities, the police usually have a public relations person—a media liaison (either in name or in effect)—who writes up stories and hands them over to the press. This makes the daily work of keeping up with crime very easy for those in the media.

In this way, the daily crime reporting that needs to be done by newspapers and television news people is almost always accomplished through the existence of an on-going, **symbiotic relationship** between the police and the press (Giles). The police make the job so easy that in essence they often do the work *for* the press. In return, the police inject their slant in daily stories reported consistently. And no one cares or makes a fuss over this. Why would they? How could they? Who in the reading or listening audience knows that this is how things work?

For more specific pieces, "theme" pieces, the media still rely on the police. Any story that purports to do thoughtful analysis about increased gang activity, or the sale of a new type of drug, or increased violence on the streets (and so on) is usually constructed by the media asking the police, "What's the story?" The police are assumed to know all about gangs, all about drugs, all about guns, all about violence—all about crime. The fact that the police have a great deal of knowledge about one side, but *only* one side of such stories, is passed over. This is not to say that the police do *not* know about these things. They know a great deal about them. It is their business to know this. The important point here is that the take or spin that the police might want to put on such issues is forever being written right into the media's reporting.

But all of this—this symbiotic relationship and nepotistic association between the media and the police—goes by the wayside when even the hint of scandal surfaces. The media, as conservative as they might be in general, will pounce upon the local police if anything racy comes up. This has to do with the competitive nature of news coverage in our contemporary age. The media want people to watch or read what they have to say, and nothing sells like a scandal. As the great newspaper man H. L. Mencken once noted, "Dog bites man. That's not news. Man bites dog. That's news!"

It is another paradoxical situation: the media, almost always supportive of the police and operating within this ongoing symbiotic situation, seem to "turn on the police" if so much as a hint of corruption or brutality surfaces. Like vultures, a term that many officers use to label reporters at such times, members of the press take on an entirely different persona when scandal breaks.

This section has only scratched the surface of the list of negatives constructed by the media with regard to police-citizen interaction. Suffice it to say that in blurring the line between fact and fiction, the media do no one any favors—neither the police nor the citizenry nor the best interests of justice.

SUMMATION

In this discussion we have explored several levels of myths. First, we have engaged the central myth about the media in America, namely that somehow—against all logic and evidence—there is a liberal bias out there. We then analyzed who owns and operates the media and how they create the myths that drive public opinion generally. Finally we turned to a discussion of several specific police-related myths that are accepted as gospel by millions of Americans. Along the way, we have illustrated how these myths work both to create police-directed antipathy on the part of citizens and to directly frustrate the police work in America.

Our endeavor here has been to understand how myths impact the American police officer in a world where there appears to be less and less of a difference between reality and fiction. We have visited a number of dynamics which, one piled on top of the other, tend to make American citizens believe that their local police are incompetent and dishonest. Even while generally supporting "the police" as a concept, people tend to think negatively of their local officers because of the dynamics illustrated.

Our first six chapters are now complete. Herein we have engaged numerous dynamics and paradoxes that inform the everyday lives of American police officers. In Chapter Seven, before ending Part One, we will gather all of this together to paint a picture of the police subculture: what it is, why it exists, and how it operates. In particular, we will engage the reality that the police subculture tends to be isolated from the public and operates to create and to maintain an "us against them" type of solidarity. It is toward the final, cumulative chapter of Part One that we now turn.

CHAPTER SIX PARADOX BOX

Members of the media tend to consider themselves to be "pro law and order," and corporations certainly operate to preserve the status quo in America. However, the effect of couching Dirty Harry as a "hero," of supporting the RCMP Syndrome, and of marketing violence as "sexy" is to create unreasonable expectations for the police in the minds of the public. In this way, the media are most definitely *not* supportive of the police. This leads to frustration on both sides of the police/community relationship.

DISCUSSION QUESTIONS

1. Discuss the idea that the media are "liberal." What about the example in Box 6.2 of the relationship between the C.I.A. and drug dealers? Why is this relationship generally kept as a "secret from the public, when so many investigations and books show it to be true?" In whose best interests would it be to keep such information under wraps?

2. Dirty Harry is sold to the American public as a positive role model of sorts. What is wrong with this? What is wrong with suggesting that "breaking the rules" is okay as long as the job gets done? If the police decide that someone is a "bad actor," why should they not go ahead and "frame" the suspect? Discuss the problems associated with making Harry a "hero."

3. The RCMP syndrome suggests that the police will always solve crime. Yet clearance rates show that this is not even close to true. Why is this bad? What are the negative consequences of people thinking that their local police will always "get their man?" Furthermore, what are the consequences of rookie police officers coming into police work with the same unrealistic expectations held by the public?

4. Hollywood tells millions of Americans that the Miranda warnings are issued immediately upon arrest. Is this true? Why not? When, in fact, are these warnings issued? What is wrong with people thinking that these admonitions come at the moment of arrest?

KEY TERMS

Clearance Rates: Police statistics kept to indicate what percentage of crimes reported are solved.

Cosmetized Violence: Term coined by Joseph Waumbaugh, former L.A.P.D. officer turned novelist; suggests that the media make violence exciting and, even, sexy.

Corporatocracy: An idea posited by some political scientists that American politics are so directly controlled by corporate dollars that we no longer have a democracy.

Dirty Harry is a "Hero": Sold by the media, this idea suggests that the "lone wolf" police officer who breaks procedural rules to "get the bad guys" is a hero.

Hard News: News programs, including nightly newscasts on major networks and 24-hour news coverage on channels such CNN, FOX, and MSNBC.

Hollywood Entertainment Media: Movies, television programs, and radio entertainment media.

The Individual Against the System: A romantic theme in American theater, movies, novels, and entertainment of all kinds; portrays a lone hero pitted against an establishment, often the government.

The Liberal Media: An important myth packaged and sold to the American public by corporations and conservative politicos.

Miranda v. Arizona (1966): Supreme Court case requiring the police to advise suspects of their rights against self-incrimination and to be represented by council when they are going to be interrogated.

Miranda Warnings: The admonitions presented to suspects under the *Miranda* decision above.

Media Imagery: Images sold to the American public by media outlets and corporations.

The News Media: Newspapers, radio, and television sources of news.

RCMP Syndrome: The idea that, like the Canadian Mountie, the American police always solve crimes.

Scandal Sells: The idea that the media will amplify scandalous behavior in an effort to improve viewer ratings.

Symbiotic Relationship: A relationship wherein both parties or entities support the other.

Spin: The process of taking troublesome statements or negative events and changing their impact in the media in a positive direction.

Talking Heads: News media stars who report the news and comment upon current events.

ADDITIONAL READINGS

There are many analysts who have discussed the myth of the "liberal media" in contemporary America. Given how widespread the belief in this myth is, this might be surprising. Perhaps the most widely read and well-respected is Michael Parenti. He has two different works that focus upon this area: a more general work, *Inventing Reality: The Politics of News Media, 2nd Ed.* (Wadsworth, 1992), and his tour de force *Dirty Truths* (City Light Publishers, 2001).

Regarding the idea of American and worldwide "corporatocracy," Jeffrey Grupp wrote *Corporatism: The Secret Government of the New World Order* (Progressive Press) in 2007. The original controversy over this topic was spawned by an oft-cited and always debated book, *Confessions of an Economic Hit Man* (Plume, 2005) by John Perkins. While millions around the world are embracing this idea, and much is being written about it, Grupp and Perkins's works give the student an excellent and insightful introduction to the topic.

The nexus between the C.I.A. and drug dealing is so troublesome to many conservative Americans that, as is the case with the liberal media myth, they find it difficult to believe. A dozen authoritative works have been produced about this problematic marriage, including *Cocaine Politics: Drugs, Armies, and the CIA in Central America* (University of California Press, 1991) by Peter Dale Scott and Jonathan Marshall; *The Big White Lie: The CIA and the Cocaine/Crack Epidemic* (Thunder's Mouth Pub., 1993) by Michael Levine and Lana Kavanau-Levine; and *Drugging America: A Trojan Horse Legacy, 2nd Ed.* (Silverpeak Enterprises, 2005) by Rodney Stich, a former federal agent. The student who reads one of these (or similar) works might dismiss it as unimportant. But taken together, these and a dozen other works will convince even the most ardent of agency supporters that the Central Intelligence Agency of the United States has, indeed, been involved in drug dealing for more than a generation now.

Police-media relations are addressed in *Beyond No Comment: Speaking with the Press as a Police Officer* (Kaplan Publishing, 2009) by Patrick Morley. This is a practical guide for police officers. An analysis of how "controversy and scandal sell" is included in *Good Cop/Bad Cop: Mass Media and the Cycle of Police Reform* (Criminal Justice Press, 2003) by Jarret S. Lovell. And the social construction of reality surrounding the police use of force is the central focus of *The Politics of Force: Media and the Construction of Police Brutality* (University of California Press, 2000) by Regina G. Lawrence.

We refer in the chapter to Joseph Wambaugh, the former L.A.P.D. Sergeant-turned-author, and students might be interested in his early novels. They are all about police work and have been universally hailed by police officers as being realistic and thoughtful. In 1971, he wrote his first police-related novel, *The New Centurions* (Little, Brown, and Company), which became a best seller and was later turned into both a feature length movie and a television series. Two years later, he wrote *The Blue Knight* (Dell, 1973), which was also made into a movie. Three years after that he wrote *The Choir Boys* (Dell, 1976), which was *also* turned into a movie. Wambaugh now writes novels about myriad subjects other than the police and is one of the best-selling authors in the world today.

CHAPTER 7

The Subculture

Chapter Seven Outline

To some extent, our object here is to synthesize the previous six discussions. We have been engaged with a set of topics that paint a picture of the experience of policing the streets of America. We have considered in particular what it is like to be a rule applier and a power broker. Over the course of these six chapters, we have at once engaged frustrating paradoxes and developed a healthy respect for the women and men who take up the daunting task of policing the streets. Now it is time to draw this all together and to talk about something that is engaged in every study ever made of the police: the **police subculture** (Adler *et al.*).

What is a **subculture**? We often hear the term but seldom stop seriously consider its meaning. To begin with, a subculture is "a culture within a culture." That is, a subculture is a subset of the **dominant culture** that exhibits some norms and values different from those of the dominant culture. Therefore, a subculture is, by definition, "deviant." It is deviant because it involves deviations from accepted norms, values, customs, and mores. We have to be careful to remind ourselves that this type of deviance is not *necessarily* something negative. Being different can be negative, but it can also be something positive—to the extreme. Benjamin Franklin, Thomas Edison, Henry Ford, and Bill Gates are all examples of famous Americans who were—there is no doubt about this—different. All innovators, experimenters, inventors, and revolutionaries are different and, therefore, deviant. It is from positive deviance that all innovation and progress comes.

But let us consider this list for one more moment. It is most definitely a good dynamic that some people are deviant when they innovate, experiment, and invent. Those who "push the envelope" in life can be extremely important to this or any society. However, we have also noted that revolutionaries are deviant. There are good revolutions and there are bad revolutions, and therein lies the problem. Not all deviant subcultures are negative, but not all **deviant subcultures** are positive either.

Let us begin our consideration of the police subculture by discussing subcultures and deviance in a more specific way.

A "DEVIANT" SUBCULTURE

As noted above, to deviate from the norm is to behave in a different way—that is all it means. It does not necessarily imply anything negative. Michael Jordan, as an example, lives an "abnormal" lifestyle that deviates profoundly from the lifestyles of "normal" people. On the basketball court, he was the ultimate innovator—considered by many to be the greatest player who ever lived. And the deviant lifestyle he led when playing basketball, including training, travel, and so forth, was something out of the ordinary, to be sure. Now he is a multi-millionaire and, thus, continues to be "deviant" in some sense. Michael Jordan is a hero to millions and deserves to be. Thus, the point is made about positive deviance.

The police subculture is known for its **isolation** and for its **solidarity** (Crank). Police officers have tended to band together—in a tribe of sorts—for generations now, and the feeling of togetherness experienced by members of the subculture is palpable. So much is the subculture known for its solidarity that sociologists who

BOX 7.1

THE DEVIANT OLYMPIC ATHLETE

Deviance is not necessarily a bad thing. Many people and subcultures have sets of norms and values that deviate from those of the dominant culture. Take Olympic athletes, for example. They value fitness and athletic performance to such an extent that for years on end they will cleave to lifestyles that involve incredible sacrifices. They will train hard, eat right, avoiding excesses, such as "partying," put off normal activities, such as starting a family, delay finishing their educations, and forestall beginning careers—all for the mere chance at success on the Olympic stage. Thus, they live a "deviant" lifestyle.

study and write about subcultures in general often point to the police subculture as one that exhibits how much solidarity such a group can develop. Membership in this group can sustain the individual police officer in several ways.

First, there is the physical side of police work to be considered here. We have visited the idea that with respect to danger and violence, nothing even approaching what Hollywood would have us believe occurs in real police work. And we have embraced the idea from Skolnick that in lieu of being confronted by violence at every turn, the police are nevertheless focused upon potential violence on a regular basis (Skolnick, Justice Without Trial). The threat posed to police officers by interacting often with hostile citizens is palpable enough to be ever-present in the minds of the police. And thus, the police subculture exists, in the first instance, as a check against the feeling of being vulnerable all of the time. The police cleave to each other in a brotherhood/sisterhood sort of arrangement in order to protect themselves from physical harm. Consistently depending upon each other for "**cover**," the police form a group that stands together (metaphorically) and faces outward against hostile forces.

Second, there is the psychic side of police work. There are numerous stresses and strains that visit the everyday officer as a part of the routine of policing the streets. So numerous are these multiple sets of frustrations experienced by the individual police officer that it appears the only avenue for support is other officers (Kurke and Scrivner). After all, only other police officers understand the frustrations visited upon the police. It becomes, in a very real sense, an "**us against them**" type of situation. And the "us" in this worldview can come to include only those who police the streets in uniform. Even police administrators, who may have worked on the beat years before but who no longer go out everyday in uniform, can be considered part of "them."

So the subculture is not only known for its solidarity, but also for its isolation. It is isolated from the citizenry and from everyone other than a very small group of like-minded and like-experienced individuals. Solidarity and isolation: these are the two bywords for the police subculture. They are what drives the subculture's creation and what helps to rationalize the deviant values held by "us."

VARIATIONS

So much is said and written about the police subculture that it behooves us here to acknowledge that there is not one, specific, unique type of police subculture. There are certainly as many types of subcultures in the police world as there are styles (or types) of police systems. In Chapters Nine and Ten we will discuss different styles of police organizations—four of them—and we will make the point that there is no one type of policing any more than there is one type of jurisdiction. Not only are there four distinctive types of police organization, but there are differences in policing that relate to geography, politics, and history. Added together, they form a sort of patchwork quilt of policing types and, concomitantly, of police subcultures.

In addition to style of police organization, several other factors influence police work in a way that creates varying police experiences and, thus, varying police subcultural norms. Most obviously, police work is differentiated by jurisdictional type. Local history, population mix, and size of population are all variables. Policing in America is done in rural areas, where there is little in the way of crime and where the policing experience is often driven by boredom more than anything else. Policing is done in suburban areas where there is a great deal of homogeneity but where there can be odd crime patterns, suburban gangs, affluent citizens with unrealistic expectations, and calls for service that involve a sort of "baby sitting the teenagers" type of approach to police work. And policing is done in major cities with diverse populations, substantial crime problems, ethnic minority enclaves, and so many calls for service that there is little time between details. In the city, there is not much in the way of discretionary time to utilize for routine patrol. In the country, there is nothing but extra time for routine patrol. These variables all work to create subcultural differences.

History, too, can impact upon police subcultural variability. Local political history can be important, because in some areas the police have been an important element of local politics and sometimes have been controlled by them. In such places, police norms can be linked with political norms. Especially in large Northern cities where "**political machines**" used to operate, police values can be quite different from those in operation elsewhere (Brezina; McCaffery). The history of the police themselves can also drive the police experience in one direction or another. In a jurisdiction where there is a history of police corruption of a systematic sort—ongoing, organized payoffs and graft that was supported by the subculture—the police will have very different contemporary mores than they will in a jurisdiction that has historically avoided such scandalous behavior. Furthermore, reform comes to police organizations in fits and starts. The Reform Era came very late in some jurisdictions. And because subcultural values are hard to change, in places where reform has happened only recently there will tend to be different norms than in places that experienced reform long ago.

However, having made the point that there are different police subcultures in different places, it is also important to remember that some police experiences are universally felt. Some of the dynamics that we have discussed in the first six chapters are common to all police officers, no matter where they may work. And taken together, these dynamics, frustrations, and paradoxes form the central rationalization for why police officers tend to think that people outside of the policing experience just "don't get it."

All police officers in all jurisdictions experience the problems associated with police goals being multiple, conflicting, and vague. This reality exists everywhere in the world of the police. Wrestling with the question of what to prioritize and the ongoing conflict between order maintenance and law enforcement is something with which all police officers must deal, and it drives them to bind with those who understand these dynamics.

All police officers stereotype and, in turn, are stereotyped themselves. They must deal with the frustrating reality that they are wrong about potential violence most of the time and with the accompanying unfairness of being lumped by citizens into a monolithic group. All police officers exercise discretionary decision-making powers. They can all experience the inhibiting realization that while attempting to do a difficult job with as much intelligence and integrity as is humanly possible, they are accused by citizens of perpetuating the rule of cop on the street. All police officers suffer from the paradoxes of coercive power and, in turn, are coerced themselves on occasion. Who but other officers can possibly understand how the police can feel powerless? Indeed, who but other officers can empathize with all of

BOX 7.2

THE ORIGINS OF THE SUBCULTURE

For a moment here, let us remind ourselves of the multiple reasons why police officers tend to form a subculture. Police officers can suffer frustration and, even, confusion due to:

- Multiple, conflicting, and vague goals.
- Being unfairly stereotyped.
- Being accused of exercising Khadi Justice.
- The exclusionary rule.
- Feeling powerless.
- Unrealistic media-created expectations.

the above frustrations and with the trouble that police officers encounter in dealing with the numerous paradoxes of police work?

All police officers question the due process system—exclusion in particular—in a way that sometimes moves them to consider the very system of which they are a part to be the enemy. Finally, all police officers, no matter where their jurisdiction and no matter what variables impact their experience, must deal with unrealistic, media-created expectations. All police officers find it impossible to live up to what the television- and motion picture-watching public expect of them and, oddly enough, to live up to what they initially—when beginning their careers—expected of themselves.

So there is a litany of reasons why the police are prone to feel there is nowhere to go but to other police officers for sustenance. There is an almost ubiquitous propensity to get into an "us against them" mode of thinking and behaving. Even though there are reasons why the subculture works to the disadvantage of the administration of justice, the existence of the police subculture is completely understandable. The paradox here is that while we must understand all of the above, we must also understand the inimical consequences of the police fusing together in this way. We will visit some of these consequences below.

THE ANOMIC POLICE OFFICER

Before moving to consider the concept of **anomie**, it is important to note that any number of studies have found the personality profiles of police officers to be normal. Years ago, many people, and even police scholars, believed in the intuitive idea that police work attracts authoritarian personality types. This seemed to be true and, furthermore, it appeared that police officers might be more prone to racial prejudice or bigotry aimed at people of diverse sexual orientations. So numerous studies were done aimed at determining if any of this was true. It turns out that it is not. The psychological profile of the average police officer is akin to that of the average American. And it is with this in mind that we turn to discuss how the policing experience can impact upon an officer's psyche over time.

This chapter has focused upon the police subculture as the logical product of police experience with paradoxes and on-the-job frustrations. But officers can also deal with these multiple problems in a compartmentalized, individual way. Escape from the numerous challenges and difficulties of the police experience can be obtained through membership in the subculture to be sure. But escape can also be acquired in independent, personal ways that bring solace to the individual. In the following subsections we will engage several of these alternative modes of achieving escape from the frustrations of the job. The good news will be that alcohol, divorce, and suicide are resorted to by fewer police officers than experts have intuited for many years now.

In a famous study of suicide, the great sociologist Emil Durkheim coined the term "anomie" to refer to the **"normlessness"** felt by many people who attempt to take their own lives (Durkeim). Durkheim said that people attempted suicide

BOX 7.3

FUTURE SHOCK

In 1970, Alvin Toffler wrote a book entitled, *Future Shock*. In it, he argued that change had been incremental throughout human history until very recently. At the outset of the 20th Century, the pace of change increased so rapidly that people in large numbers became unable to deal with it. People began to be "shocked" by how rapidly a different, changed "future" presented itself. Someone born at the beginning of the 20th Century could live long enough to see everything from the invention of the airplane to a man walking on the moon. They could live from a time when the automobile was scarce to a time when thousands of miles of super-highways criss-crossed the country. In contemporary times, someone born in the '60s has seen the development of the cell phone, the personal computer, the world of digital technology, and so forth. Dealing with such massive change, occurring at an almost frightening pace, is something that Toffler suggested brings anomic feelings to the majority of people today.

(Toffler)

largely because they felt out of sync with social values. It was as if the world operated with one set of rules and the individual with another. Police officers can suffer from anomie because all of the paradoxical experiences that they encounter, because of all of the frustrations of the job, and because of the dynamics of the subculture. They can come to believe that their understanding of the world and their value structure is out of rhythm with those of the normal person. They can come to believe that somehow they have been painted out of society's picture. When this occurs, the police officer can become anomic. There is reason to believe that a pronounced percentage of police officers suffer from this feeling.

For a moment here, we will engage in several brief discussions about personal problems that can plague police officers because of their shift work, the stressful nature of the job, and the lack of understanding others possess about the job of policing.

Stress: In general, police work involves an experience laced with stress (Miller, Laurence). To begin with, it involves **shift work** (O'Neill and Cushing). Police officers are on the street 24 hours a day, seven days a week, and that means that only about 1/3 of those who police our streets work "normal" hours. Those officers that work such normal hours get up in the morning, go to work during the day, and come home at the end of the day. They spend leisure time with their families during normal, daylight and evening hours. These police officers of the "day shift" experience something like a normal work life in the sense that they might be able to take their children to school in the morning and pick them up in the afternoon. They can go to a kid's soccer or basketball game. They can attend a play or a concert to watch either their own children or professional performances. In other words, they can be regular members of their families and enjoy the average person's ability to experience entertainment as a part of their lives.

All other officers must work either the swing shift in the evening or the graveyard shift through the night. They sleep at odd hours. Their bodies develop strange biorhythms. They cannot have normal social lives if they are single. And they cannot even make love at normal times with their significant others if they are in a relationship. And their families must negotiate normal school and work hours around the "odd" police officer routine (Crank).

But since the police must work round the clock, even day shift officers may not have Saturdays and Sundays off. So even they can miss going to church with the family on Sunday or watching sports events on Saturday. And everyone else in police work has to deal with strange hours for sleeping, strange days off, *and* strange family situations. The average police officer can thus become a "part-time" father, mother, or significant other.

Vacations come at odd times. Until a police officer has been on the job a few years and obtained some seniority, there is no guarantee of getting a vacation during normal vacation times—during the summer. Younger police officers often pull a couple of weeks worth of vacation during times of the year when either their children or their significant others do not have vacations. So the simple things in life that are vacation-oriented, such as getting the family together for a camping trip or to hit a beach for rest and relaxation, are often not available to the police. A young police officer's first years can involve working from three in the afternoon until midnight, having Tuesday and Thursday off, and taking a vacation in the second and third weeks of February.

Finally, there is something not many people can understand who have never been in uniform. People's attitudes toward the police vary from time to time. In the '60s and early '70s, Americans by the millions—especially young people—had negative feelings about the police. Today, the public is a bit more accepting. We live in a more conservative world now. But nevertheless, police officers suffer an odd sort of ostracism on a regular basis, and it is difficult to understand how this makes one feel unless one has experienced it (White). People look at the police with a jaundiced eye. They often scowl and make faces at them. Sometimes they "flip off" the police for no particular reason. As noted elsewhere in our discussions, police officers can experience this type of rejection by simply getting out of their patrol cars and going in to a café to have a cup of coffee. The feelings of anomie which can be created by experiencing this type of ostracism are palpable and can be difficult to surmount.

Alcohol: As we have seen, police officers work in a stressful occupation. They are surrounded by a culture, and work within an environment, that accepts drinking on a regular basis. Students of the police have long believed that alcohol abuse is probably a major problem among the police. But the good news is that some studies have found that the frequency with which police officers consume alcohol is just about the same as it is among the general population (Davey *et al.*). Police officers are, however, more prone to binge drink than the average person—about as prone as college students. This binge drinking reality is not good news, of course. But, on the other hand, the data on police and alcohol in general is not as bad as many have intuitively expected it to be.

Divorce: Instance of divorce is similar to that of alcohol. When early studies were done, the findings indicated that they divorced more often—much more often—than the average person. Analysis indicated that the stress of the job led to this high rate of divorce. This combined with the fact that subcultural norms were misunderstood by spouses as often as they were by other non-police people. So all too often spouses ended up appearing to be members of the ubiquitous "they"—those who do not understand the police. This leads to divorce as often as not. But in recent times an odd thing has happened. The divorce rate among average Americans has soared. And it has gone so high now—up to 50 percent—that the divorce rate for police officers is still higher (60 to 70 percent) but not inordinately so. In an odd sort of way, this is good news (White, 52).

Suicide: Numerous past studies of police suicide rates had indicated police officers were more prone to suicide than members of the general public (Stack and Kelly). The analysis done in these studies indicated that access to firearms, continuous exposure to human misery, shift work, marital and alcohol related stress, and impending retirement were the culprits. But for years, such studies were always done by large departments, one department at a time—comparing the specific department's suicide statistics to those of the general public. But since there are so many types of policing, as we have noted in several places in our discussion, there was reason to wonder if such statistics held true on a nationwide basis.

So in 1999, Stack and Kelley conducted a nationwide study on the subject. They found that the national suicide rate for police officers—25.6 per 100,000—was only slightly higher than that of the general population—23.8 per 100,000 (Stack and Kelley). So as was true with alcohol use and divorce, indications are that the police are about as prone to suffer from these anomie-related problems as are members of the public. Police work may very well lead many officers to feel anomic, but it appears that this does not necessarily drive them to excesses of this type.

There can be no doubt that police officers, isolated from the citizenry and carrying in their hearts and minds subcultural value systems that differ from those of the populace, suffer from feelings of anomie on a regular basis. This is the singularly most important reason that police officers cleave to their sister and brother officers in their subculture. It is an attempt to avoid being completely immersed and overwhelmed by a day-to-day experience that presents to them situations wherein they are exposed to the confusion associated with anomie. To some extent, this reality *demands* the creation of a solid, supportive subculture.

MORALIZING FOR OTHERS

Before turning to an analysis of the particular norms and values held by the police subculture, we will briefly engage one more dynamic that influences the development of that subculture: the fact that the police spend their time **moralizing for others**. In exercising their discretionary decision-making powers, the police moralize. When deciding who goes to jail and who does not, a police officer is, in fact, making a moral judgment of sorts. He or she is deciding who *deserves* to be incarcerated. In analyzing human behavior, the police officer on the street determines what kind of abhorrent behavior is deserving of sanction and what kind can go unpunished.

In a world where so many suffer from anomic feelings—as Toffler warned us, **"future shock"** is rampant today—the police are not immune from the confusion that rapidly changing norms can bring to anyone (Toffler). But for as much as everyone might be a bit anomic now and then in such a rapidly changing world, the average person can avoid some of the psychic trauma that may accompany anomie. They can retreat into their own spheres of life and cloister themselves from confusion if they so desire.

But police officers do not have this luxury. If it is difficult for everyone to live in a fast-paced, ever-changing world, then the police have more difficulty than most. If the police must make moral judgments—if they cannot avoid doing so—then more than the average amount of confusion in life may very well be visited upon them. Moralizing for others in a shifting landscape forces a person into a situation wherein they might go in one of two different directions.

Moralizers such as the police might become perplexed, inhibited, and even immobilized in such a changing world. The pressure of being *required* to make judgments under situations involving shifting norms—of being unable to avoid doing so—can drive a person to bewilderment. While there have been no definitive studies in this regard, it may be that significant numbers of people leave police work specifically because of these dynamics.

On the other hand, moralizers might very well become hostile, bitter, and even resentful; and they can become aggressively so. And if this happens to police officers, they can be driven to put even more distance between themselves and the public. This can further drive the individual police officer into the "us versus them" dynamic that isolates their subculture from the citizenry. Thus, in a sort of cyclical way, moralizing for others can make police officers more adamant about the certainty of their own position in life. And this distances them from the public in a way that might tend to make them even more prone to moralize about how civilians do not understand life and police values.

It is now time to turn to a consideration of some of the specific, deviant values held by members of the subculture.

Some "Abnormal" Norms

After discussing what the police subculture is, why it exists, and some of the dynamics that keep in running, it is time to define in specific terms some of the norms—the **deviant norms**—that the subculture possesses. Some of what we will engage on this list makes perfectly good sense. Given the tasks set out before the police, some of their subcultural norms are perfectly understandable, not disconcerting in any way. But on the other hand, some of these subcultural norms are disturbing; they work both to create police cynicism, and they work against the best interests of justice in America.

Overkill: We have taken some pains in our discussions to point out that police work is not particularly violent or dangerous—in fact, it is rather placid and boring, compared to what Hollywood would have us think. Overly romanticizing the physical "action" involved in police work is not a good idea, because it drives both police officers and the public to expect that a sort of Wild West aura surrounds the endeavor and nothing good comes from that. However, having said that police work is not particularly violent on a regular basis, we must recall that the constant search for symbolic assailants and the constant anticipation of violence can weigh heavily upon the officer. Police officers do get assaulted, they do get into brawls at times, and especially when they are involved in crowd situations, they are always outnumbered. And they can sometimes fall into a dynamic called **"overkill."**

When two officers, for example, walk into a bar to handle a fight, the patrons in the bar tend to believe that the ratio of troublemakers to police officers is two to two. That is, there are two citizens involved in the fight and, now that they have arrived, there are two officers who have come to handle it. But that is not the way the police view it. Two police officers walking into this situation consider that there are 75 (to pick a realistic number) potentially hostile subjects and just two officers. This is the way the police see it, and it is perfectly understandable that they do so. Thus, in a simple, common bar fight situation, the police feel outnumbered—in a big way.

The number of situations that present this dynamic to the police—of being heavily outnumbered—is great. Every time there is a bar fight, every time there is a group of teenagers "hangin'" on the streetcorner, every time the police go to a high school dance or a football game, every time they get out of the car in a housing project—in these and a dozen other types of situations commonplace in police work—the police see potential violence, and they see an uneven playing field. Subcultural norms work to provide a rationalization for the use of force that helps knit the police together (Crank 64).

The logical way with which the police deal with such situations—when they are greatly outnumbered—has to do with Muir's third paradox: the paradox of face. Recall that this paradox suggests that the nastier the reputation someone brings to such a crowd-oriented situation, the less nasty they really have to be. Put another way, bringing a "bad ass rep" into such a situation provides significant insurance against being challenged. And so developing and maintaining that sort of "rep" is

BOX 7.4

OVERKILL

The police are almost always outnumbered. While they do not get attacked often, when they do there is a subculturally driven norm that suggests that they have to "win" and that they have to "win big." The idea is that "we have to be undefeated" in order to develop the nasty reputation that brings with it intimidation. As Muir puts it, this nasty reputation is necessary in order to not have to be nasty very often. So the axiom tends to be, "If anyone assaults one of us, they go to jail. If anyone hurts one of us, they go to the hospital."

something at which police officers work, whether they have read Muir's theories about coercive power or not.

How would the police "work at" developing and maintaining such a rep? The answer is as straightforward as it is troublesome: overkill. As noted in box 7.4, this involves using force in an excessive manner—not all of the time, but when there is a genuinely violent challenge to the police, as individuals or as a group. That is, when applying force in order to get a suspect handcuffed or into a car or out of a bar, excessive force is not necessary. But when people directly challenge the police to "fight it out," then overkill is rationalized as a part of the norms of the subculture. The police must send a message—so the subcultural wisdom has it—that they are *not* to be challenged by citizens without those citizens paying a heavy, physical price.

Of course, the rules that the police must follow with regard to using force require they use "only that amount of force which is necessary to overcome the illegal use of force." This rule, or something similar to it, is in every set of police departmental **General Orders**. It is pretty much the universal rule for using force, because it parallels the legal limits of police force. But such a rule, even in today's modern, professional era of policing, tends to be ignored when a direct, physical, violent confrontational challenge to the police materializes. As Crank suggests, "The law . . . is not a set of rules to bound police behavior: it's what legitimates police use of force" (Crank 65).

Noble Cause Corruption: We have already defined noble cause corruption, albeit briefly. Later on, in Chapter Thirteen, we will spend more time on the topic. But it is important to visit this idea here, too, because one of the norms of the police subculture has specific relevance to it. Those who study police corruption long ago differentiated between two sorts of levels of corruption: "**meat eating**" and "**grass eating**" (Knapp). Meat eating corruption refers to police corruption that is ongoing, organized, and methodical. Meat eating involves the sorts of payoffs, shakedowns, and monthly "protection money" payments that permeated police work in most places during the 19th century (and in some places well into the 20th century).

Grass eating—which clearly, because of the metaphor chosen, involves misconduct of a lesser level of culpability—consists of two things. First, grass eaters are police officers who occasionally take money in exchange for not doing their jobs—say, a few dollars from a motorist, in exchange for not writing a ticket. But they do not go out and actively seek payoffs and graft. Grass eating is driven by chance and opportunity, not by ongoing greed that manifests itself in schemes aimed at generating substantial amounts of income.

Second, grass eaters are those officers who may not become involved in corruption themselves but who will look the other way when it occurs. They will neither endorse nor assist in investigations into the misdeeds of other, meat eating police officers. Today, meat eating is largely gone from most police departments. What used to be a way of life for police is now only occasionally observed, investigated, and thwarted by police review systems. (Much more on this will be addressed in Chapter Thirteen.) In fact, in most jurisdictions, most modern police officers will cooperate with investigations into meat eating—"corruptions of authority" is what it is called—because today the overwhelming majority of the police see such behavior as unprofessional and demeaning to all police officers. And so along with most meat eating, the type of grass eating that "looks the other way" when this sort of corruption occurs has also gone by the wayside.

But there is a type of grass eating that still prevails in many places in policing circles: grass eating that involves looking the other way when noble cause corruption occurs. Noble cause corruption is considered within the subculture to be something quite different from old fashioned graft and payoffs. In many police circles, Dirty Harry is still accepted as a hero. Even police officers who will not involve themselves in Dirty Harry–like behavior will often tend to be reluctant to participate in, or even sanction, investigations into this type of police misconduct by others. The subcultural rationalization for this goes something like this: If the choice is between putting a cop behind bars—for, say, testilying—or putting the bad actor who was the "victim" of the testilying behind bars, then there really is no choice to be made. The bad actor goes to jail and the cop stays on the street. In this way, the police subculture tends to underwrite noble cause corruption and, in the long run, encourages its perpetuation.

Never Explain, Never Apologize: One subcultural norm that is particularly troublesome has to do with both the macho nature of the police subculture and police isolationism. Police officers seem almost universally to be convinced that they should never, ever, under any circumstances "explain themselves" to citizens. This does not just mean that police officers tend to be guarded. It means that the actions they take are considered within the subculture to be "none of the public's business." Furthermore, even worse than explaining things to citizens would be apologizing for doing something in error. Instead of seeing an apology as a sign of strength, as many people do, police officers often see it in the opposite way. Police officers, especially young ones, will associate making explanations or apologies with weakness. And to show weakness is to undercut the ability of the police to deter, to suppress, to coerce, and generally to keep the upper hand out on the streets. This subcultural norm is troublesome in several ways that will become more obvious in our later discussions. For now, it is enough to note that the isolation of the police is both the cause of and an effect of this propensity. Police officers do not want to explain themselves or to apologize because they feel isolated. And because they act in this way, they become even more isolated from the public that they police.

Police Parties and Social Lives: The police tend to be driven by a generalized feeling that there are just no people in the world who understand the police officer experience and, indeed, understand what is going on in America. The degeneration of values in contemporary America, the amount of gratuitous violence found on the streets today, and the many frustrations associated with the individual police officer experience drive this feeling in an understandable way. One of the products of this feeling is the propensity for police officers not only to band together on the job, but to do so during their off-the-job hours as well.

Police officers tend to party together. **Police parties** are "safe" in some sense. Only when surrounded by one's peers and fellow travelers along the difficult road of being an officer can the police relax completely. When people—all people—go out to party, they want to let their hair down, drink a bit, and generally be loose and unwind. How can that be accomplished by the police if there are "civilians who don't get it" around? Indeed, how can *any* collegial relaxation be accomplished with non-police people around? (Ahern, 14).

So the police often party together. They have a few beers or watch a game. They go bowling or play golf together. They even take vacations together, or in conjunction with other police families. This extension of the police subcultural reality into the off-duty world is not always in evidence. But it develops often enough that the solidarity and isolation of the subculture can be enhanced and amplified by this socializing-related extension of the subculture's reach.

The Fort Apache Syndrome: The Fort Apache metaphor is, to some extent, self-explanatory. It suggests that the police find themselves feeling as if they are surrounded by hostile savages: citizens who simply do not understand morality, crime, social problems, and a myriad of negative developments in contemporary America (Walker, T). Not only does the average citizen not understand police work, but most people do not understand the type of violence and amoral behavior on the increase in today's society. Not only can police officers be frustrated by this, they can feel genuinely offended by it. They can rail against the misunderstanding, naiveté, and (even) genuine animosity of some citizens.

An Oppressed Minority Group: As odd as it might sound, police officers can develop a similar outlook on the world as that of the members of a minority group. The police are a minority—only 800,000 of them in a country of over 300,000,000. They construct a subcultural reality that isolates them from the

BOX 7.5

FORT APACHE

For generations it has been commonplace for police officers to feel that they are outnumbered and encircled by hostile forces. They are encircled by people who just don't "get it" and who possess a great deal of antipathy toward the police. This feeling has been in evidence in the Fort Apache Syndrome: the propensity to feel isolated and surrounded by "savages" (the Indians who attacked Fort Apache in the movie of the same name from the 1950s). So much is this the case that one New York precinct in the Bronx christened itself "Fort Apache" in the 1960s and decorated its walls with arrows and spears and Native American gear of various kinds.

majority. They are grouped together in the minds of the dominant majority and stereotyped in unfair ways. They can suffer from ostracism in the eyes of the public, not only when handling details but, even, when they simply walk into a grocery store. Finally, as is true of other minority groups in America, their feelings of isolation from the public and of being treated unfairly can lead the police to consider themselves "oppressed" to some extent.

It is an odd paradox that this is true. Ever since the invention of the police, they have themselves been accused of oppressing minority groups. In fact, as we have seen, conflict theorists suggest that one of the reasons for the invention of the police in the first place was to repress minorities in the name of ruling elites. How ironic it is then that contemporary police officers can suffer from feelings of oppression as if they themselves were members of a misunderstood minority.

DRAWBACKS

So the existence of the police subculture makes sense. Its level of solidarity and isolation makes sense. And the sorts of subcultural norms and values that are created within this subculture—these also make sense. But there is a problem here: a problem of critical importance for the administration of justice on the streets of America. For as understandable as the police subculture and its norms are, there are numerous difficulties associated with the subculture. These difficulties create dynamics that are counterproductive to both the interests of the police and to those of the citizens whom they protect and serve.

First, being isolated from the citizenry and operating within a set of principles that are divorced from those of the dominant, majority population, police officers can tend to make decisions that serve the interests of the police themselves instead of doing what is best for individual citizens, for their communities, and for justice. That is, often the police might be moved to take the easier, simpler road when deciding what to do in handling a given incident. Instead of taking the extra time to work on a problem, the police can sometimes take less time than the interests of justice might dictate. For example, when dealing with a young teenager who has been arrested for a minor offense—a kid with a reasonable attitude and a clean record—the police might eschew taking the trouble to contact the teen's parents and allowing them to handle things informally. Since this takes more time, a police officer might just take the youngster to Juvenile Hall in lieu of "doing the right thing."

Second, over time, the police not only tend to develop their own subcultural values, but they can also lose sight of the values of contemporary American society. Sometimes this might be a good thing. When, as an example, the police take a "hard line" on teenagers who use violence as a part of their gang initiations, it is undoubtedly in the best interests of justice. If the police refuse to accept the idea that this development in contemporary America is merely a "generational and cultural difference"—a change occurring in the world of today's teens that the police are supposed to "understand" and to which they are supposed to "adapt"—this can be good for society. Driven by their subcultural ideas of what is right and what is wrong, the police might very well choose to go hard on violent teens involved in such initiations and push aside any propensity to be "understanding" about today's street culture.

On the other hand, as society becomes more prone to accept certain types of protests against ignorance, unfairness, and bigotry—as occurred in the 1960s and as is occurring more and more today—the police will resist such positive changes. In this case, cleaving to outdated police subcultural norms is not in society's best interests. Unfortunately, in the 1960s, America experienced an extended period of time wherein police officers did just this: they railed against positive change in America. And they did so to the detriment of their communities and the country.

Third, when the police divide the world into an "us" and "them" dichotomy, they begin to see people as the "enemy." They can become so removed from the citizenry that they adopt a war-like mentality. We will discuss the harmful

BOX 7.6

POLICE SUBCULTURAL DRAWBACKS

For as much as the existence of the police subculture is logical, and the deviant values that it constructs are understandable reactions to the pressures of the job, the police subculture tend to stimulate police officers to:

- Make judgments that are in the interests of the police and not of justice.
- Lose touch with the "normal" values of the society within which they police.
- Consider the public to be "the enemy" in some senses.

consequences of such a perspective at great length in the next chapter, when we engage in a discussion about paramilitaristic policing. For now, suffice it to say that distancing themselves from the public in a solid and isolated subculture can make the police become driven by ideas and ideals that motivate them to go into "action" everyday against their "adversaries," the general public (Fletcher).

So as much as the existence of the police subculture is completely understandable, it can work in ways that are not in anyone's best interests—not the police, police administrators, the public, nor justice. We do not wish to paint too negative a picture here. Rather, we wish to be realistic in our efforts to understand the police subculture as best we can. In the final chapter of this book, Chapter Fifteen, we will suggest ways that today's police officers might reject some of the negatives associated with the subculture. It might sound like a "wish" or a "prayer" of some sort, but it would be nice if police officers could both receive the sustenance they need and desire from the subcultural experience and, at the same time, avoid the drawbacks that make the subculture something troublesome.

SUMMATION

In this chapter, we have discussed the concept of subculture in general. We have engaged many reasons why the police subculture exists and is so solid and isolated from the citizenry. And we have considered some of the specific norms held dear in the hearts and minds of police officers. Finally, we have briefly considered the drawbacks of the subculture—the negatives that can impact not only the lives of individual officers but American justice itself.

During this discussion we remind ourselves that police officers are normal human beings and normal Americans. Nothing discussed here should move us to believe that anything unusual in their personality structures drives police officers to join this subculture. The existence of the police subculture is an environmentally created reality.

We have come to the end of Part One. Having considered the dynamics associated with police work from the individual police officer's perspective, it is

CHAPTER SEVEN PARADOX BOX

The police subculture provides not only physical protection but also intellectual sustenance to individuals who are experiencing a work atmosphere that is often filled with paradox and frustration. Membership in the subculture can appear to be essential for the psychic survival of police officers. But avoiding the isolation that the subculture brings is critical to the administration of justice because making the citizenry into the enemy—as the subcultural experience tends to—severely limits the accomplishment of police functions.

now time to turn toward more administrative topics. In Part Two we will discuss differing styles of police organization, from three classic examples known to be operative since the 1960s, to the newest form of police organization: Community Oriented Policing. It is toward these less individualistic and more synoptic topics that we now move.

DISCUSSION QUESTIONS

1. Everyone belongs to one subculture or another. Either in their work endeavor, in conjunction with some club or hobby, in relation to some sports team or commitment, or even as a student—everyone is involved in at least one subculture. Discuss the concept of subculture and relate it to subcultures to which you belong.

2. Toffler's concept of "future shock" has to do with progress being so rapid in today's world that the future gets here "before we know it." Discuss what changes—technological as well as sociological—have come about over the course of your lifetime. What about these changes makes life difficult? How are you being required to change your behavior and view of the world in order to "keep up" with our society?

3. The police moralize for others. When they make an arrest/no arrest decision they must exercise their judgment with regard to who does and does not "deserve" to go to jail. What criteria should a police officer use to make such decisions? What sorts of values and norms drive this type of decision? Are these entirely personal norms, thus turning legal decisions into personal ones? Is that appropriate?

4. In the text, we have suggested that the police subcultural propensity to "never explain, never apologize" is misguided. We have proposed that to explain oneself or to apologize is not a sign of weakness but, rather, a sign of strength. Why is this? What does this assertion mean? How does an occasional apology indicate that a person is self assured and confidant?

KEY TERMS

Anomie: Durkheim's term for the feeling of normlessness that leads a substantial number of suicide victims to do away with themselves.

Cover: Police term referring to officers who arrive at a police detail in order to add additional protection to the officer in charge of the detail.

Deviant Norms: Norms that deviate from the dominant society's norms, but that are accepted within a subculture.

Deviant Subcultures: Subcultures with deviant norms. In some ways, all subcultures deviate from the dominant culture.

Dominant Culture: A society's culture, including norms, customs, and practices that are accepted by the vast majority of people.

The Fort Apache Syndrome: The police metaphor that "we" are inside of the fort and surrounded by "them," the "hostile savages."

Future Shock: Alvin Toffler's idea that change is so rapid in today's world and society gets reinvented so rapidly that the average person has trouble adjusting.

General Orders: Manuals in every police department that set down rules of conduct and operational regulations.

Grass Eating: A type of police corruption that involves passive, reactive graft or that involves looking the other way when meat eating occurs.

Isolation (Police): The feeling that the police are isolated from the public; the Fort Apache Syndrome is an exaggerated form of this feeling.

Meat Eating: Organized, institutionalized corruption involving payoffs, graft, and regular shakedowns.

Moralizing for Others: The idea that people who apply rules to the behavior of others must moralize about behavior when making discretionary decisions.

Normlessness: Another word for Durkheim's concept of anomie.

Oppressed Minority Group: Refers in our discussions to the idea that the police can come to consider themselves an oppressed minority group: isolated from the public, misunderstood, and underappreciated.

Overkill: The police propensity to meet force with excessive force in order to send a message that deters anti-police violence; see Paradox of Face.

Police Parties: Refers generally to the propensity of police officers to get together and socialize with other police officers—sometimes exclusively.

Police Subculture: The subculture created by police isolation and by the numerous frustrations associated with the job.

Political Machines: The party apparatuses used to run big cities during the Political Era of policing; known for their corruption and favoritism.

Shift Work: Refers to the fact that police work must be done twenty-four hours a day, seven days a week, and, thus, police officers have to work day, evening, night, and weekend shifts.

Solidarity: Refers to the feelings of power and belonging that individuals in a group obtain from group membership.

Stress: The pressure and frustrations of police work tend to create a psychic strain upon the individual officer.

Subculture: A culture within a culture, possessing its own norms and behavioral patterns.

Us Against Them: The police metaphor that the police are "pitted against" the citizenry; see Fort Apache Syndrome.

ADDITIONAL READING

The definitive statement about the importance of the police subculture comes, oddly enough, in a criminal justice textbook entitled *Criminal Justice* (McGraw-Hill, 1994) by F. Adler, G. O. W. Mueller, and W. S. Laufer. Theirs is perhaps the most often cited analysis of the phenomenon. In *Police Psychology Into the 21st Century* (Lawrence Elbaum, 1995) by Martin I. Kurke and Ellen M. Scrivner, twenty-one psychologists discuss the psychological reasons for the subculture and for its profound solidarity. Finally, Ken Bolton, Jr., analyses the subcultural experience of black police officers in *Black in Blue: African-American Police Officers and Racism* (Routledge, 2004).

Emile Durkheim's classic work about anomie is *Suicide* (Free Press, 1997). First published in 1897, this work is cited as one of the primary, original works in the entire field of sociology. Alvin Toffler's development of the idea of future shock is found in *Future Shock* (Bantam, 1984), one of the most important works of any kind from the tumultuous '60s.

The analysis cited in this chapter of police suicide was written by S. Stack and T. Kelly and published as "Police Suicide" in *Police and Policing: Contemporary Issues, 2nd Ed.* (Praeger, 1999) edited by D. J. Kenney and R. P. McNamara. In an attempt to aid police officers in dealing with the multiple stresses of the job, Laurence Miller wrote *Mental Toughness for Law Enforcement* (Looseleaf Law Publications, 2007), credited as being the first book to bring genuine research to an analysis of the practical aspects of the debilitating realities of police subcultural life.

Several "self help" books have been written for police officers and their families aimed at preparing people for the multiple stresses of the job. *Force Under Pressure: How Cops Live and Why They Die* (Lantern Books, 2000) by Laurence Blum; *I Love A Cop: What Police Families Need to Know* (The Guilford Press, 2006) by Ellen Kirshman; *Emotional Survival for Law Enforcement: A Guide for Officers and Their Families* (E-S Press, 2002) by Kevin M. Gilmartin; and *Cops Don't Cry: A Book of Help and Hope for Police Families, 6th ed.* (Creative Bond, 1999) by Vali Stone are each purchased and read often by police families.

Regarding the norms and values of the subculture that are problematic, the idea of grass eating and meat eating corruption came from the *Knapp Commission Report on Police Corruption* (George Braziller, 1973), written corporately by the members of an important commission that looked into the New York Police Department in the early '70s. Finally, the Fort Apache Syndrome is a label that was largely based upon the movie entitled "Fort Apache, the Bronx" from the early '70s, which, in turn, was based upon a now many times published novel written by former police officer Tom Walker entitled *Fort Apache: New York's Most Violent Precinct* (iUniverse Star, 2009).

PART TWO

Organizational Styles

Part Two addresses how police organizations are organized with respect to which of the multiple functions of the police are prioritized. We begin with a consideration of how much, or how little, militarism should play a role in police organizations. We then work through a discussion of three standard styles of police organization and conclude Part Two with an analysis of the newest form of police organization: Community Oriented Policing.

CHAPTER 8

Paramilitarism

Chapter Eight Outline

A growing number of police organizations in America are rejecting the paramilitaristic paradigm because the drawbacks to this type of policing are becoming more and more evident. This old model is increasingly being replaced by the notion of **Community Oriented Policing (COP)**—a subject to which we will turn our attention in Chapter Ten. American policing is divided into two camps: those organizations that still embrace the paramilitaristic mode of policing and those that have moved away from it. In this chapter, we will define paramilitaristic policing and examine its strengths and weaknesses. We will discuss an awkward paradox faced by contemporary police officers and leaders: while there are solid arguments against **paramilitaristic policing** (Jefferson), it is necessary that any police organization be prepared to operate in military fashion under certain unusual circumstances. This occurs when armed adversaries are present and "casualties" are likely to occur.

This is an odd reality. The police need not—should not—operate in a martial manner *most* of the time. Ordinarily, they ought to be community oriented, working against the idea of being an occupying army, helpful and of service to their communities. They need to integrate with their communities and avoid unnecessary distance between themselves and the public. Paramilitarism works against each of these desirable ways of operating and, consequently, needs to be deemphasized as much as possible.

Police selection procedures should reject people with a militaristic approach to the job, and officer training should aim to deemphasize paramilitarism. Those who administer police organizations should avoid emulating the armed forces. Officers who approach the public in an aloof manner should not be extolled, promoted, or held up as the "best" at their jobs. Discipline ought to be accomplished in a way that illustrates to the corps as a whole that a martial attitude toward the public is unacceptable.

But the paradox is that police training must include anti-sniper training, riot training, high-risk warrant service training, and hostage negotiation training—paramilitary training, in other words. This dichotomy presents a near-impossible paradox for police officers and leaders.

DEFINITIONS

Police operations work in a semi-military or quasi-military way. Since beginning to emphasize crime fighting in lieu of the social welfare–type of policing prevalent until the early 20th Century, the police have adopted a paramilitaristic mode of operation that has been the norm in American police work for more than a generation. Such militarism has seemed logical and effective. This emphasis upon military-like operations was put into effect in an effort to do away with the rampant corruption of an earlier age of policing. The Reform Era begat paramilitarism, and the changes it wrought have been credited with ending the police excesses of the Political Era. (More about this important change in the organization of American policing in a moment.)

BOX 8.1

PARAMILITARISTIC, "SEPARATIONIST" ORGANIZATIONS

When we discuss paramilitarism, we are talking about the propensity for police to operate in a somewhat militaristic fashion. We are *not* talking about the type of paramilitarism that involves separatist groups, like the Branch Dividians, for example, that train with military equipment in anticipation of an eventual showdown with the government and the police. Such people tend to come from the lunatic fringe of American life, and our purpose is not to engage in a discussion about them. Suffice it to say that separatist paramilitary groups are a danger to the police, to peace and stability on the streets, and to the interests of law and order. As Larkin confirms in *Comprehending Columbine*, paramilitaristic groups train for violent confrontations with authority and, contrary to what their members sometime suggest, are no blessing to contemporary America.

Police uniforms are similar to military uniforms. They are universally produced in martial colors: khaki, brown, and "police blue" being the colors of choice. They have emblems on them, from the badge of authority to stripes and bars that indicate ranks. The police prominently display the tools of their trade on their **"Sam Browns"** (the large belts they wear): sidearm, handcuffs, mace, spare ammunition, night stick. These accoutrements suggest a militaristic propensity to employ force and engage in "combat."

Police command structures take their cue from the armed forces. Personnel ranking is essentially the same: the **"chain of command"** ascends from Officer (the equivalent of a military private) to Sergeant to Lieutenant to Captain. In some larger organizations, Corporals rank between Officers and Sergeants, and Majors follow Captains. In still larger organizations, Colonels follow Majors. This hierarchical organizational chart exactly parallels that of the army (White).

And there are more similarities. Largely because of the constant search for symbolic assailants, the police tend to *carry* themselves in a militaristic way. They are cautious. They learn how to enter a house without making themselves vulnerable. They learn to scan any area they enter for potential danger. They watch people's hands and eyes. They look behind doors and in closets. They keep everyone in front of them. And so forth. These are the same modes of behavior that drive military members in combat. Of course, the potential for violence is obviously much greater in the military. Nevertheless, the police keep themselves alert, aware of their surroundings, and cognizant of potential adversaries in the same manner as soldiers.

But police work was not always driven by militaristic principles and martial mentalities.

PARAMILITARISM AS A RESPONSE TO THE "POLITICAL" ERA

As briefly noted in the Introduction, the first era of American policing occurred during the "Political Era." This label is appropriate given how the police operated for the first few decades of their existence. At that time—beginning in the mid 19th Century with the advent of a uniformed constabulary—the police were a part of the era of "machine politics." This era involved utilizing all municipal employees as part of the political structure that won elections and maintained power in big cities. Long before the creation of rules prohibiting police from openly participating in the electoral process, police officers—along with fire fighters, subway workers, and a host of other municipal employees of that era—helped deliver the party vote (usually the Democratic Party vote) on election days. They did this to retain their jobs. By helping reelect those who had hired them, the pre-civil service era police participated in the ongoing reinvention of the political control mechanism that sustained itself in perpetuity for generations (Walker, Critical Analysis of Police Reform).

During this Political Era of policing, before the advent of civil service, people obtained jobs as police officers through having the right contacts or even by bribing the appropriate person. Becoming a police officer had nothing to do with competence, intelligence, or education. There were no **civil service tests**. There was no protracted process through which candidates earned a badge—they simply had to know someone on the force. Or have a relative on the force. Or slip the right person some money. This was how someone got hired in those days. And, equally, an officer kept his job (police officers were always men, back in those days) by influencing the political process. Politics dictated hiring, firing, discipline, and so forth (Walker, *Ibid.*).

In that era, all municipal institutions were involved in ongoing, meat eating–types of corrupt behavior. Police payoffs were the norm. Police work was permeated with daily corruption in a way that is difficult to understand today. Officers took small amounts of money from individual citizens, and they took large amounts of money from those who operated the rackets—gamblers, pimps, and alcohol runners, during Prohibition. They even took **"protection money"** from businessmen, as noted in Box 8.2. And corruption passed without comment because this was how municipal administration worked, at all levels, in all institutions.

Then came reform. The Progressive Era of American politics unfolded around the turn of the 20th Century. During this era, people developed greater expectations for government. They began to expect competence, honesty, and objectivity from government and from the police in particular. Along with these types of increased expectations came the institution of civil service. Taken together, greater expectations on the part of the public and civil service protections for governmental employees facilitated the Reform Era of American policing.

In a philosophical sense, police work changed from being social welfare–oriented to focusing on "law enforcement" (Peak 23). The police began to take

BOX 8.2

THE CORRUPTION OF THE POLITICAL ERA

During the Political Era, police corruption involved more than payoffs from illegal enterprisers in exchange for not being arrested. There was much more. The police in those days regularly "shook down" business owners in an ongoing way. There were monthly payoffs. If a person owned a business, they "owed" money to the police every month in order to (1) make sure that their business was protected from vandalism (that might be perpetrated at night by the police themselves), (2) make sure permits and licenses were not necessary, and (3) make sure that their territory was protected against intrusion from competitors. Cities ran on major corruption—and increased the income of police officers, sometimes by a factor of three or four times their base salaries.

"fighting crime" seriously, and many of the changes instituted during that time reflected these differences in focus.

Tests were developed to determine who was hired. **Police accountability** became an issue for the first time. **Police academies** were created. Police attire came to resemble military uniforms. Before that time, in some places, the police were only identified by their badges (Walker, Police In America). Police salaries expanded, because it was no longer assumed that graft would augment pay—they had to be paid a living wage so that the expectation that they act in a legal manner could become realistic. And paramilitaristic policing came into vogue. It might seem odd, but this change from the Political Era to the Reform Era was not a major "movement" that swept the nation at any particular moment. Reform occurred city by city over an extended period of time. From as early as 1910 until as late as 1940, scandals rocked virtually every major police department in the nation. A scandal would erupt, the local police administration would be replaced, and reform would arrive—city by city, scandal by scandal.

This is important to understand for our discussion because the change to paramilitaristic policing was part of the reform. In an effort to eradicate rampant corruption, chains of command were tightened. The **lineup** was invented—officers stood at attention and were inspected before their shifts. Systems for investigating citizens' complaints about police misconduct were installed. Police officers were given training that was, over time, taken seriously. Competence, efficiency, and honesty became the goals of the police. Of course, not all of these ideals were realized at once. But the changes that reform fostered had an important influence. Police work in America changed forever.

And all of this worked. It worked, almost everywhere, to control the police in the same way that chains of command, inspections, and discipline in general work to control people in the military. Much of the change brought about by the Reform Era was positive. It changed the face of American policing because it changed who was hired, how they were trained, how they were disciplined, and the image of the police. It created a palpable feeling among a steadily increasing number of police officers that theirs was a noble profession, and that they could take pride in it. Administering the police force like a military organization effected much of this change. Police officers, who then and now operate alone and without immediate supervision most of the time, began to *feel* that they were being consistently monitored and controlled. Even if this was not the case—not then and not today—police officers began to sense that theirs was an occupation that was consistently held accountable.

So paramilitarism was an idea embraced by just about everyone at the time. The public liked the newly invented, more accountable and competent police. Politicians favored the removal of police from the political mix—a sometimes uncontrollable variable in the world of politics was gone. Police administrators liked the new-found control they had over their charges. And, finally, police officers grew to appreciate their increased paychecks and the increased status that became theirs as time went on. While we look back today and consider that these changes did not usher in a genuinely "professional" era (see Chapter Fifteen), the roots of the professionalization movement had taken hold.

Paramilitaristic policing did away with rampant corruption. But there are additional positive and utilitarian reasons for students of the police to embrace this mode of organizing and administering.

THE USES OF PARAMILITARISM

The logical reasons for paramilitarism begin with the most obvious one. A paramilitaristic focus begins with putting police in uniforms, and this is important for several reasons. First, uniforming the police allows citizens to identify police officers *before* they take action—when they need them. If the police are to be helpful to the citizenry, then any citizen should be able to identify a police officer when he or she sees one. Second, uniforming the police is important so that police can be identified *when* they take action. Only if police are designated by uniform can they demand cooperation from citizens—and sanction citizens when their lawful orders are resisted. If the police dressed in plain clothes, then a citizen that delays or obstructs officers could not fairly be held accountable for resisting their lawful efforts. In other words, if the police are not identifiable, then citizens can argue they "didn't know it was the police" if charged with resisting arrest, for example.

The third reason for placing police in uniform has to do with our American tradition of **limited government** (Locke). Americans do not, by and large, embrace the idea that the police—being powerful agents of the government as they are—should operate amongst us in plain clothes as "spies" of sorts. The ongoing undercover operations of the Drug War aside for a moment, our tradition of limiting the power of government creates in Americans an antipathy to having the police working around us without our knowing who they are. We are repelled by the idea of having governmental "secret agents" on the streets unbeknownst to the public. Long ago, the French had an experience with such plain clothes police officers, and it was one of the reasons that led the French people to revolt and perpetrate the most important revolution in the history of the Western world. So these reasons rationalize the first and most obvious element of paramilitaristic policing—that of putting police on the street in uniforms.

A second set of reasons for paramilitarism has to do with controlling this group of powerful individuals. As noted in our discussion of the Reform Era, the operations of paramilitarism work to keep police officers controlled—to keep them "in line." Uniforms, chains of command, lineups, and military-like ranks all work as behavior control mechanisms. As is true in the military, the trappings of paramilitarism operate to make police officers think they are more accountable than they actually are. Most of police work is done on the beat, alone, without supervision. However, putting this reality aside, uniforms and chains of command make police officers *think* they are constantly being held accountable. It might sound silly and even simplistic, but paramilitarism works; it works both in the military and in police work to instill discipline and (even) a sort of "fear"—the fear of being sanctioned for misconduct or incompetence by one's supervisors—in the hearts and minds of the police.

Third, paramilitarism creates a kind of aloofness. The uniforms and trappings of paramilitarism, the stern **military carriage** of this type of approach and the no-nonsense "I want the facts, Ma'am, only the facts" type of acting this engenders, is positive in several ways. It makes police less prone to operate with favoritism. It makes their decisions more objective. It also tends to make police decisions more "correct" in a legal sense. Removed from the public in a military-like way, the police tend to make decisions that are more legitimate in all of these ways. We must remember that paramilitarism was ushered in to deal with the rampant corruption of the Political Era, and this is one reason for its continuation.

Fourth, paramilitarism intimidates. Many people rail against this sort of intimidation, but putting a group of individuals in like uniforms and having them present to the public with a military-type carriage amplifies the ability of the police to deal with groups when they are outnumbered. As Muir tells us when discussing the paradox of face (Chapter Five), when this intimidation factor is in place—when the police maintain this type of "nasty" façade—the police are not often called upon to *prove* their nastiness (Muir). Uniforms, ranks, insignia, and a martial carriage all work to control people in a way that seldom requires the police to use force.

Fifth, as is true in the military, this type of approach tends to instill in the individual officer an *esprit de corps*. The discipline inherent inculcates the police officer corps with a level of commitment similar to that of the military. This spirit not only reinforces some of the positive dynamics discussed above—legal correctness and control over corrupt tendencies—it also instills in people an intense feeling of duty: a duty to the corps and its mission. This can be critical in police work.

BOX 8.3

THE POWER OF "DUTY"

Under fire, soldiers and sailors will risk their lives to save wounded comrades. In fact, they will even risk their lives to retrieve the bodies of dead comrades. Such is the power a feeling of duty has over people in combat. In police work, officers will go into hot details—alone and without any chance of cover arriving soon—because of the same dynamic—they believe it is their duty. Paramilitarism helps create in the individual officer the sense of duty that drives this type of heroism.

The ability of a sense of duty to control people's behavior is incredibly powerful. People will charge into certain death to live up to their duty. People who study military history often address how this works. The chronicles of war are replete with examples of men entering situations of almost certain death to fulfill their duty. Under such circumstances, the power of duty outweighs the fear of death. Put another way, in combat, the most important fear that drives soldiers is the fear of failing their comrades—*not* the fear of death. This dynamic is responsible for most of what we call "heroism" in war.

Similarly, the power of duty in police circles also motivates officers to take unusual, even heroic action. The hot detail handled without cover is the classic example. Going into a hostile environment without any backup—into a bar with a known police-hating clientele or a crowd situation involving belligerent gang members, for example—is the type of action police officers will take, driven by a feeling of duty. This is powerful stuff, and it is an important positive that comes out of the paramilitaristic way of policing.

Thus there are good reasons for embracing this approach to policing. So why do so many observers suggest that paramilitarism in policing is a bad thing?

THE ARGUMENT AGAINST PARAMILITARISM

Unfortunately, while there are numerous ways in which police paramilitarism can be rationalized, there are many reasons why it is counterproductive. Tony Jefferson wrote the quintessential book about this counterproductivity entitled *The Case Against Paramilitary Policing* (Jefferson). In it, Jefferson outlines powerful arguments against this form of organization. We will engage some of his arguments here.

In our consideration of why paramilitarism makes logical sense, we noted that it removes police from the citizenry to some extent. This aloofness can be considered a good thing when it generates more objective, fair, and legally correct decisions. However, a negative dynamic can result from this propensity for detachment—it can produce anti-police sentiment among citizens (Balko).

One criticism of paramilitarism that spurred the movement toward Community Oriented Policing (COP) is that the police have worked at being aloof and removed from the public for several generations now. This distance has developed a pronounced "us against them" attitude among police, which is not good for either the citizenry or the interests of justice. So what can function as a positive aspect of paramilitarism, as noted above, can also have negative effects. In Chapter Ten, we will examine in depth the COP movement and discover the operation of a cyclical reality: paramilitarism developed to combat negative aspects of the Political Era—namely corruption—but now, several generations later, facets of this initially positive approach are a detriment to modern policing.

A second drawback that parallels the above involves the intimidation factor (Kraska and Kappeler). Militaristic uniforms and carriage work to create an effective deterrent, a look and feel that coerces people, especially groups of people. Paramilitarism can foster a brutal reputation that does not often have to be proven. But the intimidating nature of paramilitarism creates more distance between police and citizenry, and people often resent this dynamic. Across the country, both internal and external police review systems receive thousands of complaints every year wherein citizens object to police officers acting like an occupying army. Often heard is the suggestion that police officers behave "like the Gestapo" or "Nazi storm troopers."

A third criticism involves the propensity for chain-of-command–type management to induce rigid, mindless deference to authority. That is, when following orders that descend a chain of command, officers are inhibited from thinking things through on their own. We are in the midst of an era of policing involving serious attempts to change this way of thinking—or non-thinking, to be more precise. Modern, contemporary police officers are encouraged to think of themselves as agents of change, capable of engaging crime in a proactive manner. They are encouraged to utilize their intelligence and education to become thinking and creative individuals who operate as "criminologists in uniform" on the streets. They are motivated to problem solve on a regular basis, attempting to discern patterns of deviant behavior and ongoing community problems that require thoughtful, enlightened solutions in lieu of knee-jerk, reactionary responses.

Observing chains of command—following orders without question that come down from higher up—is antithetical to these contemporary developments. This type of military thinking might be essential on a battlefield, where lives can be lost if people question orders. But it has no place on the modern American police beat where officers are sufficiently educated, intelligent, and well-trained to operate independently. COP in particular requires that today's police officer analyze problems utilizing not only the above (intelligence, education, and training) but, in addition, pragmatic experience. In other words, the modern officer has the ability to use specific knowledge garnered on a beat, to combine it with expertise gained through today's extended educational and training systems, and make a genuine difference in the administration of justice. Following the orders of those who do not possess this type of beat-specific knowledge is counterproductive and irrational.

BOX 8.4

"WARS" ON CRIME AND DRUGS

For there to be a "war" there has to be an "enemy." Who is the enemy in the War on Crime? In the War on Drugs? Is it everyone who has broken the law—are they all "criminals"? Is it everyone who has used illegal drugs—are they all "drug users?" If so, then any number of studies indicate that the size of the enemy force is somewhere well above 70,000,000. That's the number of people who have, at one time or another, used illegal drugs. Add to that everyone who has ever stolen anything, been drunk behind the wheel, or imbibed alcohol under the age of 21 . . . and we have an indication of how large the enemy "armies" are in these "wars."

Criticism four: in creating a paramilitary model that keeps the police aloof from the public, working in a metaphorical mode "fighting" a **War on Crime** and a **War on Drugs**, large numbers of the American public become the enemy. No good can come from such a paradigm. The war viewpoint, which is implicit in paramilitarism, is completely inappropriate for the process of policing under normal circumstances. As noted in Box 8.4, creating an enemy out of the public in general is diametrically opposed to what modern policing is supposed to be about.

In the military, during any war fought against any foe, one of the goals of basic training is **dehumanizing the enemy**. This is done so that the soldier will be able to kill when required. Racial epithets are often used, when there is a racial component to a war, so as to facilitate this process. This is a time-honored tradition in all militaries. In American history, during World War II in the war in the Pacific, the enemy became "Nips" and "Japs." During the Vietnam War, the enemy became "Dinks" and "Gooks." In today's ongoing wars against largely Muslim antagonists, the enemy has become "Towelheads" and "Cameljockeys." Again, this is a logical dynamic utilized by the military (all militaries, not just the American military) to dehumanize an enemy and create a situation wherein killing becomes acceptable—because those who are killed are "not exactly human beings."

Similar dehumanization sometimes occurs in police work (Crank). The public can become "the assholes." Prisoners in county jails (policed by Deputy Sheriffs) can become "the animals." Even racial epithets are sometimes heard in the contemporary police world, despite several generations' worth of progress in limiting such bigotry. To make generalizations—to refer to people in generic, slanderous terms—is to create an additional level of separation between police and citizenry. So we have both the police subculture (as noted in Chapter 7) and the paramilitaristic paradigm upon which departments are organized exacerbating the harmful consequences produced by the aloofness, the "us against them" mindset of police toward the public (Fletcher).

A fifth criticism has to do with the creation of an *esprit de* corps amongst the police. For a police *esprit de corps* can work in both positive and negative ways. As noted above, it can motivate individual officers to accomplish brave and even genuinely heroic deeds on occasion, But equally, sometimes it can motivate noble cause corruption, or other suspect behavior, "in the name of the corps" (Pound and Christenson). We will engage this reality in depth later in Chapter Thirteen.

Finally, there is one additional, classic problem with the paramilitary approach. Such military-type thinking can emphasize "looking professional" to the extreme (T. Adams). It can focus upon haircuts and shoe shines in a way that demeans the job of sergeants—making a part of their job as leaders the enforcement of somewhat trivial **grooming regulations**. It can produce in the locker room a concern for such trivialities. Telling grown men and women how they should tend to their personal hygiene is rather bizarre. We will discuss this dynamic further when we engage ideas on how to soften the paramilitary focus and change it in a positive direction.

Jefferson's work details more reasons to reject paramilitarism, but he had an entire book, and we have but a section. So we will end here by noting that there are numerous logical objections to paramilitarism and that these objections are particularly important when seen in the light of the movement to create a more community-friendly type of policing in America.

It is now time to swing the pendulum back. We began this chapter listing the logically defensible reasons for paramilitarism. We then moved on to critique it. Now, once again, we will discuss the circumstances under which—even in the light of the above criticisms—paramilitarism is necessary.

THE NEED FOR AN "ARMY"

Having enumerated the case against paramilitarism in America, we must at this time engage the central paradox of its operations: while paramilitarism is "bad" almost all of the time, there are circumstances under which it is absolutely necessary. The police must morph into a military force whenever certain situations present themselves. Police work is odd in this regard. The police are, to some extent, uniformed social workers when they are out on the street. They are involved in serving their communities in numerous ways, and—as we have taken some trouble to point out—their image and the job they do suffers from the drawbacks of paramilitarism. Yet when a particular type of call comes in, the police must change into an organization that operates in a military fashion.

What specific circumstances are these? When must the police become an army? While only occurring on rare occasions, the police can be confronted with hostage situations (Thompson). Or faced with snipers (Jones). Or they can get into prolonged shoot-outs. Or be required to serve high-risk warrants (Lonsdale). Infrequent as they may be, such circumstances call for a type of police organization—the paramilitary type—that is unimportant under normal conditions.

BOX 8.5

THE UTILITY OF S.W.A.T.

Specials Weapons And Tactics (S.W.A.T.) squads are considered troublesome in some jurisdictions where local politics operate to deny the police this type of training. This political reality usually prevails because people are unhappy with paramilitarism. But paradoxically, S.W.A.T. training can, indirectly, help lessen the impact of paramilitarism. If the police have a specially trained group of officers who are particularly effective at dealing with the sort of policing situations that demand a militaristic response—listed in this section—then the rest of a department is freed up, to some extent, to operate in a more communal, responsive, and empathetic manner.

When responding to such events, the police are required to morph into military mode. Guns come out. People might end up being shot (or shot at). And, thus, "who gave the order to fire" and "under what circumstances was that order given" become critical questions. When these types of circumstances present themselves, there are often subsequent Boards of Inquiry or external investigations that look into how the police handled themselves. Especially when people end up being hurt or killed—citizens *or* police officers—someone needs to be held accountable for police conduct. So chains of command and military-type control over "combat" situations is necessary because they can provide this accountability.

Riots constitute the other unusual situation under which the police must be militaristic. Riot squads may be called, guns and batons and teargas may be used against citizens, and police tactics need to be organized in a way that allows for accountability afterwards. Fixed responsibility—the sort demanded in the military—is necessary under such circumstances in a way not required at any other time in the normal conduct of police work.

So once again, the central paradox involved in paramilitarism is that while this way of organizing the police is counterproductive *almost* all of the time, it is absolutely necessary *some* of the time.

SOFTENING PARAMILITARISM

If there are so many reasons to eschew paramilitarism in American police work and, at the same time—paradoxically—so many justifications for it, then what can be done? How might the job of policing be accomplished in an effective way while softening the trappings and negative aspects of paramilitarism?

To begin with, academy training could deemphasize martial attitudes and approaches. There is no particular reason academy classrooms need function like boot camps. In many places, to ask a question in an academy classroom, a cadet

BOX 8.6

WHY STILL FOCUS UPON "HAIRCUTS AND SHOE SHINES?"

Why do we still have the "traditional" emphasis upon shining your shoes, polishing your brass, and getting your hair cut in today's policing? Why would we want to have leaders who ought to be concerned with justice and equity and a dozen other genuinely important matters focusing upon this type of trivia? Is it not possible, in the modern era of policing, that sergeants and other police administrators could trust officers to be responsible for looking presentable on their own? Is it really true that we trust them to carry weapons but not to manage their own appearance?

must raise his or her hand, stand at attention by their desk, and announce themselves, "Sir, Cadet Smith, Sir," before asking a question. Many students are reticent in classrooms, reluctant to speak or ask questions in front of large groups. Having this type of militaristic procedure in place in the academy classroom can further discourage participation, and to inhibit asking questions is to inhibit learning. (We will engage police academies directly in Chapter Eleven.)

Furthermore, paramilitarism places the entire academy enterprise on a warlike footing. It emphasizes exactly the wrong things. It sets the young police officer up to experience—indeed, to cause—all the drawbacks of paramilitarism we have discussed. It puts the entire learning process in jeopardy. If we are to proceed with the development of genuine professionalism in American policing (engaged further in Chapter Fifteen), then the entire endeavor of police academy training should (and, many would argue, must) be changed to resemble traditional college learning.

The police uniform might also be changed. Why is it necessary to have such a military-like outfit? If the public is to view the police as members of the community, then why do we continue with the occupying-army look? Is it not possible to have effective policing done by people dressed in a more "civilian" mode—as long as their outfits, blazers for example, are identifiable? Why is it that F.B.I. Agents can police effectively dressed in dark suits or pants suits (for women)? Is it impossible for us to imagine police officers dressed in this way?

As suggested in Box 8.6, might we do away with old-fashioned grooming regulations? Understanding that police officers are licensed both to use force and take away the freedom of citizens, is it not possible to trust them with the responsibility of keeping their appearance neat, tidy, and presentable? Given all of the dynamics of police work that truly must be considered important, is it not today, finally, time to do away with outdated personal grooming regulations inappropriate for our times? Can we not envision, for example, a police officer with a neatly trimmed beard doing the job effectively? In today's world, judges and attorneys wear beards. So do some Probation Officers and Parole Officers. So do Senators, Congressmen, and Supreme Court Justices. Why not the police? In several jurisdictions, these old-time grooming regulations *have* been done away with. And nothing detrimental has occurred to indicate that this is not a reasonable idea.

It seems logical that the only grooming regulations that might be appropriate in today's world would be regulations relating to officer safety. It might make sense to mandate that officers have hair that is not long enough to be used against them in a fight—by allowing an adversary to swing them around by hair on their heads or in a long beard, for example. But aside from that, grooming regulations appear outdated, illogical, and trivial to the extreme. Why not effect changes designed to make police more civilian-like in their demeanor and appearance? While some legal limitations operate to support police administrations that want to maintain such rules (Silver), these reasons have moved at least some administrators to rethink grooming regulations.

How about chains of command? Is it still necessary for the police to employ military chains of command and insignia? Some have suggested that in modern police work, only three levels of differentiation are now necessary. Modern police tasks can effectively be divided into the top level of administration (the executives), middle management, and the lower level, on-the-street police (Stamper). Why not label upper management with an appropriate designation—"executive administration," for example? Why not label "middle managers" as such? And furthermore, following the F.B.I. example above, why not call beat police "Agents?" These changes are possible and make logical sense. But they would require genuine innovators to implement them. And given the power of the subculture and of tradition, some of these changes might, in the end, prove impossible.

Finally, as noted in Box 8.5, an increased emphasis upon **Special Weapons and Tactics (S.W.A.T.)** training can have an impact here. More S.W.A.T. training would make the police capable of moving into military mode more quickly and efficiently (Snow). In some locations, S.W.A.T. has yet to be embraced. But if S.W.A.T. training were expanded, then the remaining police officers of a given jurisdiction would be free to behave in a less threatening, non-militaristic manner. So in an odd way, S.W.A.T. might very well allow for the minimization of paramilitarism in general.

These are just a few examples of changes modern students of police work have suggested to minimize the paramilitaristic focus of the police. Such suggestions are made in an effort to develop a more community-friendly, less threatening, less aggressive façade for the police. Some of these ideas are more realistic than others, given the difficulty of changing powerful subcultural values. But some warrant serious consideration.

One of the principal paradoxes of police work involves the uniforms and carriage of paramilitaristic police officers. The intelligent officer has to understand that the uniform *is* utilitarian in that it identifies police and helps them

BOX 8.7

THE POWER OF TRADITION

Our suggestions herein about "softening" the image of the police—about changes that might impact in a positive way upon the numerous drawbacks of paramilitarism—may be perfectly logical and echoed by other students of the police. But what do citizens think about this? Is the general public ready for a softer police image?

One particular idea presented in this discussion—outfitting police in less militaristic uniforms—has already been attempted in several places. The police have adopted blazers and dressed much like F.B.I. Agents. And it turned out the public did not warm to the idea. People wanted the police to look "like normal police officers" and the experiment was abandoned. People were so used to a military look from the police that this tradition in American policing was something they wanted to keep.

deter violence. On the other hand, the police must also understand that this paramilitaristic "nastiness" (Muir) is resented by many people. Quite often, it creates greater enmity between citizen and police officer than already exists due to other dynamics. As we shall see in subsequent chapters, one of the reasons for the movement toward COP in America has been a recent negative reaction to the intimidating nature of paramilitarism.

SUMMATION

The paradox of paramilitarism puts police officers and police leaders in a bind. If police organization is going to be accomplished in a logical and effective manner, the police must attempt to avoid paramilitarism as much as they can. This is essential to bridge the gap between citizen and police officer in the modern, professional era of police work. The distance paramilitarism creates between the two is unfortunate and counterproductive to the interests of both communities and justice. However, and this is what prohibits an easy solution, paramilitarism is absolutely essential at certain times and under certain circumstances. The only way to handle riots, hostage situations, high-risk warrant service, and snipers is in a military mode.

So the paradox here is that 99 percent of the time paramilitarism is a bad thing, while 1 percent of the time it is an absolutely essential element in how police organizations must operate. This paradox makes police training troublesome. It makes being a supervisor difficult. And it makes the development of police strategies, short term and long term, complicated and frustrating.

CHAPTER EIGHT PARADOX BOX

Many of the dynamics associated with paramilitaristic policing are negative and should be avoided if at all possible. The overwhelming majority of the time, paramilitarism is neither necessary nor desirable. However, on limited occasions the police must act as an army, in an effective and efficient military manner.

The next two chapters explore four different styles of organizing police systems. We will begin in Chapter Nine with a discussion of the three classic styles of police organization that have been in place for generations now. Following that discussion, in Chapter Ten, we will engage COP, a relatively new philosophy that in many places has taken police work in America in a new direction. It is adding a fourth style of policing to the panoply of police options.

DISCUSSION QUESTIONS

1. Our discussion has taken great pains to illustrate the drawbacks of paramilitary policing. But what about its pluses? There are numerous positive dynamics that come from such operational norms. What are they? Discuss the pluses of paramilitarism in police organizations.

2. In Box 8.4, we suggest that the War on Crime and War on Drugs metaphors are troublesome. To have a war one must have an enemy. Discuss who the enemy is in these wars. How many American citizens are encompassed by the group of "criminals" who have broken one law or another? With regard to underage drinking and marijuana use in particular, discuss how many "enemies" exist for the police to "war" against. Have you been—at any time in your life—one of the enemies?

3. Almost universally, police departments include grooming regulations in their General Orders. Such regulations can get very specific about length of hair, mustaches, sideburns, and so forth. The suggestion has been made in this chapter that such regulations are silly and even counterproductive. Discuss grooming regulations in the light of the suggestion at the end of the chapter that they be dropped because they are unnecessary. Are they unnecessary? Can they be dropped without any counterproductive consequences for American policing?

4. The central paradox of paramilitaristic policing is that while it is usually unnecessary it can be essential on certain, limited occasions. Discuss what those occasions might be. When is it absolutely necessary for the police to behave like an army? Why?

KEY TERMS

Chain of Command: Military structure developed in order to fix responsibility both up and down the organizational ladder.

Civil Service Tests: Tests developed during the Reform Era to insure objectivity in police selection.

Community Oriented Policing (COP): New philosophy of policing discussed at length in Chapter Ten.

Dehumanizing the "Enemy": The idea that, in order to facilitate and justify dealing with people in harsh and violent ways, the police will dehumanize citizens utilizing a "war-like" mentality, much as is done in the military.

Esprit de Corps: Latin for the "spirit of the body"; refers to the feeling of ardor, courage, or élan of military or police officers as a group.

Grooming Regulations: Regulations in police departmental General Orders that require specific hair length, mustache trimming, sideburn length, etc.

Limited Government: Principle of Western Liberalism that has been written into America's greatest documents and institutions.

Lineup: Police pre-service event that requires officers to stand in line, at attention, for inspection.

Military Carriage: Carrying oneself in a rigid, martial manner.

Paramilitaristic Policing: Style of policing that emphasizes military carriage, ranks, chains-on-command, and control.

Police Academies: Police-officer training bodies invented during the Reform Era for pre-service police training.

Police Accountability: The idea that the police must be held to answer to standards of conduct (see Chapter Thirteen).

Protection Money: Money demanded by the police, usually from businesses, in payment for protection from vandalism and violence—by the police themselves.

Sam Browns: The large, black belts worn by police officers that carry weapons, handcuffs, mace, batons, and so forth.

Special Weapons And Tactics (S.W.A.T.): Special anti-sniper and anti-hostage teams trained by the military with weapons not usually used by the police.

War on Crime: Metaphor in police work that was created during the Reform Era.

War on Drugs: Metaphor in police work first coined by President Nixon in the late '60s and then re-coined by President Reagan in the '80s.

ADDITIONAL READING

Many of the most important arguments presented in this chapter suggesting that there are severe limitations to the paramilitaristic organization of the police come from *The Case Against Paramilitary Policing* by Tony Jefferson (Open University Press, 1990). This has been a widely read and well received work since its publication. Jefferson was the first to make what now seem to be obvious criticisms of the paramilitary focus, and his arguments have now become mainstream. Academics of all sorts, and even some police administrators, have embraced his initially "racy" suggestions about the negative impact of this kind of policing.

An example of a contemporary police leader who is extremely intelligent, highly educated (Ph.D. from Harvard), and a lifelong police officer is Norm Stamper, former Assistant Chief of Police in San Diego and Chief of Police in Seattle. Stamper, in his book *Breaking Rank: A Top Cop's Expose of the Dark Side of American Policing* (National Books, 2006), speaks for a steadily increasing number of practitioners and administrators in today's policing circles who eschew paramilitarism and call for a "softening" of the police and their image.

Other criticisms of paramilitarism come in Radley Balko's *The Rise of Paramilitary Police Raids in America* (Cato Institute, 2006) and in an article written by two very famous criminologists: "Militarizing American Police: The Rise and Normalization of Paramilitary Units" by Peter Kraska and Victor E. Kappeler (in *Social Problems*, Volume 44, Number 1, February 1997). In "Plugging the Security Gap or Springing a Leak: Questioning the Growth of Paramilitary Policing in U.S. Domestic and Foreign Policy" (in *Democracy and Security*, Volume 3, Issue 3, September 2007), Stephen M. Hill, Randall R. Beger, and John M. Zanettill analyze the genuinely counterproductive dynamics of paramilitarism as they relate to national security. This work attacks the logic that creating a more militaristic domestic police force in America is good for anti-terrorism efforts.

Our discussion notes the paradoxical reality that there are several sorts of police details that, in fact, do require paramilitaristic organization. Examples of how practitioners in the field approach them are found in *SWAT Sniper: Deployment and Control* by Tony L. Jones (Paladin Press, 1995), *Hostage Rescue Manual* (Greenhill Books, 2006) by Leroy Thompson, and *Raids: A Tactical Guide to High Risk Warrant Service* by Mark V. Lonsdale (*Specialized Tactical Training Unit*, 2005).

In the last section of the chapter, we made several suggestions for moving away from paramilitarism. Included in this discussion was the idea that grooming regulations should be done away with. In *Public Employee Discharge and Discipline* (Aspen Publishers, 2001), Isidore Silver shows that due to existing case law this is next to impossible unless municipalities, police departments, and politicians all agree to it. Finally, the utility of S.W.A.T. is outlined in *SWAT Teams: Explosive Face-offs with America's Deadliest Criminals* by Robert L. Snow (DaCapo Press, 1999).

CHAPTER 9

Three Traditional Styles of Police Organization

One mistake often made by police administration textbooks is that they operate under an incorrect assumption: they discuss administering the police as if there is only one style or type of police organization. Some "how to manage the police" books avoid engaging in any discussion about what would appear to be obvious from the start—that policing is done in different ways in different places and there are, therefore, numerous ways to organize the police. A generation ago, the political scientist James Q. Wilson did a now-famous study of various police departments wherein he came up with a three-fold categorization of styles of police organization (Wilson). It is this categorization—now considered to be "the classic" differentiation in the field—that we will engage in this chapter.

Before we proceed, an important note is in order. These three are not the only styles of police organization in contemporary America. In the next chapter, we will engage a new philosophy—that of Community Oriented Policing (COP)—that is now offering a fourth way of administering the police endeavor. COP is not just *a* change—it is *the* critical change in today's American police circles. It has implications for the hiring process, training methods, patterns of leadership, and police accountability. COP is considered by many to have opened a new door in American policing: the door to a genuinely "**professional**" **era** (Lyman 56).

But before we move to consider this new philosophy and style, we will discuss the three classic styles. COP is new and has not yet become institutionalized in most places. It has not existed long enough to know how implementable or effective it will be. And there is something else. We need to give Wilson's configuration its due because the overwhelming majority of police departments in America cleave to one of his styles. COP is, to some extent, "all the rage" now in American policing. But while almost every department *talks* about its community orientation, most of the time this is merely window dressing; the community style is growing, to be sure, but even where administrators have made a sincere effort to install its philosophy, it has not yet taken hold in the subculture. Thus, in many places, COP is an ideal but not a reality. Real police work, almost everywhere, is in fact accomplished in an organization structure based upon one of the three styles outlined by Wilson.

PRELIMINARY DEFINITIONS

Wilson observed numerous police departments and came to the conclusion that there was a difference in approach among American police organizations. He posited that the differentiation between the three classic styles of policing paralleled discussions of the three sets of goals and functions of the police. That is, each of the three styles emphasized a different goal and function set. What he termed "**Watchman style policing**" emphasized order maintenance (Wilson 140). What he termed "**Legalistic style policing**" emphasized law enforcement (Wilson 172). And "**Service style policing**," of course, emphasized service (Wilson 200).

It was not long before Wilson's observations were accepted by not only academics who studied the police but by police administrators themselves. His configuration presented great utility to those attempting to make sense of a hodge podge of police systems. At the time, when the study of police by social scientists was still in its infancy, Wilson's work did more than suggest a schematic for the study. Along with numerous other scholars—among them Skolnick and, later, Muir—Wilson pioneered the serious study of the police experience and of police administration. Part of the movement toward a genuine professionalism in American policing was spawned by these social scientists and their scientific methods of analysis.

Order maintenance is the primary focus of the Watchman style of policing. The Watchman metaphor was chosen because, under its auspices, the police tend to sit back, watch, and, in a reactive way, respond to disorderly conduct when necessary. This style is analogous in some ways to **19th Century policing** (S. Walker, Critical History). Back then, policing was reactive and unobtrusive. The Watchman style involves a placid—almost pacific—method of policing. This style is representative of the American tradition of limited government. It is often said in American political philosophy: "that government governs best which governs least." It might equally be said of the Watchman style: "that police force polices best that polices least."

Law enforcement is the primary focus of the Legalistic style. The driving force behind policing in such organizations is the understanding that as functionaries in the legal system, it is the central function of the police to apply the law. In every situation, no matter how apparently minor in nature, the police attempt to ascertain whether or not there is a legal question at issue. If there is no legal

BOX 9.1

THE POLICE DEPARTMENT AS SOCIAL WELFARE ORGANIZATION

Policing in the 19th Century bore no resemblance to that of later years. There was little in the way of competence among personnel and, equally, there was little respect for the police among the citizenry. Accountability was virtually absent, and the police were largely ineffective at stemming the tide of increasing crime. But one difference from the 19th Century is interesting and unusual from our perspective: as Monkkonen discusses in *Police in Urban America, 1860–1920*, the police were a major—in fact *the* major—social welfare institution of the age. The police housed the homeless. The Philadelphia police, for example, housed over 100,000 people per year during the 1880s. They fed the starving, operating soup kitchens for the poor. In the absence of any other governmentally run social institutions, the police provided much sustenance for people during times of economic downturn. It was not until the 20th Century that the police focused upon crime in any realistic way.

question, then the police have little or nothing to do with it. Under the Legalistic style, anything and everything is either fashioned into a legal problem or it tends to be ignored. Non-legal problems and situations are considered the business of other agencies and institutions by legalistic police officers and organizations.

The Service style, as one might imagine, emphasizes service to the community. Operational only in suburban and rural areas, police departments driven by the Service style have the time to prioritize providing services—some of which are unknown in Watchman- and Legalistic-style departments. The Service style officer is much more prone to intervene in the lives of people and take legal action, than is the Watchman style officer. On the other hand, the Service style officer is less prone to intervene and take legal action than is the Legalistic officer. The Service style is an overtly public relations–oriented way of approaching police work.

Let us turn to a much more in-depth consideration of each style. As we move through this analysis, we will first present the central tenets of each style. Then we will critique them, one at a time, examining the strengths and weaknesses of each.

Watchman Style

The Watchman style emphasizes order maintenance. That is to say, the priority of police organizations utilizing this particular style is to maintain order. The police operating under the Watchman style answer calls for service, but do not tend to maintain a proactive operational norm. It is a passive style, organized under the assumption that the best policing impacts the lives of citizens the least. If at all possible, the Watchman style officer maintains order by staying out of the lives of citizens, by being invisible in some sense, and by allowing life to occur without police interference.

In some ways, the Watchman style resembles 19th Century policing. During that century, before the Reform Era, policing was not law-enforcement oriented. There was no War on Crime mentality in American policing. And it was long before the War on Drugs. Actually, since drugs were legal until the passage of the **Harrison Act (1914)** (Musto), any notion of a War on Drugs would have been considered bizarre during the 19th Century, to say the least. The police in the 1800s operated long before the creation of expectations that the government would have a proactive impact upon the life of the average person. Only after the institutionalization of the Progressive Era of American politics instilled expectations that governments, at every level, would strive to positively impact the lives of citizens would policing become a more proactive endeavor.

The Watchman style of policing ignores many common, minor violations—especially traffic infractions and juvenile offenses. Given that maintaining order on the street is the focus, motorists and juveniles might receive warnings or speechifying on a regular basis in lieu of citation and arrest. Motorists and juveniles are only engaged by the power of the police and the machinations of the law when their behavior is considered genuinely dangerous. If no threat to the peace, safety, or order of the community is perceived, then the police take no action. Under the Watchman style, the police are neither trained at the outset, nor are they motivated in any ongoing way, to enforce the law. Unless events on the street threaten peace, safety, and order, the police are reactive. They sit back, in essence, and await citizen calls for their services.

It sounds odd to people who live where policing is done differently, but under the Watchman style even a certain amount of vice crimes are ignored or, put differently, not prioritized. Gambling in particular tends to be considered unimportant by the police. Drinking is considered merely a part of everyday life. Even public drunkenness, if it doesn't involve a genuine threat to public order, is allowed. Certain prostitution—the kind not plied on the street corner (and so not troublesome in a public-relations sense)—is downplayed. All of these activities are considered "personal," in a way, and not the business of the police.

Watchman style policing classifies disputes between citizens as "private." Instead of translating disputes into legalistic terms, the **police** act as **referees**, making sure disputes are kept reasonably civil and do not upset a community's peace and quiet. Make no mistake, serious crime is taken seriously—the Watchman style officer will react immediately to violence and felonious behavior. But in general, this is reactive policing to the extreme.

In Watchman styles organizations, the police do not emphasize arrests and citations. Statistics are kept, to be sure, but they are not considered overly important or focused upon. Police officers hoping for advancement do not rack up lots of arrests, because this does not facilitate promotion in a Watchman style organization. Attempts to ascertain who is doing the best job of policing, and therefore who deserves choice assignments or promotion, are not predicated upon numbers of arrests. Other criteria, such as seniority and loyalty, tend to be emphasized when such evaluations are conducted in a Watchman organization.

Because neither acting in a proactive manner nor attempting to turn details into legal issues is prioritized, Watchman style policing involves giving a tremendous amount of latitude to the police. This means that discretionary decision-making power is exercised in the direction of *not* taking action, allowing the citizenry a great deal of leeway, and often avoiding the specific dictates of the law. As is the case with all three styles of policing discussed herein, Watchman style policing has its pluses and its minuses. Let us consider them in that order.

Advantages of the Watchman Style: To begin with, as noted earlier, a style of policing that involves limited police intrusion fits well under the general political principal of limited government. The Watchman watches and waits. Watchman style officers eschew the option of arrest whenever possible, and they allow a great deal of citizen self-determination to rule on the streets. The Watchman is not interested in interfering with the ongoing exercise of individual freedom that has always been emblematic of America. In a country that values the ideal of individual freedom as much as ours does, the Watchman style can be seen to focus appropriately upon allowing as much individual liberty as possible to the average citizen.

Because of this general operational principle, and because they seldom upset citizens by making arrests and utilizing force, Watchman style officers receive a limited number of **citizen's complaints** (see Chapter Thirteen). Citizens, by and large, do not tend to complain because there is little to complain about. The potentially adversarial relationship that the police often have with the public is handled by withdrawal. On a regular basis, the Watchman style police follow the path of least resistance. This works to dampen the propensity toward citizen-police antipathy that the role of the police can sometimes engender.

Thus, under a Watchman style, not only are there few citizen's complaints, but there are better police-community relations than often develop in contemporary times. The police are not often considered to be the enemy. In fact, when life in any given neighborhood operates in a reasonably peaceful way, the police are invisible.

The amount of latitude given to the police allows them *not* to take action as a part of their regular working personalities. In major cities, where there are large ethnic enclaves, this freedom of inaction can lead the police to allow a great deal of latitude to minorities in the name of being "sensitive to cultural differences." This concept is called "**cultural relativity**" by sociologists and cultural anthropologists (Geertz). Thus, Black on Black crime or Asian on Asian crime can be ignored as a "part of their culture." This leads, in turn, to few complaints from ethnic minorities—few complaints about racism. The argument can be made that Watchman style policing allows for ethnic variety in a way that provides many Americans with an optimum level of cultural diversity.

Another advantage develops from the Watchman style. If the police refrain from making arrests on a regular basis, then taxpayers are saved a great deal of money. Arrests mean expenses: for police work, jails, courts, probation and parole, and so on. A type of policing that generates little in the way of arrest statistics also generates little in the way of expenses at the local and state levels for the criminal justice system.

Finally, Dirty Harry does not tend to reside within the subculture of the Watchman style police organization. When no premium is placed upon arresting citizens, and a great deal of emphasis is placed upon allowing certain types of crimes to go unpunished, the police officer operating under a Watchman style regime does not tend to be motivated to operate in a way that involves noble cause corruption. Nothing within the administrative operation, nor anything within the type of subcultural norms that develop under this style, moves police officers to take the job of ridding the streets of bad actors so seriously that they will fall into Dirty Harry–like behavior. The Watchman, in other words, does not believe that taking aggressive police action is a noble cause.

Drawbacks to the Watchman Style: In critiquing the Watchman style, the first idea that comes to mind is that this style allows so much latitude to citizens that it almost encourages criminals. Not only with regard to crimes that Watchman style officers ignore, but with respect to crime in general, this style emphasizes police inaction to such an extent that they can be considered ineffectual at deterring crime. Even worse, police "not doing their jobs" can be considered a "cause" of crime from this perspective. The Watchman style's strengths aside, this way of prioritizing police *in*activity can encourage deviant behavior in general, embolden the individual criminal, and even allow gangs to take over the streets of America.

Second, by allowing so much latitude to the police, the Watchman style is indirectly responsible for the construction of different sets of rules in different parts of a town or city. With so much freedom to interpret the law, unfettered by an organizational structure to require the uniform application of the law, the police can create as many different penal codes as there are police officers. In a large, diverse city, this can mean quite different sets of rules, styles of policing, and, in turn, lifestyles in different parts of the city. This differentiation of the law can lead to confusion, unfairness, and a cynicism about the law in the minds of the public.

We noted in Chapter Two that in exercising discretionary decision-making powers the police define the law on the streets. In doing so, they can either create a better, more humane legal system—one that empathizes with individual citizens and allows for the development of justice in a fair manner—or they can create a system driven by prejudice. Here we turn a "strong point" of the Watchman style system (as noted above) into one of its weaknesses. Deferring to cultural differences can work in both a positive and negative manner. As Dr. King noted (see Box 9.2), when police do not do their jobs in the inner city it can add to the misery and hopelessness of ethnic minority populations. It does not matter

BOX 9.2

A DIFFERENT SORT OF RACISM

In an interview not long before his death, Dr. Martin Luther King, Jr., was asked by a young reporter to comment upon the amount of "police brutality" that Blacks suffered at the hands of White police in Black neighborhoods. Dr. King shocked the young man, to some extent, with his response. He began his comment by saying that the biggest problem with the White police in Black neighborhoods was not police brutality. He suggested that the most significant problem was that they didn't do their jobs there. Because the latitude they enjoyed allowed them to be inactive in the inner city, Black people were not afforded the protection from crime and criminals that they should have been. This type of dynamic is a standard operational norm in Watchman style organizations.

(Berkley)

why police inactivity occurs—in deference to ethnic diversity, for example—it only matters *that* the police are not doing their jobs. The effect upon the citizenry and justice is clear.

Finally, when we combine several operational dynamics of the Watchman style we come up with a particularly disconcerting reality. This style encourages the police to exercise a great deal of discretion. At the same time, it ignores a certain amount of crime—in particular, vice-related crime. Also, the Watchman style places no premium on proactivity; police officers are not rewarded for making a lot of arrests and, so, they tend not to do so. Taken together, these three realities almost invariably create an unfortunate dynamic. They encourage police corruption. It is a type we call "**corruption of authority**" (Perez and Moore), and it tends to be present, in one form or another, when Watchman style policing is in effect.

This form of corruption almost always accompanies **victimless crime** (O'Donnell). When there are no complaining parties present, as is usually the case with illegal gambling, prostitution, or drug sales cases (where there are no "victims" per se), and the police are allowed the freedom of inaction that the Watchman style provides, the system is almost "asking" for the police—some of them at least—to take payoffs from illegal gambling operations, pimps, drug dealers, and so forth. Thus the Watchman style tends to manufacture police misconduct.

Having dealt with the Watchman style's rather lackadaisical form of policing, we now turn to Wilson's Legalistic style, a form of policing in many ways diametrically opposed to the Watchman style.

Legalistic Style

In the Legalistic style, common situations are seen as law-enforcement oriented. Since the application of the law is paramount in the minds of Legalistic officers, even minor altercations between citizens are couched in legal terms. Family fights and neighborhood problems, such as barking dogs and loud parties, are considered to present legal issues. Law enforcement is so highly prioritized that other functions, involving service to the community, for example, are only tended to "when time permits." Non-legal functions are not considered substantial elements of the police function (Roberg *et al.*). "Real" police work, in other words, involves the application of the law—everything else is secondary.

Legalistic style officers make a lot of arrests. Not only is this true with regard to major crimes, but it also relates to traffic violations, juvenile problems, and minor crimes. Motorists obtain tickets, youths are taken to Juvenile Hall, and petty criminals are the subject of investigations and arrests. Even such minor offenses as petty theft and vandalism are taken seriously. Public drunkenness and even homelessness are couched in legal terms; drunks are taken to jail or to alcohol treatment centers, and never allowed to remain on the streets; the homeless, while not often arrested, are considered "loiterers" and "indigent persons." They are not ignored but, rather, ushered into shelters or (even) taken to jail. Under the dictates of this style, police discretion is limited. To be a police officer is to make arrests. Judges and juries decide what to do about suspects; the job of the police is to bring people before the bar, not to use their judgment in an indulgent manner. The Legalistic style of officer enforces the law and considers other police functions to be "social work."

In ethnic minority areas, the Legalistic style police do their jobs. Driven by the idea that "there are no excuses," Legalistic policing is not watered down in any way with considerations of diverse cultural values or alternative ethnic lifestyles. The police operate on the streets with a constant, unabashed focus upon being legal actors and utilizing the law as their primary tool. Non-legal, semi-legal, and informal means of solving problems on the street are rejected. This is true everywhere, even in minority neighborhoods, where the Watchman style might avoid dealing with such problems.

The Legalistic style of policing involves a great deal of proactive, energetic behavior on the part of the police. The police are aggressive and tenacious. When between specific details or calls for service, the Legalistic police consider it a top priority to go on what officers label "**fishing expeditions**" (Poteet and Poteet), looking for crime and criminals. The general operational procedure of the Legalistic police is to make lots of vehicle stops, confront groups on the street, make "**public assembly checks (PACs)**" of bars and other hangouts, and generally assert the power of the law.

In Legalistic style police departments, arrests and citations are dispensed on a regular basis. Numbers of arrests are counted and categorized as a part of ascertaining whether or not the department or even the individual officer is doing the job. If "doing the job" is associated with invoking the law and making arrests, then the priorities of the police are clear: the good, effective police officer makes many arrests—if possible, many felony arrests—in a Legalistic department. This is a priority. In every way, making good arrests is rewarded. One of the ways for a police officer to "make it to the top" is to pursue the creation of his or her reputation for aggressiveness and for making arrests. This can even entail focusing upon arrest statistics so much so that Legalistic style officers often know their "arrest totals." They keep track on a regular, ongoing basis.

So the legalistic style is monolithic, to some extent—rather than being diverse and accommodating—and it prioritizes law enforcement to the exclusion of other functions. Citations and arrests are the norm. They are the principle implements of the police, instead of merely tools utilized when other tactics fail. The focus is on making every citizen disagreement and troublesome situation into a legal issue.

Advantages of the Legalistic Style: The Legalistic style may seem rigid and even draconian, especially in light of the passive and reactive nature of the Watchman style. But there are several important advantages to policing in this manner. First, such aggressive policing is assumed to deter crime. Proactive efforts on the part of the police—to become involved in the lives of people on the street, to deter crowd and gang activities, to maintain vigilance over every situation out-of-the-ordinary—all of this works, or it is logical to think that it works, to make criminals leary of their chances at "getting away with anything." Furthermore, it works to make lawful citizens feel more safe and secure. The deterrent impact of Legalistic policing is palpable and one of the strong suits of this style.

A second, critical strength of the Legalistic style is that it works to create and maintain a single standard everywhere. There is one penal code—one set of universally applied rules for the citizenry—in every part of a Legalistic officer's jurisdiction, because the exercise of discretion is limited. So there is **one standard of conduct** for the public. Equally, there is one standard of police conduct, too. Any citizen, anywhere in a jurisdiction, encounters the same behavior from any police officer—because discretionary decision-making is kept to a minimum. In some sense, this is a more just and morally defensible way of having the police behave.

This dynamic works in a positive way with respect to the rule of law. The decisions of the police under the Legalistic style are uniform. They are, therefore, more defensible in a very real sense. The "rule of cop" is eschewed, and this is good news for those who expect equity in the treatment that citizens experience at the hands of the police. Furthermore, the decisions of the police tend to be more *legally* defensible. Officers are more often "correct" in their decisions under the Legalistic style, because they exercise so little in the way of discretionary judgments that their academy training takes over and tends to control their actions.

Finally, the Legalistic style works to inhibit corruption of authority. The style limits police discretion. And it requires the police to challenge all types of crime, even that associated with vice. When the police pursue victimless crimes aggressively, and when their system emphasizes arrests, the dynamics that often generate police corruption are disrupted. This is a critical difference between the Legalistic and Watchman styles of policing. Taken together, there are numerous important arguments in favor of policing in the Legalistic mode.

The Drawbacks to Legalistic Policing: For as much as there are distinctive pluses that can develop out of the Legalistic style, differentiating it from the Watchman mode in several ways noted above, there are also important drawbacks to its operations. No one style of policing has all the answers, and the Legalistic style can produce as many negatives as any other.

First, the criminal justice system can be clogged with cases under a Legalistic regime. The American system is already so inundated with cases and bodies that a new prison opens (on average) every week in this country. In corrections, so many convicts enter the system (at such a rapid rate) that others are released before serving full sentences. Criminologists call this the "revolving door" problem, as noted previously in our discussions. The Watchman style's propensity to ignore crime is juxtaposed to the Legalistic style's propensity to make arrests—and lots of them. Citations and arrests take up police time, jail cells, court time, and attorney time. The criminal justice system as a whole spends much more money on policing in a

Legalistic style than it does to support a Watchman style. Time, money, and costs for jail construction—all of these are consequences of this style. Furthermore, it is easy to make the argument that when the police arrest "everybody," the criminal justice system's time and money will be "wasted" on minor offenses. This can squander the resources needed to focus upon violent, felonious crime.

Second, under the Legalistic system the police are so overly aggressive that they are often perceived as combative, belligerent, and even hostile toward citizens. This is a natural byproduct of a style of policing encouraging officers to be ever-present in the lives of the citizenry. And this leads to citizens' complaints—lots of citizens' complaints (Perez). We must remember that the Legalistic officer cites drivers often, arrests juveniles with regularity, collars people for the most petty of offenses, and generally is involved in stopping motorists and questioning pedestrians in a way that is intrusive. All of these propensities tend to produce citizens' complaints because they create large numbers of civilians unhappy with their local police. Of the four styles of policing we will eventually engage, the Legalistic style draws the most complaints—and by a wide margin.

Third, and tangential to the above point, is the fact that under the Legalistic style the police make many more arrests in ethnic minority areas. An odd dynamic thus unfolds. The police under the Watchman style are given so much latitude that they tend to avoid making arrests in minority areas. They back off and tend toward laziness in the inner city. In a way, we could (perhaps *should*) accuse the Watchman style of encouraging racism by allowing them to normalize certain types of behavior, even criminal behavior, as being endemic to minority populations.

But the Legalistic officer does exactly the opposite: Legalistic policing emphasizes taking action under any and all circumstances and, thus, it often operates aggressively in the inner city, where crime statistics tend to soar. The police therefore make more arrests of minority peoples under the Legalistic style. This creates not only more citizens' complaints—more arrests *always* mean more complaints—but the police are more often accused of racism (see Box 9.3). This is ironic because it

BOX 9.3

CITIZENS' COMPLAINTS IN THE LEGALISTIC STYLE

One drawback to the Legalistic style is that its operations tend to generate a great number of citizens' complaints. This is due to the large numbers of arrests made under this style. It is also because ethnic minorities and juveniles in particular tend to be arrested at a relatively high rate and this produces two types of complaints: complaints about the police being racist and complaints from parents about the police acting in an inappropriately brusque and harsh manner when dealing with children and teens.

could be argued that in the inner city the police are, in fact, doing their jobs in a more appropriate manner under Legalistic policing—more appropriate as defined by none other than Dr. Martin Luther King, Jr.

The Legalistic style of policing is often given credit for minimizing corruption of authority. Fair enough. But the problem with this style is that it tends to encourage noble cause corruption. If a police organization emphasizes arresting citizens, rewards aggressive behavior on the part of police officers, and generally motivates the police to get the job done in a proactive manner, then Dirty Harry-like behavior may very well develop over time. And this tends to be the case.

The Legalistic style might appear in some ways better than the Watchman style on first glance. It seems more professional and mandates police to do their *real* jobs in a more honest and straightforward manner. However, upon reflection, the Legalistic style has significant drawbacks. It is different from the Watchman style—substantially different—but not necessarily better.

This moves us toward the consideration of a policing style found only in some regions, where police have enough time to prioritize service to their communities. The police, in essence, need "spare time" to be genuinely service oriented, and that luxury does not present itself in urban areas—and even in some suburban areas where crime and gang activity have increased dramatically in recent years.

Service Style

Service style policing can only be done effectively in suburban and rural areas. While all police departments will suggest that they are service oriented—often putting the words **"to protect and serve"** on their patrol cars—it is, practically speaking, impossible to accomplish a genuine Service style of policing with the volume of calls in cities that require a specific police response. Urban policing simply involves too much time-consuming activity for city police to perform Service style policing.

In the country, and in most suburbs, the police are not required to jump from call to call throughout their normal shifts. In such locales, there is a substantial amount of time available to police between details—this allows them to execute the Service style. Because of a lack of calls for specific action, the Service style police have the time to take all calls seriously. Calls involving legal issues, the disruption of the social order, and that request specific service—all of these can be treated with importance. The police can be involved with informal intervention, counseling, and protracted conflict resolution. Both order maintenance and law enforcement are a part of the job in the Service style. As noted in the introduction, Service-oriented police have the time—and take the time—to intervene more often than Watchman style officers. And they are far less prone than Legalistic officers to apply sanctions.

Policing in the suburbs and in the country involves operating in homogenous areas. A common definition of order tends to be embraced by citizens in these areas. This homogeneity makes police work easier, to some extent, because

BOX 9.4

THE HOMOGENEITY OF THE SUBURBS

It is no accident that suburban policing is accomplished in an atmosphere known for its homogenous population. For it can be argued that the suburbs were created precisely because people—almost universally White people, millions of them—wanted to live in a place with a common definition of order, to raise their children in an environment where people possessed a homogenous value system, and to avoid the tumult, conflict, and crime of the cities. Sociologists call this mass movement "**white flight**" (Avila)—the desire to get away from the increasingly diverse ethnic realities of American cities. Hence the white picket fence ideal, clean streets, single family homes with a small piece of land to "own," and rows upon rows of houses that look remarkably the same.

there tends to be far less tension between people's various expectations for the police. A common definition of norms and values entails more informal social control exercised by communities over individual citizens. This means less need for policing. In addition, when the police *are* called in such areas, there is a common understanding of what it is they ought to do. None of the strain experienced by urban officers—strain produced by varying expectations and diverse populations—afflicts Service oriented officers. There is, therefore, one uniform standard of conduct operational in Service policing. Service police exercise discretion—to treat people and situations with patience and understanding—in order to infuse justice with fairness. The police always have the time to do so.

Juvenile offences are never ignored; indeed, no calls for service of any kind are ignored. But under a Service orientation, teenagers tend to be treated informally, referred to family courts or handed over to parents when detained for misbehaving themselves. Motorists are always stopped for speeding, since safety on roadways is treated seriously. But quite often, Service officers will leave motorists with a warning or a lecture.

We noted above that serious crime, involving violence or felonies, is treated seriously in any style of policing. But serious crime takes on a particular significance in the Service style. This is because there is little crime to begin with. When, on occasion, the police are confronted with violence or felonious crime, they have the luxury to treat it as a major event. In the city, sometimes police officers have so many calls involving serious crime that they cannot give it the attention it deserves. This is never the case in the Service style.

Service style policing is community-relations oriented. Creating and maintaining good public relations is considered to be the job of everyone in police work, of whatever rank or responsibility. Rather than being reactive to problems that present themselves, the Service police have the time and the luxury to operate in a sort of "out-reach" mode. Furthermore, they have the time to be involved in public speaking to groups and, especially, schools. They can participate in teaching and education—being allowed to do so right on the job, as a part of their working hours. In a real sense, the Service style sees policing as a product to be delivered to the citizenry. The job of policing involves estimating the market and developing the product appropriately.

Finally, Service style police officers are hired and trained with an eye toward accomplishing these various tasks without receiving citizens' complaints. Each and every member of a Service organization is supposed to be an ambassador of the police department. In order to meet these goals in a measured and positive way, Service style organizations were the first to require that officers have college backgrounds as a prerequisite to hiring. While the requirement for college has expanded to all areas of modern police work, it was the Service style that first acknowledged the need for such levels of education.

The Advantages of the Service Style: For obvious reasons, the Service style is largely accepted by the citizenry in the suburbs and the country. This style gets very few citizens' complaints. Its public relations focus often makes for a positive, engaging, cooperative relationship between police and community. As we shall see in the next chapter, the new ideas and ideals of COP are easiest to "sell" to police organizations and subcultures previously Service oriented because of these positive dynamics.

Service style officers are able to handle details informally if required in the best interests of justice. They have time and latitude to do so. They can be aggressive if required—it seldom *is* required, but the capability exists. They can respond to not just community leaders but individual citizens. They have the time and are encouraged to do so.

The education levels of Service officers, combined with the luxury of time within which they work, makes this an almost idyllic type of policing. There are many advantages to it and, as we shall see, precious few disadvantages. The problem, of course, is that the wealth of time available to the police and the homogeneous community factor can only be replicated in communities with a great deal of **social solidarity** and a low level of deviance.

The Drawbacks to Service Style Policing: The drawbacks to Service style policing are few. Since the police are responsive—almost overly responsive, if viewed from the perspective of Legalistic officers—to community concerns and values, the police enjoy almost a honeymoon type of relationship with the public. They almost universally live in the areas they police. And this makes for an implicit agreement between citizen and police officer about local values and what police should prioritize. As a result, the police tend to be controlled locally, both formally and informally. They resent this sort of direct control less than city officers.

But there are some negatives associated with this style. One difficulty with Service style policing comes from the lack of "action" it entails. It is one thing to expect veteran police officers to embrace the idea that "not much happens" in the community where they police—and that this is a good thing. It is quite another to get young officers, especially rookies, to accept such a reality. Rookie police officers come to the job with media-created expectations about police work. Hollywood has told them, all of their lives, that police work is action packed and exciting. That while it can be violent and dangerous, there is a certain romanticism about it. That the police are involved in a "hero's quest" of sorts—to fight a war on crime and drugs and save America from the evils that threaten her.

When police officers who work in Service style organizations meet up with reality on the streets, they can be disappointed. They can become disillusioned. And they can get bored. Now there is nothing necessarily bad about a police officer experiencing the occasional stretch of boredom, say on a graveyard shift where nothing seems to happen. But boredom all of the time, on all shifts, everywhere he or she goes—this type of consistent, overwhelming, debilitating boredom can lead to trouble.

Young officers often come into police work dedicated to being involved in the great quest of cleaning up the streets and making them safe. They tend to be committed to fighting wars against crime and drugs. They have seen action on police programs and films all of their lives, and they expect action on the street. When they find there is next-to-nothing to do out there, it can cause them to act out

BOX 9.5

CRIME IN THE COUNTRY

How little crime can there be in a rural area? How little is there to do for the police? How bored can a rural police officer become? Here are the F.B.I.'s crime statistics for 2005 in Grand Isle County, Vermont, population 7,600, located in 5 small villages:

- Homicide/Manslaughter = 0
- Rape = 0
- Robbery = 0
- Aggravated Assault = 2
- Burglary = 26
- Larceny = 38
- Vehicular Theft = 0

Source: Uniform Crime Reports for Grand Isle County, 2005

in counterproductive ways. Young police officers with nothing to do often *make* something to do. And where there is little in the way of deviance and criminal behavior, this can entail harassing ordinary citizens.

Going on fishing expeditions in suburban and *especially* in rural areas accomplishes nothing good; it upsets the citizenry, it creates disorder where there is none, and it can make the police into a—or *the*—local problem. Such bored Service style police officers can present their police administration and their community—usually a community with few genuine problems to address—with unsettling situations.

On the other end of the spectrum, in suburban and especially rural areas, there can be so little to do that veteran police officers will retreat into apathy. They accomplish nothing. Such officers can be found off beat, sleeping on duty, having sex on the job, and even taking second jobs that they perform while supposedly policing. In this way, veteran Service officers can degenerate, in some sense, into non-working drags upon the system. And so, in these ways, Service policing can develop problems of a diverse nature, involving rookie and veteran police officers alike.

Having outlined these three styles, and having discussed in some depth the strengths and weaknesses of each, let us synthesize our analysis and address some over-arching questions about these various types of police organization.

WHICH STYLE IS "BEST"?

Any indirect comparison of styles begs the question: which one is best? The answer to that question is, it depends. Styles of policing are so inexorably linked to their locales that it is almost impossible to approach this question realistically. We might rephrase the question and ask, which is the best style for my city or town? Unfortunately, the answer would be the same: it depends. There is no one "best" style. Furthermore, styles of police organization are so difficult to transfer from one locale to another that coming up with an answer to the "which is best" question for any particular location isn't really necessary. Each city, town, and village across the country has a style of policing that has evolved over time and, in some sense, is "perfect."

As noted, there exists everywhere a symbiotic relationship between the police and a community. However it works in any given location, this relationship has been produced by a combination of factors. Local and political history are important. The history of the police, of police leadership and corruption (or lack thereof), is important. Community variables are of critical importance. What is the population? Is that population homogenous? Is it evenly distributed or are there various enclaves about the city or town? What is the crime situation? What types of deviant behavior are ever-present? What types of local crime is "normal"? What is the pattern of citizen calls for police service? All of these things matter.

An analyst, say a new Chief of Police, may look at a given police organizational style operative in a specific location and determine that this style "does not fit." Such an analyst might suggest an alternative style. And, in theory, he or she might be "correct" in some sense. But changing from one style to another is profoundly difficult. When it occurs it can take generations to make such a change. If someone—perhaps an incoming Chief or Sheriff—were to attempt such a change, numerous adjustments would have to take place.

First, political powers would have to be "on board" with the change. It might cost money. It would most assuredly create troublesome dynamics. The media might be drawn into it. Local politicos would have to be accommodating. Second, the entire command structure would have to "buy in" to the change. It might take some manipulating, encouraging, exhortation, cajoling, and even some threatening (coercion) to make it happen. The entire command structure would have to be enthusiastic about change.

Third, the police officers themselves, both the formal leadership (union representatives, for example) and the subculture would have to change. This is no mean feat. The police subculture is so influential that it could delay change—for years—or derail it altogether. For some changes to take place—if considered monumental by the rank and file—it might necessitate an entire officer corps being removed for effective change to proceed. That is, everyone hired and trained within the existing style would have to live out their careers and retire before change could be effectively implemented and maintained.

One further point needs making about change. Because of the differences between styles of policing, the dynamics of changing from one style to another are also different. Some change might very well be unrealizable. First, it is next to impossible to switch from either the Watchman or Legalistic styles to the Service style. This is because the Service style only works in certain circumstances. And it will not work in the city, where the other two styles constitute the options.

Second, changing from the Service or Watchman style to the Legalistic style can be all but impossible, too. If the local populace is used to either the laid-back

BOX 9.6

WHAT TYPE OF OFFICER FOR WHICH DEPARTMENT?

While this list is not definitive, the different styles *do* tend to require different types of backgrounds. As a general rule, these are the types of police officer backgrounds often prioritized when recruiting for:

- The Watchman Style = Local people "born-and-raised" in the area.
- The Legalistic Style = People with military backgrounds.
- The Service Style = People with college educations.

nature of the Watchman style or the comforting, empathetic nature of the Service style, it would be incredibly troublesome to implement the confrontational ethos of the Legalistic style. Citizens used to a non-intrusive style of policing might be shocked, confused, and diffident—they might consciously work against such a change.

The point here, generally, is that change can only occur slowly, if at all, from one style of policing to another. One frustrating reality for police administrators and local politicos is that genuine change usually happens incrementally, over time, driven by economic or social changes—such as the death of a particularly important local industry or the creation of new economic options that bring different populations to a city or town. This type of change is more likely than the kind instituted through the conscious efforts of police leaders and politicians.

 ## SUMMATION

In this chapter, we have outlined the three classic styles of police organization first enumerated by Wilson. We have analyzed the various strengths of these types and considered their various weaknesses. We have found that there is no one, particular "best" style of police organization. Furthermore, we have determined that police organizational style is not something transferable anyway—making a debate about the best system moot in the first place.

While we are about to consider yet another style, it behooves us to remember that this typology of police organization is still relevant to—even dominant in—a vast number of police and sheriffs departments today. Although the leadership of a majority of today's police organizations will suggest that they are operating under the new philosophy of COP, this is often untrue in practice. In most places in today's policing world, COP is often merely a goal and not a reality.

Let us move now to consider COP. We will engage the history behind its development and the philosophy itself. Then, as is our practice throughout, we will move on to a critical analysis of the idea—both in theory and practice.

CHAPTER NINE PARADOX BOX

While each of these three styles has its strengths, they also have significant weaknesses: the Watchman style encourages corruption of authority, the Legalistic style encourages noble cause corruption, and the Service style can be ineffective due to police officer boredom. And since there is no one "best" style, police administrators must understand that the styles are not transferable. Thus, it isn't necessarily possible to make changes from one style to another.

DISCUSSION QUESTIONS

1. Many students who have read about the Watchman style of policing over the years have immediately warmed to it, considering it to be the best system. This is largely because they are driven by the American principle of limited government to think of it as a style of policing that is reactive, less intrusive, and, thus, best. But there are numerous, important drawbacks to the Watchman style. What are they? What is limiting about its operations? Why might we think—in today's era of increased police professionalism and of COP—that the Watchman style is outdated?

2. While the Legalistic style involves more equitable and objective policing, it is accused of fostering more racism. Why is this? How does the objectivity of the Legalistic style end up appearing racist? How are its operations more prone to create citizens' complaints from minority group members than are Watchman style operations?

3. The Legalistic style is more objective in its application of the law than either the Watchman or Service styles. Decisions made by Legalistic officers are more often legally correct. And there is one universal set of rules applied everywhere in a community. With all of these positives, how is it that the Legalistic style tends to create Dirty Harry? Why is it that Legalistic style departments tend to have scandals—noble cause corruption scandals—as often or more often than do other departments?

4. In homogenous rural areas, where people live in small towns and villages, there is little need for policing. Acting as a sociologist, analyze why this is so. Why and how do people tend to self-police in rural areas? What operates to inhibit deviance and, thus, to make things easy for the police—to such an extent that policing in rural areas tends to be extremely boring?

KEY TERMS

19th Century Policing: Both the Legalistic Style and COP have elements of this type of reactive, community-involved policing.

Citizens' Complaints: Complaints made by civilians outside of the police organization alleging police misconduct.

Corruption of Authority: Old-style corruption involving officers abusing their legal authority in exchange for personal gain.

Cultural Relativity: The idea that different cultures have varying norms, values, and rituals that should be deferred to by people on the outside looking in.

Fishing Expeditions: Police subcultural parlance for stopping citizens and vehicles in order to search for criminality.

Harrison Act (1914): The congressional act that, essentially, made drugs illegal. Before this time, people could obtain opium, cocaine, and even syringes freely, whenever they wanted them, either at local apothecaries or through the mail.

Legalistic Style Policing: The name, coined by Wilson, designating a proactive, aggressive policing that emphasizes arrests and one community standard of conduct.

Police as Referees: The idea that police officers in the Watchman style merely "referee" disputes between citizens; most disputes are considered "private."

Professional Era: Today's era of policing (see Chapter Fifteen) emphasizing expanded education for police officers and social science research aimed at determining the most effective methods for the police.

Public Assembly Checks (PACs): Police parlance for briefly stopping by bars, restaurants, dancehalls, sporting events, et cetera to discover and stop criminal behavior.

Service Style Policing: The name, coined by Wilson, designating a style of policing, practiced exclusively in suburban and rural areas, that emphasizes good public relations and informal application of the law.

A Single Community Legal Standard: One of the consequences of Legalistic style policing; citizens are treated in the same way anywhere in a community.

Social Solidarity: The idea that societies and sub-societal groups develop among their members a common feeling of belonging and togetherness.

To Protect and Serve: Contemporary police motto in hundreds of jurisdictions.

Victimless Crime: Vice-related crimes where there is no individual citizen complainant; the "victim" is the people of the state.

Watchman Style Policing: The name, coined by Wilson, designating a style of policing that emphasizes 19th Century–type, reactive, passive policing that de-emphasizes arrests.

White Flight: Sociological term for the phenomenon of white people "fleeing" urban areas and relocating in newly created suburbs in the 1950s and '60s.

ADDITIONAL READING

This chapter's discussions about three styles of police organization are, of course, based upon James Q. Wilson's classic work *Varieties of Police Behavior* (Harvard University Press, 1968). This work is of critical significance not only due to the substantive points Wilson makes but also because it is one of the earliest works of social science research in the field of police studies. Later, in Chapter Ten, we will hear from Wilson again, because he helped create the impetus for the community policing movement.

In "Policing Styles and Organizational Priorities: Retesting Wilson's Theory of Local Police Culture" (in *Police Quarterly*, Volume 8, Number 4, 2005), Jihong "Soloman" Zhao and Kimberly D. Hassell examine Wilson's categorization three and a half decades after his initial research. Dovetailing with Wilson's findings, they determined that by that time (2005), American municipal government had been sufficiently homogenized such that there was little control over the police exercised by local political culture.

Other excellent studies of differences in police organizational styles include *Styles of Urban Policing: Organization, Environment, and Police Styles in Selected American Cities* by Jeffrey Slovak (N.Y.U. Press, 1988) and "The Influence of Environmental and Organizational Factors on Police Style in Urban and Rural Environments" by Cohn P. Crank (in *The Journal of Research in Crime and Delinquency*, Volume 27, Number 2, 1990). Unlike Wilson, who studied only urban and suburban departments of large and intermediate size, Crank takes the time to study and reflect upon rural policing styles as well. He finds what seems intuitively logical: that there is great variance between urban and rural police systems.

In *Organizational Structure in American Police Agencies: Context, Complexity, and Control* (SUNY Press, 2003), Edward R. Maguire finds that there is great resistance to the stylistic change from traditional forms toward COP. This information is important not only here but in the next chapter.

Along the way in this discussion, we have briefly touched upon the "revolving door" idea in American corrections. This was first suggested long ago in *Revolving Door* by David J. Pittman and C. Wayne Gordon (Glencoe Free Press, 1958), who studied the recidivism rates of inebriates. Now this concept is applied to the entire prison-industrial complex in America in such works as *Downsizing Prisons: How to Reduce Crime and End Mass Incarceration* by Michael Jacobson (N.Y.U. Press, 2005) and *Prison Race* by Renford Reese (Carolina Academic Press, 2006).

Finally, when discussing the Service style of policing we referred briefly to the idea of "white flight." In *Popular Culture in the Age of White Flight: Fantasy in Suburban Los Angeles* by Eric Avila (University of California Press, 2006), this dynamic from the 1950s and '60s is engaged and analyzed in a contemporary context as part of a sociological analysis of the American (Los Angeles) suburbs.

CHAPTER 10

Community Oriented Policing

Chapter Ten Outline

Community Oriented Policing (COP) is also known as Community Based policing. The more popular acronym deriving from **"Community Oriented Policing Services" (COPS)** is also used by an office within the Department of Justice that supports community policing efforts (*www.cops.usdoj.gov*). COP is not merely a new style of police organization. It is, in fact, a new philosophy of policing. Its implications reach into every corner of the policing experience: selection, training, leadership, and accountability. The movement toward implementing COP is the singularly most important ongoing process in contemporary policing in America. It represents nothing short of a revolution in thinking on the part of academics who study the police, political actors interested in developments in the field, and police administrators. It is impossible to overestimate the importance of the COP movement. This is because it holds the promise of changing police work from being merely an "occupation" into a genuine "profession."

In our discussions, we have referred to COP several times already. Now we assert it is the most important development in the field of police work in many years. If this is the case, why have we waited until Chapter Ten to specifically consider the elements of this philosophy? The reason is that to develop an understanding of COP we first had to provide a solid rendering of the individual police officer's experience and the machinations of the police subculture. Furthermore, we had to engage in discussions about police paramilitarism and the classic styles of policing, because a thorough understanding of COP must be based on a solid grasp of the reasons for it and of those organizational philosophies that preceded it. The idea of COP was created in an effort to respond to the dynamics of the subculture, to react to the drawbacks of paramilitarism, and to amalgamate the best elements of classic, preexisting organizational styles.

The movement to bring COP into the world of policing is, to some extent, a unique enterprise in the history of public organizations. Never before has such a complete change in philosophy in the "real world" been driven by theories developed in the academic world. The philosophy of COP represents a logical, measured change in outlook for an entire institution and for the large number of people working within it. It was not something invented as a response to scandal, as was the case with the changes of the Reform Era. COP was first mused about by academics, later refined by practical police leaders, and is being implemented with the wholehearted efforts of both groups—in concert with politicians who possess the insight and, indeed, the courage to involve themselves in change that is not a response to any emergent condition.

Sometimes in police work we hear jaded voices suggest that the norm is **"administration by crisis."** COP represents something new and important that is being constructed logically and with a view toward synoptic analysis, in lieu of responding in a knee-jerk fashion to scandal, public sentiment, and crisis. Again, in this sense, it is a unique movement, and something toward which students of the police must lend their complete attention.

Let us begin our consideration of COP with a brief discussion of its historical roots and the academic rationalizations for its invention.

HISTORY

During the 1960s, crime in America rose to levels no one had ever experienced since the advent of modern statistical tracking (Lykken). Crime went through the roof, metaphorically, and the fear of crime grew along with this increase (Mayer). While the rate of increase abated somewhat, the numbers still increased over the course of the 1970s. Both violent crime and property crime grew, almost exponentially. What is more, by the end of the '70s, the growth in gangs that has become a central reality in today's America began. Politicians, police officers, and citizens alike were upset and perplexed about what was happening on the streets of America. This increase in crime was the first in a series of problems that coalesced to create the impetus for the movement toward COP that followed.

In the 1960s and '70s, the police world reeled from several troublesome realities stemming from that tumultuous era of protest and change in America. The police were on the defensive, in a political sense, for two reasons. First, **riot commission reports** universally suggested that the police had to get their collective "act together" (President's Commission On Law Enforcement; To Secure These Rights; Skolnick, Politics of Protest). Focusing upon major, violent, deadly riots that had occurred in Los Angeles, Detroit, and elsewhere during the '60s, these commissions counseled that the police needed to have better education, training, leadership, and accountability. These commissions universally concluded that the ongoing antipathy that inner city, minority group populations held toward the largely White, male police of that era was partially responsible for the riots. And they resolved that the police needed to become more empathetic toward inner city peoples, more knowledgeable about the causes of crime, and more responsive to legal developments, including the U.S. Supreme Court's entrance into the lives of the work-a-day police officer.

These commissions called for the police to have college educations, not only to do away with police ignorance of constitutional principles, but in order to insure that they caught up with developments in the modern world. The practical requirements of police work had begun to change. For the first time, the police were required to do more than break up bar fights and handle family beefs. The *new* police needed to understand everything from search and seizure law to the civil rights and anti-war movements on the streets and college campuses. They needed to have a far more sophisticated approach to their tasks, and college educations appeared to be one way to insure that such a level of sophistication would develop.

The commissions called for a number of other changes. They suggested that civilian review boards should be formed to exercise control over the police. They suggested that police academy training be expanded and that it include more than just classes on the law and defensive tactics. The police needed to understand social conditions, contemporary history, and criminological theory. These commissions charged the police with lacking discipline, insight, and intelligence when dealing with the numerous problems and movements of the '60s. Some commission

BOX 10.1

THE WICKERSHAM COMMISSION

In 1929, President Herbert Hoover empanelled a commission to look into the causes of crime and violence in America. While its initial focus was upon Prohibition, the final report—issued in 1931—contained some shocking conclusions about the police in America. Focusing especially upon the interrogation tactics of that era, which regularly included the beating of suspects ("**the 3rd degree**"), the **Wickersham Commission** concluded that the American police were, in essence, "lawless." This report preceded those of the 1960s by several decades, of course, but its tone was similar to what would come later: it concluded the police were operating without concern for the basic constitutional principles of the American system. And they needed to make some profound changes if Americans were to enjoy those freedoms for which our country was *supposed* to stand.

(Wickersham)

reports were scathing in their tone and suggested that police leadership had failed the nation, in a time of need.

The calls for police discipline and training related directly to a second dynamic of the times. The police in the 1960s had often been undisciplined and out of touch with reality on the streets of America's inner cities and on the campuses of the country's colleges. On numerous occasions, they had reacted to civil rights and anti-war protests with a collective rage. They had been unprofessional, counterproductive, and even dangerous. In an important book written in 1972, Rodney Stark enumerated the several occasions during the '60s when groups of police officers "rioted," breaking the bonds of control and discipline that ordinarily governed their behavior. In ***Police Riots***, Stark provided stirring accounts of how police officers broke ranks, waded into crowds, and delivered violent, indiscriminate "curbside justice" (Stark).

A final push for changes in police work came from the general public. In the '60s and early '70s in America, change was in the air. The civil rights movement was in progress. The "women's liberation" movement (now entitled the "feminist" movement) had gained momentum, after a century of slow, halting progress. Concerns for gay rights and Native American and "Chicano" rights (now called "Latino" rights) were all in the process of expanding, first on college campuses and then among the general populace. And of course there was the war. Anti-Vietnam war protesting became a way of life during the late 1960s. Many of these movements began on college campuses and expanded into the general

American consciousness. In fact, they coalesced and became "the counterculture" or "the movement" (Anderson).

Unfortunately, the police were on the "wrong" side of all of these developments. Uneducated, poorly trained, and largely reactionary in their response to growing political and social tensions on the streets, the police were unable to couch these movements in proper context—as emblematic of the rights of American citizens to petition their government for redress of grievances and, more generally, as a part of the democratic process (Skolnick, Politics of Protest). As a group, the police were wrong on all of this and the public knew it. There was a great deal of general anti-police feeling at the time. For these reasons, politicians, police leaders, and community activists were moved to call for change.

Some change did occur. Federal money was provided, through the **Law Enforcement Education Program (LEEP)**, to cover the college costs of thousands of police officers (Roberg *et al.*). Academy training expanded in many jurisdictions. The "Field Training Officer" concept was invented, requiring that veteran officers be schooled in how to educate rookies on the street (we cover FTO programs in Chapter Twelve). In some locations, civilian review boards were created. In many more jurisdictions, police internal review systems were made more professional and began to take more seriously the business of holding the police accountable for their actions.

On the street, change was very slow in coming. As we have taken great pains to note, the police subculture is powerful and solidly composed. The power of the subculture illustrated its profound solidarity at the time by showing great resistance to many of the changes suggested. One thing police administrators did do was create a new, public relations–oriented entity within hundreds of police departments: the **Police-Community Relations unit** (Roberg *et al.*, 70). The idea involved an attempt to build bridges between the police and the citizenry. They had some officers take the time to interact with citizens in an informal manner by creating special programs that presented a more polished and empathetic façade for the police and by opening up store-front police substations in many places. These substations were supposed to be less intimidating to the public than the large, impersonal, centralized stations.

These Police-Community Relations units were not particularly effective in any substantive sense (Larson and Garrett). They were more about creating the *appearance* of change than altering the way the police operated. And they did not last long. Police-Community Relations units were in essence—as several analysts agreed at the time—band aids being placed upon large, gaping wounds. The public saw through these artificial efforts and never embraced the idea. Already driven by the anti-police cynicism of the times, people correctly intuited that these units represented public relations strategies. Nothing of substance had really changed.

More importantly, the police themselves saw these units for what they were: efforts to put a smiling face on police work. The units operated on their own, "on the outside" of police work, while the vast majority of police officers and police administrators went on with police work "as usual." The subculture attitude was quite jaded about this development at the time and regularly ridiculed police officers who had dropped out of doing "real" police work and, instead, were baby-sitting public opinion. Without the support of the rank and file, and being understood by the citizenry to be a cynical attempt to manipulate public opinion, Police Community-Relations units did not endure.

One more element led to the COP movement having to do with the central paradox engaged in the last chapter. Recall that paramilitaristic policing came into effect as a part of the Reform movement in order to put an end to rampant police corruption and to generate a new level of competence and pride in the police. Paramilitarism ushered in such changes as military-like uniforms, traditions, and carriage for the police; a new focus on crime fighting; and an aloofness from the public. All of this made sense at the time and worked to clean up police corruption. Within a generation or so, in most places, the subculture had changed, and the police had become, in fact, a sequestered, belligerent group of individuals. In a book that came to be known as "the Bible" for police administrators, O. W. Wilson, and later Wilson and McLaren, extolled the virtues of this approach and compiled a tome that explained how to operate a police department along paramilitaristic lines (Wilson and McLaren).

After these changes were instituted, along came the 1960s. This era presented America not only with a dramatic increase in crime but also with a different outlook toward the police among the citizenry. People began to complain about the very changes that reform had wrought. Some did not like the more aloof police and called for them to be more open and engaged in their communities. Some did not like the military carriage, likening it to the Gestapo of Nazi Germany. Some complained that the police did not live in the neighborhoods that they policed, as they *had* done in years past.

Some people did not like the idea of rotating police officers from one beat to another. Citizens began to feel that the police were, in some sense, **anonymous people in uniform**—that each time the police were called, somebody new showed up. The idea of rotating beats had been instituted originally to make ongoing "protection schemes" impossible for the police to organize. Now, a generation or more later, people were calling for police officers to be put on beats on a semi-permanent basis so that citizens could get to know their local officers. In these and other ways, the American public railed against some of the trappings and behavior patterns that were emblematic of paramilitarism.

Riot commission reports about police ineffectiveness in the inner city, reports about the police themselves rioting, the spike in crime occurring for more than two decades, the aborted attempt of the Police-Community Relations movement to bring about some sort of change, and the drawbacks of paramilitarism—all of this had an impact. To some extent, these developments of the '60s and '70s paved the way for new thinking about police work that materialized in the early 1980s.

PLANNED CHANGE

The unusual thing about COP is that it was the brainchild of academics—people who had never worked a day as police officers—and was brought from a world of ideas and theories into the real world of policing. Driven by the reasons for change enumerated above, people in the political world, in the police world, and in the academic world attempted "thinking outside of the box" (H. Goldstein). In an effort to come up with something different, something that might have an impact upon crime, many mused about who the police were, how police work was organized, and why police work was done the way it was done. What the police were doing was certainly not "working." Crime had skyrocketed during the '60s and the police seemed to be (1) ineffective in having any deterrent impact upon the growing rate of crime and (2) a part of the problem in some ways. What to do?

Ask criminologists to explain what causes crime, and they will answer that there are a litany of causes. Crime is caused by greed, poverty, racism, economic stratification, certain kinds of mental problems, and hopelessness. Scholars, knowledgeable politicos, and police leaders knew that the police could not do much about most of these causes in the grand scheme of things. But equally, they knew that there was probably something—something very different—that they could do to affect crime patterns and life on the street.

The idea of bringing police closer to their communities came to the fore over the course of the '60s and '70s in numerous places. But COP did not take off as an idea worthy of institutionalization until the 1980s. Largely given credit for its invention were George Kelling and James Wilson (the same Wilson who developed the explanation and names for the three organizational styles discussed in the last chapter). In the early '80s, they wrote several articles, published both in academic journals and in the mainstream press, which set COP in motion. In their article

BOX 10.2

BROKEN WINDOWS

The Broken Windows Theory (Wilson and Kelling) suggests that one broken window can quickly lead to buildings full of broken windows. And buildings full of broken windows tend to impact the feelings of safety held by members of the public. So do other signs of dilapidation and neglect. Broken windows, burned out cars, uncollected garbage, streetlights that do not work, uncut lawns . . . these and a dozen other signs of indifference and disintegration can affect the sense of **quality of life** felt by people in their community. A feeling of hopelessness, a lack of connection to the community, and a fear of crime can all be generated in the hearts and minds of people who live in a neighborhood where such signs of indifference are in evidence.

"**Broken Windows**," they argued that crime in the inner city in particular was largely produced by residents feeling a profound disengagement from their communities (Wilson and Kelling). When a neighborhood degenerates, when there is evidence of physical neglect and deterioration, and when there are signs of human disorder on the street, people can begin to feel apathetic. They can think that things have gone past some imaginary point of no return and there is no hope for their community. They can think that caring about their neighborhood is a waste of time, and so is cooperating with the police. In short, they can come to believe that the quality of life in their area is so poor that they "give up" on being engaged in community life.

This realization led to several logical deductions. The first had to do with the physical degeneration of neighborhoods. Fixing broken windows in a neighborhood (not to mention picking up the garbage, cutting the lawns, fixing street-lamps, and a dozen other endeavors) could perhaps make people who had "given up" reconnected with their communities. The second had to do with police patrol. When citizens interacted with police officers on foot patrol, as opposed to prowling the streets in cars, it turned out that they felt safer. They believed their streets were safer, even if crime statistics did not support this feeling. Foot patrol was important, then, in a psychological sense. The third deduction had to do with a host of proactive efforts with which the police could become involved. It appeared that the police *could* impact crime. There were any number of programs and practices that they could utilize to influence people to become more engaged in their communities and, indirectly, to deter crime.

This is the history behind the philosophy. It is now time to directly engage the principles this philosophy has inculcated in American policing over the past two decades.

THE NEW PHILOSOPHY

There are as many explanations of COP as there are criminologists who study it and police officers who attempt its implementation. In fact, one of the criticisms of COP is that it is not clearly defined. Definitions are vague, overlapping, and, at times, contradictory. We will attempt to steer a center path here and give the reader a general idea without participating in the debate about which definition of COP is best. In the following subsections, we will outline several of COP's major elements agreed upon by most experts (Friedman; Kelling and Coles; Skogan).

Police-Community Partnership: As the label implies, this new philosophy is community based. One of its central themes is the idea that the police should interact with the community on a regular basis. They should eschew the aloofness that has characterized the police since the onset of the Reform Era. Of course, members of any given community, even elected representatives and community leaders, do not directly manage police departments. But the idea here is that community input is essential. The taxpayers of any given city, town, or county have ideas about what the police should prioritize, and the police should be responsive to those ideas. The police are so few in number that they cannot, on their own, fight crime, deterioration, and disorder. An ongoing, interactive relationship between police and community is essential. And when COP came along, this type of relationship had not existed in most places in America since the days of the Political Era of policing.

A Broader Definition of the Police Function: Another principle included in the philosophy is the idea that the police function should be more broadly defined, placing an emphasis upon law enforcement, order maintenance, *and* service, all at the same time. Furthermore, under COP, the service element expands to include any number of tasks foreign to the police in recent generations. They need to be proactive in numerous ways, one of which has to do with opening up and maintaining communications networks with the community, as mentioned above. They should work together with communities to identify ongoing problems and troubleshoot solutions. They must consider themselves to be in the business of deterring crime, utilizing strategies never attempted in the past. By counseling potentially troubled youth, being of service to the elderly, interacting with schools to preemptively deal with vandalism and drug use on campus, and dealing with street people in a way that inhibits the development of disorder—in these and a dozen other ways, the police under COP are supposed to be proactive and engaged in their communities.

Personalizing Police Service: Face-to-face interactions with the public are prioritized. Foot patrol, bike patrol, and even horse patrol (where possible) are emphasized. Officers who work in patrol cars are encouraged to exit their vehicles and interact with the public whenever possible. Officers are assigned to beats on a semi-permanent basis so that they can develop this personal, service orientation toward the citizens on their beats. The police should take the time to meet with local small business owners and get to know them by name. Having police officers who are considered "anonymous" by members of the community is counterproductive and illogical. As has always been the case with the Service style of policing, COP demands that police consider their work as a "business" of sorts, that they package and market it to the community.

Proactive Crime Prevention: COP involves ongoing problem solving that again, includes members of the community whenever possible. Members of the honest, hard-working, law-abiding public must take part in the maintenance of order—in partnership with the police. Now this does not imply that citizens become involved in any sort of "**vigilante justice**." What it means is that people need to trust in, cooperate with, and feel free to ask the police for help. And the philosophy of COP suggests that in order to do this, a comfort zone needs to be created that does away with the aloofness for which the police had become known during the paramilitarism of the Reform Era. For their part, the police need to take a more serious approach to the minor violations and disorderly conduct that impacts quality of life. Reactive policing—driven by specific calls for service from citizens—is only a small part of the police function. They need to engage in overt, ongoing, proactive order-maintenance activities.

Decentralization: As an operational principle, police work under COP becomes more decentralized. The police are given a great deal of latitude within which to pursue the above goals. Discretion is expanded. And lower level expertise is utilized. That is, the fact that today's police officers are more intelligent, better educated, and better trained than ever before is acknowledged and exploited. Today's officers are "criminologists in uniform" to a real extent, and the expertise that they obtain on the beat should be put to good use. The "old fashioned" chain-of-command way of doing things is eschewed in favor of team-oriented problem solving. Led by more experienced and, perhaps, higher-ranking officers, police who patrol the streets are encouraged to develop anti-crime strategies as a group. Such strategies are a product of their individual and collective expertise.

What sorts of strategies are we talking about? Here is an example: Let us imagine that the police observe an increase in daylight burglaries in a certain part of town. In the days before COP, such an observation would lead to some sort of brief analysis on the part of the command structure. This in turn would lead to a strategic memo, generated from "above," outlining what commanders want done about the problem. Then the orders encapsulated in the memo would pass down the chain of command to those who work the street. Finally, the street police would do what they were told to do.

Today, under COP, such a problem might be engaged by an ad hoc group of beat officers—a team composed of those who understand and work on a daily basis in the area in question. Perhaps this group would be led by more experienced beat officers, or a street Sergeant, or someone in middle management (a Lieutenant or Captain). The group would problem solve and come up with a strategy. This might be done in consultation with community leaders. The strategy would then be implemented by the very people who developed it.

The idea is to have at once a more democratic problem-solving system in place and a system that is more effective—because it takes advantage of the expertise of those officers who are on the street and engaged in beat life. This method of operation may also attempt to use input from, say, the local high school principal, the leader of a **Neighborhood Watch** group, or the members of **Neighborhood Block Organizations** (Peak). In this way, lower level expertise is plumbed and utilized, police decision-making is decentralized, and the entire process becomes a collective endeavor involving beat officers, commanders with experience, and local community leaders.

Department-Wide Acceptance: COP is a new philosophy and set of strategies. It is not pure public relations, as was the Police-Community Relations movement. In some sense, it changes everything in police work: it calls for the employment of a new kind of officer; it changes almost everything about training, management and leadership, and how the police are held accountable. Furthermore, COP can employ volunteers from the community. Neighborhood organizations can be created, advisory boards developed, civilian review of the police instituted, and citizens can even participate in ad hoc ways on occasion. The "partnership between police and citizens" idea is a powerful concept drawn all the way through the organization and operation of COP.

All of this is revolutionary. It impacts upon who the police are and what they do in a profound way. In order to change police work in such a direction, it is absolutely essential everyone in the police organization back the effort. This cannot be a band aid–type of attempt at image polishing. It must be seen by everyone, top to bottom, as an important change to which they become committed. Any feeling that COP is something "some of us" do, while others revert to "normal" police work, is counterproductive.

So the general principles herein outlined (and this is not an all-inclusive list) include, but are not limited to, the idea that (1) COP is a new philosophy and strategy, requiring department-wide acceptance; (2) it takes a proactive approach to deterring crime in the first instance and to developing long term solutions for existing crime patterns; (3) it involves a new type of personalized delivery of police services; (4) it is responsive to community input and seeks it out whenever and wherever possible; (5) it broadens the definition of the police function; and (6) it involves decentralized decision-making that seeks to take advantage of the intelligence, education, and training of today's new, modern police officer corps (Roberg *et al.*, 67–102).

Now there are dozens of books about COP and, as noted in Box 10.3, an entire federal office within the Department of Justice dedicated to the concept and to instituting its operational principles. So our several brief pages here only highlight an endeavor that is much more far-reaching. (See Additional Readings at the end of the chapter for references to numerous other, more synoptic treatments of the philosophy.)

BOX 10.3

COMMUNITY ORIENTED POLICING SERVICES (COPS)

The Office of Community Oriented Policing Services within the Department of Justice is an agency that has supported this new type of policing since 1995. It has invested more than $12.4 billion in aid to encourage the effort. Over 13,000 state, local, and tribal agencies have been assisted with monies used to pay for officers, training materials, and a host of publications (CDs and DVDs included) that expand knowledge in the field.

(www.cops.usdoj.gov)

COP IN ACTION

Having put forth the over-arching philosophy of COP, and having discussed some of the major principles associated with it, we will briefly give some specific examples of how it looks in action—of the sorts of programs and tasks included in this style of policing when operational. Box 10.4 includes a list of some examples of COP-type policing. Most are self-explanatory, but we will take a moment to explicate several that either might not be or for which the rationalization isn't perfectly clear.

One of the important insights of the broken windows idea is emphasizing the importance of disorder in shaping the quality of life in a neighborhood. Disorder indirectly causes crime by creating an atmosphere of despair and apathy on the part of honest, hard-working citizens. For generations, the police focused on serious crime—sometimes to the exclusion of a concern for many types of "minor" crimes—because of how penal codes divide crimes into felonies and misdemeanors. COP suggests that given the above nexus between disorder and crime, some types of disorderly conduct that used to be considered unimportant are, in fact, of major importance with respect to creating crime patterns. And the police need to attend to these "minor concerns"

Wesley Skogan, one of the important authors in this field, has divided COP concerns about disorder into two groups: human disorder and physical disorder (Skogan 21). In operating within the COP philosophy, the police focus upon human disorders directly. They must engage public drinking, corner gangs, the harassment of women and the elderly in public places, the sale of drugs on the street, noisy neighbors, and street-level prostitution. These are the lower level, minor occurrences that impact quality of life and, thus, the crime level of a given neighborhood. The police need to utilize all tools at their disposal—legal, semi-legal, and non-legal skills and powers—to deter such behavior.

Skogan's list of physical disorders includes vandalism, dilapidation and abandonment, and rubbish. The police can do something about vandalism in the first instance, by taking it seriously in a way that they have not before. But the other categories involve things out of the hands of the police. What COP suggests as a part of its philosophy is that among their many varied tasks on the street, the police—operating within the newly expanded definition of their functions—should work with other agencies and community organizations to improve the quality of life on the street. In this case, the police themselves are not going to pick up unattended garbage, install new lighting, and fix broken windows. But they might very well contact the local refuse company and advise them of a garbage pick-up problem. They might report faulty public lighting to the electric company. And the might report broken windows in the local teen center or public building(s). These are but a few examples of what police might do to deter crime by dealing with its indirect causes.

Given our discussions above, it is no surprise that foot patrol, bicycle patrol, and even horse patrol are all a part of COP. The face-to-face interactions that these endeavors bring between police and public are direct reflections of the idea that police work needs to become more personalized under COP. With regard to proactive crime prevention, the police under COP have become more directly involved with programs like D.A.R.E., **"Just Say No,"** and Police Athletic Leagues (PAL). In some places, police officers volunteer to help students directly with studies or athletic endeavors.

Another program, **"Knock and Talk,"** is a proactive endeavor that involves police officers going to the homes of at-risk youth and interacting with parents. In Kansas City, for example, the police have a program in place where they contact the parents of teenagers who are known to be involved with local gangs but have managed to keep their records clean. The police make a deal with the parents: if they allow the police to search their kid's room, and the police find anything (drugs or guns, for example), the police confiscate it and the teenager is not charged. Thus the parents are allowed to handle the situation informally.

Finally, the partnership part of the philosophy can involve civilian participation in police policy development on advisory boards, in neighborhood organizations, and in holding the police accountable. **Civilian review boards** (see Chapter Thirteen) present such an opportunity. While police officers have tended to be against civilian oversight historically—thinking that it might be unfair to police officers—in practice civilian review is not result in unfair treatment of police officers. In fact, it involves citizen participation in police administration in a direct and non-threatening way. (More on civilian review follows in Chapter Thirteen.)

These are but a few of the many programs and police-citizen types of cooperative projects that have developed under the auspices of COP. It is an ongoing,

BOX 10.4

SOME SPECIFIC EXAMPLES

Here are some examples of the types of programs and police activities that operate, or have operated, to further the interests of COP:

- D.A.R.E. and "Just Say No"
- "Knock and Talk"
- Neighborhood Watch
- Police Athletic Leagues
- Foot patrol
- Bike patrol
- Horse patrol
- Civilian Review Boards

expanding, evolutionary endeavor that will change and morph in the years ahead. COP is *supposed* to include such adaptations. It is supposed to expand and contract over time in response to changing conditions on the street, changing expectations among the citizenry, and changing technologies.

Critique

COP has become so popular as a goal in police circles, and there has been so much emphasis placed upon it, that is has become difficult to talk about in some sense. This is because it has come to be defined in too many different ways. The COP label has been utilized to describe too many different programs. Two scholars, Greene and Mastrofski, have gone so far as to write a book about whether COP is real or just a new form of rhetoric (Greene and Mastrofski). Specific definitions are numerous and vague, and there are some substantial criticisms of COP in action. In addition to the charge about vague definitions, here are but a few standard criticisms:

Lack of Rank and File Acceptance: All students and practitioners familiar with the subject agree that COP is a philosophical change that requires acceptance everywhere within any police organization that attempts to implement it. The implication is that this new style will not work—cannot work—if the power of both the entire administration and the subculture is not behind it. But this is exactly what has been found to be the case in many locations. COP has been opposed by the entrenched establishment of rank and file police officers in enough places that this lack of commitment is regularly discussed in literature within the field. Since COP is meant to be a complete change of attitude, strategy, and administration, it can be thwarted by any lack of acceptance at any level of policing. As can be the case with any form of change in police work, the power of subcultural tradition can be the death knell of progress.

Recall that one of the problems with the Police-Community Relations movement was that in most locales the rank and file considered it to be window dressing of a sort. It was something that involved a few officers but, in the long run, was considered an unwanted nuisance that operated "on the side"—while the rest of the police continued to be involved in "real" police work. This has been the case in some locations with COP. Indeed, in some departments police administrators have amplified this problem by creating "COP Units" just as was done with the Police-Community Relations units. And when those units have operated independently, outside the dominant administrative model, then the chance for changing the entire police culture and management style is nonexistent. COP has to be considered "real police work" by everyone in any police department, large or small. It cannot be thought of as something that operates on the side or in the shadows. The police subculture in particular must be brought on board lest COP die a quiet death—the type that defeated the Police-Community Relations movement.

Middle Manager Resistance: So one criticism of COP is that rank and file police officers often tend to resist the change it represents. What is more troublesome than this is that some middle managers also rebel against its operational realities. This happens because authority sometimes does not parallel responsibility in the COP style. Any reluctance on the part of middle managers to buy in to COP can be detrimental at the least, confounding to the entire endeavor at the very worst. COP can be defeated by middle managers just as easily as it can be defeated by the rank and file.

The principle that authority must parallel responsibility in complex organizations is a basic idea found in just about every introductory textbook in the fields of both public and business administration. It suggests that if they are to be held accountable for the effectiveness of subordinates, it is only fair to administrators that they be given authority over those subordinates. If an administrator does not have authority to command and control what is done by a group of subordinates, then how can the poor performance of those subordinates be "held against" the administrator?

Whether they know it or not, many administrators and supervisors are against the violation of this principle. This is apparent when a supervisor complains about **"micro-management"** (Chambers). Micro-management is the practice of someone from higher up in an organization's structure to come into a sub-organization (a division of a large company, for example) to make changes—and then later hold a supervisor accountable for the fact that the changes did not work. In this scenario, the supervisor's authority over the group has been violated and, therefore, he or she can rightfully complain that it is not fair to hold them accountable for the group's performance.

Perhaps we can best illustrate this with an example. Let us return to the burglary problem illustrated earlier. Recall that in a chain-of-command type of operation, in the "old way" of doing things, the strategy for attacking a burglary problem in a given part of town would be developed by someone in a middle or upper level management position and then passed down. When the strategy was evaluated later, whoever came up with it would be held responsible for its effectiveness or lack thereof. This would be perfectly fair to whomever had come up with the strategy, whether it ended up working well or not. In the COP example—of how this same problem might be strategized—remember that a group of officers, led by a middle manager, develop a strategy in a collegial and, to some extent, democratic way—it is not "commanded" by the middle manager.

The point here is that a practical problem has occurred in some police jurisdictions that have attempted to put COP into practice. While the new philosophy has created a communal or collegial way of problem solving, the middle manager still tends to be held accountable if things do not go well. Having lost the ability to "command and control"—that they possessed under the old system—middle managers under COP are sometimes still held responsible for the lack of success of a strategy when it fails. And when this happens, middle managers rebel against COP because it appears to be unfair to them. They were not "in charge" of the strategy in the first place—not completely—and, therefore, they should not be held solely accountable for it. Add this sort of "rebellion" to that perpetrated by lower level officers in many organizations and we have a recipe for disaster—for the failure of COP no matter how effective its philosophical principles might be in theory.

Evaluating COP: A third point of contention has to do with evaluations. Americans have a propensity to expect accountability where their tax dollars are concerned. COP represents a huge change in how the police do *everything*. Thus people will be driven by the desire to know if it is effective or not. If COP is effective, then crime statistics should go down, correct? According to the theory behind the philosophy, this partnership between community and police should work to decrease crime in the long run. Its effectiveness should manifest in cold, hard numbers. But there is a paradox involved in COP.

What if crime statistics do not go down? What if crime goes up under COP? Would that prove that COP is *in*effective? The paradox here is that this would not necessarily be the case. If a greater degree of trust were to develop between the public and the police, then people would turn to the police more often for help and, in addition, they would more often aid in police investigations. If this happened, then crime—as indicated by the number of crimes reported (which is the standard that we use)—might very well go up under COP. More community support with police investigations would mean that more crimes would be solved, and this is a good thing. But it might also be true that more crimes would be *reported*, because citizens develop a higher level of trust in the police, and that would mean that crime statistics—which, again, is how we measure crime—would increase. Paradoxically, this increase in crime may very well occur *because COP is working well*.

In fact, this is the case. In some places, COP has produced comforting statistics: crime has gone down. In other places, the unfortunate reality is that crime has risen under COP (Roberg *et al.*, 96–98). But as we are suggesting, that does not mean that this new philosophy is not working. And so crime statistics are by no means definitive as gauges of police effectiveness under COP's auspices. What can be done about this? How can COP be effectively evaluated?

Under COP, many schemes have been created to evaluate the performance of individual officers, groups (or teams) of police officers, and police organizations in general. Such schemes seek to evaluate the "quality of life" or the "feelings of safety" on the street in the minds of the citizenry. If the quality of life goes up and the feeling of safety increases, then, in theory, COP is "working." This is true regardless of whether or not crime levels are changed in a statistical sense. So evaluations of citizen perceptions have to be attempted.

Evaluation strategies—individual assessment tools—have also sought to determine the effectiveness of the job done by police officers under COP. The assessment measures involved are complicated and protracted research tools that are different in virtually every location (Roberg *et al.*, 97). And their substantive ability to develop any realistic picture of the effectiveness of officers is debated at every turn.

Both of these types of assessments—those that assess citizen attitudes and those that assess the job the police have done—are complicated, vague, and sometimes difficult to understand and evaluate. Put another way, evaluating the "quality of life" in any given jurisdiction is difficult at best. And evaluating the job done by individual police officers, or even groups of police officers, is equally difficult. Without going into a long and complicated list of specifics, it is enough for our brief discussion here to note that the evaluation of COP is problematic, and this means that millions of dollars can be spent without any way of "proving" they have been spent in a wise, efficient, and effective manner.

Re-Inventing Past Problems: Fourth, the movement toward COP involves a recycling of sorts in policing. Even its most ardent supporters acknowledge that it is somewhat "like 19th Century policing." This is because it involves foot patrol. It involves officers remaining on one beat or in one area for extended periods of time, if not for their entire careers. It involves the re-definition of the police function in a way that suggests they become more social-welfare oriented. Under COP the police are closer to the community and supposed to develop long-term, personal ties with local business people and community leaders. All of this is being done with the best of intentions.

But we must accept the assertion that COP is like 19th Century policing and then ask, what was 19th Century policing like (Walker, Critical History, 24)? Yes, the police were closer to the community and remained on their beats for extended periods of time. But they utilized this reality to create ongoing payoff schemes that bilked local businesses and controlled communities in a very un-democratic

BOX 10.5

"OLD WINE IN NEW BOTTLES"

The metaphor of "**old wine in new bottles**" is often used to discuss supposedly "new" ideas that are, in reality, old ideas framed in a different way. Several critics of COP have suggested that this "new" philosophy is merely a way of going back to the 19th Century, and that this is undoubtedly a bad idea. Among them is Samuel Walker, a police historian, who points out that the history of policing in the 19th Century is misunderstood by the champions of COP. In particular, he suggests that COP theorists have painted a flowery and unrealistic picture of 19th Century police officers that ignores the corruption, incompetence, and politicized nature of policing in that century. Walker suggests, among other things, that going back to the "good old days" of the 19th Century might not be a very good strategy.

(Walker, Broken Windows)

way. Yes, the police had much more discretion then they have had in recent years. But they used this latitude to convolute the law and make it work for the police and against the interests of justice. Yes, the police took a minute-by-minute interest in the maintenance of order on the streets, and because they were on foot they engaged directly those who were drunk, sold illegal substances, were involved in prostitution, and so forth. But they utilized this reality not only to further their own corrupt interests but to apply excessive force so often that they were known for prosecuting "curbside justice" on a regular basis.

If COP is anything at all like 19th Century policing, then we should be very leery of its recreating corrupt practices, the application of excessive force, and a general tendency for the police to utilize the law for their own purposes rather than furthering the best interests of their communities. While we do not have the same types of officers on the street today as were then, 19th Century policing was done away with precisely because of the latitude the police possessed. Are we in fact asking for such problems to recur if we go "back" in some sense to that era? Who knows?

Problematic Assumptions: The COP philosophy is based upon several assumptions that in practice might prove false (Roberg *et al.*, 95–99). It assumes that citizens will participate actively and consistently. Sometimes, it turns out, citizen participation is great when COP "arrives," but it wanes over time. On the other side of the formula, police interest too can be high to begin with and then fade over time. The police can "revert to form"—to dealing with crime-related problems amongst themselves without reference to community input.

COP assumes that the communal development of strategies will result in the implementation of tactics that mirror those strategies. It turns out that when on the street, police officers often revert to solving problems utilizing their own, personal philosophies and experiences. COP has spawned a different type of police training. And it assumes this training will have a long-term effect upon police behavior on the street. But while some research indicates the police who finish community-oriented training leave with a solid understanding of its principles, other research indicates that when they hit the streets traditional subcultural values tend to take over and drive decision-making. The philosophy of COP also suggests that an ongoing reevaluation of strategies, tactics, assessment tools, and so forth is a part of the process. It is assumed that this reevaluation process will keep strategies fresh and responsive to new developments in a community. But it turns out that the nature of the bureaucratic experience—the tendency to institutionalize "the" way of doing things and stick to it—often inhibits such ongoing creativity.

Taken together, several of the assumptions that undergird the philosophy may not hold up over time. And, thus, what COP really means in operation can be questionable. The nexus between theory and reality is not yet firmly realized. COP is too new to know how effective it will be in the long run.

This list of criticisms is troublesome. It has to be taken seriously. And efforts are being made to answer these critiques of COP in action. But we must keep something in mind. It is important to remember that the police officers of today are not those of the 19th Century. In terms of intelligence, education, training, and subcultural commitment to integrity and competence, contemporary police are not likely to become mired in the problems of the past.

We do not wish to imply with our criticisms here that COP is not an important idea and cannot work. COP is absolutely critical to the future development of the police in America. As we shall see in Chapter Fifteen, it is an integral part of the critically important drive to create and maintain a genuinely professional outlook in the police field. And nothing is more important to American police than this drive toward the achievement, finally, of professionalism.

SUMMATION

Over the course of the past twenty years, COP has become the newest style of police organization. On the one hand, it holds great promise for positive change. On the other, the jury is still out on COP, and it will take more time for its principles to be so sufficiently institutionalized that we can know its long term effects. While we do not know—cannot know—where COP will take American policing, no study of policing today can avoid this central reality: COP is destined to change the face of policing forever, and in ways that we cannot even anticipate.

In Part Two, we have discussed the various forms that police organizations can take at the most basic level—that of deciding what the overall philosophy of the organization will be. In Part Three, we turn to several chapters wherein we will study police work at a more operational level. To begin with, we will analyze police hiring practices. In Chapter Eleven we will talk about standard practices in police selection and then critique them. In the process, we will engage still more paradoxes of police work. In particular, we will find that this absolutely critical process involves, in essence, attempting to do something that is, in fact, impossible: to quantify the evaluation of character.

CHAPTER TEN PARADOX BOX

COP is an excellent idea in theory. But it involves a call to go back in history; to a time when there was so much police discretionary latitude that corruption of authority was rampant. Because of this, there is a danger that COP will do more harm than good. Furthermore, the changes which it calls for can often be opposed by both rank and file police officers and by middle managers in a way that can negate its positive potential.

DISCUSSION QUESTIONS

1. The Police-Community Relations movement failed largely because most police officers did not accept it. Every discussion of COP suggests that department-wide acceptance is essential for its success. Given what you know about the power of the subculture, discuss how such attempts at change can be thwarted by subcultural norms and the power of tradition.

2. Discuss the theory of "Broken Windows." What do broken windows have to do with crime? Why is there such a focus upon this little idea in today's policing? What's the theory behind the entire endeavor of COP?

3. COP advocates call for the decentralization of police authority and power and even for changing the entire process of decision-making. Is this realistic? Could such changes be instituted effectively, given that we have already found middle managers frustrated by COP at times? Discuss why middle managers can be frustrated by COP.

4. One criticism of COP is that it might very well bring back old style, 19th Century–type corruption. Do you think this could happen? Why or why not? What about today's police officers and organizations would mitigate such developments?

KEY TERMS

Administration by Crisis: The idea that change almost always occurs in police work due to scandals and crises.

Anonymous People in Uniform: One of the criticisms of the rotating beat practice that paramilitaristic policing brought into effect.

Broken Windows: Title of the article written by Kelling and Wilson largely given credit for creating the impetus behind COP.

Civilian Review Boards: Police review systems populated by civilians that operate outside of police departmental systems (see Chapter Thirteen).

Community Oriented Policing Services (COPS): An office in the Department of Justice that provides information and services supporting the COP movement.

Decentralization (of Police): The idea that CBP aims to take notice of lower level expertise and, therefore, that police decision-making must be decentralized.

"Just Say No": Anti-Drug program of the 1980s supported by First Lady Nancy Reagan.

Knock and Talk: Program that sends police officers out in a proactive manner to talk with parents of teenagers determined to be "at risk" of joining street gangs.

Law Enforcement Education Program (LEEP): Federal program in the 1960s and '70s that put millions of dollars into police education and research.

Micro-management: The idea that sometimes managers in complex organizations subvert the chain-of-command by involving themselves in organizational sub-departments well below them on the organizational chart and "meddle" in decision-making.

Neighborhood Block Organizations: Local organizations that have existed (sometimes) for generations in major cities.

Neighborhood Watch: A proactive program aimed at getting citizens involved in crime prevention in their neighborhoods.

Old Wine in New Bottles: Associated with the criminologist Samuel Walker, this is the idea that COP involves old-style, 19th Century policing; and that it might not necessarily be a good idea because of the corruption and police abuses of that era.

Personalizing Police Service: One of the major principles of COP that requires police organizations to keep officers on the same beats for extended periods of time and suggests that police officers and community leaders develop on-going, personal relationships.

Police-Community Relations Unit: A movement from the late '60s and early '70s that was ineffective at improving police community relations.

Police Riots: Occurrences during the 1960s wherein police officers lost control of themselves and behaved like rioting citizens.

Quality of Life: An important concept of the COP philosophy suggesting that when people perceive their quality of life to be better they will take ownership in their communities, cooperate with police, and help fight crime.

Riot Commission Reports: Numerous expansive reports created during the 1960s—commissioned by governments at state and federal levels—that looked into inner city riots, college campus riots, and police riots.

The 3rd Degree: Police interrogation techniques from decades ago wherein suspects were regularly beaten and abused in order to obtain information.

Vigilante Justice: Refers to older times when groups of citizens policed the streets—especially in the West—in lieu of there being organized police forces.

Wickersham Commission: A commission that studied the American criminal justice system in the 1930s and made numerous recommendations for change, including better police accountability and police education.

ADDITIONAL READING

We began this chapter with a reference to the Community Oriented Policing Services office of the United States Department of Justice. The web site for "COPS" is found at *www.cops.usdoj.gov* where the student can find almost unlimited information about the subject.

In our consideration of the lead-up to the COP era, we discussed various commission reports, including the original nationwide commission *The Wickersham Commission on Law Observance and Law Enforcement* (U.S. Government Printing Office, 1931). Among other commissions from the 1960s are the following: *The President's Commission on Law Enforcement and the Administration of Justice* (U.S. Government Printing Office, 1967); *To Secure These Rights: The U.S. Commission on Civil Disorders* (U.S. Government Printing Office, 1968); and *The Politics of Protest: National Commission on the Causes and Prevention of Violence* by Jerome Skolnick (Ballantine Books, 1969). Also important is *Police Riots* by Rodney Stark (Wadsworth, 1972). This work is critical to any understanding of why so much pressure was brought to bear regarding changing policing philosophies nationwide.

The classic piece in the field of community policing, of course, is George Kelling and James Q. Wilson's article in *The Atlantic* from March of 1982 entitled "Broken Windows." This article was followed up not only by practical changes in the field but also by academic analysis that built upon the original idea. *Problem Oriented Policing* by Herman Goldstein (McGraw-Hill, 1990) is also considered a classic in this field.

Since that time, there have been dozens of works about COP, including *Fixing Broken Windows: Restoring Order and Reducing Crime in Our Communities* (Free Press, 1998), which was written by George L. Kelling, the original co-author of the broken windows theory, and Catherine M. Coles. Early important works in this area include Robert R. Friedman's *Community Policing: Comparative Perspectives and Prospects* (St. Martin's Press, 1992), Wesley Skogan's *Disorder and Decline: Crime and the Spiral of Decay in American Neighborhoods* (Free Press, 1990), and J. R. Greene and S. D. Mastrofski's *Community Policing: Rhetoric or Realty* (Praeger, 1988).

Now that the movement toward COP is more than two decades old, and there is a wealth of research in the field, the student may wish to consider more contemporary books, such as *Community Police: Partnerships for Problem Solving* by Linda S. Miller and Karen M. Hess (Wadsworth, 2007), *Community Police and Problem Solving, 5th Ed.* by Kenneth J. Peak and Ronald W. Glensor (Prentice Hall, 2007), and *Community Oriented Policing: A Systematic Approach to Policing, 4th Ed.* by Willard M. Oliver (Prentice-Hall, 2007).

Finally, it is interesting to note that the COP movement has become an international change in the philosophy of policing. *Community Policing: National and International Models and Approaches* (Willan Publishing, 2005) is a work by Preeti Nijhar and Mike Brogden that informs the reader of international experiences in the field.

PART THREE

Police Administration

Part Three is about several important administrative tasks performed by police leaders and police departments that are replete with paradoxes. Police selection, police training, and police accountability are all troublesome for police officers, police administrators, and citizens alike. Efforts to accomplish these functions can be effectively thwarted by either the police themselves, in the form of reluctant and diffident line officers or police managers, or by forces external to the police department, such as the media and local politicos.

CHAPTER 11

Selection

Chapter Eleven Outline

The hiring process is absolutely critical to any organization. When hiring new personnel, an organization redefines itself. An organization makes a statement about the ongoing development of its mission with each new hire. Hiring either replicates what has been done in the past or it suggests a new direction. Both the process and the substance of hiring practices are important. That is, it is important *how* the process proceeds, and it is equally important *who* the process hires. Each in their way describes what an organization believes and what it plans to do in the future.

In police work, hiring involves a prolonged series of "hoops" through which prospective candidates must "jump." Almost no other occupation or profession has so many varied and difficult hurdles for the would-be employee to surmount. In an era when so many people want to be police officers, police departments and sheriff's departments can afford to be picky. And picky they usually are. In some places, there are 8 or 10 candidates for every open position. The status of being a police officer, the benefits accorded working officers, and the retirement packages are impressive in most places. Those who make hiring decisions can select candidates who further the drive of the police to become more intelligent, more educated, better trained, and genuinely professional. Those hired today are "the best and the brightest" young police officers America has ever seen.

We begin our examination of police selection processes by engaging in a dialogue that has fascinated humankind for more than 2,000 years. Ever since the ancient Greek philosophers wrote about it, people have been debating a central question about the human experience: what constitutes good character? This is a critical issue for us because the selection of good police officers is contingent on answering that question.

THE IDEAL CANDIDATE

While having good character is *the* critical ingredient in the mix that makes up a good police officer, is it not the only thing for which the selection process searches. There are two lists of qualities important to those who make personnel decisions in police work. "**Good Character**" is the central element on the first list. The idea of good character is an amorphous concept. It is at once the most important quality that police departments are looking for in candidates and the most difficult to define.

The second list includes numerous elements. The successful candidate must possess the required intelligence level, amount of education, and skill sets. We will call this second list the "**Practical Qualifications**" (Aamedt). This second list of qualities is more easily evaluated than the first. Some elements of this list can be investigated in short order, by giving tests, checking educational transcripts, and contacting former employers and teachers. Ascertaining good character is something altogether different and problematic.

BOX 11.1

ARISTOTLE'S VIRTUES

AREA	DEFECT	MEAN	EXCESS
fear	cowardice	courage	recklessness
pleasure	insensitivity	self-control	indulgence
money	stinginess	generosity	extravagance
honor	small-mindedness	high-mindedness	vanity
anger	apathy	gentleness	short temper
truth	self-deprecation	truthfulness	boastfulness
shame	shamelessness	modesty	terror-stricken (Perez and Moore, 50)

Perez, D. W., and J. Alan Moore. *Police Ethics, 1st Ed.* ©2003 Delmar Learning, a part of Cengage Learning, Inc. Reproduced by permission. *www.cengage.com/permissions*

Good Character: Two and a half millennia ago, Aristotle discussed the elements of good character (N. Sherman)—or what he labeled **"the virtues."** He talked about character defects and excesses and determined that a person with good character was courageous, truthful, generous, and so on (see Box 11.1). The search for people who might make good police officers involves wading through a pool of applicants, searching for several critical characteristics. The central paradox of the police selection process is that it involves a serious search for candidates that possess these character elements—and yet the characteristics sought are all amorphous and hard to determine in advance.

How can we know if a person will be honest when confronted with the opportunities for corruption in police work? How can we know if a person will be courageous when faced with the duty to go into a hot detail without cover? How can we know if a person will possess the empathy and kindness necessary to be a good officer in the face of people's worst behavior on a regular basis? The answer is that we cannot. Arguably, those character values most critical for police officers are courage, self-control, honesty, empathy, and integrity. Each is both critical and vaguely defined. Each is hard to gauge, even in mature candidates with significant life experiences behind them. Let us discuss these characteristics for a moment (Cohen and Chaiken; Walker, Police in America).

Without falling into Hollywood-like exaggeration, it is fair to say that on occasion police work requires courage. It requires the physical courage to engage in coercing and, at times, combating hostile citizens. Police work equally requires self-control. Often, the officer on the street is tempted to react to people's strange, threatening, and even dangerous behavior with personal disgust and **"curbside justice"** (Kelling). On a regular basis, police work is about avoiding such a personalized response and, instead, reacting to people's worst behavior with poise and "grace under pressure."

Police work requires maximum honesty. Temptation to be dishonest are ubiquitous, and maintaining principles and behaving as an officer should can be a minute-by-minute challenge. And amidst the human misery on the street, the officer of good character needs to be empathetic not only toward victims but even suspects. Police officers must keep their humanity to avoid cynicism. Finally, the good officer needs integrity—the ability to behave in concert with one's philosophy. The tendency to be hypocritical, saying one thing and doing another, is ever-present in police work. And so integrity is almost as important as the other characteristics combined.

The ability to apply common sense to life's complexities is another indispensible facet of the good police officer's personality. Common sense, as is true with each of the virtues discussed above, is difficult if not impossible to evaluate. It is not reasonable to think any selection process could determine in advance whether or not a candidate will be able to penetrate life's complexities, apply the law, utilize non-legal tools-of-the-trade, and generally make decisions based on sound, commonsensical grounds.

So the first list of necessary qualifications, as critically important as it might be, presents a troublesome set of questions. Questions for which there are not necessarily definitive answers. Thus, even a logically constructed selection process will attempt to evaluate candidates using criteria not very well understood.

Practical Qualifications: The second list of qualification is much more specific and quantifiable. To begin with, perhaps the first, entry-level question about a potential police officer candidate has to do with intelligence. The more naturally intelligent a candidate is, the better the candidate they are. Long gone are the days when police officers were men (always men) with reasonably clean records, perhaps a military background, physical enough to be bouncers at bars—and that was *all* they were. Today's police officer needs to possess much more in the way of natural intelligence than the police officer of old. The modern officer needs to read and interpret the law, understand the nuances of case decisions, grapple with the paradoxes of police work in a sophisticated way, balance numerous delicate decisions as he or she works the street, and understand and empathize with diverse populations and cultures. This is no mean feat. Several studies indicate that today's rookies have intelligence quotients much higher than that of the average person, and this is where any model of candidacy must begin.

Of course, education, too, is a critical component. Responding to the long ago call for college educated officers, the model candidate possesses at least a two-year community college degree if not a four-year bachelor's. But there is tension operating in the police world today in this regard. It is another paradox of modern police work. While in most places a college education is something desired in the ideal officer candidate, in other locations there is an anti-educational bias. In small jurisdictions especially, where the police organization has always been populated by officers without college educations, there is still prejudice that works against expanding the educational level of the officer corps. Led by people who do not possess college backgrounds themselves, some places deride **"book learning"** and do not consider a college education something that makes for a better candidate. So the paradox is that while several hundred thousand college students across the country are majoring in criminal justice to prepare themselves for entry into the modern police officer corps, their efforts are not appreciated in some jurisdictions.

The ideal officer is mature and confidant. While rookie officers will almost always be young, every effort should be made to hire individuals with a substantial amount of real-world experience—living, working, paying taxes, wrestling with the problems of modern American life—so that they have the necessary knowledge, and, ideally, wisdom, to make decisions that impact profoundly upon the lives of others. As noted above, police officers moralize for others on a regular basis. To do this appropriately, they should know about working, raising families, birth and death—they should possess a general experience of modern American adult life.

The ideal officer has a relatively clean record. While there certainly should be latitude in this regard, it is probably not appropriate to hire people with a substantial criminal record. Felonies in particular are troublesome. The ideal candidate will understand the law is not for personal use but something that applies to everyone, and to everyone equally.

A police officer must be physically up to the job. Police work is, as many people joke, "a contact sport." For as much as the modern officer needs to be intelligent, educated, and wise, it is still necessary on occasion for an officer to enter a bar fight or wade into a street melee; to handle a suspect in a one-on-one situation, on the street at night, without help; to deal with altercations involving large numbers of people, who are often hostile and belligerent. As we have taken great pains to point out, officers are not challenged to fight very often. But they *are* challenged on occasion. When that happens, the modern officer still needs to be "part bouncer," even in today's complex world of policing.

In some locations, additional qualities might be important. In the Southwestern United States, it can be advantageous for officers to speak at least conversational Spanish. In parts of New England, it can help if police officers speak at least conversational French. In Louisiana, having some understanding of Creole is important. In some cities, there are large "China Town" areas, and officer candidates who speak Mandarin—the widest spoken Chinese dialect—might be preferable to candidates who do not. Then, too, as we shall see in the affirmative action section, a candidate's ethnic background or sexual orientation might very well be important in some areas of the country (Leinen; Belkin and McNichol). It is better for department demographics to parallel those of the population it polices.

Police work comprises several occupations. Officers today must be part lawyer, part social worker, part forensics expert, part marital counselor, part child psychologist, part martial arts expert, part weapons specialist, part local historian, part medical responder, and so on. The ability to know something about many subjects is part of the model for an ideal candidate. The necessity to understand and balance these areas of expertise is a unique skill required in police work. No other endeavor requires so much in the way of diverse knowledge sets.

Finally, it is important to understand that police work is a "**team sport**." Despite what Hollywood might suggest, there are no superhuman police officers out there, no one officer who can do the job all on their own. Working with and depending on brother and sister officers is an essential element of the job. Strong, silent, loners have no place in police work. So selection processes need to attempt to ascertain if a candidate can be a team player.

Having discussed the concept of the ideal officer in a general sense, we move on now to engage an important dynamic in many parts of the country—something that until very recently was important everywhere in America: the application of **affirmative action** principles to police hiring practices.

AFFIRMATIVE ACTION

From the 1960s until well into the 1980s, the federal government had an affirmative action policy in place. This policy required that local, state, and federal hiring procedures take cognizance of race as a part of their process (Kellough). This policy applied to all governmental jobs, including positions in police work. If a systematic pattern of discrimination had been in place in any jurisdiction, then the discriminating entity—a local police department, state run school system, or federally run parks department, for example—had to attempt to undo that discrimination. This was to be accomplished by prioritizing the hiring of whatever race (to begin with, it was usually African American) had been the target of discrimination.

BOX 11.2

BROWN V. BOARD OF EDUCATION (1954)

In terms of its impact upon American society and upon the lives of millions of individual Americans, the Supreme Court's most important decision of the 20th Century was **Brown v. Board of Education**. In this case, the Court reversed an 80-year-old decision that allowed the state to discriminate on the grounds of race as long as the separated races were treated equally. The "separate but equal" doctrine went by the wayside in *Brown*. Later cases required that any level of government that had been systematically discriminating on racial grounds not only had to stop such discrimination, it had to take "affirmative action" to undo the harm caused by discrimination. Applied to police work, this has meant profound changes in the demographics of departments across the country.

At the federal level, affirmative action is no longer required. But any number of states and major cities still have affirmative action policies in place. We take the time to discuss affirmative action here not only because it still determines part of the selection process in some locales but because it was a critical element in the changes in American policing that have occurred in the past generation.

This is not a constitutional law text and, therefore, we will not spend time fleshing the intricacies of affirmative action—how it came into being, how it was made operational, and the debate that surrounded it. For our purposes, it is only important to note that a part of the formula that defines the "model police officer" in some jurisdictions can include the race, gender, or sexual orientation of prospective candidates—and there are logical reasons for this. As noted above, there is good reason to believe that it is important for the demographics of a police department to reflect those of the city it polices. Until affirmative action was instituted in the late 1960s, many cities had almost all White police departments but populations made up of a majority of non-white peoples. In Oakland, for example, the police department had over 600 officers in the mid 1960s, and all of them (but one) were White males. This organization policed a city with a population that was more than 60 percent Black and Latino. The idea behind affirmative action was, and still is, that this imbalance is not good for police-community relations in general, and that it also can be troublesome for the delivery of justice on the streets.

So affirmative action came to the city of Oakland. Today, with a non-white population of more than 70 percent, the police department has a patrol division that almost exactly replicates that percentage demographically. This is important because there is every reason to believe that a racial disparity between police officers and citizens can produce a great deal of citizen-police (and police-citizen) enmity. As noted by the riot commissions of the 1960s, one of the reasons for the riots was this very tension between the races.

Of course, affirmative action has its own paradox. In attempting to do away with a history of systematic discrimination, the tool used is systematic discrimination (Anglin). That is, in turning an all-white police department into one that is largely Black and Latino, there have to be many academy classes made up of almost all non-white cadets. And during the years when this changeover occurs, it is extremely difficult for a white candidate to be hired. No matter how much we might accept the logic of affirmative action in theory, it has been difficult, for White males in particular, to avoid the feeling that it involves "**reverse discrimination**"—the application of racial prejudice to selection processes in a way that prioritizes candidates of diverse ethnic backgrounds over White candidates. The fairness of the civil service system is thus circumvented by affirmative action (Moran).

Affirmative action was first aimed at the Black/White dichotomy. But later, it was utilized to integrate Latinos, women, Asians, and gays into many police departments. Has it worked? Has affirmative action led to a lessoning of tensions between police and public? It is hard to tell. There is a great amount of "testimonial" evidence that having a police department that mirrors the ethnic diversity of the community it polices tends to mitigate antipathy toward police and encourage the development of good police-community networking. But there is little empirical evidence to this effect. Several studies indicate that there is a short-term, positive impact that comes from affirmative action. On the other hand, some long term studies find that statistical data does not necessarily support this conclusion. We are left to ponder whether or not it *seems* logical that affirmative action has worked in positive ways with regard to tension between races.

With regard to women in policing, some interesting findings have been observed in recent years. In the beginning, many male officers felt that women could not handle the physical requirements of the job. There was a great deal of angst about affirmative action bringing more women into the profession. But over time, several things have been proven about female officers that are truly fascinating. Female officers get far, far fewer citizens' complaints than do their male counterparts. They rarely are the subject of excessive force complaints and seldom get into altercations with citizens. Women are better at dealing with children and with rape victims. Taken together, it is clear that the addition of women to the ranks of the patrol officer corps has had a positive impact in many places and in many ways.

The same can be said of homosexual police officers. It has been found that opening police work up to openly homosexual officers not only had no deleterious effects for the public, but it generated a substantial amount of normalization on the part of straight police officers for their gay comrades (Belkin and McNichol). This, in turn, may very well create even more acceptance of gay people in general among the police.

So affirmative action has changed the face of American policing. And there is reason to believe that the changes wrought have narrowed the distance between police and public—particularly in the inner city. Of course, we must remember that the era during which these changes have occurred has been hard on the White, male candidate from the "dominant" culture.

CIVIL SERVICE AND THE CERTIFICATION PROCESS

During the Political Era of policing, hiring and firing was done on an ad hoc basis, with little in the way of deference given to competence, intelligence, or education. By the end of the 19th Century, America was turning in a new political direction. Over the course of several decades, the Progressive movement became paramount in politics. The progressives called for a number of reforms having to do with government, one of which resulted in the creation of a civil service. In order to eradicate favoritism, incompetence, and corrupt practices, **Civil Service Commissions** were created to instill objectivity in hiring, firing, and administering governmental bureaucracies (Schultz and Moranto). In police work, the entry level test—eventually a series of tests and hurdles—was instituted.

Today, it is the Civil Service Commission that officially administers exams and operates the hiring process. Candidates may go to a police department for a written test, oral board examination, or physical agility test, but these trials are in fact given by Civil Service. For written tests, and sometimes for oral board examinations, the candidate obtains a numerical grade. Seventy to seventy-five percent usually constitute a passing grade, with higher scores being (obviously) preferable. The other elements of the process are conducted on a pass/fail basis. For example, a candidate is either certified by a medical doctor to be fit for duty or he or she is not.

We will soon discuss specific tests that can be involved in selection processes, but it is important to note that once the process is completed, scores are added and candidates are determined to have passed or not. Civil Service will have a predetermined numerical cut-off point, below which a candidate is deemed "unqualified" for hiring. A candidate list, starting with the best candidates, is constructed in descending order. Again, all of this is accomplished by the local, state, or federal Civil Service Commission. Once the testing is done, in some places a candidate can obtain extra points for having a military background. While this process has fallen off in some jurisdictions, having military experience still counts extra in most places—as many as 5 percentage points can be added to a candidate's score in this way.

Then the list is complete. It is "**certified**" by Civil Service. That is, Civil Service states officially that those on the final list are qualified to be hired as police officers. The list goes to either the local Chief of Police or the Sheriff. At that point, and only at that point, does the police department have the ability to make decisions. After the objective and analytical process run by Civil Service has been completed, the police executive has the final choice to make—but only from the certified list. Lists are certified for a certain period of time. Because giving exams is a prolonged and somewhat expensive process, a Civil Service Commission normally certifies a list for at least two years. That means that everyone who made it is eligible for hiring within those two years. Thereafter, a new exam must be given and a new list formulated.

Once the list goes to the Chief or Sheriff, the "**Rule of 3**" applies. The Rule of 3 states that when hiring, the final decision-maker must take one of the top three people on the existing list (Schultz and Moranto). When a list is first certified, this means the first new hire must come from the top three people on the list. After some hiring is done—and several candidates are selected to be sworn in as peace officers—everyone else moves up the list. This process goes on as people are hired, with candidates on the list moving up in turn. But whenever a new hire is made, the Chief or Sheriff always has to take someone out of the top three on the remaining list.

Why the Rule of 3? This rule allows the chief executive of the police department some latitude in the hiring process. Certain candidates that for one reason or another become unacceptable to the Chief or Sheriff can be passed over. This gives the chief executive a small amount of discretion in the reconstruction of the department that the selection process entails. On the other hand, it is only a limited amount of discretionary power. In general, the exams and other elements of the hiring process are kept in the hands of Civil Service. This is meant to insure that objectivity prevails. We must remember that the corrupt hiring practices of the 19th Century were ended by the formulation of a selection process that emphasized the search for intelligence, education, and competence—a process that was to be kept apart from the police department itself (Schultz and Moranto).

BACKGROUND CHECKS

Arguably the most important step in the police hiring process, and often the most costly one, is the **background check**. It is the most costly because those who conduct background checks are often police middle managers—who are paid substantial salaries—and they can spend an entire week checking the background of just one candidate. This is because of how much time is spent in making sure that a candidate's application is accurate and complete (the process side of things) and that the candidate's background is appropriate for a career in police work (the substantive side of things).

Background checks look into anything and everything that might impact a candidate's ability to perform the job effectively. Educational background is checked. It is necessary to verify the high school credentials of every candidate and, in an increasing number of departments, it is also necessary to check the potential officer's college transcripts. Furthermore, a candidate's demeanor and behavioral record in school is considered. Were there any problems in high school related to misconduct? Were there trips to the Dean's office? If so, did youthful indiscretion give way eventually to some level of maturity? Did a somewhat "reckless youth" become a "fine young woman" (or man)?

Employment records are checked. What jobs has a candidate had? What types of responsibilities have been lived up to and what types avoided? Does the candidate get along well with superiors and peers? If there is a supervisory history, how did the potential officer handle having power over others? What about dependability? Did the candidate show up regularly and on time? Was sick leave taken only when appropriate? In particular, how did the candidate handle stress? Given how much stress police work causes, it is important to ascertain how the stress of a "normal" job affected the candidate.

Friends and family are checked out, too. While we are all familiar with the unfairness of **guilt by association**, a concern for the types of people who surround a potential police officer is fair game for a background investigator. The choices one makes in selecting friends can illustrate a person's character in some ways. If candidates spend time around gangsters or criminals, then it does not bode well for them as future police officers. Then, too, family background is important in that the stresses of police work are shared, to some extent, by an officer's family. Is the family squarely behind the police endeavor? Or is there reluctance to have the candidate enter into police work? Considering all of the familial stress that can be created by shift work, odd days off, and strange vacation times, it is critical that significant others accept and support a candidate's decision to enter police work.

Most obvious, and to some extent most important, is a candidate's criminal record. With regard to checking such a record, there is a "sliding scale" in place. That is, the answer to the question, "what type of criminal past might a candidate have and still be acceptable" is: it depends. There are almost no hard and fast rules with regard to criminal background. Considering felonies, it might appear straightforward;

BOX 11.3

Is Everything Fair Game in a Background Check?

What might be considered out of bounds when police conduct background checks on potential officer candidates? Anything? Is everything in a candidate's past and current lifestyle open for inspection? Which of the following might perhaps be considered inappropriate for investigation?

- A candidate's politics.
- A candidate's sexual orientation.
- A candidate's personal relationships with significant others.
- A candidate's friendships.
- A candidate's relationships with members of the police department in question.

any felony convictions, or even felony arrests, will mean disqualification. But what about non-violent felonies, especially if they occur early in a person's life? Would, say, one arrest for burglary, at the age of 18, disqualify a candidate? What if the potential officer is now 28 years old, possesses a college degree, and has had a clean record since the time of the arrest? What about an arrest for passing one bad check? What if a young teenager had one arrest for possession of marijuana at the age of 18? Would using marijuana at such a young age disqualify a candidate? Should it?

Drug use, of course, is a particularly thorny issue. With over 70,000,000 Americans having tried marijuana at least once in their lives, the debate over previous drug use is an important one. Both here and with regard to oral board examinations (see Box 11.4), the drug issue is critical. Until about 30 years ago, any drug use of any kind would automatically disqualify a candidate from entering into police service. But in a world where drug use—especially marijuana use—has become normal, can that rule be observed today? Would it be possible to construct a police officer corps made up entirely of individuals who have never had the now normal experience of experimenting with drug use in their youth? Would we *want* to have such a group—the "I have never even tried it" group—of individuals policing our streets?

If marijuana use has become normal, then those who have not tried it are, by definition, *abnormal*. Is it possible or even desirable in today's world to select police officers who are abnormal in this sense? And if we are willing to accept "some" drug use (some "youthful experimentation") in a candidate's past, then how much is acceptable? How much marijuana use, as the classic example in today's world, constitutes "experimentation?" Two experiences? Seven? A dozen? There is no hard-and-fast answer; police selection must apply a sliding scale to this question in today's world, and the application of that scale can be uneven and unfair.

What about misdemeanors? Is "an arrest or two" acceptable for such "minor" crimes? How about petty theft? How about being drunk in public? How about drunk driving? How about violent misdemeanors, such as battery? Should such records be disqualifying? Are we in fact going to assemble a police officer corps capable of handling the physical side of police work effectively if we never hire anyone who has ever been drunk or in a fight? Again, a sliding scale must be in place, and that is totally understandable. A background investigator or an oral board must assess the overall picture of a candidate's past and decide whether or not a potential officer can effectively police with a criminal record. The application of this inexact science creates the central paradox of police selection: the attempt at precision with this all-important decision-making process when precision is impossible. Deciding in advance if an individual is acceptable, even with transgressions in their past, is difficult, frustrating, and almost impossible. Nevertheless, it is the function of those who make selections in today's complex world.

Other Elements of the Process

Having discussed the critical element of background checks, let us briefly consider other elements of the process, beginning with the written exam.

Written Exams: The overwhelming majority of police organizations utilize **written exams** as the first step in the selection process. These exams are generic intelligence and problem-solving tests. They tend to measure general abilities in vocabulary, grammar, and writing. They also test deductive reasoning, inductive reasoning, and the ability to solve logical dilemmas. Such tests are akin to the basic exams taken by most people in school (Krasowski). They are designed for people unknowledgeable and inexperienced in the police field. The assumption behind them is that no one need know anything about police work to be a good candidate. A generally solid intelligence, a standard education, and some natural ability at problem solving is all that is necessary for a candidate to be chosen. (There is much wrong with this, and we will engage in the discussion about the inappropriate nature of today's tests in our "critique" section.) The written exam eventuates in a numerical score.

Oral Boards: One tradition that is both a troublesome and important part of the process is the **oral board examination**. Usually in front of three interviewers, the candidate is asked a series of questions aimed at assessing their ability to think quickly, their aptitude for dealing with people, and their common sense. While the oral board is almost entirely subjective—another problem we will engage below—it is deemed necessary in most jurisdictions to inject some life, some human interaction into the process. Printed educational transcripts, criminal records, and work histories do not tell the story of a candidate's potential. Written exams, agility tests, and physical examinations are also lifeless and officious. Thus, the oral board, despite its subjectivity, is still considered in most places an important hurdle for a candidate. If a potential

BOX 11.4

THE "DRUG USE" QUESTION

Almost all police Oral Board examinations involve a question about drug use. What is—or should be—the response to a candidate who answers in the affirmatively when asked if they have ever used illegal drugs? There are several schools of thought on this:

- No candidate who has used illegal drugs should ever be hired.
- It is acceptable if a candidate has used illegal drugs, as long as it occurred in a phase of youthful "experimentation."
- Given that a large majority of today's young people have used illegal drugs—it is the "norm"—police officers *should* have some experience with using such drugs, as this will make them more knowledgeable about the subject.

Which answer is appropriate? It depends upon one's perspective.

police officer cannot deal with the stress of being questioned by three interviewers in a quiet, calm, and safe environment, then logic suggests that they should not be entrusted with a weapon and the power of the badge. Oral board exams are usually pass/fail, but they are scored numerically in some places.

Psychological Testing: Given the amount of stress involved in day-to-day police work, given the pressure exerted upon police family life, and given the responsibility of being licensed to use force—lethal force under certain circumstances—it makes sense that police selection procedures should include **psychological profiling** (Rostowd and Davis). After all, those who are eventually hired will be given weapons, handcuffs, mace, and a tremendous amount of discretionary decision-making power over the lives of American citizens. Unfortunately, the sort of psychological testing considered optimum is extraordinarily expensive.

Only a few jurisdictions, owing to the expense, have police selection procedures that include screening by a qualified psychologist. In lieu of this expensive process, most police organizations utilize one of several written, multiple-choice exams that attempt to create personality profiles of candidates. These profiles are designed to ascertain if a candidate is overly aggressive or abnormal. The two tests most often relied upon are the **Minnesota Multi-Phasic Inventory (MMPI) II** (Megargee) and the **California Personality Inventory (CPI)** (Robertson and Myers). In some jurisdictions, after these tests are taken, candidates can be ordered to see a psychologist. In other words, the exams are used to screen for individuals who might score too high on aggressiveness and, thus, need professional evaluation. Psychological testing is done on a pass/fail basis.

Physical Exams: Before a candidate can make it onto a certified Civil Service list, he or she must take a **physical examination** administered by a medical doctor. It is to some extent obvious what such doctors are looking for. All candidates must pass a drug test for obvious reasons. They must pass blood tests for any number of communicable diseases. They must possess at least a normal person's back strength, and their knees must be in good shape. This is to insure one's ability to scale fences, carry injured officers or citizens, and lift things in general. Police work is a high-stress occupation. So physical exams include screening for any stress-related infirmities. Blood pressure, resting heart rate, and EKG results are always included in such evaluations. Physical exams are pass/fail.

Agility Tests: Americans sometimes think of police officers as overweight, out of shape, donut eaters. It is ironic that this image co-exists with the image, discussed in Chapter Six, of police officers as super-humans of some kind. Being fit in this "contact sport" is obviously important. So **agility tests** have been instituted to gauge aerobic fitness, strength, and flexibility. Such tests used to be quite simple, including merely push-ups, pull-ups, sit-ups, and perhaps some sort of strength test. But in recent years, they have expanded to include running, vaulting fences, and dragging dead weights (replicating pulling a citizen from a burning building). These elements of the test can either be done individually or they can be done in a circuit where "beating" an overall minimum time is required to pass.

Local contractual agreements between unions and cities and counties usually make it extremely difficult to utilize agility tests once officers have been hired. That is, once police officers have passed their probationary period, they cannot again be tested and told they are unfit for duty. So agility tests are almost always taken but once during an officer's career: at the entry level. Given how important it is for police to be fit, some jurisdictions allow officers to earn time off with pay if they pass fitness tests during their tenure. This provides a great incentive to remain fit for the in-service officer. Agility tests are pass/fail.

BOX 11.5

DETERRING WOMEN

Police agility tests used to be quite easy. In fact, they were so easy that only the most hopelessly unfit candidates would fail. Once affirmative action policies were in place, and an increased number of women wanted to become police officers, tests became much more difficult. This was done in an effort to keep women out of police work (Wells and Alt). But the change hasn't been bad in the grand scheme of things, because candidates now take getting fit before applying much more seriously than they used to.

Polygraphs: Polygraph examinations are so expensive that the fiscal commitment involved makes them prohibitive for most police organizations. However, even though they are both time consuming and expensive, polygraphs are still the norm in some locations. It used to be that police departments could utilize polygraph examinations whenever they conducted investigations into police misconduct. A department could require that an officer under investigation take a polygraph or be terminated. Today, however, in most places, this use of the polygraph for internal investigations is either severely limited or no longer allowed. **"Police Officer Bills of Rights"** (see Chapter Thirteen) have been passed in some states, making such polygraph exams illegal. Also, in some jurisdictions, the local contract between the police union and the city or county stipulates this same rule. In these jurisdictions, the only chance police departments have to polygraph an employee is in the pre-employment phase, where it is always legal to do so.

Polygraph exams are given on a pass/fail basis. Essentially, the information accrued becomes a part of the entire "picture" of an employee's character that is painted throughout the process. A potential employee can be deemed ineligible for hiring based on a bad polygraph result.

Bringing the Process Together: Not all jurisdictions utilize all of these procedures. Some steps are considered outdated by some departments—the oral board exam, for example. But in every jurisdiction, some process is in place, and it almost always involves putting the candidate through a long series of challenges.

Normally, it is the background check investigator that collects the information and organizes it. The successful candidate's file is then passed on to the chief executive. The final step in the selection process is the interview with the Chief or

BOX 11.6

WHAT PERCENTAGE OF DEPARTMENTS USE WHICH PROCEDURES?

- Background Investigations   =   96%
- Written Tests   =   85%
- Oral Boards   =   96%
- Psychological Testing   =   61%
- Physical Exams   =   81%
- Agility Tests   =   44%
- Polygraphs   =   21%

(Hickman and Reaves 5)

Sheriff. Limited only by the Rule of 3, the final decision belongs to them. Once a candidate has passed the multiple steps and been certified by civil service, the Chief or Sheriff makes the selection and the candidate then starts the red tape–riddled process of being officially hired.

CRITIQUE

What might we criticize about the process just discussed? First, there is reason to question the type of written exams given at the entry level. These are general intelligence and problem solving tests. They tend to cover vocabulary, logical reasoning, knowledge of syntax, basic math, and so forth. In essence, they are aimed at people with *only* a basic education (Aamedt). The assumption behind a test like this is that the police academy will teach selected candidates all they need to know about police work. What is wrong with this?

The problem with such written exams is that they require no preexisting expertise in police work. They are aimed at candidates who are intelligent but completely ignorant of criminal law, criminal procedures, constitutional law, the elements of the criminal justice system, and of a host of other topics. Why have such basic tests when thousands of candidates bring substantial amounts of knowledge in the field? Why operate a system that assumes ignorance in lieu of one that takes advantage of the growth of study in the field of police work at the college level?

In law, medicine, architecture, nursing, and many other professions, potential practitioners are given pre-professional training examinations that test their knowledge in the field. Potential lawyers must now take the LSATs in order to enter law school. Potential doctors must take the MCATs to enter medical school. While the analogy is not perfect, there is reason to believe that police work could benefit from a change in the sort of basic testing required at the entry level. Substantial change to entry level exams might allow the reorganization of police academy training, excluding much of the current curriculums and fashioning new methods of instruction. This change could allow the inclusion of new and important subjects—subjects for which there is not enough time in today's academy. Because the candidates chosen, despite being intelligent, are ignorant about criminal law, constitutional law, and the elements of the criminal justice system, these subjects have to be taught in the academy.

Why? Why do entry level exams not expect candidates to know the basic elements of the **F.B.I.'s Part One Offenses**? The holdings in *Mapp v. Ohio* and *Miranda v. Arizona*? The components of the criminal justice system? The difference between probation and parole? The difference between jails and prisons? The basics of juvenile procedures and vehicular law? Arrest and search and seizure law? Since there are several hundred thousand students on today's college campuses majoring in criminal justice, learning all of the above at their own expense, why not have entry level exams that test these things in advance of academy training?

Why spend any academy training time teaching the basics of the system and the law? Might police academy time be better spent teaching other subjects?

Couldn't police academies spend time on subjects such as the psychology of death and dying, the dynamics of marital conflict, the history of race relations in America, and a host of other subjects that are left out of academy curriculum? Why "waste" time teaching the substance of the law and the elements of the criminal justice system when it would be easy enough to require candidates to have knowledge of these subjects before they even apply? This is a primary criticism of the standard selection process.

Second, we must acknowledge that oral board exams are totally subjective. In fact, in the history of police selection, it was the oral board examination that was utilized for generations to keep minorities and women out of police work (Walker, Police In America). Black and female candidates would pass entry level written exams, but they were then found "unfit for duty" by the subjective machinations of the oral board process. We might defend oral boards by suggesting that today they are no longer utilized to keep minorities and women out of police service. But that still would beg another question.

Who is, in fact, being left out of the process? Are there new types of officers, with different backgrounds and skill sets, being blocked from police work? People who might very well hasten the progress of community policing or police professionalization? If the process is at all prone to select only a certain type of "predetermined" candidate, excluding candidates who might make excellent officers but who have different, unusual backgrounds, then the oral board element of the selection procedure is quite possibly the place where these inappropriate exclusions are being made—because of the subjectivity involved.

All exclusive groups—fraternities, sororities, service clubs, country clubs, the American Bar Association, the American Medical Association—have complete control over their own selection processes. They tend to accept like-minded individuals and exclude those with different, unusual, or unique backgrounds. This process might be defensible, if viewed from the perspective that the members of the "in group" know who belongs and who does not—because of their expertise and experience. But it might be equally criticized for being too conservative and for eschewing the chance to make changes for the better by exposing the selection process to thinking that is "outside of the box."

What types of "better police officer candidates" are we discussing here? Who is being excluded that might change police work for the better? What groups are being frozen out of the experience to the detriment of justice? (R. Kaminski) The answer to these questions is that we do not know who is being left out. There is no way to know. And that's the point.

A third criticism of the process has to do with allowing candidates extra credit for military service. Why? Why is this done? As we have seen in the previous chapter, this might make sense for a Legalistic style department. Such departments operate in a manner that suggests candidates with military backgrounds might provide a distinct advantage to the organization. On the other hand, a militaristic carriage and focus is not the optimum choice for Service or Watchman style departments.

Furthermore, there is reason to believe that a military background might actually be a hindrance when hiring for a COP styled organization. Nevertheless, adding points for a military background is almost universally done.

Why not college points? Why not award extra points to anyone with a two-year degree and still more points to anyone with a four-year degree? This occurs in only a limited number of jurisdictions, but it makes more sense than extending the traditional military advantage. And what about other background characteristics? Why not give a candidate extra points for speaking Spanish in a Southwestern department? Why not give a candidate extra points for speaking French in a North-eastern department? While such skills do lend an advantage to the candidacy of recruits who possess them, why not institutionalize such advantages with a specific points system?

The overall question for those wishing to critique the existing selection process is: Who is left out? And, unfortunately, the answer is that we have no idea.

SUMMATION

The central paradox of police selection processes is that they attempt to do the impossible. The most important question at issue in selection is the evaluation of character. And for as much as police organizations attempt to do everything in their power to assess it, character is something too amorphous to measure with any accuracy. So the goal of police selection procedures is, to some extent, an impossible one: to quantify the unquantifiable and predict the unpredictable.

Furthermore, while police hiring processes become more sophisticated and produce a cadet corps superior to those of the past, they can also work to preserve the status quo while inhibiting progress—especially toward the institutionalizing of community policing.

Next, we will engage the topic of police education and training. Focusing mainly upon the academy, we will once again discuss standard operations and then turn to critique them. We will focus not only on the curriculum included in most police academies, but also on the operational tone used in most police academies. In doing so, we will once again engage the pluses and minuses of paramilitarism.

CHAPTER ELEVEN PARADOX BOX

Selection is crucial: it involves an ongoing attempt to re-invent the police organization. But selection involves ascertaining the character of a candidate. And this is impossible to accomplish with any level of certainty, no matter what tests are applied.

DISCUSSION QUESTIONS

1. Aristotle's list of "the virtues" has become famous worldwide. Take a look at the list. Is it all-inclusive? Aren't there additional, important virtues, such as kindness or integrity (the characteristic of acting in agreement with one's professed beliefs)? Discuss that list. Since no one is a saint, and most people rank highly on some virtues and low on others, try to prioritize the virtues. Which is most important? Which is least important? Finally, discuss whether or not there are virtues you might add to Aristotle's list.

2. Discuss affirmative action. What are the pluses of this policy? What are the minuses? How might it affect police selection in either direction? Finally, discuss what characteristics might be important in one part of the country or another—as is done briefly in the text. Might it be important for police officers in South Florida to speak Spanish? Could an officer's religion be important in one part of the country or another?

3. We have suggested in the text that a candidate's politics are "out of bounds" where background checks are concerned. Can you think of other areas of a person's life that should also be considered irrelevant in determining whether or not they should be hired as a police officer? Discuss.

4. It is a historical fact that agility tests were made more difficult in order to keep women out of policing. Now that we know women can do a fine job of policing on the street, what should be done about the upper body strength problem? Should there be two different agility tests, one for women and one for men? Or should there be one and only one test? What are the pros and cons of these two options, as seen in light of the fact that woman are actually better than men at some police tasks—and therefore it is in the best interests of police work to hire women?

KEY TERMS

Affirmative Action: Court-created process by which previous patterns of discrimination on the part of the state are undone.

Agility Tests: Strength, endurance, and agility tests given to police officers as part of the selection process. Sometimes they involve individual "events," sometimes a circuit run against a clock.

Background Check: Extensive investigation into the histories of candidates going through the police selection process.

"Book Learning": Refers, in rather derisive terms, to knowledge obtained in academe.

Brown v. Board of Education (1954): The case that did away with "separate but equal" schools in America and began the process that eventually ushered in the era of affirmative action.

California Personality Inventory (CPI): One of the standard tests often given to potential police officers as a part of their selection process. These tests attempt to construct a psychological profile that looks for over-aggressiveness in particular.

Certified Lists: A list of potential police hirees compiled by Civil Service and delivered to a Chief of Police or a Sheriff.

Civil Service Commissions: Bureaucracies created around the turn of the 19th Century to instill objectivity in governmental selection procedures.

Curbside Justice: The practice of police officers administering punishment on the streets to citizens they determine "deserve it."

F.B.I.'s Part One Offenses: The part of the F.B.I.'s Uniform Crime Reports that includes homicide, rape, robbery, burglary, auto theft, aggravated assault, larceny, and arson.

Good Character: The rather amorphous concept that comprises what police selection processes seek to determine.

Guilt by Association: An ancient concept suggesting that people should be found guilty of deviant behavior due to the guilt of their associates or family.

Minnesota Multi-Phasic Inventory (MMPI) II: One of the standard tests often given to potential police officers as a part of their selection process. These tests attempt to construct a psychological profile that looks for over-aggressiveness in particular.

Oral Board Examinations: Personal interview with potential police officers that usually involves the candidate being confronted by three interviewers.

Physical Examination: Examination conducted by a medical doctor to determine the physical fitness of candidates for the job of being a police officer.

Police Officer Bills of Rights: Sets of laws that are passed in an effort to protect accused police officers when they are investigated for misconduct.

Polygraph Examinations: "Lie detector tests" that monitor physical responses to questioning. Sometimes included in police selection procedures.

Practical Qualifications: Requirements that potential police officers must reach in order to be hired; separate from the "good character" requirement.

Psychological Profiling: Sometimes a part of police selection procedures, such testing often involves the MMPI or CPI (above).

Reverse Discrimination: The idea that affirmative action involves discriminating against people, normally White people, on the grounds of race.

Rule of 3: Administrative rule that requires a Chief of Police or Sheriff to hire one of the top three candidates on a Certified Civil Service Hiring List.

Team Sport (Policing As): The idea that the police are a team, involved in a contact sport.

The Virtues: Aristotle's 2,400-year-old discussion about human character traits that ranks them according to their "excesses," "defects," and "mean."

Written Exams: Entry level tests required of police officer candidates almost everywhere; usually given first in the selection process.

ADDITIONAL READING:

Our discussion here began with reference to Aristotle's famous discussion about character, a central theme for police selection. An excellent review of Aristotle's treatment of the topic is *The Fabric of Character: Aristotle's Theory of Virtue* by Nancy Sherman (Oxford University Press, 1991). Also, Perez and Moore (cited elsewhere) take Aristotle's analysis and apply it directly to the issue of police officer character.

In order to understand the political realities of affirmative action, both *Understanding Affirmative Action: Politics, Discrimination, and the Search for Justice* by J. Edward Kellough (Georgetown University Press, 2006) and *The Affirmative Action Dilemma* by Kirklin Anglin (BookSurge Publishing, 2006) give good overviews of not only the law involved but the political struggles associated with the process.

We have already cited several works about African-American police officers. In addition, Stephen Leinen's *Gay Cops* (Rutgers University Press, 1993) discusses the dynamics associated with the movement to allow gay people into police work for the first time, beginning less than 20 years ago in San Francisco. A more recent work is A. Belkin and J. McNichol's article "Pink in Blue: Outcomes Associated With the Integration of Open Gay and Lesbian Personnel in the San Diego Police Department" (in *Police Quarterly*, 5:63–95, 2002). These works engage the idea directly that police departments need to reflect the demographics of the populations they police.

The invention of civil service is a critical historical development for our discussions in several chapters in this book. *The Politics of Civil Service Reform* by David A. Schultz and Robert Moranto (Peter Lang Publishing, 1998) gives the student a good overview of the history of the idea's evolution as well as some insight into the political realities of contemporary civil service commissions.

Focusing more specifically upon police work, Michael G. Aamedt has put together a collection of research data about selection processes in *Research in Law Enforcement Selection* (Brown Walker Press, 2004). In *A Handbook for Psychological Fitness-For-Duty Evaluations in Law Enforcement* (Routledge, 2004), C. Rostowd and R. Davis offer an analysis of the process from a more practical, how-to perspective.

There are any number of books written for would-be police officer candidates. *Master the Police Officer Exam, 17th ed.* by Joe Krasowski, ed. (Thomson Peterson, 2005), is one such book that has been in print for many years.

Finally, Stephen A. Baker discusses changes in police selection procedures (among other topics) in a book focused upon the contemporary drive to accredit police departments across the nation. The book is *Effects of Law Enforcement Accreditation: Officer Selection, Promotion, and Education* (Praeger, 1995).

CHAPTER 12

Education and Training

Chapter Twelve Outline

The educational requirements for today's modern police are odd in the sense that there is no one clear cut, particular path down which a person should travel in order to obtain the knowledge necessary to become a police officer. What a modern, competent officer needs to know includes information about a broad range of subjects and skill sets. Ideally, the officer needs to experience several different levels of education. There is neither merely one type of knowledge to possess nor is there only one place to go to obtain it. In this chapter we will engage in a discussion of the substance of what today's officer needs to know and also in a consideration of the process through which this education and training is garnered.

To become an appropriately educated and trained officer in today's officer corps, one needs the combined experience of high school, college, academy training, and in-service training. As is true in other professions, the education of a modern police officer never ceases. In fact, one of the selling points used by recruiters to convince intelligent young people to enter police service relates to this specific point: police work is a challenging and rewarding profession for the person interested in life-long learning. It is a profession meant for those who want to grow and expand their knowledge base and expertise in life in a way that means they will continually be "going to school" throughout their career.

The education of police officers can underwrite the status quo by passing along "the way things are done" from one generation of police officers to another. Or it can engage modern officers with new directions in a philosophical and operational sense. It involves either cleaving to paramilitarism or eschewing it in favor of a more progressive model. Thus, debates about which direction modern policing should take find their way into police educational debates and, indeed, into the halls of police academies. This discussion is constantly in flux in the world of police work; how are we going to educate rookie police officers and what are we going to teach them?

Let us take a moment to consider the various elements that make up the educational experience necessary for today's police officer.

A PATCHWORK QUILT OF EDUCATIONAL REQUIREMENTS

Certainly, the base line educational requirement for police officers is the high school education. It was not long ago that this was the only education required for the job. In today's police work, high school is merely the starting point for officer education. Before the modern era of policing, it was enough for an officer to read and write, to be able to handle the physical, **"contact sport"** side of the job, and to be able to exercise common sense. Obviously, the requirements of the job still involve possessing these three elements. But important developments over the course of the past several decades have created an entirely different kind of policing and, in turn, an entirely different set of educational requirements. What are the developments that have spawned this expanded set of educational prerequisites?

First, there is the exclusionary rule. The police today must understand constitutional law in a way that was irrelevant to their predecessors on the beat. Since

BOX 12.1

THE ELEMENTS OF POLICE EDUCATION

To be a truly educated police officer, a member of what Jerome Skolnick and David Bayley have labeled "The New Blue Line" (Skolnick and Bayley), an officer needs to have:

- A high school education.

- A two-year college degree; community college programs offer introductory, general education classes and additional core courses that give students a basic understanding of the criminal justice system and criminological theory.

- An upper division, four-year college experience; this entails getting a broadly based, liberal arts education that includes history, psychology, sociology, political science, and a host of other subjects that allow a person to be well-rounded and informed . . . as well as more specific, law and criminal justice–oriented courses.

- The police academy experience.

- Field training with an F.T.O.

- Specific training for a specialized assignment, such as being a Field Training Officer (FTO), a K-9 officer, or a forensics technician.

- On-going, in-service training.

the dictates of the Constitution have now been translated into minute-by-minute police work, the police need to have much more than just a passing understanding of it. Furthermore, search and seizure law in particular has become an area of study in which today's police need to be experts of sorts. Once the Supreme Court began making decisions that impacted upon police officers in direct ways, it opened a Pandora's box; today's officers have to be familiar with stop and frisk law, search warrant requirements, interrogation law, vehicle stop and vehicle search cases, and so forth. A job that once left the specifics of case law to attorneys is now driven by it daily.

Second, as noted in Chapter Four, today's officer must understand the delicate balancing act required when applying substantive law. The problem with catch-all penal code sections is something about which every beat officer must be wary. Thus, a sort of political savvy—an understanding that the police have to be careful when applying catch-all sections—has become essential knowledge in the field.

Third, there have been technological developments with which the police must be knowledgeable. Until recently, no one associated with the American legal system needed to know anything about **DNA testing**, for example (Semikhodskii).

Today, even beat officers must understand how developments in this and other areas change the nature of investigations.

Fourth, the expectations of the citizenry have changed with regard to what police officers should know about a host of issues. Today they are expected to control suspects in "humane" ways. Even discussions about how prisoners of war are treated have made their way into the police literature (Amnesty International). They are expected to be able to deal with the homeless and with gangs. They need to understand basic human psychology and the subfield of adolescent psychology. They must grasp the basic principles of sociology, including problems associated with death and dying, gang membership, and marital strife. They need to be conversant with American history, especially that of the civil rights movement and the turbulent '60s. And they must understand basic political science, including how American governmental institutions interact and the principles of our system of checks and balances.

Last, and perhaps most important, COP has brought to the fore a host of new requirements. Taken together, they mean that police officers have to be part local politician, part community organizer, and—of critical importance—part criminologist. The proactive philosophy of COP requires that today's officers understand the root causes of crime at the outset. They must be able to problem solve and come up with anti-crime strategies that require a sort of synoptic knowledge of American culture and life on the streets. The average patrol officer today needs to possess an understanding of these subjects that was possessed only by police managers in the past. Put another way, being a line officer today requires the type of broadly based knowledge that was required of Lieutenants and Captains in the past.

So not even a good, solid high school education avails today's officer of the substantive knowledge needed to work a beat. High school provides merely the tools necessary to enable the modern officer go out and learn what is required. Unfortunately, in contemporary America, all we can expect of a high school graduate is that he or she can read and write and knows basic math skills. Anything further is no longer required to graduate. Therefore, a high school education is just the starting point.

After high school, there is the requirement of attending college-level courses and obtaining a college degree. This is no longer an "option." Below, we will discuss the debate about what such a college education should entail. For now, let us just acknowledge that today's police officer cannot function effectively without one. Today's officer must understand the paradoxes of police work. He or she must be comfortable changing from one role to another. Studying the nature of roles, in sociology courses—not to mention the nature of subcultures, also garnered in sociology courses—is just one of the important pieces of knowledge this college level experience should provide to the modern officer.

Once a candidate is hired, there is the police academy experience (discussed at length below). After that, there is learning occurs in the field. Field training involves interacting with today's Field Training Officer (FTO) and living up to expectations more involved than those of past eras. In the past, after an officer was hired, he or she needed only to "keep their noses clean" for a year—then they were past their probationary period. Today, they have so much more to learn when they hit the street that the system works to weed out officers that cannot live up to expectations. Thus, the probationary period is serious business. A substantial minority of probationary police officers today are either terminated or resign, a fact unheard of in previous days.

Additional training can be required, depending upon what specific areas of police work an officer engages. Special training is necessary to be a K-9 officer, a Forensics Technician, an F.T.O., a member of S.W.A.T., and so on. Such training is not required of all police officers, of course, but an increasing number are required to specialize and focus upon one area of expertise or another.

Finally, there is in-service training. In an effort to require that officers keep current in the field, as is the case for other professionals, in-service training hours are not only encouraged but required. As we shall see shortly, this makes for an ongoing learning process that is an integral part of today's modern police officer's career.

Let us engage the elements of this patchwork quilt in logical order.

Higher Education

Four decades ago, the call went out for the education of police officers to be improved through the creation of college programs in criminal justice (L. Sherman). Over the next twenty years, advanced by federal monies granted through the L.E.E.P. program (and others), the movement gathered momentum (Korbets). After the call for college-educated police officers has become almost universal, there still exists an ongoing debate about how much college education is necessary for the average police officer and, furthermore, about what *kind* of college education is optimal. Some students of the police maintain that the best college background is that of a **liberal arts education**, not necessarily aimed at police work (Muir). These people argue that the breadth of knowledge obtained in this kind of generalized course of study will best inform the police officer on the street. A liberal arts education takes seriously the goal of attaining knowledge in a diverse set of fields—exactly the sort of broadly-based academic experience with which a police officer should be conversant.

Others point out that there is so much to learn in the particularized, focused field of police work that the undergraduate experience should take a straightforward run at the profession. These people argue that criminal justice studies should be the focus. This debate has made its way into the field of criminal justice, criminology, and "police science." Within the academic culture that focuses upon such major courses of study, this argument—about police officers obtaining either a generalized education or a more focused one—is constantly debated.

The debate goes further. In the world of academia there are two distinctively different types of criminal justice programs. One emphasizes a sociological approach to the study of crime, criminology, and the criminal justice system. It is analytical and critical. This type of criminal justice program is driven by the idea that modern police work requires officers to have the broadly based, liberal arts background discussed above. The idea here is that police work demands that officers understand multiple roles and that they become able to change at will from one role to another.

For example, today's officer must be a member of the criminal justice system's prosecutorial staff, in a sense, while they search for guilty parties and put handcuffs on them. This is clearly one role they must play. But then, if they are going to interrogate a suspect, the police must immediately change roles and become part of the defense team. They must advise suspects of their rights under the Constitution and, oddly enough, tell suspects that questions are going to be asked of them and that they *need not be answered*. So at a moment's notice, the modern police officer changes roles, jumping from one side of the fence to the other.

As another example, today's officer must avoid the pitfalls of paramilitarism most of the time. As discussed at length in Chapter Eight, the modern police officer's role as community servant requires that he or she do this. But in an instant, if presented with a hostage situation, for example, officers must change their method of operation and morph into members of a military unit. They must respond to chains of command that require military-type accountability. Again, they must be capable of changing instantly from one role to another.

The **sociologically based college programs** view the process of role changing as one that might best be understood by those who have taken a broadly based

BOX 12.2

AN UNUSUAL BODY OF KNOWLEDGE

There is no profession quite like policing with regard to the breadth of subjects upon which a competent officer must be expert. In no particular order, a partial list includes:

Criminal Law	Case Law
Forensics	Investigation Strategies
Interrogation Techniques	Firearms and Other Weapons
Defensive Tactics	First Aid
Local History	Local Politics
Sociological Theory	The Psychology of Death and Dying
Gang Theory	Counseling Strategies
Adolescent Psychology	Departmental Regulations

set of courses. Having a generalized educational background will avail the pre–police experience college student of the tools necessary to accomplish the myriad tasks and play the numerous roles required by modern policing.

Then there are the **practical college programs**. These programs involve a curriculum aimed at preparing the undergraduate to work the street as soon as they graduate. Courses in these programs encompass pragmatic concerns, such as how to work a beat, how to make a search, fire arms training, and so forth. Sometimes, these programs emulate police academies, simply expanding the curriculum of the academy into a college-length experience. Most of these programs are located at the community-college, two-year level of higher education. But some are four year programs. Aimed at those who wish to prepare for police work (and only for police work), such programs provide less in the way of broad knowledge and more in the way of "nuts 'n bolts."

In the academic world, the debate between protagonists supporting each type of program is ongoing. The sociological programs tend to call the more practical programs "**cop shops**," and claim that, from their perspective, such programs are unnecessary, since they merely replicate academy training. The more practical programs claim that, from their perspective, a lot of time is "wasted" in sociological programs—wasted studying subjects of no value to police officers. They tend to make fun of the "theory" that a liberal arts education includes.

There is no definitive answer to the question of which type of program is "best." Each has its strengths and weaknesses. It can be said with relative certainty that the sociological programs better prepare officers to enter into COP-styled departments, and that the practical programs better prepare officers for Legalistic style departments. The good news for modern police work is that both types of programs expand police officer education in the direction of turning it into a genuine profession. From the perspective of most police managers, it makes no difference which is "better."

The Optimal Pre-Employment Education: Perhaps the best overall educational formula for the modern police officer would involve the following set of experiences. (1) A solid high school education that teaches one to read and write—especially to write essays that are logically constructed and that abide by the basic rules of English grammar and syntax composition. (2) A two-year community college experience that engages the student with general education courses and some basic, introductory criminal justice classes. These introductory criminal justice courses include criminology, the organization and processes of the criminal justice system, criminal law, and introductory courses about police and corrections. Such courses at the community college level tend to be of the more practical sort discussed above, and they establish a baseline for would-be officer college education. (3) Two upper division years at a college or university that provide a liberal arts education and criminal justice courses that are sociologically based. This provides the student with a critical, analytical perspective on crime, criminals, victimization, the nature of law, the sociology of police work in America, and the concept of justice. The experience of hiring college-educated police officers has been found to "work," in the sense that such officers out-perform their non–college educated counterparts, so this is a development that is most definitely here to stay in American police work (Truxillo *et al.*).

It is now time to turn to a consideration of the modern police academy. We will first outline two sorts of academy foci, then discuss the standard academy curriculum, and, finally, offer a critique of it.

The Academy

For the first century of American policing, in most locales, there was no serious effort to give police officers any training in advance of their street experience. Police work was a blue collar job—thus, the expectation was that everything an officer needed to know would be learned in an informal manner by associating with more experienced officers. Police work was so inexorably linked to the operations of political machines that it did not seem necessary to take police training very seriously. It would have made more sense to give 19th Century rookie police officers training in politics rather than in the law and criminal procedures. The law did not have much to do with what the police did at all until well into the 20th Century.

Then, as we have seen, the Reform Era arrived and changed much about police work. And one of the substantial changes was the development of the police academy. Given that the efforts of reformists were largely aimed at generating control over police behavior (or misbehavior, to be more precise), police academies were engineered to instill discipline and engender a militaristic chain-of-command–type of operational norm. Since the era of reform, police academies in many jurisdictions have maintained exactly this same focus and tenor. But since additional change has been in the air in American policing for a generation now, we must discuss the contemporary debate over how academies should be organized and operated.

The Tone: There is an ongoing debate about police academy training in American policing that parallels the general debate about paramilitarism. The world of police academies is now divided into two types of approaches. The first type features **stress-based academies** that emphasize paramilitarism and a **boot camp mentality**. Inspections occur regularly. Such a program "typically includes paramilitary drills, intensive physical demands, public disciplinary measures, immediate reaction to infractions, daily inspections, valued inculcation, and withholding of privileges" (DOJ *Special Report* 9). The entire focus is aimed at creating a military-like experience that prepares police cadets for work in a paramilitary organization. A self-reporting study done by the Department of Justice found that 15 percent of academies report their training to be mostly stress-based and 38 percent report "more stress than non-stress" based programs (DOJ *Special Report* 10).

As briefly noted in Chapter Eight, the classroom in such stress-oriented academies has a boot camp tone. Cadets who wish to participate in discussions must rise from their desks, stand at attention, identify themselves, and then ask a question.

This is exactly the sort of atmosphere that permeates training in military boot camps. The stress level experienced by cadets all through their time at the academy is meant to prepare them for the tensions of life on the street as a police officer.

Second, there are those academies that attempt to avoid military boot camp training in favor of a more **collegial style of teaching and learning**. Their operations are driven by the idea that a college-like atmosphere will produce more thorough and in-depth learning. Such academies even encourage analytical and critical thinking about contemporary issues in police work, much as is done in the sociologically based college program. Marching is eschewed, because when do police officers ever march together? Fitness is encouraged, but military drill is avoided. Forty-seven percent of today's academies are non-stress based (DOJ *Special Report* 10).

The non-stress type of academy is on the rise. The change toward them is driven largely by COP-based ideals—by the idea that police academies are supposed to encourage cutting edge thinking and problem solving that is creative and resourceful. Only time will tell whether or not such low stress academies are the wave of the future. Since there can be a case made for both types, it is difficult to know in which direction academy training is headed. We will discuss this further below and make the point that some sort of compromise or combination of the two strategies is probably best.

Standard Curriculum: Chart 12.1 indicates those courses of study (and numbers of hours for each) required for a police academy to be certified by the **Peace Officer Standards and Training (P.O.S.T.)** Commission of the State of California. Such regulatory agencies are found in almost every state, whether or not they are officially labeled as "P.O.S.T." commissions (U.S.D.O.J. *Special Report*). These commissions set requirements for police academies and a host of other police-related training courses, such as K-9 courses, FTO courses, and leadership courses. Experienced police executives, such as in-service or retired Chiefs of Police and Sheriffs, populate such commissions. They are a part of the self-regulation of police work that is increasing across the country. In Chapter Fifteen, we will consider how important this self-regulation is for the development of police professionalism.

If it is true that the competent police officer needs to know something about a great number of subjects, then it should be equally true that the police academy should cover a great number of subjects. And so it is. The academy curriculum in most places is made up of another patchwork quilt of sorts. There are, as noted in the accompanying chart, several dozen separate subject areas that are treated in today's academy. There are the strictly law-related topics. Of course criminal law takes precedence in this arena, but cadets are subjected to a dozen different types of law in addition to their studies of the penal code. Vehicle law, alcohol-related law, and juvenile-related law are covered because the police face situations controlled by such laws much of the time. Then, too, in order to provide a feel for them, other types of legal discussions can touch on fish and game law, parks and recreation law, animal control law, and mental health-related law. The cadet is, to some extent, bombarded with a litany of legal topics.

CHART 12.1

MINIMUM CONTENT AND HOURLY REQUIREMENTS

REGULAR BASIC COURSE (RBC)—STANDARD FORMAT

DOMAIN NUMBER	DOMAIN DESCRIPTION	MINIMUM HOURS
01	Leadership, Professionalism, & Ethics	8 hours
02	Criminal Justice System	2 hours
03	Policing in the Community	18 hours
04	Victimology / Crisis Intervention	6 hours
05	Introduction to Criminal Law	4 hours
06	Property Crimes	6 hours
07	Crimes Against Persons / Death Investigation	6 hours
08	General Criminal Statutes	2 hours
09	Crimes Against Children	4 hours
10	Sex Crimes	4 hours
11	Juvenile Law and Procedure	3 hours
12	Controlled Substances	12 hours
13	ABC Law	2 hours
14	Laws of Arrest	12 hours
15	Search and Seizure	12 hours
16	Presentation of Evidence	6 hours
17	Investigative Report Writing	52 hours
18	Vehicle Operations	24 hours
19	Use of Force	12 hours
20	Patrol Techniques	12 hours
21	Vehicle Pullovers	14 hours
22	Crimes in Progress	20 hours
23	Handling Disputes / Crowd Control	8 hours
24	Domestic Violence	10 hours
25	Unusual Occurrences	4 hours
26	Missing Persons	4 hours
27	Traffic Enforcement	16 hours
28	Traffic Collision Investigations	12 hours
29	Crime Scenes, Evidence, and Forensics	12 hours
30	Custody	2 hours
31	Lifetime Fitness	44 hours
32	Arrest Methods / Defensive Tactics	60 hours

33	First Aid and CPR	21 hours
34	Firearms / Chemical Agents	72 hours
35	Information Systems	2 hours
36	People with Disabilities	6 hours
37	Gang Awareness	2 hours
38	Crimes Against the Justice System	4 hours
39	Weapons Violations	4 hours
40	Hazardous Materials Awareness	4 hours
41	Cultural Diversity / Discrimination	16 hours
42	Emergency Management	16 hours
	Minimum Instructional Hours	560 hours

The minimum number of hours allocated to testing in the Course are shown below[1]

TESTS	HOURS
Scenario Tests (40 hours test administration; 18 hours Scenario Demonstration)	58 hours
Written Tests (25 hours test administration; 15 hours examination review)	40 hours
Pre-Course Test (Non-scored test administered prior to instruction) Knowledge Tests (LDs 2, 3, 5, 6, 7, 8, 9, 10, 11, 12, 15, 16–19, 20, 25, 26, 28, 31, 34, 36, 37, 39, 40, and 43)	
POST-Constructed Comprehensives Tests Mid-Course Proficiency Test (Assesses LDs 2, 3, 5, 6, 7, 8, 9, 10, 15, 16, 20, and 39)	
End-of-Course Proficiency Test (Assesses LDs 2, 3, 5, 6, 7, 8, 9, 10, 11, 12, 15, 16, 19, 20, 25, 26, 31, 36, 37, 39, 40, and 43)	
Exercise Tests (Physical Skills Pilot Tests)	6 hours
Total Minimum Required Hours	664 hours

[1]Time required for exercise testing, instructional activities, and the Work Sample Test Battery is included in instructional hours.

From the California Commission on Peace Officer Standards and Training (POST), *http://www.post.ca.gov/Training/bt_bureau/TrainingSpecs/RBC_MINIMUM_HOURLY_REQUIREMENTS.doc , July 2008*

Then there is the time spent in developing practical, beat-operational skills, such as how to operate a patrol car, make a traffic stop, frisk a suspect, enter a dwelling, and so forth. In addition, there is preparation for the physical side of the job; fitness classes, defensive tactics classes, and firearms training are engaged. And several miscellaneous topics are covered, such as first aid, CPR, public relations, and computer data entry.

As Chart 12.1 indicates, the overwhelming majority of time in the academy is spent learning about law enforcement and the practical skills involved in working a beat. Little time is spent on COP issues like community relations, handling disputes/crowds, domestic violence, persons with disabilities, gang awareness, and culture, diversity, and discrimination. The total number of hours allotted to these topics is 78 out of more than 600 hours of required training.

The police academy experience is like no other in the world of education. Because so many different topics are covered, and because experts are brought in as teachers from many different arenas, the experience is rather disjointed. A day at the academy may include two hours of criminal law, two hours of learning patrol techniques, two hours of first aid, and two hours of criminal procedure. At day's end, there might be an hour or two of physical fitness training. Each day is cut up into blocks of time filled with different topics. Academy training lacks the normalization of other academic experiences—one day is not like the next, and the sequence of classes is never the same.

Textbooks are usually eschewed in favor of individualized notebooks prepared by the academy. The numerous instructors involved in the process often bring articles or memos to share with cadets. Cadets usually put together their own notebooks made up of such handouts and their own notes. Exams are given on a regular basis—normally on one day per week—and at the end of the experience, the graduated cadet has several notebooks filled with information. The breadth of information covered is substantial, as the chart indicates. However, when viewed another way, it is heavily law-enforcement oriented. This is one of the obvious criticisms made of standard academy curriculum. And it is toward an analytical criticism of such standard curricula that we now turn.

Academy Critique: In beginning a critical analysis of standard police academies, the first and foremost criticism is that police academy training is almost universally aimed at the law enforcement function. Since so little of what the police do is law-enforcement oriented, this is an obvious problem. But, as noted in the previous chapter, there is little that can be done about this until and unless entry level tests are designed to expect police-specific, substantive legal knowledge on the part of candidates. Only if such a change were made, and everyone entering an academy class already possessed much of the law enforcement-related information now taught at the academy, could the academy curriculum be changed to include more COP-related topics. In other words, if cadets entering a police academy had already taken courses in criminal law—and passed entry level exams proving they'd learned the material—then basic, introductory criminal law classes could be omitted from the academy curriculum. And this, in turn, would create space for other topics. Less than half of America's police academies include training in COP, and this is just one, specific example of the training expansion possible if such changes were made (DOJ *Special Report* 7).

Second, the paramilitaristic focus of many academies is also problematic—in obvious ways (Berg). We spent an entire chapter discussing paramilitarism and focusing on its central paradox: the distance it creates between police and public is counterproductive—but paramilitarism is essential under certain circumstances. The police academy experience ought to mirror this paradox. It should avail the cadet of some militaristic discipline and training aimed at those situations that demand a paramilitaristic response. And equally, it ought to inform the cadet of the drawbacks inherent in maintaining a paramilitaristic demeanor all of the time. This "balancing act" should be front-and-center in the minds of police cadets as they create for themselves their working personalities.

This outlines the difficulty with the stress-based academy. Beginning a young officer's police experience with such a paramilitaristic focus only exacerbates the numerous problems involved in this style of policing. Furthermore, paramilitarism works against COP in numerous ways (as pointed out in previous chapters). The point here is that having *some* paramilitaristic focus is appropriate and important. But creating a police academy aura that replicates the stress level experienced by military boot camps is probably not a good idea.

A third standard criticism has to do with **ethics training in police academies**. In a nationwide survey, it was discovered that the average police academy in America includes 3 ½ hours of discussion about police ethics (Das, Police Training in Ethics, 70)—out of 400 to 600 hours of academy training! To begin with, this is woefully inadequate. Spending so little time on such an important subject implies to cadets that the topic is of little importance.

A second problem relates to the *type* of training done with regard to ethics.

As Box 12.3 suggests, academy training in ethics involves discussing ethics "backwards." That is, such training almost universally consists of lectures about

BOX 12.3

ETHICS DONE "BACKWARDS"

The standard police academy curriculum involves very little in the way of time spent discussing ethics. In fact, so little time is spent that when it occurs it takes the form of simplistic lectures given by Internal Affairs investigators. Such lectures tend to be driven by the idea that to be a good officer is to "not screw up." Such a limited initiation into what ought to be a central theme in police work—accomplishing good works in an ethical manner—conditions the cadet to think of ethical policing as merely an incidental consideration to the modern police officer.

how "not to screw up." Looking at ethics from this negative perspective is more than inappropriate; it is wrong. If the goal is to instill a personal ethic in police officers that approaches police work from the perspective of what good officers *ought* to do—which, undoubtedly, such training should entail—then the existing perspective comes at ethics from the wrong end of things. This is because current training focuses upon what good officers *ought not* to do.

Constructing **a personal ethic** should include building an understanding of the positive requirements of ethical behavior from the ground up—deriving from a baseline discussion of what it means to be a good person and police officer (Perez and Moore). Today's academy cadet is both intelligent and educated enough to do this—to understand basic philosophical principles relating to being ethical and doing good works in life. So it would appear essential that today's young cadets be taught with an eye toward taking advantage of their intelligence and education levels. Instead, academy training almost universally ignores the intellects of today's "new" cadets and treats them to the outdated approach of a "thou shalt not" type of message.

Here is an example: One classic topic in the field of police ethics has to do with the free cup of coffee. Giving free coffee to police officers is a time-honored tradition in America. Waitresses and coffeehouse managers like to do it because when the police are around citizens behave themselves, they pay their tabs, and they *certainly* do not rob the place. In some locations today the police will reject free coffee, but in many places it is still a tradition. And some citizens do not like this. They resent seeing the police treated to such "**freebies**." So this topic is often engaged when ethics are discussed in the academy. In the past, the academy lecture on ethics included a brief suggestion that taking a free cup of coffee "is the same thing as taking money from drug dealers." Neither the Internal Affairs officer giving the lecture nor the cadets listening believes this. And thus, when they hit the streets, rookie officers ignore the lecture.

But today's intelligent, college-educated cadet can engage in a very different discussion: one that assumes their ability to comprehend the philosophical issue behind it. Today's officer can engage with the idea that when people give the police free coffee there can be an assumed **quid pro quo** involved implying they will be treated differently than other citizens if they are, for example, stopped by the police. The tacit understanding is that free coffee "purchases" a degree of latitude from the police for the waitresses and coffee house managers who provide it. And, thus, it should be avoided to circumvent the potential ethical problem it might pose for an officer. This is a more logical and sophisticated way of engaging a touchy issue. And in today's world of the modern police officer, this is the correct way to do it.

A final and rather simplistic area of concern has to do with the learning process in police academies. It is almost unheard of for police officers in training to be required to read textbooks as they go through the academy process. Why is this so? Why aren't required books read as part of the academy experience? There are any number of good texts that could be utilized for weekly discussions about relevant topics. This, too, would create a more collegial atmosphere and learning model in the modern police academy. Today's police cadet is certainly capable of reading, understanding, and discussing basic textbooks in the field. Furthermore, such textbooks would then be available indefinitely as reference sources to the cadet. Police academies need to take advantage of the intelligence and education levels of today's cadets. Extensive reading might very well provide a richer understanding for the cadet-in-training.

It is time now to consider the final element in our patchwork quilt of police educational requirements: post-academy training for rookie and, even, veteran officers throughout their careers.

Post-Academy Training

Once a contemporary officer is sworn in and has completed the police academy requirement, he or she "hits the street." In past eras, that was the end of the formalized learning process. In today's world of policing, there are additional, continuous requirements for all officers, not just those seeking specialized training.

The Field Training Officer (FTO): After the academy experience, in most jurisdictions today, the rookie officer is assigned to an FTO program. There are many variations on the theme, but the general idea is to pair someone with a substantial amount of experience and aptitude for teaching with an inexperienced officer. FTOs should themselves be excellent officers with enough of an achievement orientation to act not only as teachers but also as role models. Rookie officers are not only taught and mentored by FTOs: they are also evaluated by them on a regular basis—daily, in some places (Haider).

FTO programs can either last a relatively short time, or they can be quite involved and extensive. Ideally, there are steps in such a program that require the rookie to work with different FTOs for extended timeframes (4–6 weeks). This provides a series of evaluations rather than just one. At the end of several monitoring and evaluating periods, rookies go solo for a few weeks. In the final step of the process, a plain clothes FTO rides with the rookie for a few weeks and evaluates him or her for final approval—if the evaluation is positive, the FTO certifies the rookie to work alone thereafter. This is how the FTO process works under ideal conditions.

There is good news and bad news about FTO programs. On the positive side, the movement requiring young officers to pair with FTOs can be seen as an important step toward inculcating modern principles in personnel from the outset. Instead of learning things from veterans in a piecemeal fashion, the FTO (in theory) has both an aptitude for teaching and the substantive knowledge to make the experience an important one. Thus, in an organized and disciplined way, the rookie learns a little bit about a lot of subjects and becomes expert in a few—such as the "nuts 'n bolts" of working a beat.

BOX 12.4

THE FTO: PLUS OR MINUS?

This used to be done informally, but since the 1970s, FTO programs have been installed in most jurisdictions to mentor young police officers. While the FTO idea has institutionalized something that had always been done, it has not changed the central problem for the segue from academy training to the street; FTOs have the same opportunity that their predecessors had to subvert academy training by suggesting to the rookie that he or she "can forget what you learned in the academy, now you'll find out how police work is *really* done."

The bad news is that FTO programs do not necessarily work in the ways they are supposed to. First, because such programs involve a great deal of paperwork and extra effort, many departments have trouble fielding FTOs. Several studies indicate that the most experienced officers—ideally those who would make the best teachers—tend to avoid the process. Second, the average amount of experience in police work required to become an FTO is only about 2 years (Langworthy *et al.*). This is troublesome, since the whole idea is to have veteran officers involved in teaching younger officers—and two years on the street does not qualify most people as "veterans." Third, extra pay for FTOs is meager—hardly an incentive. Finally, if a rookie is dropped from a department—does not achieve final certification—that rookie can (and sometimes does) sue for damages. When this occurs, the FTO is a party to the suit along with the police department. For these reasons, the utilitarian theory behind the FTO process is not necessarily achieved in practice.

Finally, as noted in Box 12.4, there is no guarantee that the FTO process works against a long-term problem from which police work has suffered for generations: the idea that once an officer hits the street, they are told to forget what they have learned in the academy and start learning about *real* police work. FTOs can fall into this trap as easily as other veterans. And if FTOs do so, then they can inhibit the development of the COP philosophy and of genuine professionalism.

In-Service Training: Once an officer passes their probationary period, there are "**in-service training**" requirements in virtually all police departments. Ranging from as little as 40 hours per year to more than 90, police departments in the modern era tend to require that officers involve themselves in continuing education (Hickman and Reaves). In some locales, college courses may substitute for police-delivered training. Furthermore, modern technology allows in-service updates on changes in the law, new search and seizure decisions, and so forth to be provided to officers right in the squad room, before they go out on the street. This constant updating for officers is important to the process of professionalization.

It is *almost* universally true that every police officer is required to complete the FTO experience and, in addition, keep up with in-service training requirements. Additionally, there is specialized training for officers interested in expanding their knowledge in one direction or another, particularly in an effort to obtain experience that helps with advancement. There are schools for K-9 officers, requiring certain types of training with one's dog in order to make a K-9 patrol and remain on it. Officers can garner extra training in forensics that, in some jurisdictions, allows them to work certain types of cases to lessen the burden placed on crime lab personnel. In some places, these officers earn a "Forensics Tech" distinction and are awarded incentive pay. S.W.A.T. training is another option. Most officers taking such courses are interested in advancement and want more than just patrol experience on their resumes when the time comes to be considered for promotion.

SUMMATION

Police education has shown a pronounced improvement during three eras in American police history. First, as the Reform Era arrived, the police academy was invented. With it, citizen expectations for the police expanded, and the level of competence exhibited by police grew. Also, police discipline, confidence, and status improved dramatically. After the 1960s came the invention of the FTO and the creation of ongoing, in-service training requirements. Finally, in recent years, academies in many places—but by no means everywhere—are taking a more collegial approach to training, aimed especially at COP-style policing and the achievement of genuine professionalism.

Each of these developments has been positive, inspiring progress toward the illusive "professionalism" that has been a long-term goal of police leaders for generations now. But there are two central paradoxes involved in police education. First, strictly paramilitaristic academy training has persisted in many locations. Without acknowledging *both* the strengths and weaknesses of paramilitarism, such

CHAPTER TWELVE PARADOX BOX

While police academies have grown in their sophistication and comprehension levels, a substantial minority still tend to be operated in a paramilitaristic, "high-stress" fashion with Law Enforcement being the key focus. This works against both the progress of COP and the development of modern police professionalism. Furthermore, because of cynicism on the part of some veteran officers, FTO programs can have a similar effect: to retard progress toward COP and professionalism.

an academy experience works against the modern COP movement. Second, for all of their promise, FTO programs sometimes—often in some jurisdictions—reinforce existing subcultural norms and values that academy training attempts to reject. In this way, the FTO and the academy can be working at odds with each other.

It is now time to consider the controversial topic of police accountability. American citizens often rail against the misbehavior of politicians and bureaucrats of all stripes. But nothing has quite the emotional impact on the public that police misconduct does. Americans support their local police "in theory"—from a distance—but when the blue lights go on and they are pulled over by the local beat officer, they tend to respond with an old-fashioned, "Yankee," chip-on-the-shoulder attitude about governmental power. And this attitude, as we shall see, presents police accountability mechanisms with numerous paradoxical realities.

 ## DISCUSSION QUESTIONS

1. As the text relates, there are two different types of college criminal justice programs: those that are sociologically based and those that are more practical. What is the difference? Do you know examples of each? Which type of college background best informs the police officer experience in the long run?

2. There are "stress-based" police academies and there are those that are more collegial. Which is best? Which makes for the optimal learning environment in the short run and why? Which makes for the optimal training experience in the long run and why?

3. Refer to the Chart in the text including the P.O.S.T. Minimum Requirements for police academies in California. What sticks out when you look at the curriculum? Do you agree that law enforcement is over-emphasized? What, if anything, is under-emphasized? How might academy training be changed to make the chart's list of topics more closely approximate the list of knowledge areas necessary for police officers from Box 12.2?

4. Discuss ethics training in police work. What kind of training is it? Is it appropriate for the job, both in terms of the amount of time spent on it and content discussed? How might ethics training be changed in order to better serve the interests of the police and, at the same time, the interests of justice?

 ## KEY TERMS

Boot Camp Mentality: The idea that some police academies attempt to approximate the mentality of military boot camps.

Collegial Style of Teaching and Learning: Academy learning paradigm that approximates that present in college classrooms.

Contact Sport (Police work as): The idea that despite modern requirements to understand an ever-expanding body of legal and sociological knowledge, police work still involves a physical side that is of critical importance.

Cop Shops: Somewhat derogatory term used by proponents of sociologically based college programs to describe the more practical type of program.

DNA Testing: Modern forensic system of identifying people by utilizing traces of their genetic materials.

Ethics Training in Police Academies: The attempt to inculcate ethical values into police officers before they go out on the beat.

"Freebies": Goods or services offered to police officers as a "courtesy" by citizens or businesses.

In-Service Training: Post-academy training in police work requiring a minimum number of credit hours each year for a police officer to remain qualified to work on the job.

Liberal Arts Education: A college educational philosophy that emphasizes giving students a broadly based background in a number of general subjects in addition to what they learn in their major field of study.

Peace Officer Standards and Training (P.O.S.T.): State level commissions that set standards or training for police academies and advanced officer training.

A Personal Ethic: Refers to the idea that a police officer should be conversant enough with ethical philosophy that he or she develops their own, personalized philosophical approach to the profession.

Practical College Programs: College-level educational programs for police that focus on practical police operations, such as how to work a beat.

Quid Pro Quo: Latin for "something for something"; that which a party receives or is promised in return for something done or promised.

Sociologically Based College Programs: Programs of higher education for police officers that emphasize a critical, analytical, and liberal arts education.

Stress-Based Academies: Police academies that emphasize a militaristic, boot camp–type of approach to police training.

ADDITIONAL READINGS

As we have noted several times in our discussions, the suggestion for increased police education, including expanded academies and college, began with the commissions of the 1960s (cited elsewhere). Early on, one of the most important scholars in the field of police studies, Lawrence W. Sherman, wrote ***Quality Police Education*** (Proquest Info and Learning, 1978), a set of recommendations for what specific type of expanded education was needed. Ten years later, in a work about police reform and experimentation around the country, Jerome H. Skolnick and David H. Bayley, also critically important authors in the field, discussed police education (among many topics) in ***The New Blue Line*** (Free Press, 1988).

An analysis of how college educations have impacted police officer performances was conducted by Donald M. Truxillo, Suzanne R. Bennett, and Michelle L. Collings in 1998 entitled "College Education and Police Job Performance: A Ten Year Study" (***Public Personal Management***, Volume 27, Number 2). They found that along almost any evaluation parameter, college education improved the quality of policing in America. Only with regard to discipline had college-educated officers not out-performed their non-college-educated counterparts.

Our chart illustrating the hours spent at police academies in California came from the California Commission for P.O.S.T., Bulletin 95-9, May 12, 1995 (published by P.O.S.T., Sacramento). To get a feeling for the operations of P.O.S.T. commissions, the student may go to *www.post.ca.gov* and visit the California Commission's site.

Analyzing and critiquing police academy training (and police training in general), James O'Keefe wrote *Protecting the Republic: The Education and Training of American Police Officers* (Prentice Hall, 2003) wherein he focuses upon how the behavioral sciences should be more emphasized in academy training. *Critical Issues in Police Training* by Maria R. Haberfield (Prentice-Hall, 2002) discusses academy training, too, and engages the idea that there are two types of academies in operation today, as noted in our discussion above. Howard S. Cohen and Michael Feldberg wrote *Power and Restraint: The Moral Dimension of Police Work* (Praeger, 1991) wherein they make the argument for police officer ethics training to start "from the ground up." The book *Police Ethics: A Matter of Character* by Perez and Moore (cited elsewhere) is a short work aimed at academy cadets utilizing this "from the ground up" framework. For an international look at police training, see *Police Education and Training in a Global Society* by Peter C. Kratcoski and Dilip K. Das (Lexington Books, 2007).

Glenn F. Kaminsky writes about basic concepts in *Field Training Concepts in Criminal Justice Agencies* (Prentice Hall, 2000), as does James T. Haider in *Field Training Police Recruits: Developing, Improving, and Operating a Field Training Program* (Charles C. Thomas, 1990), a short, how-to book. Finally, at the C.O.P.S. website (*www.cops.usdoj.gov*) the student can find information about F.T.O. programs, manuals for trainees, manuals for trainers, and more.

CHAPTER 13

Accountability

Chapter Thirteen Outline

Of all the topics relating to police work, **police misconduct** is the one that most often hits people "where they live." People are quite emotional when they discuss police misconduct—excessive force, in particular. American citizens are driven by an age-old desire to be both supportive of their government in a patriotic sense and, at the same time, suspicious of governmental power. It is a part of our heritage. And the power exhibited by the police is, to some extent, the most obvious, ever-present sort of governmental power with which we are faced on a daily basis. The police walk among us, they carry weapons, and they wear military-style uniforms. They are licensed both to take freedom from and visit force upon citizens. Deep within the American psyche, there is an inbred aversion to the exercise of these types of powers by agents of the state.

This paradoxical feeling on the part of Americans—at once supportive of the agents of "law and order" and possessing antipathy toward them—produces numerous difficulties and problematic dynamics where police accountability is concerned. The subject is replete with misunderstanding on the part of citizens and police officers alike. And, like the issues so far covered, police accountability is plagued by troublesome paradoxes (Perez).

First, members of the public cannot identify police misconduct. Most citizens possess an incomplete and incorrect understanding of what it entails. Often driven by misconceptions created by Hollywood, American citizens frequently believe the police guilty of misconduct when, in fact, they are not. Second, there is the troublesome reality that the public often applauds police misconduct of the "noble cause" type. Dirty Harry is a "hero" of sorts to many Americans (Klockars). When a Dirty Harry–type officer engages in "curbside justice" aimed at a local bully, for example, people tend to be very supportive—supportive of this type of misconduct. Third, there are numerous layers of procedural safeguards that protect police officers accused of misconduct when they are being investigated. The consequent complexity of the police accountability process can mean that police officers *factually guilty* of misconduct will be cleared by the review process.

Fourth, both police officers and citizens hold prejudicial, preconceived notions regarding what to do about police misconduct when it occurs. Citizens tend to believe that some sort of external, civilianized review will "solve" the problem of police misbehavior. The thought here is that civilian review will be tougher on the police than they would be on themselves. Conversely, police officers believe that civilian review would be unfair and abusive. They tend to think civilian reviewers will always find them guilty, irrespective of the facts. Research indicates that neither of these beliefs is true—but police officers and American citizens cleave to them in a way that inhibits the effectiveness of police review systems.

So this chapter's discussions are filled with paradoxes, illustrations of misunderstandings, and prejudicial notions about police accountability. Let us begin by discussing police misconduct.

MISCONCEPTIONS ABOUT MISCONDUCT

To begin with, the first major difficulty involved in the debate about police accountability is that citizens often misunderstand the subject. Most citizens are not lawyers. They are not experts on the law. So they often misunderstand how police officers are supposed to behave in a legal sense. As noted in Chapter Six, a classic example has to do with the *Miranda* admonitions. Having seen suspects admonished at the moment of arrest on television and in the movies, the average citizen genuinely believes that the police have been incompetent when they do not follow suit with such Hollywood-created imagery.

Second, citizens are not police officers. They know next to nothing about how the police are trained or the hundreds of rules and regulations included in any police department's General Orders (hereafter, the "G.O.s"). As illustrated in Box 13.1, this often leads to citizen misunderstanding about standard police practices. Again, this means that members of the public will often believe that the police have been guilty of misconduct when they have not.

Third, there is the problem of differing perspectives. No matter what the law says or what departmental rules indicate, the police are in the business of making judgments on a regular basis. Citizens observe these police judgments

BOX 13.1

A Citizen's Complaint

An upper middle class citizen who has seldom interacted with the police before, and who certainly has never seen the back seat of a patrol car, is arrested on a Friday night for DUI. On the following Monday morning, he comes into Internal Affairs (I.A.) and wants to make a complaint. He says, "In front of my family, I was treated rudely and humiliated by the arresting officer." When the I.A. Investigator asks what the arresting officer did to humiliate the citizen, the complainant states that he was, "Handcuffed and frisked . . . like a common criminal."

Does this constitute police misconduct? Of course it doesn't. In fact, the officer would have been guilty of violating the Department's General Orders if he *had not* frisked and handcuffed the suspect. But the citizen believes that this is misconduct. And he wants an investigation. Here we have illustrated both a misconception about police misconduct and a demand for police services—I.A. services—that is an unreasonable waste of time and taxpayer money. How should a police review system deal with this "case"?

being made all of the time. Sometimes they consider the decisions of the police to be inappropriate. When people view police discretionary judgments being made, it can appear that police officers are guilty of misconducting themselves. For example, officers will often decide to let teenaged drinkers off with warnings instead of arresting them. Kids may be made to pour out their beer and move along. Citizens sometimes observe this perfectly legal and proper exercise in police discretion and believe it to be misconduct. Driven perhaps by religious tenets against drinking alcohol, or even by having been the victim of a drunk driver, citizens can feel perfectly within their rights to complain about such "police misconduct."

Citizens tend to have particular difficulty differentiating between appropriate and reprehensible police behavior where force is concerned. What constitutes "excessive" or "appropriate" behavior with regard to the application of force? Some people believe that every time the police put their hands on a citizen they are using inappropriate force. These people believe it ought to be possible to police the streets without ever using force. Other citizens are of the mind that the police should exercise "curbside justice" and "teach a lesson" to thugs on the street. Thus, these citizens are supportive of almost any application of force by the police. These varying expectations make for a great deal of confusion and can create trouble for police review systems.

And there is more. The police must answer to multiple standards of conduct. As was the case with the goals and functions of the police, so it is with these sets of standards: they are multiple, conflicting, and vague (Wildavsky). The police play three roles on the street. First, they are legal actors. Everything they do must stand up to legal scrutiny. They enforce the law on a regular basis and must be held accountable to it themselves. Second, the police are political actors. They must answer to the public. Especially in an era of COP, the police must ascertain and then respond to the desires of the citizenry. Finally, they are administrative actors. They must be held accountable to hundreds of general police practices and specific rules included in their G.O.s.

The problem is that these three sets of standards can conflict with each other. In particular, members of the community can ask the police to do things that are not strictly legal. People want them to "clean up the streets," and they do not much care how this is accomplished. People want the police to lower crime rates, to get guns out of their neighborhoods, to run gangs out of town, and to stop drug trafficking. And the average American citizen does not care one bit about constitutional and legal processes that may stand in the way of accomplishing these tasks. They want action, not excuses.

In demanding action, and not caring about the exigencies of law, people can ask the police—directly or indirectly—to behave like Dirty Harry. The public will usually support any effective tactic that gets the job done. This support can be troublesome for attempts to hold the police accountable to legal and departmental standards.

So the definition of police misconduct is debatable. And there is, in some sense, nothing that anyone, inside or outside of police work, can do to synthesize the differing perceptions and perspectives of public and police. Let us now define what *really* constitutes police misconduct.

A Typology of Police Misconduct

In constructing a typology for police misconduct, Table 13.1, which accompanies this section, was developed (Perez and Moore 127–140). The labels in the table's four boxes are determined by asking two basic questions about police misconduct. First, was the misbehavior done in the name of **personal gain**? That is, did the police officer(s) involved seek to profit personally from the misconduct? Whether it takes the form of money, goods, services, or other types of trade-offs, when police officers misbehave they are either looking to enhance their own material well-being or they are not.

Second, did the misconduct involve the **misuse of legal authority**? That is, did the officer(s) "sell the badge" in exchange for something? Whether it involves protecting criminals from arrest or arresting certain criminals to enhance the business of others, police officers sometimes use their state-granted authority as a bargaining tool to get something improper accomplished. On the other hand, sometimes police misconduct has nothing to do with the abuse of legal authority.

Once these two questions are answered, police misconduct can be classified into its five major types. Four of the types fall within the bounds established by the table and one exists outside of them. This may seem an academic exercise, but it is not. The consequences, methods of investigation, punishment, and political fall-out associated with these five types of misbehavior are different—sometimes very different—from each other. Let us discuss these types individually.

Corruption of Authority: Police officers are guilty of what we label "**corruption of authority**" when they misuse their legal authority (badges) to obtain personal rewards. This takes several forms. Payoffs are sometimes obtained by police officers to protect certain criminal enterprises, such as gambling, prostitution, or drug sales. Money changes hands, and arrests are not made. Shakedowns are sometimes undertaken wherein police officers proactively demand money from people, normally small business operators, in exchange for "letting them off easy" with regard to city ordinances and so forth. Graft can be accepted on an individual basis, from a motorist in exchange for not being given a ticket, for example, or for not administering the law in an impartial manner.

Corruption of authority was the sort of misconduct that permeated police work before the Reform Era (Walker, Critical History). (There is much less of it today.) It is further differentiated into the categories of "meat eating" and "grass eating," as noted in earlier discussions. This is the sort of misconduct to which most people refer when they use the generic term "police corruption."

Noble Cause Corruption: Here we are confronted directly by the Dirty Harry problem. Some officers ignore the due process limitations of the law during investigations or in handling non-legal details. They do this to get the job done (Caldero and Crank). That is, to deter criminals or to prosecute people they believe guilty of criminal deeds, police officers falsify reports ("**creative report writing**"), harass citizens, or use excessive force. When noble cause corruption involves lying on the witness stand to obtain a conviction, it is called "**testilying**." (Perez and Moore 134) These sorts of behaviors involve police officers misusing their legal authority in inappropriate ways, but they are not doing it for personal gain. "Getting the bad guys behind bars" (instead of making money) is the rationalization here.

Police Crime: Sometimes, police officers will become involved in criminal activities while on duty that do not involve the use of their legal office. This is known as "**police crime**." Officers will sometimes use the opportunities that being on duty (particularly at night) affords them to burglarize businesses or residences. Sometimes, when a theft has already occurred, police officers take extra merchandise or money and report it as part of the original theft. When this type of misconduct happens, the police are misbehaving to obtain personal gain. But they are not trading off their legal authority to do so (Kappeler, Sluder, and Alpert). Thus, this type of misconduct is considered to be different from either of the above two types.

Ineptitude: There are many transgressions against departmental G.O.s considered police misconduct but involving neither personal gain nor the misuse of legal

BOX 13.2

POLICE CRIME

At a construction site where new homes were being built, more than a mile out in the country and, thus, far away from "prying eyes," several Deputy Sheriffs decided to take advantage of the fact that the site was left unguarded all night long. They began stealing hundreds of brand new, still-in-the-box garbage disposals and microwave ovens kept at the site. A few at a time, over the course of many months, the officers developed a thriving business selling these items to unscrupulous developers in other locations. When the theft ring was finally discovered, three officers went to prison for thievery and three others were terminated for knowing about it and not taking action. This is an example of police crime. It is the product of greed and opportunity.

authority. This category is made up of such common violations as sleeping on duty, showing up habitually late, having sex on duty, drinking on duty, writing poor reports, failing to respond to calls, and ignoring orders. While these can be serious violations when investigated, they are neither criminal nor corrupt in their nature. They are thus considered "merely" the product of **ineptitude**.

Personal Misconduct: This category contains the sort of personal (and sometimes even criminal) misconduct that reflects on an individual's image as a police officer but occurs off duty. Examples include alcoholism, adultery, off-duty drunk driving, and so on. This category does not fit in the types-of-misconduct table because it does not directly relate to a person's on-duty actions as a police officer.

However, we should not make the mistake of thinking that off duty police officer behavior is unimportant. It can have great significance. For example, when an officer does not pay his or her bills, it can have a tremendous, negative affect upon community confidence in the police. This is especially true in a small jurisdiction. Thus, a police officer can be found guilty of **"conduct unbecoming an officer"** even if the conduct has no relation to anything he or she does on duty. This is because perceptions held about the police are critical to maintaining legitimacy in any police organization.

These then are the forms that police misconduct takes. But where does it come from? Why do police officers misbehave? We now turn to that important discussion.

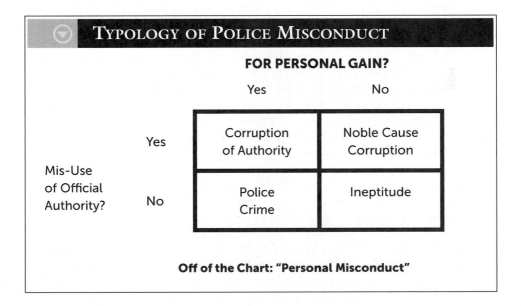

TYPOLOGY OF POLICE MISCONDUCT

| | | **FOR PERSONAL GAIN?** | |
		Yes	No
Mis-Use of Official Authority?	Yes	Corruption of Authority	Noble Cause Corruption
	No	Police Crime	Ineptitude

Off of the Chart: "Personal Misconduct"

Causes of Police Misconduct

The causes of police misconduct are numerous. They range from individual frailties in officers to subcultural norms and values that "push" the police to misbehave (Klockars, Ivkovic, and Haberfeld). Furthermore, even American culture as a whole—the dominant culture—can be blamed for some misconduct. Let us begin with the most obvious causes.

Crime Analogies: When one studies criminology, one studies the causes of crime. We learn that crime has multiple causes and, thus, that it must be treated with multiple strategies. Crime is caused by the sort of crippling poverty that creates hopelessness. It is caused by a system of **economic stratification** that divides the rich and poor in America by income differences that almost stagger the imagination. Top-income-level Americans earn 200 times what people earn at the bottom of the economic pyramid—a figure unheard of anywhere else in the developed world. Crime is caused by racial and sexual barriers that can make competing in the marketplace, and even obtaining a subsistence level of income, impossible for many. Crime is caused by a lack of intelligence and education. It is caused by a health care system that leaves so many millions of people uncovered that one debilitating disease or injury can scuttle an entire family's chances of living a good life. Crime is caused by genetically and chemically induced imbalances in people's brains. None of these causes affect police officers. The police have incomes that provide reasonable comfort, they have health care, they are intelligent and sane, and their lives are lived securely based in the American middle class.

But some crime also stems from individual greed combined with chance and opportunity. And so it is with police misconduct. On the job, police officers are presented with multiple opportunities and chance occurrences that might lead the greedy to misbehave. The police are around business areas in the middle of the night and on weekends when no one else is present. On occasion, they may chance upon an unlocked storefront or unguarded property of one kind or another. Thus, they are presented with the opportunity to steal or burgle, if they are so moved by their individual greed. The police sometimes interact with business people or individual citizens who are willing to purchase their favor. Some people will reimburse the police for taking an action and others will pay them for *not* taking action. Such opportunities can lead either to corruption of authority or to police crime.

Furthermore, the police are responsible for monitoring several types of victimless crimes. Victimless crimes, such as illegal gambling, prostitution, and drug use, all possess several key elements: (1) there is an ongoing demand for the goods or services provided (gambling, sex, and drugs); (2) there are usually no independent, personally injured citizen-victims when the police confront perpetrators (and thus, no "witnesses"); and (3) there is a great amount of money (in the case of drugs, an astronomical amount of money) involved in the "business" of providing these goods and services to the public. These elements invariably combine to create official corruption—what we have labeled corruption of authority (Schur). The history of the policing of gambling, prostitution, and drug sales is replete with examples of police officers succumbing to temptation and becoming involved in this type of corruption. We must recall that the movement to reform the police was created out of a concern for the type of misconduct—corruption of authority— that often accompanies the prosecution of such victimless crimes.

So to begin with, we engage the idea that some police misconduct is the product of the same type of greed, opportunity, and chance that leads some civilians into crime. But there are other, more troubling causes for police misbehavior.

Subcultural Rationalizations: Unfortunately, the police subculture can lead to police misconduct and equally rationalize it in several ways. First, as has been found to be the case with criminal subcultures, the police subculture can aid the individual officer in rationalizing corruption of authority or police crime. Research has found that police officers involved in these sorts of misconduct for personal gain will offer several "standard" rationalizations for it—and sometimes these rationalizations are accepted by brother and sister officers. Some officers suggest they are involved in such schemes because theirs is a tough job and it is only "right" that they take full advantage of opportunities presented to them. Some corrupt officers argue that they "get no respect" on the streets, and that they should receive money in lieu of respect they are "due." Sometimes their argument is as simple as this: "If I don't take it, somebody else will." Then, too, officers will engage in what criminologists label as **"denying the status of the victim"** (Barker and Carter). If money is taken from a drug dealer, for example, the argument made is that the drug dealer had no right to it in the first place; the money was ill-gotten and, thus, the drug dealer is denied the status of "victim."

Then there is Dirty Harry–like behavior. Almost everywhere in American policing, and for a long time now, modern police work has moved beyond the era wherein corruption of authority was rampant. We live in an age where that type of corruption is a rarity. But noble cause corruption is quite another matter. While the overwhelming majority of police officers in the field today would never become involved in corruption of authority, many will engage in Dirty Harry's type of noble cause corruption, because that involves getting the job done.

As pointed out, the problem with noble cause corruption is that it comes with its own rationalization: Dirty Harry gets the bad guys and makes the streets safer. The feeling that Harry is policing effectively can provide support for officers who might be prone to such behavior. But the problem goes deeper than that. For some officers will support noble cause corruption indirectly by refusing to cooperate with police review systems when they pursue it. Thousands of officers who would never become involved in noble cause corruption themselves look the other way when Dirty Harry is around. Even in today's modern and enlightened era, many officers who will cooperate with investigations into corruption of authority will *not* cooperate with investigations into noble cause corruption.

As noted several chapters ago, the rationalization for this type of indirect support for police misconduct is logical enough. When a police officer is investigated for **"framing"** a case around a bad guy, the alternative outcomes for the investigation are several. On one hand, if the erring officer is found not guilty of misconduct, then the bad guy stays behind bars, and the police officer continues working on getting the job done. On the other hand, if the officer is found guilty of framing a suspect (by testilying, as an example), the officer is incarcerated and the bad guy goes free. Many of today's modern, educated, otherwise virtuous police officers will simply not become involved in an investigative process that involves Dirty Harry's noble cause. In these ways, the police subculture can effectively inhibit attempts to limit noble cause corruption.

American Culture: There are also American cultural realities that can impact upon the propensity for police to misconduct themselves. In numerous ways, American culture creates, undergirds, and rationalizes police misconduct. The first way involves the use of force. The police are licensed to use force. In fact, they *must* do so as part of their responsibility to control crime and criminals on the street. They must use enough force to overcome the illegal use of force. This much is clear.

What is perhaps not so clear is that this guarantees that the American police will be the most violent police anywhere in the industrialized world. If American society is the most violent, most prone to be armed society in the industrialized world (Harries), then the American police—in order to overcome this level of violence—must necessarily be more violent than police elsewhere. And when police use force there is always the perception on the part of some citizens that misconduct was involved, whether this is technically correct or not. The more often force is used, the more often misconduct—real or not—is perceived to have occurred.

A second cultural reality has to do with the level of crime, economic stratification, and hopelessness in today's society. The crime rate in the United States is greater than that of any other industrialized nation and *far* greater than most (Kalish). Economic stratification in the United States is also greater than anywhere else in the developed world. The gap between rich and poor is twice that in any other advanced nation (Judd). As students of crime causation, we know this will produce not only more crime but more stress between the economic classes in the United States than elsewhere. Of course, the police stand amidst the strain and frustration that such realities produce—and the consequent crime. In confronting these inequities, the police in America will often be accused of repressing the underclass in favor of society's elites. And they will be accused of this more often than law enforcement in other, more equitable societies.

This might sound like a diatribe "against America" in some ways. It is not meant to be. It is merely a statement of the facts—perhaps uncomfortable facts but facts nevertheless. And if we are to understand and improve police work in America, we must engage such facts with an open mind.

BOX 13.3

PEOPLE LOVE DIRTY HARRY

A police officer finds that an elderly man's home has been burglarized by a local ne'er-do-well who became an assailant when the old man came home to find the burglar there. He pushed the 90-year-old man down a set of stairs and almost killed him. At the very moment when the police officer and the old man's neighbors were hearing the story, the assailant happened to walk around the corner. The police officer lost his temper and pummeled the assailant in front of about a dozen citizens . . . and the citizens applauded the officer's actions—they *applauded*! (This is a true story.)

The point here is that when citizens support such Dirty Harry–like behavior it is almost impossible to dissuade police officers from engaging in this sort of "noble cause corruption."

Finally, there is the reality that, in the long run in America, "people get the policing that they want." That is to say we live in a relatively democratic society, and over time, what the police do will mirror what people want them to do. When a great deal of support exists for noble cause corruption, as it in fact does, then the police are being "encouraged" to misbehave in some sense.

Before we discuss what can be done about police misconduct, there is one more point to make about the causes of police deviance.

Excessive Force—Multiple Causes: Excessive force is the area of police misconduct that most elicits a visceral reaction on the part of American citizens (Nelson). Historically, the use of unnecessary force by the police has been *the* most emotional issue behind the call for civilian review. In our analysis of the causes of police misconduct, we find that excessive force is troublesome due to its multiple roots.

First, some excessive force is caused by bigotry on the part of the police. This form of misconduct is labeled as ineptitude. While fewer and fewer modern police officers make it through the selection gauntlet and into uniform possessing pronounced levels of racial bigotry or homophobia, there are still officers that seek to "punish" certain groups. Second, some excessive force is produced as an off-shoot of corruption of authority; it is utilized by corrupt officers to maintain control over their nefarious enterprises. Finally, some excessive force is noble cause–related. Either in an effort to obtain information from suspects or to punish "bad" citizens directly, police officers can become involved in issuing curbside justice on the streets.

Because it presents such an emotional issue to most Americans, and because of these multiple types of causal patterns, excessive force is perhaps the most volatile form of police misconduct. Again, a concern about excessive force often drives calls for civilian review and, in turn, creates a gap between police and civilian expectations for police review systems.

The Limits of Reform

Before we engage in a comparative discussion of the forms that police review systems take, we must first consider the severe limitations to which police accountability in America is subject. There are multiple layers of procedural protections afforded a police officer accused of misconduct. Investigations into misconduct allegations can be cumbersome, legally complicated, and troubling because of the same dynamic that affects the criminal justice system as a whole: legal technicalities can result in the factually guilty escaping punishment.

Due Process: To begin with, it is important for us to differentiate between criminal investigations into police misconduct and **administrative investigations** (Perez). Criminal investigations into police officer misconduct function the same as those for which citizens can be the focus. In the end, the potential sanctions awaiting officers found guilty are fines, imprisonment, or even death. Because this is so, the procedural rights afforded police officers being investigated are exactly the same as those afforded accused citizens. The right to counsel, the right to a jury trial, the right against unreasonable searchers and seizures—all of this is the same for anyone accused of a crime, including police officers (Aitchison).

For administrative investigations, the rules are different. While police officers under investigation have some procedural rights, those rights are limited. Given that the potential sanction of an administrative investigation is "only" the loss of a job, the police do not possess as many safeguards. As one appeals court once put it when handing down a ruling about police officer rights, no one has a constitutionally guaranteed right to be a police officer."

Since we are surveying the entire field of police work, we do not have the time to delve in depth into the rights of accused officers. But we can and must note one procedural rule for administrative investigations that is of particular importance. The accused police officer has no right against self-incrimination. Police officers under investigation must make truthful statements to investigators. If an officer refuses to make a statement when being investigated, he or she can be disciplined for this refusal and even terminated. Police officers also do not have the right to be represented when interrogated. It might appear that because of these particular procedural rules police officers are at a distinctive disadvantage when being investigated administratively. But as we shall see in a moment, this is not necessarily the case.

Police Officers' Bills of Rights: Beginning about 30 years ago, a movement to "protect" police officers who are under investigation for misconduct began to crystallize and gain momentum behind the idea of what are called **"Police Officers' Bills of Rights" (POBRs)**. These state level legislative acts provide police officers with far more procedural safeguards then they used to receive under existing case law (Aitchison). Today more than 22 states have enacted such legislation. There is even a movement to enact a nationwide, federal bill that would cover all officers in the United States.

Many POBRs contain provisions that allow police officers to be represented when interrogated. Usually, this means that they have the right to have a union representative present. Some POBRs contain limitations on the length of interrogations. Some disallow the use of the polygraph. Some limit the time of day when interrogations may occur, such as "during the officer's normal waking hours"—which means that an officer who works the graveyard shift can only be interrogated when on duty or during the evening hours before work. Some POBRs state that an officer under investigation must be advised of the nature of the investigation before interrogation.

Certain POBRs attempt to limit the ability of citizens to complain. Several state that police officers under investigation have the right to be informed of the identities of all witnesses against them. Citizens who know this might very well fear retaliation and, therefore, decline to complain. Several POBRs require complaining citizens to notarize their statements—to make them in front of a sworn Notary Public. Since citizens are not lawyers, by and large, this last requirement implies that if the accused officer is not found guilty of misconduct, the citizen will be jailed for "making a false police report." This is not, in fact, true—it merely means that the statement given has to be "true to the best of your knowledge." But in essence, this provision dissuades citizens from making complaints, even valid ones. These two provisions effectively subvert the right of citizens to "petition their government for redress of grievances"—a right granted to all Americans by the Constitution. Finally, in several states, POBRs will not allow investigations into anonymous complaints, no matter how egregious the misconduct involved. Taken together, POBRs substantially limit the ability of investigations to find police officers guilty of misconduct (Perez). But there is more.

Local Contracts: Collective bargaining agreements between police unions and cities or counties have always included provisions about salaries, medical benefits, vacation days, overtime pay, and a host of other issues relating to working conditions. This is their main reason for existing. But in recent years, such agreements have also included provisions relating to how police officers (members of the local police union) must be treated when under investigation for misconduct. In some locations, for example, officers have the right to representation by counsel—not by a union representative, but by an attorney—and that counsel is even paid for by the city or county doing the investigating. Such collective agreements then provide still another layer of procedural safeguards for accused officers. So far, we have discussed the normal, court-allowed due process safeguards afforded to accused officers, additional safeguards created within POBRs, and still additional safeguards instituted by collective bargaining agreements. But there is *still* more.

Civil Service Review: Regulations vary from city to city and county to county, but it is almost universally true that when a police officer is given any substantial punishment for misconduct, the local Civil Service Commission has an automatic responsibility to review the case. Because it is Civil Service that officially hires police officers, it must also officially fire them. Generally speaking, Civil Service was invented insure that those who work for the state are hired, fired, managed, and disciplined in a fair, impartial, non-political manner. These are its functions relative to the police.

Such a **Civil Service review** process may seem just a formality. One might think Civil Service commissions would tend to "rubber stamp" decisions made by chiefs of police. But this is often not the case. Driven by the desire to be tough on crime and support their local police officers, Civil Service commissions regularly restore fired officers to their positions or reduce the severity of punishments handed out by a Police Chief (Perez). While this is disconcerting to chiefs of police, it provides still *another* layer of protection for police officers accused of misconduct.

Taken together, and added to the propensity of both the police subculture and many citizens to support noble cause corruption, these procedural safeguards severely limit the ability of any review system to find the police guilty of misconduct—no matter the circumstances. Now it is time to consider several forms such police review systems take.

BOX 13.4

OVERLAPPING LAYERS OF PROTECTION

Police officers accused of misconduct can be shielded from guilty verdicts—even if they *are* factually guilty—by:

- Due process rights afforded them by case law decisions.
- Rights afforded them by "Police Officer's Bills of Rights."
- Rights afforded them by local collective bargaining agreements.
- Civil Service review.

Comparative Police Review Systems

Since the Wickersham Commission of the early 1930s, the idea of having someone other than the police themselves review allegations of police misconduct has been a central theme among those who discuss police accountability (Wickersham). First attempted in just a few places, and not with much staying power or success, civilian review boards have now been established in a substantial number of locations across America.

Of course, the overwhelming majority of allegations of police misconduct occur—and are dealt with—within the police organization itself. These are allegations of ineptitude, and they are invariably dealt with by police supervisors (as they should be). But often enough, allegations of police misconduct come from outside the police organization—from citizens—and the study of police review systems is about analyzing who should deal with such "citizens' complaints" and how they should go about it (Walker, New World).

There are three main types of police review systems that accept, investigate, adjudicate, and impose appropriate sanctions regarding citizen allegations. There are internal, police-operated review mechanisms. There are civilian review boards. And there are "hybrid" systems that include elements of both. Let us briefly consider each.

Internal Affairs: "Internal Affairs" (I.A.) is a generic term that refers to all police review systems operated by sworn police personnel within the police organization itself. The law in most states requires that police departments have in place a system for accepting and investigating citizens' complaints. And this is always the case. But most police organizations receive so few complaints of police misconduct that their case load is very small. Thus most police organizations investigate citizen allegations of misconduct on an ad hoc basis. Such investigations are usually assigned by the Chief of Police to a trusted middle manager. Only in a few, very large departments are there enough complaints to warrant having a separate body called I.A.

I.A. processes are completely "in-house." Allegations are accepted at police headquarters; initial statements are given to police investigators; investigations are done completely by the police; outcomes are decided by I.A. personnel (in consultation with the Chief, in most places); and sanctions are handed out by the Chief of Police when officers are found guilty of misconduct. These investigations are truly considered "internal affairs." They are conducted in secret, and the results are kept from the public, even from complaining citizens (Perez).

The central rationalizations behind allowing the police to conduct the investigations of their own people are several. First, it is assumed by most people in police work that because of their investigatory expertise, police investigators will do the most thorough and effective job possible of investigating such allegations. Second, it is assumed that police investigators and managers are driven by concerns of maintaining the "cleanest" organization possible. Not only with regard to individual cases, but with respect to keeping the image of the department clean, the idea is that the police are the best people to conduct such inquiries. Police investigators will consider themselves the guardians of the department and police professionalism in general.

Third, it is assumed no one from outside of a police organization will be familiar enough with the multiple standards of conduct to which the police must be held. Only police officers will know the law, general police practices, and also the specific regulations included in departmental G.O.s well enough to hold other officers accountable. Fourth, it is argued that no one outside a department will understand enough about the specific operational realties of how beats, high crime areas, and personnel issues are handled within that department—and, thus, no one outside the department can effectively know how and why operations are carried out the way they are.

A fifth reason put forward in favor of internal review is that if the Chief of Police is not given authority over such investigations and resulting disciplinary decisions, then it is not fair to hold him or her accountable for either specific investigations or operations of the department in general. Here again we see the principle that "authority must parallel responsibility." Those who hold that this type of review is best believe that if the Chief of Police cannot be trusted with such investigations and with meting out discipline in a fair and appropriate manner, then the Chief should be replaced; this is what a Chief of Police is hired to do.

Civilian Review Boards: Initially just an idea considered by those who did not trust the police, the concept of civilian review has grown pronouncedly in the past few years (Walker, Police Accountability). Today there are approximately 70 civilian bodies operating in America that share at least part of the responsibility for investigating citizen complaints against the police. While some of these organizations are, in fact, "hybrid" systems (see below), it is important to note that the expansion of civilian review is evolving quickly. As the name implies, civilian review boards are not made up of law enforcement employees—they are comprised of citizens who accept, investigate, and adjudicate the public's complaints about police misconduct.

There are a number of good, logical reasons for civilian review. These boards offer complaining citizens an alternate, civilian-run forum for making initial complaints. It is assumed some citizens are leery of going to police headquarters to file a complaint about the very people who populate the building. So one argument in favor of civilian review is that it is more accessible to the public. A second reason for civilian review is that its investigations are conducted by non-police personnel. It is assumed by proponents of this type of review that such investigators will bring more objectivity to the process and conduct investigations unaffected by conscious or subconscious police subcultural bias.

A third rationalization for civilianizing police review has to do with the general openness of the process. Not only are investigative files made available to the

BOX 13.5

POLICE EXPERTISE

A citizen walks into I.A. and wants to make a complaint. The woman says she was stopped for creeping through a red light and that "about four police cars and eight officers showed up." She claims this was unnecessary and intimidating. That is her complaint.

The I.A. Investigator asks where and when she was stopped. She tells him. He immediately knows what happened and explains to her that the traffic stop occurred at the very end of a police shift—the swing shift—and near the police station. The "extra" officers were about to go off duty and simply came by to cover the traffic stop. The woman accepts the explanation. The I.A. Investigator suggests that he talk with the supervisor of the shift in question and ask him or her to relate the incident to line officers and tell them to avoid such behavior in the future. The woman is satisfied. A complaint is avoided. The taxpayers are saved some money.

This is an example of one of the strengths of internal review. There is good reason to believe that a civilian investigator who did not work for the police department would not have such an immediate understanding of what had happened.

public in most places—the antithesis of "internal" affairs—but public hearings are often conducted that bring the issues involved into the open. Such semi-judicialized hearings include participants from both "sides" of the investigation.

So the process of civilian review is done in the open and by non-police personnel, from beginning to end. One final twist to the process is that, in most jurisdictions, the Chief of Police still determines the appropriate disciplinary measures for errant officers. Only a few jurisdictions attempt to circumvent the Chief's authority in this regard (because of the logic discussed above): the Chief's job includes meting out discipline, and if the Chief cannot be trusted with this power, then the Chief should be replaced.

Hybrid Systems: As we shall see in a moment, there are important strengths to each of these processes. But each also has its drawbacks. So in some jurisdictions, "hybrid" systems have been developed. They attempt to take advantage of the strengths of both internal affairs and civilian review boards without sacrificing the integrity of the process. These hybrid systems are different in almost every location. One operates in Kansas City, Missouri, and it is this system we will discuss briefly here (Perez).

The **Office of Citizen's Complaints (O.C.C.)** in Kansas City allows citizens to make complaints either at a police station (any police station, and there are several in Kansas City) or at the O.C.C. offices. Civilians interview complainants, outline allegations, and initiate complaint cases. Then the complaints are handed over to the police department's I.A. for investigation. O.C.C. monitors these investigations. O.C.C. civilians can suggest investigative strategies at the outset, and I.A. investigators' findings can be rejected if O.C.C. auditors are not satisfied. Complaint investigations that have been finalized are open to public scrutiny. That is, unlike in I.A. systems, the O.C.C.'s investigations are available for perusal by anyone outside the police department.

Police officer guilt or innocence is determined by the Director of the O.C.C. Reviewing complaints initially outlined by civilian personnel, then investigated by police personnel, the Director makes the initial decision about outcomes. The Director then advises the Chief of Police about this decision. On those rare occasions when the Director and the Chief do not agree, the two confer, review the investigation, and come to a mutual agreement. Thus the O.C.C. system is partly civilianized and partly operated by the police.

Comparative Analysis: Before we compare these systems directly, it is important to note several non-intuitive research findings relating to police review systems. First, comparing systems operating in parallel, it turns out that I.A. tends to find police officers guilty of misconduct slightly *more* often than does civilian review—such findings have been reported in several jurisdictions. Second, it has been found that a large majority of police officers working in jurisdictions that *do not* have civilian review are against the idea. Driven by pre-judgments about how unfair civilian review would be to police officers, such findings are universal. However, when officers who work in jurisdictions that *do* have civilian review are surveyed, they believe it to be a good idea—and by a large margin. It appears that real life experience with civilian review does not move police officers to reject its operations. With these rather counterintuitive findings in mind, let us turn to a direct comparison of these systems (Perez).

The major strengths of the I.A. system are several. First, professional, experienced police investigators conduct the inquiries. They are conversant with the law, with how police are trained, and with the pragmatic operations of local departments—including beat differentiation, shift assignments, crime patterns, and so forth. Second, today's internal police investigators tend to take their responsibility very seriously; they see themselves as the guardians of the police image and of police professionalism. Rank and file officers take internal review seriously, too, because it means review by their peers. Investigated officers tend to "learn from their mistakes" if they are found at fault by other police officers. Third, the system allows the supervisory staff complete authority over the process, and, thus, it can be held accountable. The weaknesses of I.A. review are: (1) it operates in secret; (2) it suffers from the perception—externally—that it is unfair to citizens; and (3) it may conduct investigations with an inappropriate deference to subcultural values.

The strengths of the civilian review system are also several. First, it is much more open to the public than internal review, accepting all complaints and never subverting the right of citizens to complain. Second, its investigatory findings are open to the public. Third, the decision-making phase includes open hearings, which provides not only complaining parties but the public in general an opportunity to witness the process. The weaknesses of civilian review are: (1) sometimes its investigators are not conversant with police practices and local police operations; (2) police officers tend to ignore its dictates, considering them to be irrelevant to their profession; and (3) it is expensive.

Civilian review is expensive because when it operates in a genuinely independent way, completely removed from the police departmental apparatus, it usually functions in parallel with internal systems. The law requires police to conduct their own investigations, so there are two systems operational—the internal one and the external one. And the taxpaying public foots the bill for both.

Which system is best? The answer seems to be that the balance between civilian review and internal review presented by the hybrid system is best. It enjoys several of the advantages of the internal system: (1) investigations are done by police officers; (2) sanctioned rank and file officers must respect the fact that experienced police officers have found them culpable; and (3) it leaves disciplining to the Chief and the chain of command. Research indicates that it is accepted and respected by police officers (Perez).

The hybrid system also enjoys several advantages of the civilian system: (1) it is more accessible to receiving complaints at the input stage of the process; (2) it is much more open than the internal system, allowing the public access to its findings; (3) it is largely run by civilians, with a civilian administrator making final decisions in concert with the Chief of Police; (4) the hybrid system is not expensive because there are not two systems operating in tandem (it costs about as much to run the hybrid system as it does the I.A. process); and (5) the externally perceived legitimacy of the hybrid system—what citizens think of it—is greater than that of the I.A. process.

This discussion has attempted to simplify a complicated and politically volatile subject. There has been a wealth of research and debate over the topic for many years now. Suffice it to say that the hybrid system seems to utilize the strengths of each of the other major forms of police review—and it does so in a fiscally responsible way.

Discipline

A police review system must do one of three things when it investigates an allegation of misconduct. It must either (1) find the accused officer not guilty of misconduct; (2) terminate the offending officer if his or her offense is of significant gravity; or (3) attempt to change the behavior of an errant officer in a positive direction if he or she has done something wrong that doesn't warrant termination. How is this done? What happens when a police officer is found guilty of misconduct? We will answer that question in two ways. First, we will discuss traditional, punitive forms of sanctions; second, we will briefly outline an emerging and controversial system of sanctioning without fault.

Traditional Sanctions: The traditional, punitive sanctioning system used by police departments for more than 150 years (O.W. Wilson), begins with the "verbal warning." Sometimes, especially with regard to ineptitude, supervisors will sanction minor offenses with such a personal chastisement. This may or may not be noted in an offending officer's permanent record. After this level of sanction, punishment can escalate to the "written warning" level. Such a penalty *is* kept in the permanent record of the errant officer. In some police organizations, minor sanctions, such as verbal and written warnings, can combine over time to become something more substantial. That is, if an officer is continually punished in these ways, greater punishment can ensue. Misconduct can "add up."

Often in modern police organizations, minor offenses can be taken care of with required training. Depending upon the issues involved, re-training can be administered as a response to poor report writing, poor physical technique when using force, or inappropriate driving. These are just several examples where training would be perfectly appropriate as a sanction.

The next level of punishment in the traditional system involves "time off without pay." This is, in essence, a fine. And because it affects an officer's income, most jurisdictions allow an automatic semi-judicialized Civil Service review of any case resulting in a substantial amount of time off without pay. The point at which such a review becomes automatic is different from jurisdiction to jurisdiction. In some locations, such a Civil Service review occurs punishment entails 30 days or more without pay. But in other places, even as few as two days off without pay can eventuate in a hearing before Civil Service. Some Chiefs of Police eschew such punishments unless absolutely necessary in their estimation, because Civil Service can overturn sanctions levied by a Chief.

Finally there is the ultimate sanction for an administrative investigation—termination. This always results in Civil Service review, but sometimes, especially when the charge is excessive force or corrupt behavior of some kind, chiefs feel they have no other option. Sometimes police officers misbehave in a way that indicates they can no longer be entrusted with the job. This is the worst-case scenario, of course, but it is sometimes necessary for the integrity of the organization and the good of the community.

The problem with the traditional, punishment-oriented system is that police officers often resent it. Instead of motivating them to change errant ways when negatively sanctioned, guilty officers can become diffident, cynical, and counterproductive. Anyone involved in disciplining others knows this. We are left with the question: "Is there any alternative to such a system?"

No-Fault Systems: There have been experiments in a limited number of jurisdictions with what are called **no-fault disciplinary systems**. This idea was first created in the private, corporate sector and then made its way into police work a few years ago (Iannone *et al.*). Under the no-fault system, officers who have done something wrong that does not warrant termination are subjected to less-formalized sanctions. This type of system combines the written warning process with retraining as often as possible. When officers are "sanctioned" under such a system, they are given written explanations of what it was that they did wrong, what retraining is in order, and what an officer should do to direct their behavior in a positive direction.

The no-fault system has several interesting twists to it. On the one hand, as is true of written warnings in the punitive system, if numerous episodes of misconduct form a pattern of disregard for positive suggestions and retraining, then this unchanging misbehavior can lead to termination. On the other hand—and this is something officers like about such systems—if officers do change the negative behavior, their disciplinary experience is expunged from their record after a prescribed period of time—six months to two years, depending on the severity of the misconduct. In this way, the no-fault system allows police officers to err, to change their behavior, and to avoid any long-term repercussions. Thus being found guilty of misconduct may not impact an officer's chances for advancement or choice assignments if they desist from misbehaving themselves.

Again, this no-fault idea is still an uncommon experiment. But it bears watching due to the propensity of police officers to become cynical and jaded regarding traditional disciplinary systems.

 ## SUMMATION

In this chapter we have seen that police misconduct is often misunderstood by citizens. We have also seen that the causes for genuine misconduct are numerous and troublesome; they are troublesome because some police deviance is caused and supported by not only the police subculture but members of the public as well.

CHAPTER THIRTEEN PARADOX BOX

There are two central, over-arching paradoxes relating to police accountability. First, even though "old-style" corruption of authority is very rare in today's policing world, Dirty Harry lives on—supported by both police subculture and substantial numbers of citizens. Second, internal review tends to be effective at curbing police misbehavior, but is not trusted outside police circles. On the other hand, civilian review tends to go easy on the police and to be ignored by them altogether—but it *is* trusted externally.

We have engaged the reality that holding the police accountable for genuine misconduct is made extremely difficult by several sets of overlapping procedural safeguards meant to guarantee the integrity of the system.

We have discussed several classic forms of police review and compared them directly. The hybrid system seems to be optimum, as it attempts to take advantage of the strengths of both internal and civilian review, without succumbing to their various weaknesses. Furthermore, it is cost effective. Finally, we have engaged in a brief discussion of traditional, punitive sanctioning systems and of controversial, no-fault systems. The no-fault alternative seems to present great potential, but it only exists in experimental stages in a limited number of jurisdictions.

It is now time to discuss police leadership. We will find that the Sergeant is, in some ways, the most critical leader in any police organization. Unfortunately, sergeants can be plagued by several paradoxes having to do with being supportive—and at the same time critical—of their subordinates. Then, too, we shall see in Chapter Fourteen that a Chief must play a difficult, paradox-laden role in modern police organizations. Let us now turn to engage the paradoxes of police leadership.

 DISCUSSION QUESTIONS

1. The text suggests that there is a fifth type of police misconduct that does not fit in the table: personal misconduct. This type is troublesome because it occurs off duty. Discuss what sort of off-duty deviant behavior occurs in a police officer's personal life that can become "the business" of a police department—and why. What limits should be placed upon the type of personal conduct that is "the chief's business?"

2. Some police misconduct—police crime in particular—is caused by the combination of greed and opportunity. Discuss what opportunities for such criminal behavior regularly presents itself to police officers in the line of duty.

3. What constitutes an "excessive" use of force? How much force is excessive and how much is appropriate? In fashioning your discussion, take note of the fact that the biggest problem with regard to this term is that there *is* no definitive meaning for "excessive." And because we cannot define it specifically, it is always troublesome to talk about and make sure police officers don't use it.

4. The classic debate about police review revolves around this question: who should review allegations of police misconduct? Should it be veteran police officers or civilians outside of the police organization? Discuss both sides of this argument, taking each side in turn. First, make the argument that only experienced and educated police officers can do this job effectively. Then make the argument that only people outside of the police subculture can (or should) review police conduct.

KEY TERMS

Administrative Investigations: Investigations into police misconduct that are non-criminal and can eventuate in civil sanctions including termination.

Civil Service Review: The process by which Civil Service Commissions review any substantial punishments meted out by a Chief or Sheriff.

Conduct Unbecoming an Officer: Generic, "catch-all" form of misconduct found in the G.O.s of virtually every police department.

Corruption of Authority: Police misconduct involving the abuse of official authority for personal gain.

Creative Report Writing: Police subcultural term for writing misleading and dishonest reports in order to obtain convictions.

Denying the Status of the Victim: Term used for rationalizing deviance wherein the deviant person suggests that the Victim is worthless.

Economic Stratification: Concept describing the disparity in income and savings between society's upper and lower levels of wealth.

Excessive Force: When police officers use more force than is absolutely necessary to overcome the illegal use of force.

Framing: Creating a case against a citizen that is without substantive merit.

Hybrid Systems: Police review systems that utilize some elements of civilian review in conjunction with some elements of internal review.

Ineptitude: Type of police misconduct that involves neither personal gain nor the abuse of official authority.

Misuse of Legal Authority: The "selling of the badge" by a police officer.

No-Fault Disciplinary Systems: Systems that attempt to use positive reinforcement and training as sanctions for police misconduct.

Office of Citizen's Complaints (O.C.C.): Hybrid review system of Kansas City, Missouri.

Personal Gain: Key concept in determining police misconduct to be of one type or another.

Personal Misconduct: Police misconduct that occurs off duty.

Police Crime: Police misconduct that does not involve the abuse of official authority but is for personal gain.

Police Deviance: Generic term for a multiplicity of forms of police misconduct.

Police Misconduct: Generic term for a multiplicity of forms of police misbehavior.

Police Officer's Bills of Rights (POBRs): State legislation that allows police officers under administrative investigation more procedural rights than they are afforded by the courts.

Testilying: Lying on the witness stand in an effort to convict citizens in a criminal trial.

ADDITIONAL READING

There are several excellent works in the field of police deviance. This is not surprising given the always volatile nature of the subject. In 1994, Barker and Carter wrote *Police Deviance, 3rd Ed.* (Anderson); in 1998, Kappeler, Sluder, and Alpert wrote *Forces of Deviance: Understanding the Dark Side of Policing, 2nd Ed.* (Waveland Press); and in 2002, Edwin J. Delattre wrote *Character and Cops: Ethics in Policing* (American Enterprise Institute). These are considered to be *the* critically important works in the field. Each of these books is synoptic and affords the student a solid, wide-ranging introduction to the field of police deviance. In 2004, Klockars, Ivkovic, and Haberfeld drew together contemporary thinking and research in the field in *The Contours of Police Integrity* (Sage), which includes significant discussion about the multiple causes of police misconduct. Regarding the point made in our discussion that American society contributes to police misconduct, Keith D. Harries's work *Serious Violence: Patterns of Homicide and Assault in America* (Charles C. Thomas, 1997) cogently illustrates the phenomenon of American violence.

With regard to the critically important study of Dirty Harry–like, noble cause corruption, an excellent work by Caldero and Crank is *Police Ethics: The Corruption of Noble Cause, 3rd Ed.* (Anderson, 2009). This work is an insightful and thought-provoking treatment of this area in the field. Jill Nelson's *Police Brutality: An Anthology* (W. W. Norton and Co., 2001) covers the most controversial of all police-related topics, the use of excessive force.

Police review is covered in two works that involve definitive treatments of the civilian review debate. Douglas W. Perez's *Common Sense About Police Review* (Temple University Press, 1994) is a research-oriented, comparative study of internal, external, and hybrid review systems. Samuel Walker's *The New World of Police Accountability* (Sage, 2005) includes an argument in favor of civilian review. Taken together, they give the student a balanced approach to the subject.

Fallen Blue Knights: Controlling Police Corruption by Sanja Kutnjak Ivkovic (Oxford University, 2005) presents a more traditional approach to the question of what to do about police misconduct once it has been discovered and investigated. Outside of the field of criminal justice studies, Richard C. Grote's *Discipline Without Punishment* (AMACOM, 1995) gives the student a look at no-fault disciplinary systems. His work is being utilized everywhere in the field of business and public administration. As noted in the text, experiments with this type of system are growing in contemporary American police work. Iannone, Iannone, and Bernstein approach this same idea—labeling it "upward discipline"—in *Supervision of Police Personnel, 7th Ed.* (Prentice hall, 2008). Their work points out the pluses and minuses of what may very well be the police disciplinary system of the future.

PART FOUR

Futures

Part Four concludes our discussions by focusing on current changes that impact the future of policing in critically important ways. We first engage the ever-changing field of police leadership, followed by a discussion of the professionalization movement. Both of these analyses are colored by the issues and paradoxes covered to this point.

CHAPTER 14

Leadership

Chapter Fourteen Outline

I.   Introduction

II. Command and Control

III. Coaching
   A.   The Sergeant as Teacher
   B.   Middle Management
   C.   The "Vulnerable and Corruptible" Chief
   D.   "The Good Ol' Boys"

IV. Summation

Absolutely crucial to the operations of any complex organization is the top-to-bottom leadership exercised by its supervisors. Leaders are involved in socializing new members into an organization. In police work in particular, leadership must endeavor to instill appropriate norms and values that mitigate the negatives of subcultural norms. Leaders are involved in planning and instituting change. Modern police leaders must work to educate officers about police professionalism and about COP. Leadership involves motivating like a coach and teaching like a classroom professor. Police supervisors must motivate officers to engage the dictates of the law in a realistic, creative way with an eye toward the always illusive ideal of justice. Leadership also involves evaluating and punishing misconduct and inefficiency. Police managers need to control the excesses of overzealous officers. Of principal importance, all of these police leadership tasks must be accomplished with an understanding of how the paradoxes of police work frustrate and limit police morale and effectiveness.

In this chapter, we begin by visiting the traditional "**command and control**" system of police leadership, a system based on the military model (Seddon). As many analysts have in recent years, we note that this model is outdated and inappropriate for police work *almost* all of the time. Then we discuss the analogous aspects of police managing and coaching, noting that some of the skills involved in being a good coach can translate into being a leader of police officers. But that analogy only goes so far. While there are substantial similarities, there are also differences between a coach and a police supervisor. So we then study the Sergeant as teacher—how he or she imparts important principles and operational norms to rookies and veterans alike. After a brief discussion on middle managers, we finally consider the paradoxical situation in which chiefs of police find themselves.

To begin, let us engage the troublesome reality that many police organizations adhere to forms of command and control management even though it is antithetical to logic, the philosophy of COP, and the development of police professionalism.

COMMAND AND CONTROL

The command and control model of management comes from the military. It suggests that management involves some fairly simple tasks. Managers decide what is to be done. Then they communicate their decisions down a chain of command by ordering subordinates to do this or that. They then monitor the actions of their subordinates and exercise direct control over them. In this way, little discretion is allowed, and the command structure is in control at all times (O.W. Wilson and McLaren).

This way of doing things makes perfectly good sense in the military. To begin with, boot camps instill both a fear of commanders and a propensity to follow orders in a knee-jerk fashion. Second, in the military, subordinates—the troops—are almost universally under the immediate supervision and control of their superiors. While soldiers or sailors or marines are exhorted to **"adapt and overcome"** when they are without supervision, this is rare. Usually, commanders are with their troops and direct control is what prevails. Because of the movement toward paramilitarism that occurred during the Reform Era, this is the type of organizational management model that has been followed in police work for generations now.

But the command and control model does not suit police work for several reasons (Meese and Ortmeier). First, it involves controlling people exclusively through coercion. As pointed out in Chapter Five, people do not like to be coerced. They tend to rebel against it. In the case of police officers, who themselves exercise power over citizens, being the objects of such rigid power is not well accepted. And as experts in power manipulation themselves, if they are motivated to do so, for one reason or another, police officers can behave in any number of ways that work to limit the impact of command and control–type management.

Second, command and control requires immediate supervision. It does not work well if supervisors issue orders and then only occasionally monitor the impact of those orders. In police work, supervision is almost never immediate. Sergeants who are supposed to "control" line officers see them at the beginning and end of their shifts. In the middle of a standard shift, the Sergeant will move from beat to beat, checking in with his or her subordinates. And, if logistically possible, they will visit numerous details to monitor their officers. But in the grand scheme of things, minute-by-minute supervision is rare in police work. The discretionary decisions made by police officers—to stop a vehicle or not, to invoke the dictates of the law or not, to use force or not—are made alone and without supervision. There is no realistic way for police commanders to "control" almost anything that happens most often on the street.

Third, because of the amount of information and expertise possessed by today's COP officers on patrol, the ability of supervisors to know what to do in the first instance is limited. Beat officers have always possessed substantial amounts of particularized knowledge about their beats unknown to their managers. But in today's world of COP, where such a great amount of discretionary power is afforded to individual officers, it is doubly difficult for supervisors to issue "orders" that are meaningful in any sense. Supervisors are at a disadvantage—they know far less than the officers they are supposed to control.

Fourth, in the command and control model, supervisors are sometimes required to be **"swift and ruthless"** about misconduct. In the military, this makes perfectly good sense, since any break in the chain of command can cost soldiers or sailors or marines their lives. But in police work, being swift and ruthless is almost never appropriate (Glenn). As we shall discuss later, when an officer errs, exactly the opposite is usually called for; the police leader needs to be measured and empathetic.

Finally, and without deprecating the intelligence and abilities of police leaders, the lack of substantive expertise on the part of police elites can be viewed from below as more than ignorance: it can be seen as incompetence. As noted

BOX 14.1

THE PETER PRINCIPLE

"**The Peter Principle**" is a humorous book first published in 1969 that makes a serious point about management. It notes that in any complex organization, people move up the ladder of management by showing their competence and abilities at each level. In the competition for promotions, being competent allows a person to advance. But at some point, people tend to rise to their level of *in*competence. That is, they get to a point that is one level above their ability—where they remain and cannot advance. The thrust of the principle is that most people involved in the management of most organizations are *in*competent at what they are attempting to accomplish.

(Peter and Hull)

in Box 14.1, some who move up the chain of command in any organization can ultimately occupy positions where they are working beyond their capacities to be effective. That is, they rise to their level of incompetence. Add to this the above point about supervisors' lack of beat-specific knowledge of crime-related patterns and individual perpetrators, and we see that many supervisors can have only a minimum level of impact upon specific strategies on the street today.

So the old fashioned command and control model of police supervision is considered by progressive police leaders to be almost completely irrelevant to today's police organizations. But the key word here is "almost." As noted when discussing the drawbacks of paramilitarism, there are situations under which command and control becomes necessary. When hostages are taken, when riots occur, or when guns are drawn, it is necessary to issue commands and to control police forces. This is a central paradox of police management.

For all of the reasons listed above, in some places—where the limitations of command and control are appreciated and analyzed—the world of police management has been searching for alternative methods of supervision for a generation. Modern analysts suggest that police leaders resemble coaches or teachers more than commanders. And it is toward an analysis of the police leader as coach that we now turn.

COACHING

Being a police leader is like being the coach of a team in some ways—in many ways, actually. The rhetoric of COP in particular suggests that modern police management should be modeled after coaching (Cordner). The team analogy often seems perfect. The police dress in uniforms, they work the street in unison, they are outnumbered, and they are involved in a "contact sport." They must coordinate efforts, possess discipline, and have an appropriate esprit de corps. Viewing the policing endeavor as a team enterprise seems logical and utilitarian. And if the police are a team, then it follows that their leaders are coaches—some of the time.

But the analogy breaks down at other times. As noted in our discussions about the limitations of police subcultural norms, the drawbacks of paramilitarism, and how today's COP philosophy is supposed to work, the police can engage in many counterproductive behaviors if they focus too much on the "us against them" dynamic. And this us-against-them conceptualization is central to the sports team idea. In other words, the sports team analogy works some of the time, in some ways, but it is not appropriate at other times, in other ways.

So leading police officers is like coaching at times. It involves the same dynamics and entails utilizing the same skill sets (Gardner). Football coaching in particular seems to present us with a good analogy. There is danger on the football field. People get hurt out there, sometimes badly, and sometimes—on rare occasions—players even die on the football field. So the danger factor is similar, and the need to work together in a disciplined fashion—to achieve an overall success level—is sometimes appropriate. The leadership mechanism is also similar: the Head Coach is like a Chief of Police; Offensive and Defensive Coordinators are like middle managers; and football captains—who play on the field with other players— are like sergeants.

There are several lessons both police managers and football coaches must learn. First, a football coach learns that the rules for the team must be set up and administered so that every athlete knows they are applied equitably. Everyone must be treated in the same way, or the integrity of the coaching staff will suffer in the estimation of the players on the team (see Box 14.2). To have favorites or to make excuses for players is antithetical to good coaching. And so it is with supervising police officers.

However, the paradox here is that everyone's situation is not the same in life. People live in different family situations. They have different levels of experience, intelligence, and maturity. They have differing capabilities and expectations. They have different histories on the field or on the job. In order to be a good coach/ police supervisor one has to understand this. And in administering subordinates, this central paradox is often in evidence; you must treat everyone the same way, and yet you cannot treat everyone the same way.

This leads to another coaching axiom: unless it is unavoidable, it is not appropriate to discipline an athlete in front of the team. Doing so can create a level of animosity in the erring player that makes him diffident and, even, an enemy of sorts. Even if he does not literally quit the team, a coach can "lose" an athlete by embarrassing him in this way. So even if a football player knows he has messed up, his chastisement needs to be done quietly, on the side. An errant police officer needs to be dealt with in this same way. Anything said to the officer should be done quietly and in private. And as is true with athletes, this rule should never be broken unless a player has messed up often enough that disciplining him publically has become something a leader needs to do in order to make a point to others. So it is with football and so it is with policing.

Still another coaching point that is critical in police work has to do with giving positive feedback when someone has erred. In coaching, they talk about **"the sandwich technique,"** and this, too, is relevant in police work. The sandwich metaphor relates to engineering a conference with an errant subordinate in a three-tiered way. First, the coach/supervisor says something positive about the athlete/officer. Second, "the bad news" is delivered (about whatever misconduct has occurred). And third, the coach/supervisor ends with something positive. As simplistic as this might appear, it works. When supervisors have negative news to present, this little technique can often make the experience end up being positive.

A final coaching point has to do with having a generally positive attitude whenever possible. This, too, might sound simplistic, but in police work it is all important. Because of the multiple, overlapping frustrations faced by police officers on a regular basis, they can become jaded and even cynical—about people, the job, and life in general. Nothing impacts more positively upon this than a supervisor's ongoing, positive, "you can do it" attitude.

BOX 14.2

THE CENTRAL PARADOX OF COACHING

The Head Coach of a high school football team sets out a rule. "We have had some people missing practice, for one reason or another, and I have had it. From now on, you will not play on Friday night unless you attend every practice, all week long." Too many players have used faulty excuses to escape a practice here or there, and the team's performance on game nights is suffering. There will be no excuses; this policy applies to everyone equally—it is understandable and fair. And it is in the team's best interests.

Then, on a Thursday afternoon, his starting tailback, the team hero, has to leave school to take care of his brothers and sisters while his mother goes to the hospital Emergency Room with the flu. The player misses practice. The kid is being a good son and a good brother. He is living up to the idea that family comes first in life. He is not missing practice due to any capricious or silly reason. He's being dependable.

What will the Coach do on Friday night, when his all-star tailback—the kid that the team cannot win without—is ineligible to play because of the attendance rule? Does the Coach "bend" the rule, because this was an unusual circumstance? Or does the Coach stick by the rule—and, thus, lose the game—because to break it would be to lose integrity?

So far in discussing police leadership we have focused upon the concept of supervision as a generalized idea. Now, we will talk—in order—about the particularized leadership of sergeants, middle managers, and chiefs.

The Sergeant as Teacher

The Sergeant is the key person in any police organization. Sergeants are the glue that keeps things together (Muir). While those above them occupy important roles also, police sergeants are the only supervisors who work the streets as police officers in uniform. Officers know and respect this reality. When the sh%! goes down, the Sergeant is out there, on the street, working and struggling with us. This is the perspective of the average line officer.

Sergeants are the critical link that joins upper level policy developers with rank and file officers who actually interact with the populace on the street. Their efforts at coaching, mentoring, and teaching beat officers bring meaning to the otherwise sterile dictates of the law and police administrative policy. Let us discuss some coaching and teaching dynamics with which the effective and creative Sergeant must be familiar.

First, perhaps the most important teaching job required of sergeants is that they nurture in their subordinates an understanding of and a feeling for the paradoxes of police work. While many sergeants do not necessarily label them as such, they understand a great deal about these paradoxes. In their roles as teachers and mentors, it is absolutely essential that they prepare young officers in particular for the frustrations resulting from these paradoxes that will afflict them on the street. Only if officers intellectually understand these conundrums will they be able to avert some of the emotional stress that results from experiencing them.

Second, it is critical that the Sergeant allow young officers in particular to try out different ways of doing things. The idea that there is only one way to solve any type of detail is nonsense. Police officers can handle people with confidence and poise, with intelligence and logic, and even with humor. It depends upon the officer and how they deal with people. Sergeants not only have to understand this, but they have to be ready to allow that mistakes will be made as an officer feels his or her way through the creation of a working personality. Sergeants must be creative in knowing how to chastise an officer for making mistakes while at the same time understanding that the harsher their discipline, the less likely their officers will attempt experimentation (Muir). As noted in Box 14.3, being supportive when an officer is wrong is absolutely crucial to police officer morale, learning, and professionalism.

A third important element of the Sergeant's role has to do with police ethics. We noted in Chapter Thirteen that today's officers are intelligent and educated enough to be expected to develop a sophisticated understanding of ethics from the ground up. That is, in lieu of **"trying not to screw up,"** the modern officer should be engaged with the idea of being a good police officer and accomplishing good things (Perez and Moore). Today's officer needs to take seriously the job of developing a personal ethic. Along the path to creating such an ethical framework, the Sergeant needs to encourage officers to think about and study ethics, to talk about it with other officers, and to accept becoming a serious, ethical person as a critical element of their jobs and lives.

A fourth important area of teaching for the Sergeant relates to the use of power and force. Since there is no definitive understanding of what appropriate force is—what does "excessive" mean? (Klockars, "Controlling Excessive Force")—the Sergeant is the key person in developing the circumspection police officers must have regarding the use of force. With empathy and compassion for the difficulty of the job, the Sergeant must illustrate how critical the use of force is and how police officers must think about it a great deal—they must come to terms with the paradoxes involved. In particular, the Sergeant needs to work consciously on the subcultural norm of overkill. While understanding the paradox of face, and why police officers cleave to the idea that they have to "win and win big" when confronted by citizen violence, the Sergeant must attempt to dispel the idea that excessive force has any place in police work.

Fifth, and in conjunction with the above point, the Sergeant needs to do everything possible to dissuade police officers from adhering to those subcultural norms most inimical to the best interests of justice. Aside from overkill, the Sergeant must endeavor to lessen the "distance" between police and public. In particular, a good Sergeant will teach police officers that to explain or apologize is neither a sign of weakness nor counterproductive to the interests of the police themselves. The contemporary police officer must understand that COP requires a closely knit relationship between police and public. In order to create and to maintain this relationship, explanations of how the police operate (and why) should be offered to citizens whenever possible. In the long run, this produces cooperation and respect for the police among the citizenry.

Finally, the Sergeant must do everything possible to aid the young police officer in avoiding one of the difficulties often presented to anyone who works with people in a bureaucratic capacity. In the helping professions, there is a tendency for workers to treat citizens as "cases." So many individuals pass through bureaucratic systems that they can come to be seen as cases instead of people. The objectification of people can be a tendency into which doctors, nurses, social workers, and a host of other helping professionals can fall.

Of course, make people into cases can be a positive thing if it is utilized to lessen the tension sometimes experienced by doctors or nurses, in the operating room, for example. Or it can be positive if it helps police officers to be more objective and correct in their decision-making. But the objectification of citizens feeds a negative dynamic if it leads a professional to lose touch with his or her humanity and become jaded and cynical. The creative Sergeant must warn the young police officer about this tendency to objectify people. Guarding against such cynicism is something rookie police officers in particular need to work on, and it is part of a Sergeant's job to help them do so.

Our discussion has focused on the substance of what a Sergeant must teach. Then, too, we have related, albeit briefly, that empathizing with subordinates and allowing for experimentation and error is critical in a procedural sense. There is still another, final element to our brief treatment of the tasks that confront a sergeant. And that has to do with the Sergeant as role model (Kleinig).

A Sergeant cannot be "one of the gang." The requirements of the position will not allow for such an attitude. The Sergeant must be firm and resolute and, at the same time, empathetic and understanding—sometimes a difficult mix of characteristics to achieve. The Sergeant must be circumspect about his or her own behavior, not just on the street, but also in social situations involving other officers. Most important is a Sergeant's integrity—the relationship between what one teaches and what one does. Our final coaching axiom is something all coaches know: you cannot give speeches to athletes about commitment, punctuality, loyalty, intensity, or proficiency if you do not live up to these things yourself.

BOX 14.3

ALLOWING FOR MISTAKES

A young police rookie shows up at the scene of a domestic disturbance. When the rookie suggests to an irate husband that he must quiet down or he'll be "taken outa here," the husband responds with indignation and states, "If you think you're man enough." The young officer immediately bristles at this challenge to his manhood and grabs the man by the shirt. The man responds by grabbing the officer by his shirt.

The rookie's Sergeant arrives at that moment. He calms the husband, who, in fact, is not really any threat to the police. He separates the two, and he handles the detail without incident or arrest. Later, the Sergeant sits the young officer down and talks him through the event, suggesting a number of alternative strategies for its resolution. The Sergeant believes that the rookie has performed poorly—has made several important mistakes—but he understands the macho mentality of the young man, remembers how young and inexperienced the rookie is, and handles the entire situation informally, in a "just between you and me" manner. In this way, the Sergeant acknowledges the rookie's mistakes, encourages learning, and, at the same time, develops a level of trust upon which he can depend in the future. The Sergeant is "allowing for mistakes" without being too officious or judgmental. And he has probably taught the young officer several important lessons.

Middle Management

Our discussion here about middle management will be brief, because this topic involves an entire field of police study that is growing more complicated all the time. Along with the changes instituted with the advent of the COP movement, police middle management has become replete with a host of programs aimed at making the development of strategies, their implementation, and their evaluation more effective. And we cannot do justice to this broad set of developments in the space we have.

So we will engage the middle manager's role in two ways. We will briefly discuss the traditional role under the command and control model and then outline the middle manager's newfound responsibilities under COP. Under command and control, the middle manager serves as the intersection point between upper level policy makers and line officers on the street. Policy is developed on high and descends the chain of command to the middle manager. Middle managers develop day-to-day strategies aimed at implementing the policies from above. The strategies of the middle managers are passed down to the line officers, and they are implemented. Then, as the second part of their job, middle managers evaluate implementation efforts, and they evaluate police officers. This is the command and control model in a nutshell, and it is fairly straightforward and easy to understand.

In our modern era, with COP strategies being instituted around the country, the role of the middle manager has expanded. It still includes some of the basic elements of command and control. When policy is decided above, the middle manager is still charged with implementing it at lower levels. And the middle manager is still responsible for generating police accountability systems that evaluate officers below. This much is the same. But under COP there is much more. Today's middle manager must learn to implement any one of a number of management systems that have come into vogue in the police world. We will briefly mention one, the system most often utilized around the country: **Total Quality Management (TQM)** (Peratec). Introduced into police work from the private sector, this system seeks to inculcate some of the basic principles of COP by creating more specifically targeted strategies and developing measuring instruments (Walsh and Vito). TQM is currently attempted at thousands of police departments around the country.

The qualitative dimension of TQM includes several key concepts that are a part of the COP movement. First and foremost, middle management today is all about teamwork. Managers are required to seek lower level expertise and input before making key decisions. The best way to improve work quality is to seek such input. Top-down, command-and-control–type management is strongly discouraged. Today's middle manager is often meant to play **the role of facilitator**. Gathering input from those at the lower level who actually meet the public and do the police work, middle managers become the leaders of groups of decision makers—and not necessarily the primary decision-makers themselves.

Second, where discipline is concerned, managers are encouraged to spend their time focusing upon the management of the 95 percent of their subordinates who do not cause problems. The focus of management in the past has often been on the 5 percent who *do* cause problems. TQM encourages prompt and fair dealings with problem employees but suggests that as little time as is possible should be spent in this negative direction.

Third, TQM emphasizes allowing for and encouraging creativity in subordinates. As we have mentioned with regard to sergeants, the middle manager should coach, motivate, and facilitate. They should allow for honest mistakes, understanding that they will be made if subordinates are being creative and attempting to develop alternative strategies and ways of doing things.

Fourth, TQM's qualitative dimension involves a focus upon citizens as "customers." Evaluating whether or not customers are obtaining what they want is critical. Surveys are done to ascertain citizen feedback, and the information obtained is taken seriously and included in future decision-making. Citizens' complaints are understood not as individual problems, but as departmental feedback that brings more data into the decision-making process.

The quantitative dimension of TQM involves the use of research and statistical techniques in evaluating organizational effectiveness and efficiency. Here and elsewhere, middle managers are supposed to focus upon data-driven problem solving in lieu of making decisions based upon emotion. As noted above, both departmentally generated surveys and citizens' complaints provide data upon which decisions should be made. One example of the type of new statistics involved in TQM is the idea that counting numbers of "problems solved" is more important than focusing upon arrest statistics.

Of course, as is always the case, there are problems with TQM. Literally hundreds of types of surveys have been attempted in different locations, some generating results of questionable value. Evaluating "problems solved," for example, is difficult given the amorphous nature of the categories involved. Then, too, police officers must accept and "buy into" such creative ideas, and this often does not happen. The surveying and generalized research orientation of such modern systems can be seen as a waste of time at best—and the unwarranted addition of extra work and angst at worst. Line officers sometimes complain that TQM has turned police departments into survey research centers.

Furthermore, we must recall that in Chapter Ten we engaged the idea that today's middle managers often exist in an awkward reality. Under this new philosophy, middle managers tend to feel that they have lost their ability to command those beneath them. and yet they are still held responsible for the actions of subordinates. Today's middle managers are caught in an odd position that can make their job extremely difficult.

So we've now scratched the surface of a set of issues about which entire textbooks and police operational manuals have been written. Our efforts here have only been aimed at pointing out the existence of evaluation and implementation systems such as TQM and, in addition, to note that the progress of such systems is halting and problematic at times. The paradox presented to middle managers is that during the past generation of American policing they have operated amidst a sea of change, and while expected to embrace this change, they can often be left rudderless, without the sort of clear-cut focus they used to enjoy under the command and control model.

The "Vulnerable and Corruptible" Chief

William Muir's work includes not only his insightful explanation of the paradoxes of coercive power but, in addition, an important discussion of the role of the Chief of Police. Muir suggests that the Chief is **"vulnerable and corruptible"** (Muir 263). In this section, we will begin by engaging what Muir meant by this. In general, we are going to talk about how the Chief of Police lives a sort of **fishbowl existence**, wherein his or her decisions and even personal behavior are viewed with both interest and skepticism. And because of the power that others can exercise over the Chief's tenure, the Chief is vulnerable to being removed from office at a moment's notice.

Because of this vulnerability, the Chief can become corruptible. We do not mean to say that the Chief may tend to fall into corruption of authority. Almost everywhere, the time when that was true has long passed in American policing. But chiefs of police are susceptible to noble cause corruption. Just as is true of beat officers, the Chief can be the recipient of requests to "do anything to get the job done." And because they occupy such a vulnerable position, chiefs can be prone to respond to such requests, even when they are totally inappropriate.

Tenure: Chiefs of police are vulnerable in that their **tenure** is not guaranteed in any way. Chiefs are appointed by Mayors or City Councils or Boards of Selectmen

BOX 14.4

THE "CORRUPTIBLE" CHIEF

While the average police officer can get feedback from the community when he or she behaves like Dirty Harry (as we have noted elsewhere), the Chief of Police is even more prone to obtain positive feedback when police officers do "anything that works" to get the job done. "Mr. and Mrs. John Q. Public" care little about the exigencies of the United States Constitution. They do not care to hear excuses about what the Chief can or cannot do legally. They want the police, and the Chief in particular, to "clean up the streets" using whatever methods available. Furthermore, as noted in Chapter Six, Hollywood regularly sells images to the public indicating that when the police break procedural rules they should be considered "heroes."

or even by City Managers. While they are civil servants during the rest of their careers, when they move to the head position, they are not afforded Civil Service protections. They serve **"at the pleasure of"** whoever appointed them. This means that they do not have to be removed for "good cause." They can be removed whenever the powers that installed them decide they are no longer effective. Such decisions can be made using whatever grounds these powers deem reasonable to make such a determination. Thus, chiefs are vulnerable to being discharged at any time. A major corruption scandal, a controversial political fight over police policies, or an individual incident involving police misconduct of some egregious sort—these are just a few examples of the sorts of events that might lead to the firing of a Chief of Police. This makes the Chief vulnerable on a daily basis.

In some places, there have been attempts to create a more solid level of stability for the Chief. Understanding the various pressures that make the position vulnerable, some jurisdictions have sought to allow tenure to the Chief. The idea is to place the chief executive police officer on more sound footing and thus make it possible for the Chief to behave ethically when confronted with elements in the community that may lobby for the expedient and inappropriate thing (witness our example in Box 14.5). In Los Angeles, for example, the City Charter has been modified to allow the Chief of Police a 5-year contract that is renewable only once. During the 5 years of the contract, the Chief is only **removable for "cause."** This is an effort to free the Chief from political powers that sometimes operate in opposition to just and professional decision-making.

Sheriffs, on the other hand, are elected. The American Sheriff administers the county's policing as long as he or she continues to be popular enough to win re-election. Thus, the Sheriff is also vulnerable, but only in a once-in-a-while, political sense. Sheriffs enjoy a sort of tenure denied to chiefs. But they too often receive calls to do inappropriate and even illegal things.

The important point here is that both chiefs and sheriffs can be responsive to calls for inappropriate, overly aggressive, and even illegal police action—much as the individual officer is responsive to calls for Dirty Harry–like behavior. Theirs is a position that can be compromised by falling into noble cause corruption in an effort to create a more stable work situation for themselves.

So police executives can be vulnerable to political elites. Unfortunately, this is just the beginning of the list of characters to whom the Chief must respond.

Media Influence: As we have discussed at some length, the media in America tend to be very supportive of the police in general. But when controversy of any kind rears its head, the media will pounce. Controversy means increased television ratings or newspapers sales—or at least that is how the media perceive things. So police executives must manage their images in the local press. And since this involves keeping away from controversy, chiefs of police tend to work constantly at public relations management. They work at comforting local politicos. They work at appearing tough and effective at fighting crime. They work at polishing their individual images.

This is usually an easy enough task, given the symbiotic relationship enjoyed between the police and the media (noted in Chapter Six). But it can become impossible when anything out of the ordinary occurs. One operational norm to which chiefs adhere is the **"rotten apple syndrome"** (Perez). This idea suggests that when corruption or misconduct of any kind becomes manifest enough to be covered in the press, the police executive's internal review system must find a culprit. And that culprit is always an individual officer or group of officers—not the police administration itself. Individual officers are "sacrificed," to some extent, sold to the media as "rotten apples" (Perez 70). This metaphor suggests that the barrel full of apples (the police department) is clean, effective, and ethical; the problem (whatever problem) lies in a few rotten apples that might "spoil the barrel." Thus, internalized review systems work to do two things at once: they get rid of such rotten apples and, coincidentally, they facilitate the avoidance of having to deal with larger questions about executive-level competence. In other words, by discharging officers involved in misconduct and labeling misconduct as "unusual," the Chief avoids questions about whether the roots of misconduct might lead to the Chief's office. Here again, the Chief can become involved in noble cause corruption in order to curry local media favor.

Police Unions: An odd paradox faced by chiefs of police is that they are supposed to be in command of police organizations, but, at the same time, in some locations, they can be vulnerable to being controlled by the very people they are supposed to manage—line officers. Modern police unions can be incredibly powerful (Delord *et al.*). And unions can be so powerful in some locales that they can operate to get the Chief discharged. There are numerous examples of this happening in places where the police union is extremely powerful. Being aware of the possibility, chiefs of police can sometimes feel required to placate union leadership. Not only can the Chief be vulnerable to union power moves, but this reality can work to dissuade the Chief from taking action that would otherwise be considered logical and progressive. Thus—and this is only true where unions have obtained a substantial amount of political power and independence—the Chief's job is made more vulnerable by the very officers the Chief is supposed to administer and control.

Personal Life: Chiefs of police must maintain unsullied personal lives. They cannot avoid their fishbowl-like existence. So they must behave in a way that is unimpeachable. Chiefs must pay their bills—on time. They must pay their taxes—on time. They must sleep with their significant others and no one else. They must avoid the police subcultural propensity to become involved in public drinking. In these and a hundred other ways, chiefs of police must be circumspect about their own behavior and image in the community.

As the head of the police organization, the Chief of Police must be a role model both within and without the police department. One method of sending a positive message is to be no-nonsense about discipline. Internal review systems must be organized and operated in a way that tells everyone within the rank and file that the Chief is serious about I.A.'s performance. One way to do this is to appoint to I.A. people who are "the best and the brightest" in the department. In most police organizations, it is traditional to assign the fastest rising, most intelligent, and most career-oriented types of investigators to the Homicide detail. In many modern departments, chiefs have also begun to appoint such people to I.A. This issues an ongoing message to everyone: the Chief is serious about departmental discipline.

Legality and Democracy: The Chief of Police must operate within still one more ongoing paradox: that of having **to teach democracy and legality** at the same time. Muir points out that both of these concepts are critical to modern policing. Police officers must be hired, trained, and disciplined on a regular basis with an eye toward insuring that they have an appreciation of the law. Everything they do must be done legally, and this must be a serious principle that drives the organization.

But also, the police must have an appreciation for democracy—for the rule of the people. Especially in an era of COP, they must understand that they serve the citizens of their community and that they need to be as responsive to public concerns as they can possibly be. Thus, as noted in Chapter Thirteen, the police

BOX 14.5

THE CHIEF AND DIRTY HARRY

In contemporary America, supported by the most conservative Supreme Court in American history, the Constitution is being interpreted by many lower courts in such a way as to allow numerous powers to the police that many argue are inappropriate. For example, the police are allowed a great deal of latitude within which to make warrantless searches. Appeals courts in several locations have accepted random "sweeps" of public housing. In some places, such sweeps tend to be popular with political elites, as they appear to show how tough on crime a given city or county administration is. And since such sweeps are aimed at poor, politically disenfranchised people, there is little danger they will be met with much protest.

But while the police *can* make such searches, the question is, *should* they? Or, led by the Chief of Police, should local police organizations eschew such searches in favor of a more progressive and civil rights–friendly view of their powers? Does the Chief placate the politicos—and behave in a Dirty Harry–like way—or do the right thing? Because of the Chief's vulnerability, it is difficult for most chiefs to avoid such draconian actions if they operate in jurisdictions where local politics will support such extremes.

must be both legal and political actors. But to do both things at the same time is often impossible, because "the people" will sometimes call for the most outrageous of police actions. To ignore calls for illegal action from the citizenry, and thus ignore the principle of democratic rule, is to observe the law. And this can produce even more angst in the world of the Chief of Police. Following the law and doing what is right becomes a political liability.

The "Good Ol' Boys"

Police work has come a long way in America in a short period of time. It was only 50 years ago when the majority of those who were brought into police work had limited educations, limited training, and were essentially state-hired bouncers and crowd control experts. Today, as American policing approaches genuine professionalism, just about everything has changed: who is hired, how they are trained, how they are disciplined, and the entire philosophy underwriting the endeavor. It is a new world for policing just about everywhere in just about every way.

But in saying that policing is new and different "just about everywhere," we acknowledge a critical reality: in some places, there is an entrenched subcultural system—"old school thinking"—that inhibits the development of modern police leadership in appropriate directions (Brown). There are still places in America where, despite over 100 years of Civil Service operations, police officers tend to be hired because of who they know or who they are related to. In some small town departments, the local police organization is populated by siblings and in-laws.

BOX 14.6

GOOD OL' BOY LEADERSHIP

In a small, rural police department, several officers—including the Chief of Police—were fired because of their use of a taser gun on a restrained and handcuffed suspect "just for the fun of it." Several years later, the department went through a second scandal relating to a scheme involving kickbacks to officers from local small businesses. How could this have happened? How could a "new" reform administration be brought into town and have such a limited impact upon the police culture and how things were supervised? The answer is that even though this happened recently—in the 1990s—the officers who replaced those who were fired (because of the first scandal) were relatives of the terminated, offending officers. And they resisted even the suggestion of change of any kind—in hiring, training, or managing the department. This sort of "good ol' boy" thinking may be diminishing, but it is not yet gone from American policing.

This happens in more locations than one might imagine. And in such locales, the call for the type of leadership that we have herein discussed does not fall upon receptive ears.

Just as was the case when we discussed police education two chapters ago, in some places there is a sort of reactionary push against modern police management principles. The "good ol' boy" network is still in place in many small, rural jurisdictions. In those departments, not only is the modern college-educated police officer unappreciated, but modern leadership principles are rejected in favor of command and control. "This is the way we've always done it," runs the typical rationale. In discussing police professionalism in our next and final chapter, we will revisit this reaction against progress. For now, we will note that that the tension between the old and the new in police work can be observed to this day. Some police leaders do not want to hire the modern, more-educated officer. They do not want to embrace more sophisticated training regimens. And they do not want to develop more up-to-date supervisorial strategies. Such change threatens to undo not only their personal worldviews but the nature of their control over local police systems.

Thus, our discussion about the power of the police subculture to inhibit change of any kind applies equally to command structures in some locales. It is not merely the line officer who resists change. Such resistance can be observed in police management as well, especially in small-town policing.

SUMMATION

In this chapter we have explored the limitations of the traditional command and control method of police leadership. We have seen its weaknesses and engaged some more modern ideas about how police supervisors and, especially, modern sergeants need to operate in order to avoid the drawbacks of the traditional model. We have seen the relevance of the paradoxes of paramilitarism extended to the world of the police supervisor. To wit, command and control is almost always a bad way of administering the police, and it is almost always unnecessary. Almost. But on some occasions—the same types that necessitate paramilitaristic policing—it is absolutely necessary.

We have discussed the Sergeant as coach and as teacher. And we have briefly touched upon the role of middle managers in today's police world. We have noted

CHAPTER FOURTEEN PARADOX BOX

There are several paradoxes involved in police leadership, at different levels. Perhaps the most important one involves the Chief of Police. The Chief is supposed to be in control of the police organization, is supposed to lead by example, and is particularly charged with being the guardian of the department's ethical compass. Yet Chiefs can be so vulnerable that they can sometimes be manipulated into becoming involved in noble cause corruption.

that both of these police actors need to teach and to motivate their subordinates with an understanding of the many paradoxes of police work. Finally, we have considered the vulnerable and corruptible role of the Chief of Police and visited several paradoxes involved in their difficult fishbowl-like existence.

Along the way we have examined numerous paradoxes that inhibit progress toward modern leadership and supervision. And, in turn, we have discovered that the changes in contemporary police work that have been embraced by so many are not necessarily well received everywhere.

In Chapter Fifteen we will engage police professionalism. This chapter will first seek to engage the debate about what professionalism actually means. Then, we will discuss how close the police are to achieving genuine professionalism. Finally, we will consider what it would take—what changes need to occur—to achieve the goal of genuine professionalism in American policing.

DISCUSSION QUESTIONS

1. What is the "command and control" philosophy? How does the command side of it work? How does the control side of it work? Even though this is the most traditional form of police leadership, we argue in the text that it does not fit well with today's COP philosophy. Why not? Are there elements of command and control that *can* be utilized effectively in today's policing?

2. Box 14.1 discusses The Peter Principle. What does the Peter Principle state? What does it mean? Is it true? If so, what does it say about police leadership and the ability of the police to make progress toward both COP and genuine professionalism today?

3. Muir suggests that for all of the power ostensibly embraced by the Chief of Police, these powerful actors are still vulnerable and corruptible. Why is this so? What makes the Chief vulnerable? What are the multiple ways in which the Chief can be corrupted? What, if anything, might be done about it?

4. What is the "rotten apple syndrome"? How does it work to protect police administrators from criticism? Is it true that police misconduct is cause by individual, misbehaving officers? Or are there sometimes patterns of misconduct that might have something to do with poor management and ineffective leadership?

KEY TERMS

"Adapt and Overcome": Catch phrase or motto in both the military (Marine Corps in particular) and police work.

Allowing for Mistakes: Important operational principle for sergeants and middle managers when teaching subordinates.

"At the Pleasure of": Legal phrase describing the tenure of chiefs of police under most circumstances in most places. Without any civil service protection, chiefs may be terminated instantly when their behavior displeases those who appointed them.

Command and Control: Traditional military and police form of supervision.

Fishbowl Existence (of the Chief): Metaphor illustrating how public the Chief of Police's role is, both in professional and private life.

The Peter Principle: In complex organizations, most administrators rise to their level of incompetence.

Removable for Cause: The standard necessary to terminate police officers under Civil Service protection (and some chiefs of police who enjoy expanded tenure under contracts).

The Role of Facilitator (Middle Manager as): Under COP, the central role of the middle manager has become facilitator in lieu of being a "commander."

Rotten Apple Syndrome: Metaphor illustrating the propensity of management to avoid questions about inefficiency, ineffectiveness, or incompetence on its part by making examples of individual police officers when misconduct occurs.

The Sandwich Technique: Coaching principle suggesting that when an athlete needs admonishing, it should be "sandwiched" between two positive statements.

"Swift and Ruthless": One of the principles of supervision associated with the command and control model. Under this philosophy, when subordinates make mistakes, supervisorial response must avoid any tendency to be empathetic or accommodating.

Tenure: The amount of time a professional has in office, whether guaranteed or problematic.

To Teach Democracy and Legality: One of the paradoxes of the role of Chief of Police is to do both of these simultaneously.

Total Quality Management (TQM): System of managing and evaluating modern complex organizations used in the private sector and, recently, in police circles.

"Trying Not to Screw Up": The traditional focus of police-academy training where discussions about ethics are concerned.

Vulnerable and Corruptible: Muir's conceptualization of two dynamics that make the role of Chief of Police extraordinarily difficult.

ADDITIONAL READING

Our discussion here begins with references to the command and control model of police management. Two excellent works that analyze and issue critiques of this antiquated method of supervision are *Freedom from Command and Control* by

John Seddon (Productivity Press, 2005), and *Training the 21st Century Police Officer* by Russell W. Glenn (Rand Crop, 2003). Glenn focuses in particular on how the command and control model must give way to methods of supervision commensurate with COP.

Our text here makes reference to the "Peter Principle" early in the chapter. This idea can be found in the best selling book *The Peter Principle* by Laurence J. Peter and Raymond Hull (Bantam, 1969), which has been reprinted many times since its first printing in 1969.

Muir's work (cited elsewhere, numerous times) focuses directly on the importance of considering the Sergeant as teacher. This idea is echoed in *Common Sense Police Supervision: Practical Tips for the First-Line Leader* by Gerald W. Garner (Charles C. Thomas, 2008). In *The Ethics of Policing* (Cambridge University Press, 1996), John Kleinig discusses the importance of this teaching role, among a host of other topics. As noted in the text, Muir also treats us to the idea that the Chief of Police can be vulnerable and corruptible.

In *Supervising Police Personnel: The Fifteen Responsibilities, 6th Ed.* (Prentice Hall, 2006), Paul M. Whisenand suggests a list-like approach to police supervision that, while a bit on the dry side, is nevertheless indicative of a more traditional approach to the topic. Counter-posed to this traditional focus is *Leadership, Ethics, and Policing: Challenges for the 21st Century* by Edwin Meese and P. J. Ortmeier (Prentice Hall, 2003), which suggests that such an "old style" approach will not work and that, indeed, the new philosophy of more collegial problem solving is the appropriate approach for the future of policing. With regard to the ever-expanding field of alternatives to traditional police supervision, the idea of practicing "upward discipline" is embraced by Nathan F. Iannone, Marvin D. Iannone, and Jeff Berstein in *Supervision of Police Personnel, 7th Ed.* (Prentice Hall, 2008).

The principles of TQM have been explained in dozens of books in recent years. One very recent work is *Total Quality Management* published by Peratec Ltd. (Springer, 2009), which gives a brief, general outline of the idea. *Strategic Management in Policing: A Total Quality Management Approach* by William F. Walsh and Gennaro F. Vito (Prentice Hall, 2007), engages the reader with a more police-focused approach.

CHAPTER 15

Professionalism

In the Introduction, we noted that the drive toward creating a genuine "professionalism" in police work is the most important contemporary development in the field. We also suggested this subject of professionalism would be alluded to in almost every subsequent chapter—and, indeed, this has been the case. Now, at the end of our journey, we directly engage the issue in the light of everything we have learned. We will discuss the historical roots of the movement, the progress achieved, and what is necessary for this drive to reach final fruition. Operating in parallel with the COP movement, progress toward this goal has been substantial in many places and halting in others.

What does it mean to be a professional? Are police officers professionals? If not, why not? How might the police achieve membership in the world of the genuine professionals? Our discussion here will approach the first question with a consideration of several different definitions of "professionalism." There is considerable debate about what police professionalism might look like, and it is this discussion we initially engage.

The answer to the second question is straightforward enough. The police are *not* considered true professionals in America at this time. So our final focal point addresses what would have to happen for the police to become professionals. What changes are necessary for the police to reach this long-held dream? In engaging this question, we will find that in some areas progress has been substantial; in others, it has been difficult; and in still others, profound changes in approach will have to occur in order to reach this final goal.

But to begin with, we consider: what *does* it mean to be a professional?

WHAT IS A "PROFESSION"?

Who are the genuine professionals in American society? What constitutes professionalism? What elements do all professions have in common? In the field of police work there has been considerable debate over the answers to these questions. To attempt our own answers, we must first engage several definitions of professionalism. We will discuss them in order, from the least to the most sophisticated.

A Lay Definition

We begin with a rather simplistic, commonplace definition of profession. A profession is anything that a person does for money. More specifically, it is anything that a person does to support their family and their lifestyle. It is different from a hobby or an avocation. Thus, high school basketball players are amateurs, and women who play in the WNBA are professionals. Candy stripers at hospitals are volunteers, and nurses are professionals. And so forth. This **lay definition of professionalism** describes a common differentiation, and it is particularly appropriate where sports are involved.

However, this differentiation is not sophisticated enough for our purposes. People intuitively know that there is a difference between those people involved

BOX 15.1

HAIR CUTS AND SHOE SHINES

During the Reform Era, the police "lineup" was created. The lineup used to involve exactly what it implies: police officers would stand at attention for inspection every day before going out onto the street. This inspection was all about "looking professional." It involved having a clean uniform, shined shoes, polished brass, cut hair, and a clean-shaven face. This is what "professional" meant to the police in the 1900s.

in the genuine "professions" and those involved in common "**occupations**" or "**vocations**." Professionals do not have "jobs," they have "**careers**." They do not work for hourly wages—they receive salaries. And so merely doing something for money is not an appropriate definition. It lacks the depth necessary for our analysis of modern police work.

Paramilitarism as Professionalism

A second definition of a profession has a militaristic tinge to it. Generally speaking, people will often remark that someone on the job "looks very professional." Or supervisors in any number of occupations will often suggest that their subordinates clean themselves up or take a rigid, serious posture and thus "look professional." Such reflections can be aimed at just about anyone, from a store clerk to a burger flipper at McDonald's to a police officer (Fogelson). What people mean to say when they assert that a person looks professional is that they look neat, clean cut, and presentable. Such a statement has to do with appearance and not behavior. It is a part of our culture to consider someone who looks presentable as being professional.

This is a militaristic view of the idea of a profession. In police work it has very specific and important implications. When the Reform Era of policing replaced the Political Era, many people misunderstood a critical part of that changeover. As we have noted in several places, numerous changes instituted to reform the police were paramilitaristic in nature. Given the rampant corruption of authority at the time, this made perfectly good sense. Paramilitarism did the job of undoing corrupt practices immediately in some places and gradually mitigated that particular form of misconduct over the course of several generations in others. Paramilitarism eventually changed subcultural norms and reconstructed police systems. It made the police into "crime fighters," when for more than half a century they had been, in essence, "social workers" and political operatives (Walker, Critical History of Police Reform).

But paramilitarism was not professionalism—neither then nor now. And numerous people made the mistake of believing this to be the case. Many police officers, police leaders, politicians, and even scholars mistook the Reform Era as a "Professional Era." The two are not the same. While there is nothing wrong with police officers getting hair cuts and shoe shines, keeping their uniforms cleaned and pressed, and presenting themselves in a serious, attentive, intelligent manner, this sort of appearance-oriented façade manipulation does not constitute professionalism.

A Sociological Definition

Having found two characterizations wanting, we move to a more sophisticated and appropriate definition, accepted by sociologists, of "profession." In differentiating jobs, occupations, and vocations from the genuine professions, sociologists have isolated a number of indicators (Larson). The genuine professions—those of medicine, law, architecture, teaching, engineering, and so forth—all have specific elements in common. While there are several different typologies even among sociologists, we focus here on six critical elements common to all professions.

Academic Experience: First, professions require their members to go through a prolonged and sophisticated **academic experience** (Roberg *et al.*). Members obtain an education—not merely a degree, but a genuine education—at what Plato called his "Academy." When we refer here to entering into academe, we are talking about obtaining a bachelor's degree at a university as a starting point. This is where the professional becomes an educated person—in exactly the way Plato envisioned several thousand years ago. But this is only the beginning.

In most professions—including all of those listed above—there is specific training that follows this generalized experience. And that additional training takes substantial amounts of time. Medical school takes four years. Law school takes three years. Many engineers, architects, and teachers obtain graduate degrees and participate in prolonged apprenticeships. It is only after high school *and* college that members of the professions obtain their specified "training."

Of course, we must be careful when talking about the police with regard to this specific training experience, because they all attend police "academies." The fifteen- or twenty-week-long experience involved in these academies is not what we are discussing here. Police academies constitute important elements in the overall police officer educational experience, but their courses of study are much shorter and they do not develop in police cadets the breadth of knowledge an education in academe provides.

Substantive Knowledge: The second characteristic common to all professions involves what the would-be professional obtains in academe—namely, a **systematized body of knowledge** unknown to those outside professional circles (Freidson). This body of knowledge is substantial in both depth and breadth. That is, it is not easily obtainable in terms of time spent, and it is equally difficult to obtain in terms of the intellectual powers necessary to engage the knowledge.

Furthermore, this body is scientifically constructed (Cullen; Geison). Outside of the profession, the specifics of this knowledge are so unknown that we—collectively, as a society—give great deference to the professions. Their members know something—a great deal, actually—that we do not know, and we accord them a special status because this is so.

Collegial Problem Solving: A third characteristic involves a specific methodology with which obstacles and difficulties are solved in the professions: **collegial problem solving**. In most occupations, decisions are made in a command and control manner, whether it is labeled as such or not. That is, decisions are made on high and passed down the line of communication. This is true in retail businesses, factories, white-collar workplaces, and so on. In police work, of course, this is called the chain of command. But it is not necessary to label it as such. There is an organizational chart in all complex organizations, and the fact that those above dictate policies and strategies to those below is universal.

In the professions, this is not the case. Problems are solved "collegially" in the professions. That is, when difficulties present themselves, expert professionals from anywhere in the organization get together to troubleshoot and problem solve. Difficulties are not surmounted through a hierarchical process (Roberg *et al.*). Professionals pool their intelligence and expertise and attempt to create solutions that are, in essence, democratically constructed. Perhaps an example is in order. When surgeons come upon a troublesome case, right in the operating room, they will pool their intellects, their expertise, and their experience. They will work to save the patient's life collectively, without regard to chains of command. The most experienced surgeon participates as an equal colleague with the least experienced surgeon in this endeavor.

Self-Regulation: Fourth, and this is directly linked to points one and two above, the professions are allowed to **self-regulate**. That is to say, standards for education, licensing, and behavior are determined by **professional organizations**, without outside interference (Carter and Wilson). As a society, we allow them to do this because we defer to their knowledge base. So deep is our collective respect for the academic experience and the substantive knowledge held by professionals, that we allow them the latitude to establish and enforce their own standards. Who but a lawyer knows what a lawyer needs to learn in law school? Who but a lawyer knows who should be allowed to practice at the bar? Who but a lawyer knows what particular licensing steps a would-be lawyer ought to take in order to earn the privilege of practicing law?

All genuine professions have an absolute, unquestioned authority over their own endeavors. Ordinarily, no one outside a profession purports to have much to say about these things, and on those rare occasions when they do—when lay people suggest they should be involved in the regulation of a profession—such suggestions usually do not go very far. Our collectively constructed understanding of how the world works operates in favor of the professional under such circumstances.

BOX 15.2

RESPECT FOR PROFESSIONALS

A mother's 3-year-old daughter has broken her arm. She rushes her to the hospital, races into the Emergency Room, and tells the story to the first person she sees. The mother is a medical student. She is concerned but not hysterical; she knows what has happened, and she knows exactly what needs to be done. A nurse takes the little girl away on a gurney, and the mother is asked to "sit down and wait in the lobby."

What does she do? What does a person with her intelligence level and expertise do? Does she protest and suggest she should accompany her daughter to the E.R.? Does the mother argue that she won't be in the way and that she just doesn't want to lose contact with her little girl? Or—despite her intelligence, education, and experience level—does she do what she is told, defer to the expertise of the professionals, sit down, and wait? This is a true story, and the mother sat down and waited; she did what she was told because she trusted the expertise of the professionals, even though those working in the E.R. were complete strangers and she was in the process of becoming a doctor herself.

Self-Disciplining: The professions are allowed to **self-discipline**. Because of the same rationalizations listed for self-regulating, the professions are considered capable of policing themselves. Accusations of misconduct made against professionals are handled by organizations populated by other members of the appropriate profession. Committees or boards or commissions of practitioners are responsible for looking into such allegations, and they are given great latitude in doing so. While members of the public who consider themselves victims of professional incompetence, slothfulness, or dishonesty have the right to petition for redress, such petitions are considered by experienced professionals (Roberg *et al.*).

Who but a college professor would know if a student has been given an inappropriate grade by another professor? Who but a licensed engineer would know whether or not another engineer has mismanaged a construction project? Who but a surgeon would know if the death of a patient was due to the incompetence or laziness of another surgeon or if it was due to natural causes, poor luck, or an honest mistake? Some people outside of a profession may disagree with the granting of this power, but the true professionals of the world are allowed the greatest degree of latitude where alleged misconduct is concerned.

An Internalized Ethic: Finally, genuine professionals are known to possess an internalized ethical code. During their acquiring of systematized knowledge, professionals learn an ethical framework within which they base their craft. They are socialized into accepting this ethical framework, and then they operate in its shadow without external interference (Pollock). The behavior of professionals is controlled in this way by values and norms that are socialized into their working personalities during the professionalization process.

For the purposes of analyzing whether or not the police can be considered professionals—and, if not, what would be required to make them such—we shall utilize this sociological definition. But before we make these evaluations and prescriptions, we will engage a conceptualization of what it means to be a professional in an individualistic sense.

MUIR'S PROFESSIONAL OFFICER

Our discussion of various definitions has focused upon the professions as collectivities. We have debated how and why a given group of workers might be labeled professionals. Before beginning a specific analysis of police professionalism on a macro level, let us first consider an intriguing idea of Muir's. He suggested that to be a professional, a police officer needed to possess several specific world views. His was an individualistic definition of professionalism. Muir did several years of research that involved riding with dozens of officers. He witnessed their achievements and limitations, their strengths and weaknesses, their successes and defeats. In the end, he categorized them and established four distinctive officer types. The substance of the questions he used to derive this calculus involved, in his words, "passion and perspective" (Muir 50).

Passion

Muir began by suggesting that there were two different types of "**passion**" within the personality structures of the officers he observed. He focused on the use of coercive power, which, as we saw in earlier discussions, was central to his studies of the police. Muir claimed that in observing police officers in the line of duty, they approached the use of coercion in one of two ways. Officers were either comfortable with coercing others or they were not. And this differentiation was critical, in his estimation.

Some officers had integrated into their working personalities the ability to coerce comfortably. That is, they had no trouble with the reality that a person who coerces is, to a real extent, a "bully." Getting people to behave how you want by threatening to harm them or something they value is bullying, plain and simple. Some officers were comfortable playing this role and some were not. Muir did not take issue with those who could bully with ease—he did not see bullying as a bad thing, necessarily. In fact, he suggests that without the ability to rationalize bullying, an officer cannot be effective on the street.

The point here is that "**principled violence**" is what coercive power *should* be all about (Muir 50). When exhortation and reciprocity fails, the effective police officer knows coercion is the next and last resort. There was nothing wrong with this in Muir's estimation. In fact, in his opinion, police officers who were conflicted about the exercise of such bullying tactics were incapable of handling some types of details. As long as officers did not coerce for inappropriate reasons—as long as their bullying was principled—they could be effective at doing their jobs and producing desired behavior from citizens.

An illustration is in order. When a police officer threatens an obnoxious drunk at a ballpark with arrest and gets the man to go home and sober up, an important task has been accomplished. When a group of rowdy juveniles is harassing patrons at a convenience store, and the police order them to disperse "or else," and the youths do, another detail has been handled appropriately—and without either arrest or violence. Principled bullying is an important tool and, as Muir pointed out, not all officers are comfortable with this reality. Thus, he divided his group of officers into those who had what he called an **integrated understanding of coercion**—that is, of the morality of principled bullying—and those with a **conflicted view of coercion**. This is how he defined and applied the concept of "passion" in order to create his typology. By passion, then, Muir means the ability to threaten in the name of doing good (Muir 50–51).

Perspective

Muir then suggested that another differentiation among his police officers was equally critical. He called it **perspective**. His officers divided into two groups with regard to this concept as well. There were those who had the **tragic perspective** of life, and there were those who had the **cynical perspective**. He clearly believed that the tragic perspective was optimum.

Muir begins his discussion of police officers possessing a tragic perspective of life by suggesting that this includes a feeling for the suffering of others. All people yearn to be treated with dignity, no matter what they may have done criminally. A sort of "religious understanding" that no person is worthless is integral to the tragic perspective. Everyone deserves some modicum of deference due to their value as a "soul" in the world. There are three specific elements to the tragic perspective.

First is an understanding of what Muir calls **the unitary experience of life**. All people share a common reality. They all struggle against odds; they all suffer tragedies of sorts; and they all are capable of doing both good and evil. This is true of everyone, no matter their specific circumstances. The police officer with this perspective, therefore, takes time to attempt an understanding of even those suspects who have perpetrated the most heinous crimes—this officer seeks to empathize with the injustices suffered by anyone and everyone (Muir 178).

Second, the tragic perspective includes an understanding of the **complex causal patterns of life** (Muir 179). Deviance is the product of chance and necessity at times and does not always evolve out of free will. Yes, some people look at alternatives, make calculations, and *decide* to steal or murder. They exercise free will in making such decisions. But life is not always that simple. Chance plays a part in deviance, and so does necessity. The causes of crime are complicated and numerous—sometimes it is produced by poverty, tragic circumstances, and even bad luck. A police officer with the tragic perspective looks for the complex causal patterns behind whatever type of deviant behavior they face.

Third, a person with this perspective understands the **precariousness and necessity of human interdependence**. Human solidarity and community is critical to the meaning of life (Muir 180–181). We are communal animals, and it is essential to understand that the maintenance of community and interaction is the way in which humans have become not only capable of living together but of conquering nature and ruling the planet. Humans only accomplish this through collective and cooperative efforts. Maintaining relationships—person to person and, even, police officer to person—is a necessary condition of the human experience.

The "cynic" holds opposing views (Muir 225–226). The **cynical perspective** denies that everyone struggles with life's tragedies and adverse circumstances; the cynic believes there are, quite simply, good people and bad people. Life does not involve a unitary experience. The cynic, therefore, believes there is nothing complicated about deviance; bad people choose to be bad and that is the end of it. Nothing complicated, nothing difficult to understand is involved. The cynic involves himself or herself in individual fault finding and moralizing. Trying to discover and to understand people's motivations and tragic experiences is a complete waste of time to the cynic: there are no complex causal patterns, only simple-to-understand villainy. Furthermore, the cynic insulates himself or herself from psychic harm by denying interdependence. Cynics make themselves invulnerable by spurning civility and denying that there is any moral conflict in the world.

Muir's police officers were thus divided along these lines; there were those driven by tragic and those driven by cynical perspectives. He then took these several sets of differentiations and used them to construct a four-fold table of police officer types divided by different modes of "passion and perspective" (see Table 15.1).

Let us consider the four types of police officers that Muir found operating on the beat (Muir 57).

CLASSIFICATION ACCORDING TO PROFESSIONAL POLITICAL MODEL

	MORALITY OF COERCION	
	INTEGRATED	CONFLICTED
Tragic perspective	Professional	Reciprocator
Cynical perspective	Enforcer	Avoider

Other-Than-Professional Officers

Before engaging **Muir's Professional** directly, we will briefly discuss his other three types. Officers who are conflicted about coercing others—who are uncomfortable about bullying—and who have a tragic perspective of life are labeled "**Reciprocators**." These officers operate on the street with a sort of passive resistance to deviance. Since they are conflicted about coercion, they use reciprocal power as often as possible. In order to work their beats, Reciprocators worked at developing relationships wherein citizens owe personal obligations to the police. Favors are exchanged with citizens in an effort to build up a level of gratitude that can be depended on in the future. Reciprocators even allow minor illegality to proceed without sanction in order to make the public believe they are "nice" officers deserving of the public's cooperation. This propensity to allow crime to proceed without notice is particularly disturbing for Muir.

Those officers who have an integrated understanding of coercion—who have no trouble bullying people—but who possess a cynical view of humankind are labeled "**Enforcers**." These officers tend to be reminiscent of Dirty Harry. They are impatient with people and unenlightened about the causes of deviance. Theirs is a world driven by the idea that it is the job of the police to use force to punish those citizens who are naturally bad people. It is even acceptable to use two different standards in police work: rules that apply to good people and rules that apply to bad people. The inconsistency in treating people differently is lost on Enforcers. Enforcers communicate to incite people, rather than probing and discovering insights into motivations and causes.

Those officers who possess a conflicted attitude about coercion and a cynical perspective of life are labeled "**Avoiders**." Avoiders are passive and ineloquent. They are lifeless and unresponsive to human suffering. They view the job as something to be done without ever really becoming engaged in the endeavor. They do as little as possible, remaining uninterested in people's lives or motivations or in doing good work of any kind. Muir is given particular credit by practitioners for observing the fact that there are Avoiders in police work. Most outsiders have always taken the stereotypical view that the police are "all" aggressive, domineering, and boisterous personality types. As all police officers know, this is not true. Avoiders *are* present on the job, and they make more work for those who actually do their jobs honestly.

The Professional

This brings us to what Muir considers the optimum police officer personality set: those officers with an integrated understanding of the morality of coercion and who possess the tragic perspective of life. These are the "**Professionals**." The Professional is gregarious and works at teaching people on the street. They teach not by asserting the naked power of the law but by shaping events through communicating to the populaces they police that a great deal is gained by living within the legal framework and behaving oneself. Professionals are not afraid to explain things to citizens. In fact, they are comfortable with the idea that providing explanations about officer decisions and how the law works is a central part of what the police are supposed to do.

Muir considered the Professional to be the optimum police officer. He thought officers should be open, convivial, "people-oriented" individuals—that there is no place in police work for the "strong, silent type." Police officers should be gregarious—they should enjoy "shooting the breeze" with citizens, as this not only opens up lines of communication in general but may result in garnering important information. They should proactively engage with people's problems and do their best to create solutions. The Avoider does none of this.

Of course, police officers must respect the dictates of the law. While they enjoy some power of mutability via their discretionary decision-making, the police must understand that the law is not something to be treated cavalierly. They must avoid acting the Reciprocator, allowing some people to get away with criminal conduct in an effort to appear "nice." And, certainly, the professional officer needs to avoid the aggressive and, at times, abusive excesses of the Enforcer.

So Muir gives us a more individual officer-focused idea of professionalism. The modern COP movement aims to foster the development of Muir's Professional officer. Armed with this information, we now engage the central question of the chapter: are the police professionals? If they are not, then what would it take to make them so?

ARE THE POLICE PROFESSIONALS?

So, in many ways, when it comes to contemporary policing in America, this is *the* question that needs asking: are the police professionals? And ascertaining the answer is not as easy as it might appear at first glance (Greene). Our discussion so far provides two levels to approach the subject. We can ask if the police are professionals in Muir's individualized sense of the word. Or we can ask if the police are professionals as defined collectively by sociological analysis.

Regarding Muir's conceptualization, we might wonder if police work today is generating a professional officer corps. The answer is yes. The good news about contemporary developments in American policing is that through the application of increased educational standards, the expansion of police officer training, the leadership of enlightened and insightful police supervision, and the development of COP, a substantial number of today's police officers are, as defined by Muir, professionals. And there is reason to believe that this number is increasing over time. Today's police officer corps undoubtedly includes far fewer Enforcers, Avoiders, and Reciprocators than previously. This is good news for everyone concerned—the police, police administrators, politicians, the public, and the criminal justice system in general.

Then there is the other way of approaching the question. Taken together as a collectivity, are the police professionals as defined by sociologists? And the correct answer to this question is: almost. Over the last 100 years, developments in

BOX 15.3

ACADEME

Since Plato's time, the idea of going to an "academy" or obtaining an experience in "academe" has meant participating in a learned society or attending an institution of higher, theoretical learning. But Plato's academy was situated in a park with a gymnasium for physical training. Plato specifically acknowledged the importance of intellectual pursuits and of physical fitness in parallel. This seems perfectly appropriate as a touchstone experience for police officers, since they are involved at the same time in both a complicated intellectual endeavor and a contact sport.

the field have propelled American police work in the direction of professionalism, moving it close to the sociological definition. To determine what this means, let us examine the elements discussed above that transform an occupation into a genuine profession.

Do the police have an educational experience that replicates that of Plato's Academy? Not exactly, but that is changing. As the push for more education gains traction, the two years now required for hiring in many places will probably change into what many assume to be the requirement of the future: a four-year degree for everyone in the profession. When this happens, the police academic experience will begin to approximate that of other professions. Post-college police training is expanding in many places, too. The basic 15 weeks of academy training is growing. Nationally speaking, the amount of academy time has risen to an average of 761 hours—the equivalent of about 19 weeks (*DOJ Special Report* 6). Longer academy training, longer FTO training, and, finally, in-service training of substantial proportions—all of this makes up today's training regimen. As this propensity continues, police education will soon—in the lifetime of today's police academy cadet—approximate that of the educational experiences required for other professions.

Does the substantive scholarship and information that today's police officer must possess form a "systematized body of knowledge, unknown to the lay person outside of the profession"? Yes, it does. There is no doubt that the combination of knowledge in the fields of legal studies, sociology, psychology, political science, deviance, criminology, forensics, firearms, and pragmatic police operations required by police officers today constitutes such a body of knowledge. An illustration is in order.

Almost all lawyers possess more substantive knowledge about criminal law than do police officers. But unless they *practice* criminal law, most attorneys are not familiar—in the way that the modern, accomplished police officer is—with the combination of legal issues a beat officer must know. Today's serious, committed, professional officer is aware of criminal law, criminal procedure, constitutional law, and specific case law relating to searches and seizures and interrogations in a way that sets them apart from both their predecessors and the average, non–criminal law attorney. What is more, the legal expertise required to be a good, effective officer involves but one of numerous fields required in modern police work. So modern police do embody this element of the sociological definition of professionals.

With respect to collegial problem solving, the movement toward COP is apposite. One of the critical elements of the COP philosophy has to do with utilizing lower level expertise and decentralizing decision-making. When this is done in an appropriate way, it involves the same sort of collegial problem solving as does other professions. That is exactly the point of the team-oriented, collective-problem-solving model that COP presents. So as COP becomes more and more institutionalized across the nation, this element of professionalism will be more and more inculcated into police work as a standard operational norm. Collegial problem solving has arrived, but it hasn't yet been "institutionalized."

What about self-regulation? Again, today's police are close to achieving this requirement. As noted elsewhere, each state has a P.O.S.T. (or near-equivalent) commission empanelled to make decisions about standards for police education. So the basic requirements for academy and in-service training are, in fact, set by members of the profession itself. Academy examinations are controlled in a like manner, by experienced police officers. So is initial entry into the occupational group—while Civil Service has a role in giving exams and operating selection mechanisms, the types of exams and requirements in place are always constructed by police executives. As is true with other professions, great deference is given to the police within public bureaucracies and within the criminal justice system itself. Where police officer regulation is concerned, the operative norm among other political and justice system elites gives control to experienced police officers because who else would know what is required?

With regard to the next requirement for genuine professionalism—that of self-discipline—the police fall short. Many practitioners believe the police self-regulate because of the existence of Internal Affairs. But this is not an appropriate analogy to the self-disciplining done in other professions. Internal police review systems are operated by police departments, not by police professional groups. If the police were to discipline themselves, they would be disciplined by police unions. Do police unions take discipline seriously and become part of the process? Do they attempt to inculcate appropriate behavior patterns in their own operatives while at the same time creating more respect and trust in the minds of the public? This is done in medicine, law, and so forth. Is it done in police work?

Unfortunately, nothing could be further from this in police work today. In contemporary police work, professional organizations—unions—commonly work against holding the police accountable. No matter how egregious the behavior of errant officers, **police unions** invariably fight *against* accountability. This is universal—and a disturbing reality for proponents of professionalism, because it allows agents outside law enforcement to curtail efforts to increase the status, income, and power of the police in general (Perez).

Finally, do the police live by a personal ethic that is internalized and self-operational? The answer, again, is—almost. A consistently applied, universally understood professional ethic is in the process of being constructed in American policing. It is not here yet. But it is on its way. Unfortunately, the reluctance of many contemporary police officers and of the subculture (in some places) to embrace the principles of COP, the aversion that most police unions have to taking responsibility for police accountability, and the inability of police training to embrace the concept of creating a personal ethic from the positive side—eschewing the idea that to be a good officer is to avoid screwing up—all work against the implementation of this element of the formula.

In analyzing police professionalism, it is of critical importance to note that what the police do in a substantive sense—whether or not they live up to either Muir's or the sociological definition—composes only part of the formula. Police professionalism will never truly be a reality until and unless the American public accepts the police as professionals and affords them the status that goes along with this acceptance. In other words, public perception is crucial. The American public accepts doctors and lawyers as professionals, and, thus, these occupations are afforded a great deal of status and latitude within which to regulate, discipline, analyze, recreate, and perpetuate their own professional milieus. The police have yet to reach this level—but we have good reason to believe this status will, eventually, be accorded them.

So the police are close to being professionals. The police academic experience is growing in its sophistication and baseline requirements. The substantive body of knowledge imparted to police officers during the education process is substantial and growing. COP is helping to institute collegial problem solving. Self-regulation is already a reality. Only in the areas of self-disciplining and possessing an internalized, universally accepted ethic are the police substantially short of obtaining the status of professionals.

In the next section we will engage in a brief discussion of what might be done to overcome obstacles that delay the professionalization of the American police.

FUTURE DIRECTIONS

If the police are not yet genuine professionals—not completely—then how might they become such? What are the critical steps in the process? We have just reviewed what has been accomplished already. What remains to be done? In this section, we will consider first the **European model of police professionalism** and then move on to offer several suggestions about future directions for the American system.

The European Model

One option we might engage before our final analysis of the America model of professional policing has to do with how policing is organized in many European countries (Das and Dolu). In Europe, police work is organized along bifurcated lines. Those who police the streets in uniform have similar backgrounds and training as do American police officers. Although the training process has achieved a genuinely professional level—for example, in Austria, it takes two full years of academy training to reach street-deployment status—the system is otherwise similar in terms of command structures, FTO requirements, and so forth.

But in Europe police administration operates in a completely different way. The entire upper level of the command structure is educated at the graduate school level. Those ranking above Captain do not work their way up from the ranks. Instead, they are educated in graduate level programs that involve nothing in the way of practical policing at the beat level. European police are organized in a way analogous to an American corporation—one that produces, say, automobiles.

In such a corporation, supervisors and managers are college educated and rarely, if ever, have production line experience. It is not considered necessary at General Motors, for example, for supervisors to have worked at the business of actually making cars with their hands. It is understood that the information and expertise obtained in college, through majoring in business administration, is sufficient. If managers know about budgets, personnel administration, organizational theory, and marketing they are well suited to supervise and make corporate policy. And so it is with the police in Europe. Commanders are sent through graduate schools to earn the equivalent of a master's degree or Ph.D. in police management. They then enter the upper echelon of the police hierarchy and supervise those who work on the streets.

In America, policing has always worked under the assumption that to be an effective supervisor it is necessary to have worked a beat, making one's way up through the ranks. Is this truly necessary? Or might an effective route to professionalism in American policing be to emulate the European model? This is not likely to happen, given the strength of the police subculture and more than 150 years of history. But it does provide an interesting point of reference for our discussions here. How effective might it be to keep the lower levels of the American police system the way they are but change the upper management

BOX 15.4

THE EFFECTIVENESS OF ROUTINE PATROL

In 1974, a report was issued about the first and perhaps single most important piece of police research ever done. In Kansas City, Missouri, an experiment was constructed to ascertain the effectiveness of routine patrol. Long believed to deter crime, the movement of patrol vehicles on city streets was found to have a negligible impact on crime. This, of course, changed our understanding of the importance of routine patrol. But it also ushered in today's era of constant research into police effectiveness.

structure by bringing in experts in managing police systems—in the same fashion as corporations and public bureaucracies? Would this or could this accelerate the development of professionalism and even COP in America? Would it be better for the public? Would it be more in the interests of the delivery of justice on the streets? Our answer, for now, must be: who can say?

The Research Component of Professionalism

How scientific is police work? How much is done because officers, administrators, or scholars have systematically collected evidence indicating that certain methods are effective and efficient? It turns out that much of what police officers do derives from tradition and intuition. Practical applications of street officers tend to be effective because they make common sense, have worked in the past, or follow the dictates of police traditional lore.

But in the last several decades, policing has become much more scientific thanks to information generated by myriad research projects (Caiden). Police professionalism has expanded dramatically because, about 30 years ago, social scientists studying the police from the outside were embraced by police leaders. Instead of resenting such "outsiders," it is to the credit of many such leaders in the late 1960s and early 1970s that they had the foresight and courage to expose their operations to dozens of different studies. Almost all aspects of police work have now been, or are in the process of being, studied. The information garnered in these studies has advanced the cause of professionalization rapidly. And all of this works to increase the scientific nature of the systematized body of knowledge possessed by the police.

Spurred by several riot commissions that called for more scientific policing and more police education, in 1965 federal funds were committed to police research under the **Office of Law Enforcement Assistance (OLEA)**. Hundreds of millions of dollars were committed to this effort (Roberg *et al.*). COP in particular was partly driven by research that questioned paramilitarism, the effectiveness of random and reactive patrol, the need for rapid response, and the effectiveness of criminal investigations. The police began to understand that utilizing research in order to solve problems was more logical and effective. Not only has police procedure been dramatically changed, but our understanding of the causes of crime and what to do about it has expanded. This research component of modern policing is one of the reasons genuine professionalism is within reach.

Police Review

The genuine professions enjoy the privilege of disciplining themselves. This is possible because of the latitude society grants them due to their academic experience and substantive knowledge base. But such latitude has never been granted the police. And in contemporary times, the call for the civilianization of police review has expanded. Research has discovered that civilian review does not unfairly punish police officers (Perez). At the same time, several studies suggest that it enhances the externally perceived faith in police operations. Therefore, external police review is expanding rapidly (Walker, New World of Police Accountability).

While civilian review has its drawbacks, as noted in Chapter Thirteen, hybrid systems seem to provide both an effective accountability mechanism and an efficient use of taxpayer dollars. And there is something else. Police professionalism is underwritten by such open review systems because they generate more citizen support for police in the long run. And on the police officer side of things, opening up review to a more broadly based perspective can instill a more COP-oriented view of who should control the police and why. That is, the partnership ideal of COP moves closer to fruition through civilianized review.

COP

Much of what we have discussed—many of the problems associated with the police not yet achieving genuine professionalism in America—is addressed by the movement toward COP. Here we need only remind ourselves that COP encourages more logical, scientifically defensible police operations. It suggests more collegial problem-solving and more decentralization, which both empower the individual police officer. It inspires officers and managers to behave in any number of intelligent and educated ways—behavior that is emblematic of a genuine profession. Everything about COP influences the drive toward genuine professionalism in a positive way.

So these are the types of programs and movements operating today to encourage and develop police professionalism. Progress in this direction, so incremental and halting for several generations, has now escalated. There is good reason to believe that the genuine professionalization of the police is within the grasp of its practitioners.

THE LIMITS OF REFORM

In this book, in one place or another, we have explored the numerous roadblocks in the way of police professionalism, but a final summarization is in order.

Media Imagery

The media tend to sensationalize police work, focusing on anything negative when it appears. While day-to-day coverage is positive, the amplification of police misconduct and occasional failures can retard the drive to professionalize the police. This is because part of the achievement of genuine professional status—when it finally arrives—will be in the eyes of the public. The media sell inaccurate images to the American populace that mitigate respect for the police in the minds of millions of citizens. Then, too, the media are so focused on the elimination of crime that they do not care how it is achieved. They tend to accept and even demand noble cause corruption on the part of everyone in police work, from the beat officer on up to the Chief or Sheriff.

American Cultural Resistance

American citizens are born and raised with a penchant for resisting governmental power. And since the police exercise power over the lives of citizens in an obvious, public, and even violent way at times, the public will always be reluctant to accord them the sort of professional status given to doctors, nurses, teachers, engineers, architects, and the like. Also, as is true with media, the public tends to demand that the police minimize crime and render streets safe no matter the method. Thus, noble cause corruption is accepted and, at times, even encouraged and applauded by the public.

However, having said this, it is interesting to note that when surveyed today's average American places their respect for the police above that of politicians, journalists, bankers, business leaders, and lawyers. [Gallup News Service, 14 Dec 2006]

Paramilitarism

Keeping themselves aloof from the public through the machinations of paramilitarism only exacerbates the propensity for people to denigrate the police and refuse them professional status. Even though, as noted, paramilitarism has its place in police work on limited, extraordinary occasions, it can create a feeling of separation in the hearts and minds of not only police but citizenry as well. And this feeling works against the achievement of professional status. Paramilitarism also works against the sort of interactive and partnership-oriented approach toward the public that COP, and, thus, professionalism, demands.

Good Ol' Boys

Those in police work who operate with an old-school-thinking-is-best mentality are of no help whatsoever in promoting professionalism. "Good ol' boys" operate in an unprofessional manner, are not apologetic for this, and work directly against any efforts to professionalize police work. While this sort of policing is becoming anachronistic, it still impacts rural policing, in particular, and inhibits the growth of status and respect for officers everywhere.

Subcultural Resistance

There is little *overt* resistance to professionalism within the police subculture. After all, achieving the status accompanying this change would mean increased respect and fiscal stability for all police officers. The sort of subcultural resistance that exists is latent, taking the form of support for Dirty Harry and grass-eating misconduct, for overkill and never explaining oneself, for resistance to police accountability and the changes involved in COP. In these ways, the police subculture actually works against the interests of the police in general by standing in the way of the professionalization movement.

We revisit these numerous roadblocks that inhibit the development of police professionalism to make our discussion balanced and fair. This reiteration is not meant to imply that these inhibitors will thwart the adoption of professionalism forever. No one versed in American policing and its history believes this. Police professionalism is coming, and, in the long run, nothing is likely to stop it.

 ## SUMMATION

Police professionalism is most definitely on the rise. The move toward this long-sought goal has accelerated. In terms of who the police are, how educated they have become, how they are trained, how they comport themselves, how they are supervised, and how they are disciplined, the American police have made great strides in the direction of professionalizing what has for generations been a blue collar occupation. On the public's side of the equation, American citizens are beginning to accord police the status traditionally reserved for professions.

Even though the logic of police professionalization remains unchallenged, there are forces that operate to thwart progress in this direction. Even some elements of the police work against professional development. But the die appears cast. In short order, the police will take their well-earned position among the professionals of America.

Having now worked through the fifteen chapters of this book, we will take a moment for one more, brief discussion in the Epilogue. Therein, we will synthesize several of our most important topics. Let us now turn to that final review.

CHAPTER FIFTEEN PARADOX BOX

The professionalization of the police is an important goal for police practitioners, citizens, and the administration of justice as well. Its pursuit is an admirable endeavor. But numerous dynamics in America work directly against the development of police professionalism. From citizen support for noble cause corruption, to paramilitarism, to police subcultural resistance, to the "good ol' boy" network, the effort to institute genuine professionalism in American police work is an uphill battle. There are police officers, institutions, and even American citizens who work *against* professionalization, even though to do so is not in their own best interests.

DISCUSSION QUESTIONS

1. Our discussion in this chapter makes short work of the paramilitaristic defini-tion of professionalism, opting instead for the sociological definition. What about the paramilitaristic definition? Why is this appearance-oriented defini-tion of limited utility? Discuss.

2. In this chapter, we note that the police are "close" to being professionals (as judged by the sociological definition). But a troublesome stumbling block inhibiting professionalism is a lack of self-disciplining. Police professional or-ganizations (unions) fight against accountability instead of taking the lead in attempting to produce it. Why is this? Can this be changed? Might police unions begin to take police misconduct seriously? Why or why not?

3. Muir's professionals have the passion to use "principled bullying" in the name of getting good things accomplished. What exactly does Muir mean by this? Can you think of examples of principled bullying? Discuss this idea and see if you can come up with instances from parenting, being President of the United States, and being a police officer.

4. In the last several chapters, we have several times decried "the good ol' boys." Who are they? Do you know of any examples of towns or cities run by these types of anti-intellectual, anti-progressive police officers or leaders? What does the future hold for them? Or, put another way, what are they likely to do to retard the development of police professionalism in the long run?

KEY TERMS

Academic Experience: A necessary element of the sociological definition of the "professions" involving substantial amounts of time being spent in college and in specific, profession-oriented training.

Avoiders: Muir's officers who possessed a conflicted view of coercion and the cynical perspective of life.

Careers: Differentiated from "jobs" or "occupations," genuine professionals travel career-oriented working paths in life.

Collegial Problem Solving: A necessary element of the sociological definition of the "professions." This involves approaching problem solving in a demo-cratic way instead of using command-and-control methods of operation.

Complex Causal Patterns of Life: A part of the tragic perspective of life involv-ing a sophisticated approach to understanding people's motivations.

Conflicted View of Coercion: What Muir considers to be a lack of "passion."

Cynical Perspective: One of Muir's police perspectives of life.

Enforcers: Muir's officers who possess an integrated passion for coercion and a cynical perspective of life.

European Model of Police Professionalism: Involves upper level managers who have graduate school educations and no experience as beat officers.

Integrated Understanding of Coercion: A part of Muir's element of "passion" involving the coercer being comfortable with principled bullying.

Lay Definition of Professionalism: Involves the rather simplistic notion that anyone who does anything for money is a "professional."

Occupations or Vocations: Different from "professions," occupations and vocations are "jobs" and not "careers."

Office of Law Enforcement Assistance (OLEA): Federal bureaucracy that poured millions of dollars into police research in the 1960s and 1970s.

Muir's Professional: A police officer with an integrated passion for using coercion and the tragic perspective of life.

Paramilitarism as Professionalism: The idea that to be a "professional" means to look clean and presentable and to carry oneself erect and in a serious manner.

Passion: One of Muir's elements that determine types of police officers. Relates to whether or not a police officer rationalizes principles bullying.

Perspective: One of Muir's elements that determine types of police officers. Muir divides police officers into those who possess the tragic and those who possess the cynical perspectives.

Police Unions . . . Against Accountability: The unfortunate historical reality that police unions, in a misguided attempt to protect their membership, invariably fight against the development of professional accountability.

Precariousness and Necessity of Human Interdependence: Part of the tragic perspective of life involving an understanding of the importance of community in the human experience.

Principled Violence: The idea that it is moral to use coercion as long as it is in the pursuit of morally defensible objectives.

Professional Organizations: Organizations created by and operated in the interests of groups of professionals, such as the American Medical Association (AMA) or the American Bar Association (ABA).

Reciprocators: Muir's police officers who possess a conflicted view of coercion and the tragic perspective of life.

Research Component of Professionalism: An important element in the drive toward professionalism—it seeks to make police work more scientific.

Self-Disciplining: One element of the sociological definition of the genuine professions. Involves professionals in determining the appropriateness (or lack thereof) of the conduct of other professionals in their field.

Self-Regulation: One element of the sociological definition of the genuine professions. Involves professionals in determining appropriate requirements for professional education, training, and certification in their own fields.

Systematized Body of Knowledge: One element of the sociological definition of the genuine professions. Refers to the knowledge obtained by a professional at the academy, knowledge unknown to lay person.

Tragic Perspective: One of Muir's perspectives of life for police officers involving an understanding of the unitary experience of life, complex causal patterns and the necessity of human interdependence.

Unitary Experience of Life: Part of the tragic perspective of life involving an understanding of the commonality of people's life experiences.

ADDITIONAL READING

Early in this chapter, we discuss—and dismiss—the paramilitaristic definition of professionalism. Many scholars have accepted this definition, declaring the Reform Era to be the age of professionalism. Perhaps most influential, because of the insightful and important work he's done in the field, is Samuel Walker's misunderstanding of this concept, illustrated in *A Critical History of Police Reform* (Lexington, 1977).

With respect to the sociological definition of professionalism, Magah Sarfatti Larson discusses this concept in synoptic fashion in *The Rise of Professionalism: A Sociological Analysis* (University of California Press, 1979). She emphasizes the idea of the internalized ethic as the critical element in professionalism. In *Professional Powers: A Study of the Institutionalization of Formal Knowledge* (University of Chicago Press, 1988), Eliot Freidson focuses almost exclusively on the idea of the systematized body of knowledge necessary for the achievement of professional status.

The article "Measuring Professionalism of Police Officers" by Lycia Carter and Mark Wilson, which appeared in *The Police Chief* magazine, analyzes the professionalism of contemporary policing. Theirs is a rather paramilitaristic conceptualization, which includes in their definition the idea that professionals operate in "a manner that exudes authority and control."

Jack R. Greene largely embraces the sociological definition of professionalism but stops short of analyzing whether or not the movement has actually achieved that goal. His analysis is a good example of the (rather) "traditional" idea of police professionalism, meaning that he agrees, to some extent, with both Carter and Wilson's piece and with Walker's idea from a generation ago. Greene's treatment can be found in *The Encyclopedia of Police Science* (CRC Press, 2006).

A more synoptic and contemporary look at the movement toward police professionalism can be found in *Understanding Today's Police* by M. L. Dantzker (Criminal Justice Press, 2005). Dantzker agrees largely with our analysis that the police are moving toward the illusive goal, but that they have substantial progress to make before its realization.

And, of course, we must once more credit William Muir, Jr. (cited elsewhere) in this chapter for his individualized conceptualization of police professionalism involving passion and perspective.

EPILOGUE

Our various discussions have traversed fifteen sets of topics and unearthed more than two dozen paradoxes in police work. We have analyzed the individual police officer's experience in detail and mused about the power and importance of the police subculture. We have discussed paradoxes relating to the organization and operation of police systems, not to mention those that have to do with selection, training, and accountability. And we have considered the critical importance of leadership and professionalism as the police move toward an uncertain future. After such a trek, it seems only right that we stop to consider, if only for a moment, the principal paradoxes and reiterate their operational dynamics and importance.

If one had to explain the paradoxical nature of American police work in encapsulated form, what would one say? Which issues and dynamics associated with our paradoxes are the most important? How would we summarize our many discussion points for the layperson and provide them with a brief but significant understanding of the police experience?

To begin with, police paramilitarism presents a profoundly difficult paradox. In an era when many Americans expect officers to grow closer to their communities, closing the gap created between police and citizenry during the Reform Era, militaristic structures and behavior embody the antithesis of this. The many drawbacks of an occupying-army mindset are ever present in contemporary America. It makes sense for insightful police officers and leaders to work—consciously and consistently—to reduce the emphasis on paramilitarism. It behooves citizens and law enforcement personnel alike to facilitate the "de-militarization" of the police, allowing (and motivating) them to behave as community members, social welfare workers, and agents of positive change.

And yet America is still the most violent society in the industrialized world. We have more guns in our homes, and use them on each other more frequently, than the people of any other developed nation. So the police *must* be ready to react to violence at a moment's notice. They must be capable of protecting themselves and citizens from gang warfare, sniper situations, hostage dilemmas, and a host of predicaments involving violence and guns. This is a part of their charge, and it is no less important than the other, more peaceful elements of the job. When doing so, when confronting genuine "battle situations," the police must be disciplined and circumspect about the utilization of firepower. They must be held accountable for their actions in such situations, and they need efficient and powerful chains of command to assume this responsibility.

Further complicating things is the fact that long ago—in the name of reforming an era of rampant and organized corruption in police work—paramilitarism was instituted *consciously*. It was no accident. And it worked. It worked almost everywhere to instill more discipline and control over the police and to do away with corruption. Therefore, when suggesting that paramilitarism needs to be de-emphasized, we are purposefully undoing something that was intentionally done. And backtracking might seem to be asking for trouble.

Thus, the paradoxes associated with paramilitarism are manifest and frustrating. For it seems impossible to operate without a paramilitaristic focus while being totally prepared to do so. Albert Einstein, commenting on the international arms race, once stated: "You cannot simultaneously prepare for both war and peace." And so it is with regard to the police and violence: they cannot simultaneously prepare for and reject it.

A second, ever present set of paradoxes has to do with noble cause corruption. Ever since the United States Supreme Court began handing down decisions that require the police to understand and defer to the stipulations of the Constitution, it has been necessary for the police in this country to be more intelligent and educated than ever before. Today's police officer must be conversant with the general principles of constitutional law and possess a sophisticated understanding of contemporary court decisions. Exclusion has done this.

Encouraged by their leadership, exclusion has motivated today's police to achieve ever-expanding levels of competence and effectiveness. It has been good for the police to do so, enhancing their status among the citizenry and expanding their salaries and benefits. Beginning in the 1960s, America needed the development of a "new blue line" of more intelligent and sophisticated officers. We now have them. Today's police are responding in every way to the numerous challenges associated with the due process revolution of the '60s.

But exclusion has also cut the other way. Frustrating those whose business is to focus upon factual guilt, the due process system's contemporary machinations have created a backlash. Some police officers, motivated to get the job done at any cost, have become enemies of the system. Dirty Harry, in all of his forms and manifestations, has become a central, paradoxical problem in police work. Egged on by conservative politicians and those who would profit from his excesses, Harry lives and thrives amidst today's police officer corps. Within a subculture that a generation ago began eschewing other forms of police misconduct—such as police crime and corruption of authority—the noble cause corruption associated with Dirty Harry represents a step backwards in time. It is bad for the police, bad for the public, and bad for the administration of justice.

Noble cause corruption is supported not only by certain police officers and norms of the subculture. The problem goes deeper. It is also encouraged and applauded by millions of American citizens, the media, and local politicians. Calling for the police to do "whatever it takes" to get results, these groups are often so supportive of this type of misconduct that it makes holding the police accountable a paradoxical endeavor. Thus, taken together, the paradoxes of the due process system operate to create police misbehavior and mitigate some of the progress made toward demilitarization and professionalism.

Community Oriented Policing is critically important in today's America and it presents another set of paradoxical dynamics. Redefining the function of the police, making policing more personal, generating an ongoing, close relationship between police and public, and re-organizing police systems in a way that is more logical and responsive to contemporary demands—these are the elements of COP. As change occurs in this direction, we are in the process of creating a new type of police work and, indeed, a new type of police officer. These changes are logical and practically defensible. And they are worthy of the efforts of the thousands of officers, politicos, and citizens who are working hard for them.

But COP does not come easy. It involves changing everything in American police work. And change always cuts the wrong way when somebody's interests are threatened. Line officers used to the standard way of doing things have been reluctant to embrace COP in many places. Middle managers, upset at their responsibility not being paralleled by authority, have sometimes been equally reluctant to embrace these changes. And "the gold ol' boys" at every level, afraid that COP minimizes their expertise and threatens their careers, have worked against it. Even certain scholars, afraid that COP may, paradoxically, return us to an era of corrupt police practices and excessive police powers, have been unwilling to embrace it.

So for as much as the evolution of policing in the direction of COP makes good sense to many, it has been slow in coming to some jurisdictions. And even in places where a majority accepts it, subcultural resistance—in pockets, here and there—has been effective at deterring its development. Only time will tell if COP will become institutionalized and universally acknowledged as *the* new philosophy of policing everywhere. Or, for all of its promise, COP might end up as a short term set of ideas thwarted in the long run by subcultural, political, and personal defiance.

Inexorably linked to COP is the drive toward police professionalism. Begun long before the ideas of COP entered the minds of its creators, the professionalization movement has made profound strides in recent years. The police have become more educated and sophisticated about their charge, and organizational dynamics are slowly changing in positive ways. Collegial problem solving is on the rise. In cooperation with academic institutions of higher learning, the systematized body of knowledge in the field is expanding, and police professionalism is enhanced in parallel. Self-regulation exists in most jurisdictions, and even the personal ethic associated with the genuine professions is on its way to being accepted everywhere within police circles.

But professionalism has its detractors and its rational limitations. And they are very much analogous to those that operate to limit the progress of COP. The "good ol' boys" are not interested in this sort of progress. The media talk about it in a positive way, but, in some ways, they are not prepared to grant the status and allow the latitude necessary for police to become genuine professionals. And some of the police themselves, those that champion paramilitarism as the only way to operate and who support the noble cause corruption of Dirty Harry, often oppose professionalism in either tacit or obvious ways.

So professionalism too has its paradoxes. And taken together, all of these paradoxes—those associated with paramilitarism, noble cause corruption, and

COP—often make the reality of being a police officer, or of attempting to lead and supervise officers, a frustrating one.

Perhaps the singularly most important paradox of police work has to do with the fact that officers have become America's fall guys and gals. As noted throughout our various discussions, the police are expected to deal with the most violent, vulgar, disgusting, and despicable sorts of human behavior imaginable—and much that is nearly unimaginable. They are entrusted with keeping our streets safe and peaceful in the face of derision and forces that work toward deviance and anarchy. This they are entrusted to do, they *must* do, in whatever ways that are pragmatic and effective.

But the police are forever enjoined to accomplish these tasks within the legal framework. Confronted with unrealistic media imagery, political forces that sometimes disrespect them, and internal and external accountability mechanisms that show no mercy with regard to the paradoxes they face, the police must cleave to sanitized, idealistic, even romantic notions of perfect legality. What is worse, the police are left alone to wrestle with the practical realities of the nasty, imperfect, dirty nature of what they are supposed to accomplish on the streets; no one besides police officers completely understands the unfairness of the expectations they face.

At the end of our endeavor, it is important to the author that the reader understands something: engaging in a prolonged discussion of the paradoxes of police work and the numerous frustrations visited on today's police officer should not be misconstrued to suggest that police work is either impossible or unsatisfying. The author considers police work to be an engaging, exciting, and (even) sometimes wonderful experience. The job may be difficult, but it is an important one—one of the most important professions to which any person could commit themselves.

Police work is dynamic. It changes over time. It presents different challenges and different opportunities to the police officer in service throughout his or her career. Furthermore, a commitment to becoming the best police officer one can possibly be involves a life-long responsibility. It entails ongoing study and analysis. It requires the development of a well-thought-out personal ethic to which an officer must commit with integrity. It involves committing oneself to one's community, to a professional officer corps, and to the law.

To be a police officer today is to embrace change and to commit oneself to the most honorable of professions. It is both an enthralling and a challenging experience. It is both physical and intellectual. It is frustrating and engaging. It is often boring and sometimes exciting. It takes intellect, education, and courage. It is an endeavor to which any person can become obsessively attached—in either a bad or a good way. It rewards like almost no other form of professional experience. There is nothing quite like it.

WORKS CITED

Aamedt, Michael G. *Research in Law Enforcement Selection*. Boca Raton, FL: Brown Walker Press, 2004.

Abrahams, Jeffrey. *The Mission Statement Book*. Berkeley: Ten Speed Press, 1999.

Adams, Charles Francis, ed. *The Works of John Adams*. Boston: Charles C. Little and James Brown, 1851.

Adams, Thomas F. *Police Field Operations, 7th Ed*. Upper Saddle River, NJ: Prentice Hall, 2006.

Adler, F., G. O. W. Mueller, and W. S. Laufer. *Criminal Justice*. Columbus, OH: McGraw-Hill, 1994.

Ahern, James. *Police in Trouble: Our Frightening Crisis in Law Enforcement*. New York: Hawthorn Books, 1972.

Aho, James. *This Thing of Darkness*. Seattle: University of Washington Press, 1995.

Aitchison, Will. *The Rights of Law Enforcement Officers, 5th Ed*. Portland, Oregon; Labor Relations Information Systems, 2004.

Albrecht, Steve. *Surviving Street Patrol: The Officer's Guide to Safe and Effective Policing*. Boulder, CO: Paladin Press, 2001.

Alpert, Geoffrey P., and Roger G. Dunham. *Understanding Police Use of Force: Officers, Suspects, and Reciprocity*. New York: Cambridge University Press, 2004.

American Academy of Child and Adolescent Psychology. "Children and TV Violence." 13 Nov 2002.

Amnesty International. *Understanding Policing: A Resource for Human Rights Activists*. The Netherlands; Amnesty International, 2006.

Anderson, Terry H. *The Movement and the Sixties*. New York: Oxford University Press, 1996.

Anglin, Kirklin. *The Affirmative Action Dilemma*. Charleston, SC: BookSurge Press, 2006.

Avila, Eric. *Popular Culture in the Age of White Flight: Fantasy in Suburban Los Angeles*. Berkeley: University of California Press, 2006.

Baker, Stephen A. *Effects of Law Enforcement Accreditation: Officer Selection, Promotion, and Education*. Santa Barbara, CA: Praeger, 1995.

Baker, Thomas E. *Effective Police Leadership*. Flushing, NY: Looseleaf Law Press, 2005.

Balko, Radley. *The Rise of Paramilitary Police Raids in America*. Washington, D.C.: Cato Institute, 2006.

Banks, Cyndi. *Criminal Justice Ethics: Theory and Practice. 2nd Ed*. London, UK: Sage, 2008.

Barker, Thomas, and David L. Carter. *Police Deviance, 3rd Ed*. Albany, NY: Anderson, 1994.

Becker, Howard S. *Outsiders: Studies in the Sociology of Deviance*. New York: Free Press, 1997.

Belkin, A., and J. McNichol. "Pink in Blue: Outcomes Associated with the Integration of Open Gay and Lesbian Personnel in the San Diego Police Department." *Police Quarterly*, 5, 63–95, 2002.

Berg, B. L. "First Day at the Police Academy: Stress-Reaction Training as a Screening Technique." *Journal of Contemporary Criminal Justice*. 6, 89–105.

Berkley, George. *The Democratic Policeman*. Boston: Beacon, 1969.

Berlin, Isaiah. *The Age of Enlightenment: The 18th Century Philosophers*. New York: Plume, 1984.

Black, Donald. *The Behavior of Law*. St. Louis, MO: Academic Press, 1980.

———. "The Social Organization of Arrest." *Stanford Law Review*. 1971, Volume 23, 1087–1111.

Blum, Laurence N. *Force Under Pressure: How "Cops Live and Why They Die*. Herndon, VA: Lantern Books, 2000.

———. *Stoning the Keepers at the Gate: Society's Relationship with Law Enforcement*. Lantern, 2003.

Bodenhamer, David J. *Fair Trial: Rights of the Accused in American History*. New York: Oxford University Press, 1991.

Bolton, Ken, Jr. *Black in Blue: African-American Police Officers and Racism*. New York: Routledge, 2004.

Bouza, Anthony. *The Police Mystique: An Insider's Look at Cops, Crime, and the Criminal Justice System*. Jackson, TN: Perseus, 2001.

———. *Police Unbound: Corruption, Abuse, and Heroism by the Boys in Blue*. Amherst, NY: Prometheus, 2001.

Boychuk, M. K. "Are Stalking Laws Unconstitutionally Vague and Overboard?" Northwestern University Law Review, Volume 88, Number 2, 769–802, 1994.

Bramsted, Ernest Kohn, and K. J. Melhuish. *Western Liberalism: A History in Documents, from Locke to Croce*. White Plains, NY: Longman Press, 1978.

Brezina, Corona. *America's Political Scandals in the Late 1800s: Boss Tweed and Tammany Hall*. New York: Rosen Publishing, 2003.

Brody, David. *Labor in Crisis: The Steel Strike of 1919*. Santa Barbara, CA: Greenwood Publishing Group, 1982.

Brown, M. K. *Working the Street: Police Discretion*. New York: Russell Sage Foundation, 1981.

Burris, John L., and Catharine Whitney. *Blue vs. Black: Let's End the Conflict Between Cops and Minorities*. New York: St. Martin's Griffin, 2000.

Caiden, G. E. *Police Revitalization*. Lexington, MA: D. C. Heath, 1977.

Caldero, Michael A., and John P. Crank. *Police Ethics: The Corruption of Noble Cause, 3rd Ed*. Albany, NY: Anderson, 2009.

State of California. Commission for Peace Officer Standards and Training. *Bulletin 95–9*, May 12, 1995.

Carter, Lycia, and Mark Wilson. "Measuring Professionalism of Police Officers." *The Police Chief Magazine.* March 2009.

Chambers, Harry. *My Way or the Highway: The Micromanagement Survival Guide.* San Francisco: Berrett-Koehler, 2004.

Cialdini, Robert. B. *Influence: The Power of Persuasion.* San Francisco: Collins Business Press, 2006.

Cohen, Bernard, and Jan M. Chaiken. *Police Background Characteristics and Performance.* Lanham, MD: Lexington Books, 1973.

Cohen, Howard S., and Michael Feldberg. *Power and Restraint: The Moral Dimension of Police Work.* Santa Barbara, CA: Praeger, 1991.

Connor, Greg, and Gregory Connor. *Vehicle Stops, 3rd Ed.* Champaign, IL: Stipes Publishing, LLC, 2000.

Cooper, L. *The Iron Fist and the Velvet Glove.* Berkeley: Center for Research on Criminal Justice, 1975.

Cordner, G. "Community Policing: Elements and Effects." R. G. Dunham and G. P. Alpert, Eds. *Critical Issues in Policing, 5th Ed.* Long Grove, IL: Waveland Press, 2005.

Crank, John P. "The Influence of Environmental and Organizational Factors in Police Styles in Urban and Rural Environments." *The Journal of Research in Crime and Delinquency,* Volume 27, Number 2, 1990.

———. *Understanding Police Culture.* Albany, NY: Anderson, 1998.

Cullen, J. B. *The Structure of Professionalism.* Princeton, NJ: Princeton University Press, 1978.

Dantzker, M. L. *Understanding Today's Police.* Monsey, NY: Criminal Justice Press, 2005.

Das, Dilip K. "Police Training in Ethics: The Need for an Innovative Approach in Mandated Programs." *American Journal of Criminal Justice,* Volume 11, Number 1, 1986.

Das, Dilip K., and Osman Dolu. *Cross-Cultural Profiles of Policing.* Danvers, MA: CRC, 2009.

Davey, J. D., P. L. Obst, and M. C. Sheehan. "Developing a Profile of Alcohol Consumption Patterns of Police Officers in a Large Scale Sample of an Australian Police Service." *European Addiction Studies,* 6, 205–212, 2000.

Davis, Kenneth Culp. *Police Discretion.* Eagan, MN: West Group, 1977.

Delattre, Edwin J. *Character and Cops: Ethics in Policing.* Washington, D.C.: American Enterprise Institute, 2002.

Delord, Ron, John Burpo, Michael Shannon, and Jim Spearing. *Police Union Power, Politics, and Confrontation in the 21st Century.* Springfield, IL: Charles C. Thomas, 2008.

Diner, Steven J. *A Very Different Era: Americans of the Progressive Era.* New York: Hill and Wang, 1998.

Durkheim, Emile. *Suicide.* New York: Free Press, 1997.

Edwards, Charles J. *Changing Policing Theories for 21st Century Societies.* Australia: Federation Press, 2005.

Fogelson, R. *Big City Police*. Cambridge: Harvard University Press, 1977.

Freidson, Eliot. *Professional Powers: A Study of the Institutionalization of Formal Knowledge*. Chicago: University of Chicago Press, 1988.

Fleishacker, Samuel. *A Short History of Distributive Justice*. Cambridge: Harvard University Press, 2005.

Fletcher, Connie. *Pure Cop*. New York: Pocket Books, 1991.

Freidman, Robert R. *Community Policing: Comparative Perspectives and Prospects*. New York: St. Martin's Press, 1992.

Gardner, Gerald W. *Common Sense Police Supervision: Practical Tips for the First-Line Leader*. Springfield, IL: Charles C. Thomas, 2008.

Geertz, Clifford. *The Interpretation of Cultures*. New York: Basic Books, 1973.

Geison, G. L., Ed. *Professions and Professional Ideologies in America*. Chapel Hill: University of North Carolina Press, 1983.

Giles, Howard, Ed. *Law Enforcement, Communications, and Community*. Amsterdam, NL: John Benjamins Press, 2002.

Gilmartin, Kevin M. *Emotional Survival for Law Enforcement: A Guide for Officers and Their Families*. Tucson, AR: E-S Press, 2002.

Glenn, Russell W. *Training the 21st Century Police Officer*. Santa Monica, CA: Rand Corporation, 2003.

Goldstein, Herman. *Problem-Oriented Policing*. Columbus, OH: McGraw-Hill, 1990.

Goldstein, Robert Justin. *Flag Burning and Free Speech: The Case of Texas v. Johnson*. Lawrence, KS: University of Kansas, 2000.

Goodsell, Charles T. *The Case for Bureaucracy*. Washington, D.C.: C Q Press, 2003.

Green, Jack R. "Police Professionalism." *The Encyclopedia of Police Science*. Danvers, MA: CRC Press, 2006.

Greene, J. R., and S. D. Mastrofski. *Community Policing: Rhetoric or Reality*. Santa Barbara, CA: Praeger, 1988.

Greene, Robert. *Concise 48 Laws of Power, 2nd Ed*. London, UK: Profile Books, 2002.

Groeneveld, Richard F. *Arrest Discretion of Police Officers: The Impact of Varying Organizational Structures*. El Paso, TX: LFB Scholarly Publishing, LLC, 2005.

Grote, Richard C. *Discipline Without Punishment*. New York: AMACOM, 1995.

Grupp, Jeffrey. *Corporatism: The Secret Government of the New World Order*. Joshua Tree, CA: Progressive Press, 2007.

Haberfield, Maria R. *Critical Issues in Police Training*. Upper Saddle River, NJ: Prentice-Hall, 2002.

Haider, James T. *Field Training Police Recruits: Developing, Improving, and Operating a Field Training Program*. Springfield, IL: Charles C. Thomas, 1990.

Harries, Keith D. *Serious Violence: Patterns of Homicide and Assault in America*. Springfield, IL: Charles C. Thomas, 1997.

Hatch, Orrin G. *The Jury and the Search for Truth: The Case Against Excluding Relevant Evidence at Trial: Hearing before the Committee on the Judiciary, U.S. Senate*. Danvers, MA: DIANE Publishing Company, 1995.

Hawkins, David R. *Power vs. Force: The Hidden Determinants of Human Behavior.* Carlsbad, CA: Hay House Press, 2002.

Hennessy, Stephen M. *Thinking Cop, Feeling Cop: A Study in Police Personalities, 3rd Ed.* Gainesville, FL: Center for Applications of Psychological Type, 1998.

Hickman, M. J., and B. A. Reaves. *Local Police Departments.* Washington, D.C.: Bureau of Justice Statistics, 2000.

Hill, Stephen M., Randall R. Beger, and John M. Zanetill. "Plugging the Security Gap or Springing a Leak: Questioning the Growth of Paramilitary Policing in U.S. Domestic and Foreign Policy." *Democracy and Security*, Volume 3, Issue 3, September 2007.

Hirsch, Susan Eleanor. *After the Strike: A Century of Labor Struggle at Pullman.* Champaign-Urbana, IL: University of Illinois, 2003.

Hrenchir, Tim. "Miranda Readings Lack Hollywood Spin." *The Topeka Capital-Journal*, 25 January 1999.

Iannone, Nathan F., Marvin D. Iannone, and Jeff Bernstein. *Supervision of Police Personnel, 7th Ed.* Upper Saddle River, NJ: Prentice Hall, 2008.

Ivkovic, Sanja Kutnjak. *Fallen Blue Knights: Controlling Police Corruption.* New York: Oxford University Press, 2005.

Jefferson, Tony. *The Case Against Paramilitary Policing.* Columbus, OH: Open University Press, 1990.

Johnson, D. R. *American Law Enforcement: A History.* St. Louis: Forum Press, 1981.

Jones, Tony L. *SWAT Sniper: Deployment and Control.* Boulder, CO: Paladin Press, 1995.

Judd, Kenneth L. "The Growing Gap Between Rich and Poor." *Hoover Digest: Research and Opinion on Public Policy*, Number 2, 1997.

Kalish, Carol B. "International Crime Rates: Bureau of Justice Statistics, Special Report." Washington, D.C.: Bureau of Justice Statistics, 1988.

Kaminsky, Glenn F. *Field Training Concepts in Criminal Justice Agencies.* Upper Saddle River, NJ: Prentice Hall, 2000.

Kaminsky, Robert J. "Police Minority Recruitment: Predicting Who Will Say Yes to an Offer for a Job as a Cop." *Journal of Criminal Justice*, Volume 21, Number 2, 1993.

Kappeler, Victor E., Richard D. Sluder, and Geoffrey P. Alpert. *Forces of Deviance: Understanding the Dark Side of Policing, 2nd Ed.* Long Grove, IL: Waveland, 1998.

Kelling, George. "Juveniles and Police: The End of the Nightstick." *Children to Citizens, Vol. II: The Role of the Juvenile Court.* Frances X. Hartman, Ed. New York: Springer-Vertag, 1987.

Kelling, George, and Catherine M. Coles. *Fixing Broken Windows: Restoring Order and Reducing Crime in Our Communities.* New York: Free Press, 1998.

Kellough, J. Edward. *Understanding Affirmative Action: Politics, Discrimination, and the Search for Justice.* Washington, D.C.: Georgetown University Press, 2006.

Keynes, Edward. *Liberty, Property, and Privacy: Toward a Jurisprudence of Substantive Due Process.* State College, PA: Pennsylvania State University Press, 1996.

King, Leonard W. *The Code of Hammurabi.* Whitefish, MT: Kessinger Publishing, 2004.

Kirshman, Ellen. *I Love A Cop: What Police Families Need to Know*. New York: The Guilford Press, 2006.

Kleinig, John. *The Ethics of Policing*. Cambridge, UK: Cambridge University Press, 1996.

Klockars, Carl. "The Dirty Harry Problem." *The Annals of the American Academy of Political and Social Science*, Volume 452, Number 2, 33–47, 1980.

———. *The Idea of Police*. London, UK: Sage, 1985.

———. "The Only Way to Make Any Real Progress in Controlling Excessive Force By Police." *Law Enforcement News*. 15 May 1992.

———. *Thinking About Police*. Columbus, OH: McGraw-Hill, 1983.

Klockars, Carl, Sanja Kutnjak Ivkovic, and M. R. Haberfeld. *The Contours of Police Integrity*. London, UK: Sage, 2004.

Knapp Commission Report on Police Corruption. New York: George Braziller, Inc. 1973.

Kolm, Serge Christophe. *Reciprocity: An Economics of Social Relations*. Cambridge, UK: Cambridge University Press, 2008.

Korbetz, R. W. *Law Enforcement and Criminal Justice Education Directory, 1975–1976*. Gaithersburg, MD: International Association of Chiefs of Police, 1976.

Krantz, Sheldon. *Police Policy-Making: The Boston Experience*. Lanham, MD: Lexington Books, 1979.

Kraska, Peter, and Victor E. Kappeler. "Militarizing American Police: The Rise and Normalization of Paramilitary Units." *Social Problems*, Volume 44, Number 1, February 1997.

Krasowski, Joe, Ed. *Master the Police Officer Exam, 17th Ed*. Lawrenceville, NJ: Thomson Peterson's, 2005.

Kratcosky, Peter C., and Dilip K. Das. *Policing Education and Training in a Global Society*. Lanham, MD: Lexington Books, 2007.

Kurke, Martin I., and Ellen M. Scrivner. *Police Psychology Into the 21st Century*. Philadelphia: Lawrence Erlbaum, 1995.

Lane, Roger. *Policing the City: Boston, 1822–1882*. Cambridge: Harvard University Press, 1967.

Langworthy, R., T. Hughes, and B. Sanders. *Law Enforcement Recruitment, Selection, and Training: A Survey of Major Police Departments in the U.S.* Highland Heights, KY: Academy of Criminal Justice Sciences, 1995.

Larkin, Ralph W. *Comprehending Columbine*. Philadelphia: Temple University Press, 2007.

Larson, Calvin J., and Gerald R. Garrett. *Crime, Justice, and Society*. Lanham, MD: Rowman Altamira, 1996.

Larson, Magah Sarfatti. *The Rise of Professionalism: A Sociological Analysis*. Berkeley: University of California Press, 1979.

Lawrence, Regina G. *The Politics of Force: Media and the Construction of Police Brutality*. Berkeley: University of California Press, 2000.

Leinen, Stephen. *Gay Cops*. Piscataway, NJ: Rutgers University Press, 1993.

Levine, Michael, and Lana Kavanau-Levine. *The Big White Lie: The CIA and the Cocaine/Crack Epidemic*. New York: Thunder's Mouth Press, 1993.

Lieberman, David J. *Get Anyone to Do Anything: Never Feel Powerless Again.* New York: St. Martin's Griffin, 2001.

———. *You Can Read Anyone.* Lakewood, NJ: Viter Press, 2007.

Locke, John. *Two Treatises of Government.* Whitefish, MT: Kessinger Publishing, 2004.

Long, Carolyn N. *Mapp v. Ohio: Guarding Against Unreasonable Searches and Seizures.* Lawrence, KS: University of Kansas Press, 2006.

Lonsdale, Mark V. *Raids: A Tactical Guide to High Risk Warrant Service.* Specialized Tactical Training Unit, 2005.

Lovell, Jarret S. *Good Cop/Bad Cop: Mass Media and the Cycle of Police Reform.* Monsey, NY: Criminal Justice Press, 2003.

Lykken, David Thoreson. *The Antisocial Personalities.* New York: Routledge, 1995.

Lyman, Michael D. *The Police: An Introduction, 3rd Ed.* Upper Saddle River, NJ: Pearson Prentice Hall, 2004.

Lyman, Michael D., and Vernon J. Geberth. *Practical Drug Enforcement.* Danvers, MA: CRC Press, 2001.

Macdonald, Heather. *Are Cops Racist?* Chicago: Ivan R. Dee, Publisher, 2003.

Maguire, Edward R. *Organizational Structure in American Police Agencies: Context, Complexity, and Control.* Albany: SUNY Press, 2003.

Maier, Norman Raymond Frederick. *The Study of Behavior Without a Goal.* Santa Barbara, CA: Greenwood Publishing Group, 1982.

Mayer, William G. *The Changing American Mind.* Ann Arbor, MI: University of Michigan Press, 1993.

McCaffery, Peter. *When Bosses Ruled Philadelphia: The Emergence of the Republican Machine, 1867–1933.* State College, PA: Pennsylvania State University Press, 2008.

McGarty, Craig, Vincent Y. Yzerbyt, and Russell Spears. *Stereotypes as Explanations: The Formation of Meaningful Beliefs About Social Groups.* Cambridge, UK: Cambridge University Press, 2002.

Megargee, Edwin I., and James N. Butcher. *Minnesota Multi-Phasic Inventory II.* Minneaplis; University of Minnesota Press, 2001.

Merriam-Webster. *New Collegiate Dictionary.* Cambridge, MA: G. & C. Merriam Co. Press, 1949.

Meese, Edwin, and P. J. Ortmeier. *Leadership, Ethics, and Policing: Challenges for the 21st Century.* Upper Saddle River, NJ: Prentice Hall, 2003.

Miller, Laurence. *Mental Toughness for Law Enforcement.* Flushing, NY: Looseleaf Law Publications, Inc., 2007.

Miller, Linda, and Karen M. Hess. *Community Police: Partnership and Problem Solving.* Florence, KY: Wadsworth, 2007.

Miller, Wilbur R. *Cops and Bobbies: Police Authority in New York and London, 1830–1870.* Chicago: University of Chicago Press, 1977.

Mollen, Milton. *The Mollen Commission Report: The City of New York Commission to Investigate Allegations of Police Corruption and the Anti-Corruption Procedures of the Police Department.* New York: City of New York, 1994.

Monkkonen, Eric H. *Police in Urban America, 1860–1920.* Cambridge, UK: Cambridge University Press, 1981.

Montesquieu, Charles, baron de. *The Spirit of Laws.* Amherst, NY: Prometheus Books, 2002.

Moran, T.K. "Pathways Toward a Nondiscriminatory Recruitment Policy." *Journal of Police Science and Administration.* 16, 274–287.

Morley, Patrick. *Beyond No Comment: Speaking with the Press as a Police Officer.* Chicago: Kaplan Press, 2009.

Muir, William K. *Police: Streetcorner Politicians.* Chicago: University of Chicago Press, 1977.

Musto, David F. *The American Disease: Origins of Narcotic Control.* New York: Oxford University Press, 1999.

Navarro, Joe, and Marvin Karlins. *What Everybody Is Saying: An Ex-F.B.I. Agent's Guide to Speed-Reading People.* New York: Collins Living, 2008.

Nelson, Jill. *Police Brutality: An Anthology.* New York: W. W. Norton and Co., 2001.

Nijhar, Preeti, and Mike Brogden. *Community Policing: National and International Models and Approaches.* London, UK: Willan Publishing, 2005.

O'Donnell, Tim. *American Holocaust: The Price of Victimless Crime Laws.* Bloomington, IN: IUniverse, 2000.

O'Keefe, James. *Protecting the Republic: The Education and Training of American Police Officers.* Upper Saddle River, NJ: Prentice Hall, 2003.

Oliver, Willard M. *Community Oriented Policing: A Systematic Approach to Policing, 4th Ed.* Upper Saddle River, NJ: Prentice-Hall, 2007.

O'Neill, J. L., and M. A. Cushing. *The Impact of Shift Work on Police Officers.* Washington, D.C.: Police Executive Research Forum, 1991.

Orth, John. V *Due Process of Law: A Brief History.* Lawrence, KS: University of Kansas Press, 2003.

Otis, James. "Against Writs of Assistance" 1761. Bowie, MD: National Humanities Institute, 1998.

Parenti, Michael. *Dirty Truths.* San Francisco: City Light Press, 2001.

———. *Inventing Reality: The Politics of News Media, 2nd Ed.* Florence, KY: Wadsworth, 2002.

Peak, Kenneth J. *Policing America.* Upper Saddle River, NJ: Prentice-Hall, 2000.

Peak, Kenneth J., and Ronald W. Glensor. *Community Police and Problem Solving, 5th Ed.* Upper Saddle River, NJ: Prentice Hall, 2007.

Peratec Ltd., *Total Quality Management.* New York: Springer, 2009.

Perez, Douglas W. *Common Sense About Police Review.* Philadelphia: Temple University Press, 1994.

Perez, Douglas W., and J. Alan Moore. *Police Ethics: A Matter of Character.* Florence, KY: Cengage, 2002.

Perkins, John. *Confessions of an Economic Hit Man.* New York: Plume, 2005.

Perrow, Charles. *Complex Organizations: A Critical Essay.* Glenview, IL: Scott, Foresman, 1972.

Perry, Tim. *Basic Patrol Procedures.* Salem, WI: Sheffield Publishing Company, 1998.

Peter, Laurence J., and Raymond Hull. *The Peter Principle.* New York: Bantam, 1969.

Pittman, David J., and C. Wayne Gordon. *Revolving Door.* Columbus, OH: Glencoe Free Press, 1958.

Pollock, Joycelyn. *Ethical Dilemmas and Decisions in Criminal Justice, 6th Ed.* Belmont, CA: Wadsworth, 2008.

Poteet, Lewis, and Aaron C. Poteet. *Cop Talk: A Dictionary of Police Slang.* Bloomington, IN: IUniverse Press, 2000.

Pound, Roscoe, and Ron Christenson. *Criminal Justice in America.* Piscataway, NJ: Transaction Press, 1997.

Punch, Maurice. *Zero Tolerance Policing.* Bristol, UK: Policy Press, 2007.

Rahtz, Howard. *Understanding Police Use of Force.* Berkeley: Criminal Justice Press, 2003.

Reese, Renford. *Prison Race.* Durham, NC: Carolina Academic Press, 2006.

Roach, Kent. *Due Process and Victim's Rights: The New Law and Policies of Criminal Justice.* Toronto, Canada: University of Toronto Press, 1999.

Roberg, Roy, Kenneth Novak, and Gary Cordner. *Police & Society, 3rd Ed.* Los Angeles: Roxbury Press, 2005.

Robertson, T. S., and J. A. Myers. "Personality Correlates of Opinion Leadership and Innovative Buying Behaviour." *Journal of Marketing Research.* Volume 6, May 1969.

Robinson, Cyril D., Richard Scaglion, and J. Michael Olero. *Police in Contradiction: The Evolution of the Police Function in Society.* Santa Barbara, CA: Greenwood Publishing Group, 1993.

Rostowd, C., and R. Davis. *A Handbook for Psychological Fitness-For-Duty Evaluations in Law Enforcement.* New York: Routledge, 2004.

Schlossberg, Herbert. *Idols for Destruction.* London, UK: Thomas Nelson, 1983.

Schneider, David J. *The Psychology of Stereotyping.* New York: Guilford Press, 2005.

Schultz, David A., and Robert Moranto. *The Politics of Civil Service Reform.* New York: Peter Lang Press, 1998.

Schur, Edwin M. *Victimless Crimes.* Upper Saddle River, NJ: Prentice Hall, 1975.

Scott, Eric. *Calls for Service: Citizen Demand and Initial Police Response.* Washington, D.C.: U.S. Government Printing Office, 1981.

Scott, Peter Dale, and Jonathan Marshall. *Cocaine Politics: Drugs, Armies, and the CIA in Central America.* Berkeley: University of California Press, 1991.

Seddon, John. *Freedom from Command and Control.* London, UK: Productivity Press, 2005.

Semikhodskii, Andrei. *Dealing with DNA Evidence.* New York: Routledge-Cavendish, 2007.

Sherman, Lawrence. *Quality of Police Education.* Ann Arbor, MI: Proquest Info and Learning, 1978.

Sherman, Nancy. *The Fabric of Character: Aristotle's Theory of Virtue.* New York: Oxford University Press, 1991.

Silver, Isidore. *Public Employee Discharge and Discipline.* Aspen, CO: Aspen Press, 2001.

Skogen, Wesley. *Disorder and Decline: Crime and the Spiral of Decay in American Neighborhoods*. New York: Free Press, 1990.

Skolnick, Jerome. *Justice Without Trial*. New York: John Wiley and Sons, 1966.

———. *The Politics of Protest: National Commission on the Causes and Prevention of Violence*. New York: Ballantine Books, 1969.

Skolnick, H. Jerome, and David H. Bayley. *The New Blue Line*. New York: Free Press, 1988.

Slovak, Jeffrey. *Styles of Urban Policing: Organization, Environment, and Police Styles in Selected American Cities*. NewYork: N.Y.U. Press, 1988.

Snow, Robert L. *SWAT Teams: Explosive Face-offs with America's Deadliest Criminals*. Jackson, TN: DaCapo Press, 1999.

Stack, S., and T. Kelly. "Police Suicide." *Police and Policing: Contemporary Issues, 2nd Ed*. D. J. Kenney and R. P. McNamara, Eds. Santa Barbara, CA: Praeger, 1999.

Stamper, Norm. *Breaking Rank: A Top Cop's Exposé of the Dark Side of American Policing*. New York: Nation Books, 2006.

Stark, Rodney. *Police Riots*. Florence, KY: Wadsworth, 1972.

Stich, Rodney. *Drugging America: A Trojan Horse Legacy, 2nd Ed*. Alamo, CA: Silverpeak Enterprises, 2005.

Stone, Vali. *Cops Don't Cry: A Book of Help and Hope for Police Families, 6th Ed*. Ontario, Canada: Creative Bound, 1999.

Sudnow, David. *Normal Crimes*. New York; Irvington Publishers, 1993.

Terrill, William. *Police Coercion: Application of the Force Continuum*. El Paso, TX: LFB Scholarly Publishing, 2001.

The President's Commission on Law Enforcement and the Administration of Justice. Washington, D.C.: U.S. Government Printing Office, 1967.

The Wickersham Commission on Law Observance and Law Enforcement. Washington: U.S. Government Printing Offi ce, 1931.

Thompson, Leroy. *Hostage Rescue Manual*. Newbury, UK: Greenhill Books, 2006.

Toffler, Alvin. *Future Shock*. New York: Bantam, 1984.

Toobin, Jeffrey. *The Nine: Inside the Secret World of the Supreme Court*. New York: Doubleday, 2007.

To Secure These Rights: The U.S. Commission on Civil Disorders. Washington, D.C.: U.S. Government Printing Office, 1968.

Truxillo, Donald M., Suzanne R. Bennett, and Michelle L. Collings. "College Education and Police Job Performance: A Ten Year Study." *Public Personnel Management*. Volume 27, Number 2, 1998.

United States. Controller General. "Impact of the Exclusionary Rule on Federal Criminal Prosecutions." Report #GGD-79-45, April 19, 1979.

United States. Federal Bureau of Investigation. *Uniform Crime Reports*. Washington, D.C.: 2005, 2007.

United States. Department of Justice. Bureau of Justice Statistics. (*www.ojp.usdoj.gov*)

———. Office of "Community Oriented Policing Services."

———. "Special Report: State and Local Law Enforcement Training Academies, 2006." Bureau of Justice Statistics.

Walker, Samuel. "Broken Windows and Fractured History: The Use and Misuse of History in Recent Police Patrol Analysis." *Justice Quarterly*. 1 March 1984.

———. *A Critical History of Police Reform*. Lanham, MD: Lexington, 1977.

———. *The New World of Police Accountability*. London, UK: Sage, 2005.

———. *Police Accountability: The Role of Civilian Oversight*. Florence, KY: Wadsworth, 2001.

———. *The Police in America, 5th Ed*. Columbus, OH: McGraw-Hill, 2004.

Walker, Tom. *Fort Apache: New York's Most Violent Precinct*. Bloomington, IN: iUniverse Star, 2009.

Walsh, William F., and Gennaro F. Vito. *Strategic Management in Policing: A Total Quality Management Approach*. Upper Saddle River, NJ: Prentice Hall, 2007.

Wambaugh, Joseph. *The Blue Knight*. New York: Dell, 1973

———. *The Choir Boys*. New York: Dell, 1976.

———. *The New Centurions*. Boston: Little, Brown, and Co, 1971.

———. "Violence Is Not Beautiful." Bob MacKenzie. *TV Guide*. 10 November 1973.

Weisenand, Paul. M. *Supervising Police Personnel: The Fifteen Responsibilities, 6th Ed*. Upper Saddle River, NJ: Prentice Hall, 2006.

Wells, Sandra, and Betty Sowers Alt. *Police Women*. Santa Barbara, CA: Greenwood Publishing Group, 2005.

White, Michael D. *Current Issues and Controversies in Policing*. London, UK: Pearson, 2007.

Wildavsky, Aaron. *Speaking Truth to Power*. Piscataway, NJ: Transaction Press, 1987.

Wilson, James Q. *Varieties of Police Behavior*. Cambridge, MA: Harvard University Press, 1968.

Wilson, James Q., and George Kelling. "Broken Windows." *The Atlantic*. March, 1982.

Wilson, O. W., and R. C. McLaren. *Police Administration, 4th Ed*. New York: McGraw-Hill, 1977.

Wolfe, Alan. *The Future of Liberalism*. New York: Knopf, 2009.

Wrage, Alexandra Addison. *Bribery and Extortion: Undermining Business, Government, and Security*. Santa Barbara, CA: Praeger, 2007.

Wrobleski, H. M. and K. M. Hess. *Introduction of Law Enforcement and Criminal Justice, 7th Ed*. Belmont: Wadsworth, 2003.

Yellin, Keith. *Battle Exhortation: The Rhetoric of Combat Leadership*. Columbia, SC: University of South Carolina Press, 2008.

Zhao, Jihong "Soloman," and Kimberly D. Hassell. "Policing Styles and Organizational Priorities: Retesting Wilson's Theory of Local Police Culture" *Police Quarterly*. Volume 8, Number 4, 2005.

INDEX